Shojo Beat

S·A
Special A

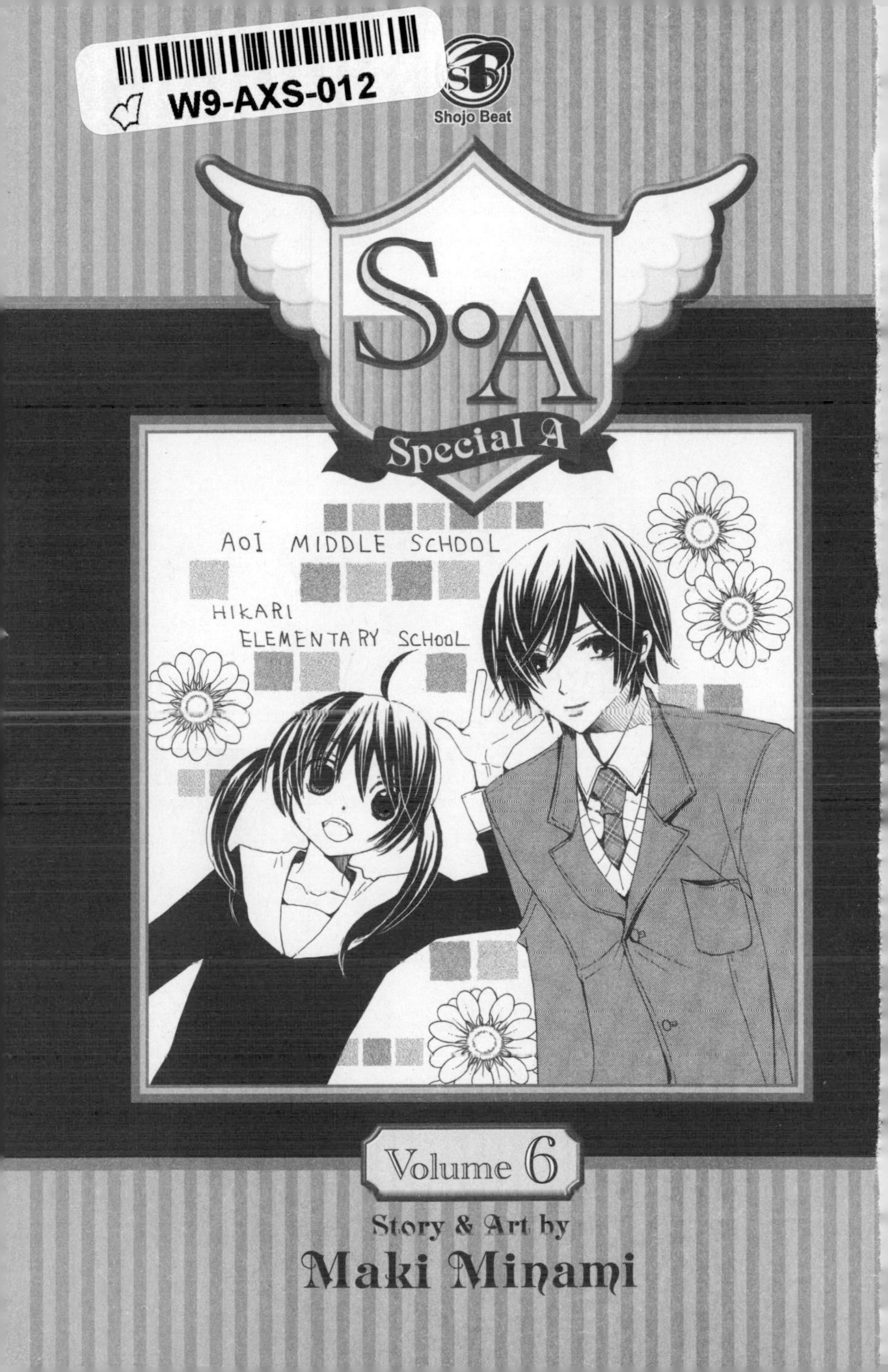
AOI MIDDLE SCHOOL
HIKARI ELEMENTARY SCHOOL

Volume 6

Story & Art by
Maki Minami

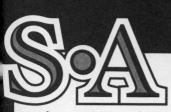

S·A CHARACTERS

Hikari goes to an elite school called Hakusenkan High School. This school divides each grade level into groups A through F, according to the students' test scores. Group A includes only the top seven students in each class. Then the top seven students from all grades' A groups are put into a group called Special A, which is considered much higher than all others. Known as SA, they are "the elite among the elite."

What is "Special A"?

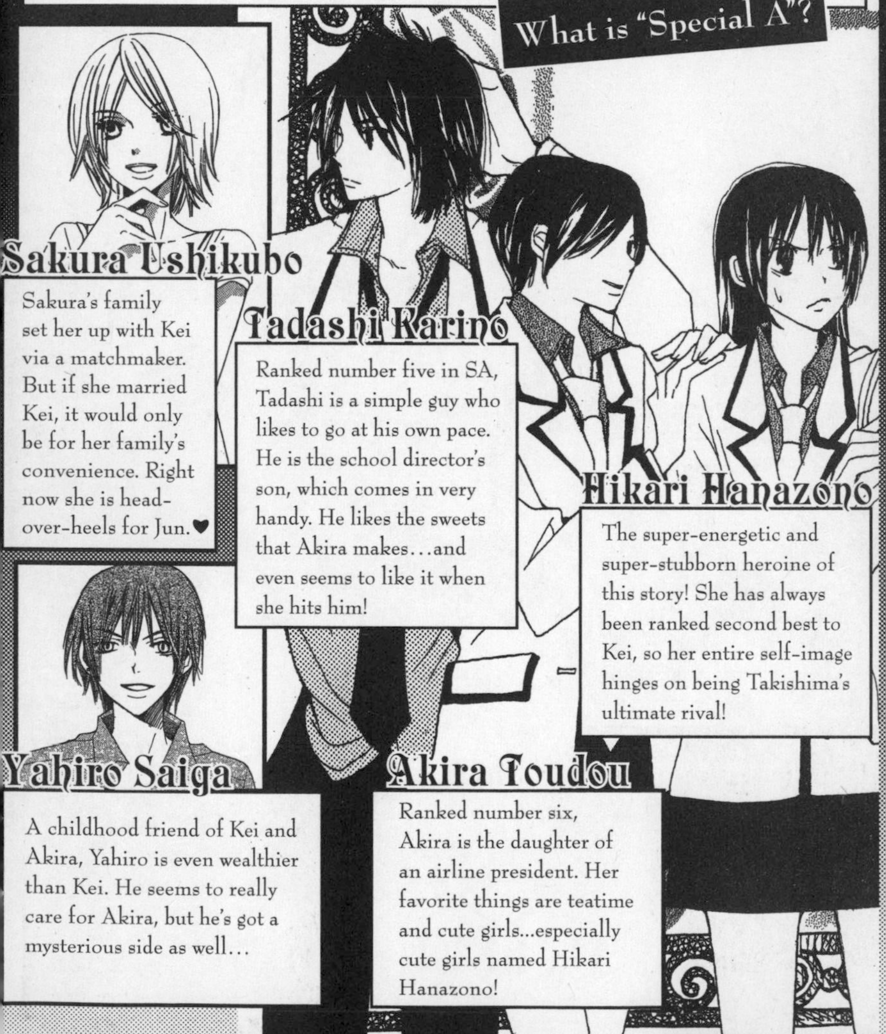

Sakura Ushikubo

Sakura's family set her up with Kei via a matchmaker. But if she married Kei, it would only be for her family's convenience. Right now she is head-over-heels for Jun.♥

Tadashi Karino

Ranked number five in SA, Tadashi is a simple guy who likes to go at his own pace. He is the school director's son, which comes in very handy. He likes the sweets that Akira makes...and even seems to like it when she hits him!

Hikari Hanazono

The super-energetic and super-stubborn heroine of this story! She has always been ranked second best to Kei, so her entire self-image hinges on being Takishima's ultimate rival!

Yahiro Saiga

A childhood friend of Kei and Akira, Yahiro is even wealthier than Kei. He seems to really care for Akira, but he's got a mysterious side as well...

Akira Toudou

Ranked number six, Akira is the daughter of an airline president. Her favorite things are teatime and cute girls...especially cute girls named Hikari Hanazono!

STORY

★At the tender age of 6, carpenter's daughter Hikari Hanazono suffered her first loss to the wealthy Kei Takishima in a wrestling match. Now the hardworking Hikari has followed Kei to the most elite school for the rich just to beat him! I call this story "Overthrow Takishima! Rise Above Perpetual Second Place!!" It's the story of Hikari's sweat, tears and passion, with a little bit of love thrown in!

★When Kei's marriage meeting with Sakura failed, Kei's grandfather ordered him to transfer to a school in London! Hikari and the rest of SA brought Kei back, but more trouble is brewing...

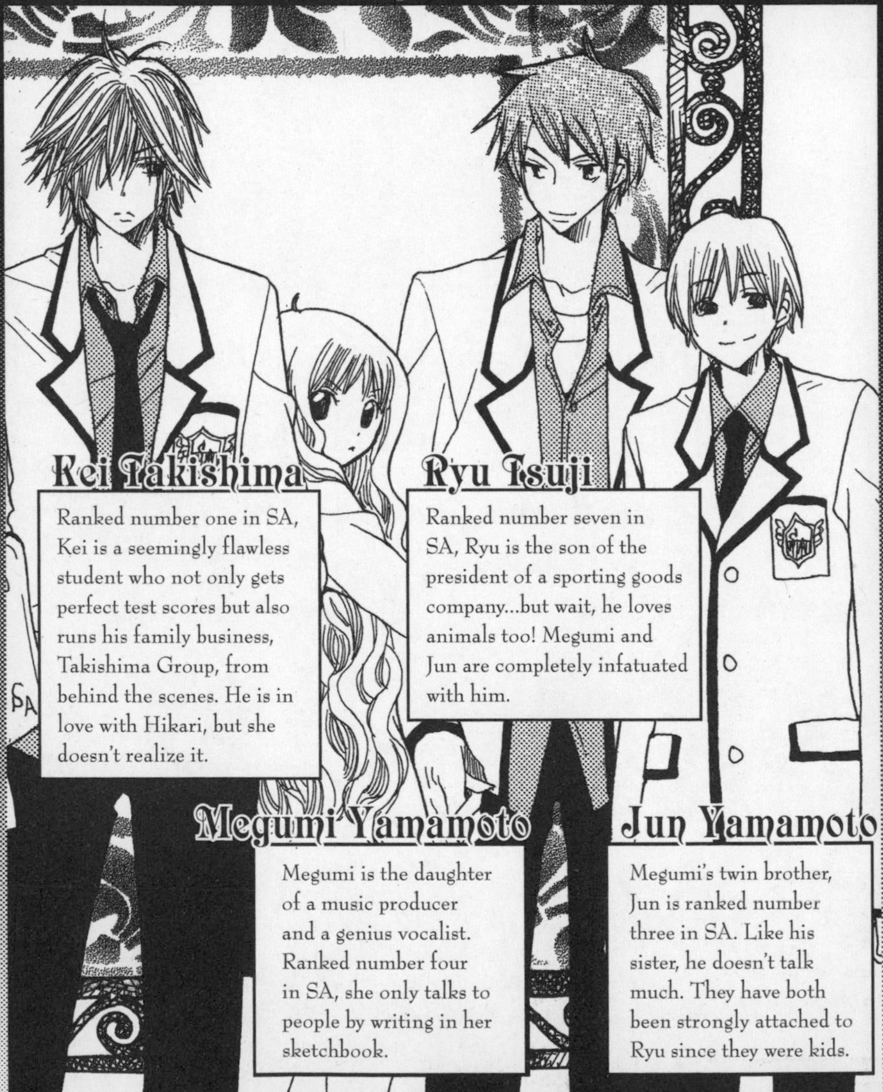
Kei Takishima
Ranked number one in SA, Kei is a seemingly flawless student who not only gets perfect test scores but also runs his family business, Takishima Group, from behind the scenes. He is in love with Hikari, but she doesn't realize it.
Ryu Tsuji
Ranked number seven in SA, Ryu is the son of the president of a sporting goods company...but wait, he loves animals too! Megumi and Jun are completely infatuated with him.
Megumi Yamamoto
Megumi is the daughter of a music producer and a genius vocalist. Ranked number four in SA, she only talks to people by writing in her sketchbook.
Jun Yamamoto
Megumi's twin brother, Jun is ranked number three in SA. Like his sister, he doesn't talk much. They have both been strongly attached to Ryu since they were kids.
SA

Contents

Chapter 29 5

Chapter 30 35

Chapter 31 65

Chapter 32 97

Chapter 33 127

Chapter 34 157

Bonus Pages 187

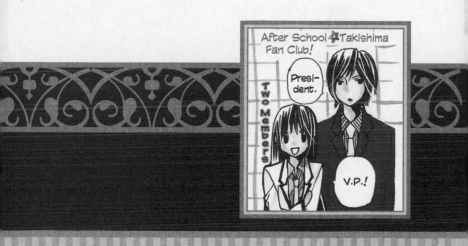

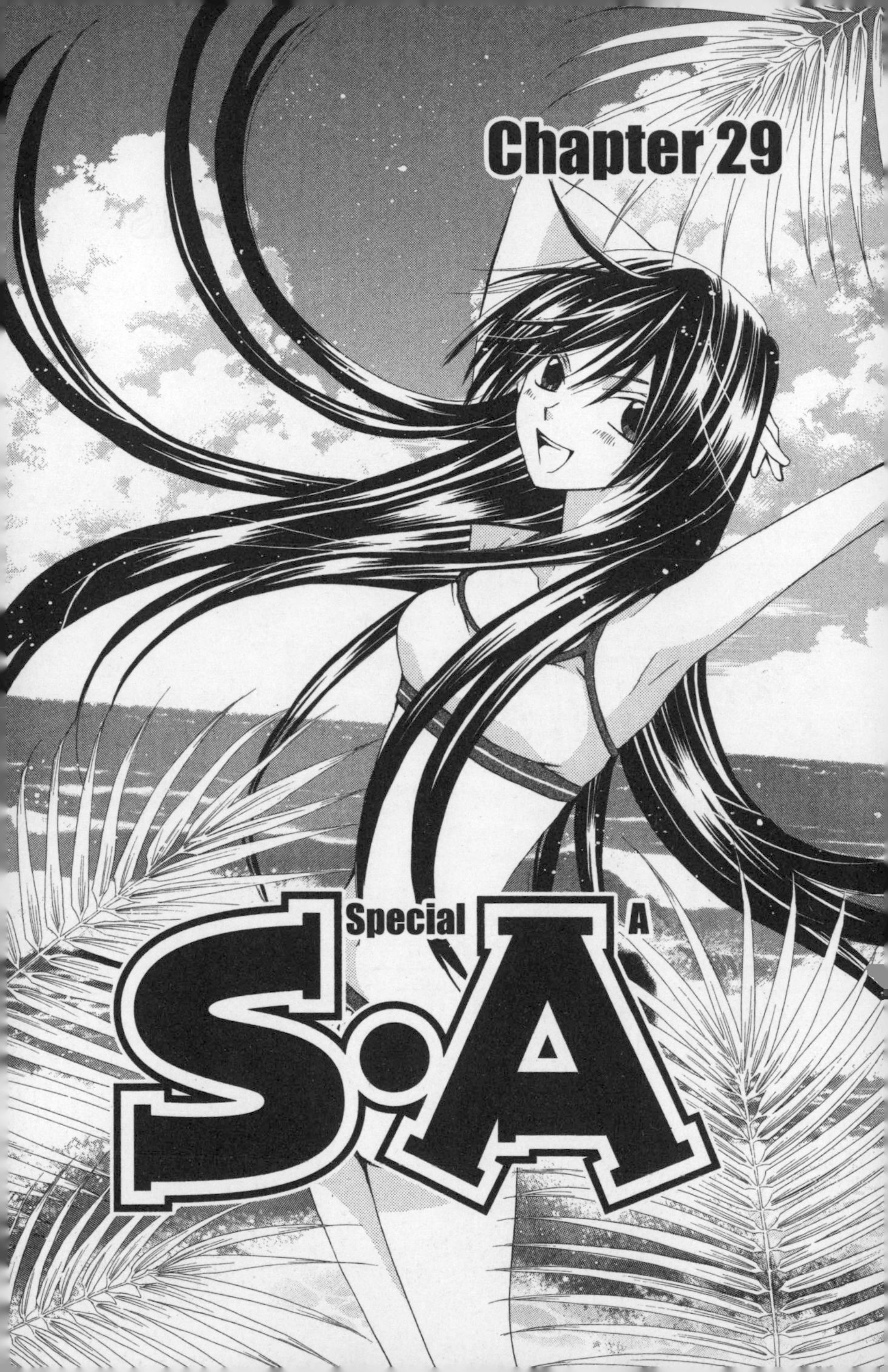
Chapter 29
Special A
S.A

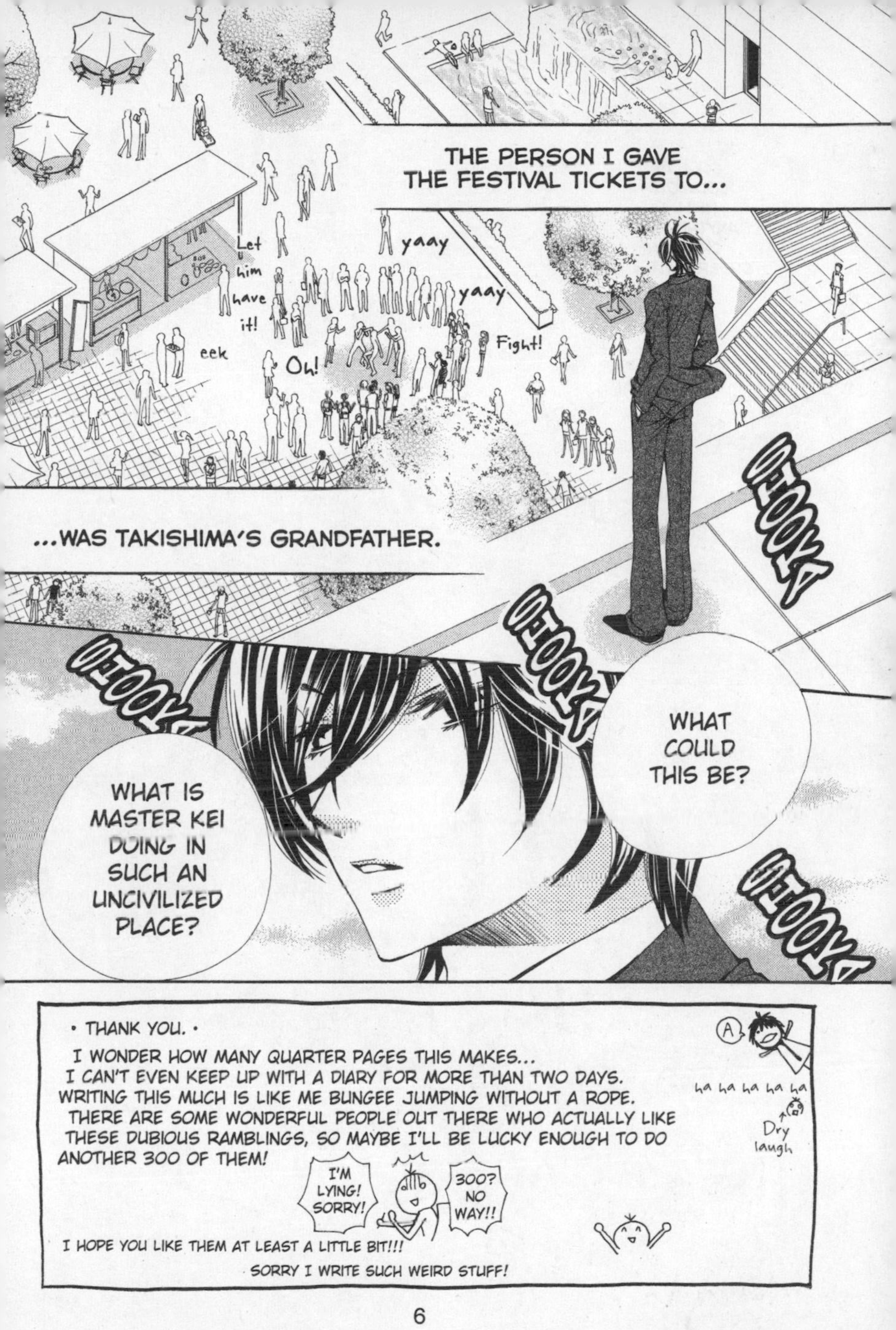
THE PERSON I GAVE THE FESTIVAL TICKETS TO...
yaay
yaay
Fight!
Let him have it!
Oh!
eek
...WAS TAKISHIMA'S GRANDFATHER.
WHAT COULD THIS BE?
WHAT IS MASTER KEI DOING IN SUCH AN UNCIVILIZED PLACE?

• THANK YOU. •

I WONDER HOW MANY QUARTER PAGES THIS MAKES... I CAN'T EVEN KEEP UP WITH A DIARY FOR MORE THAN TWO DAYS. WRITING THIS MUCH IS LIKE ME BUNGEE JUMPING WITHOUT A ROPE. THERE ARE SOME WONDERFUL PEOPLE OUT THERE WHO ACTUALLY LIKE THESE DUBIOUS RAMBLINGS, SO MAYBE I'LL BE LUCKY ENOUGH TO DO ANOTHER 300 OF THEM!

A

ha ha ha ha ha

Dry laugh

300? NO WAY!!

I'M LYING! SORRY!

I HOPE YOU LIKE THEM AT LEAST A LITTLE BIT!!!

SORRY I WRITE SUCH WEIRD STUFF!

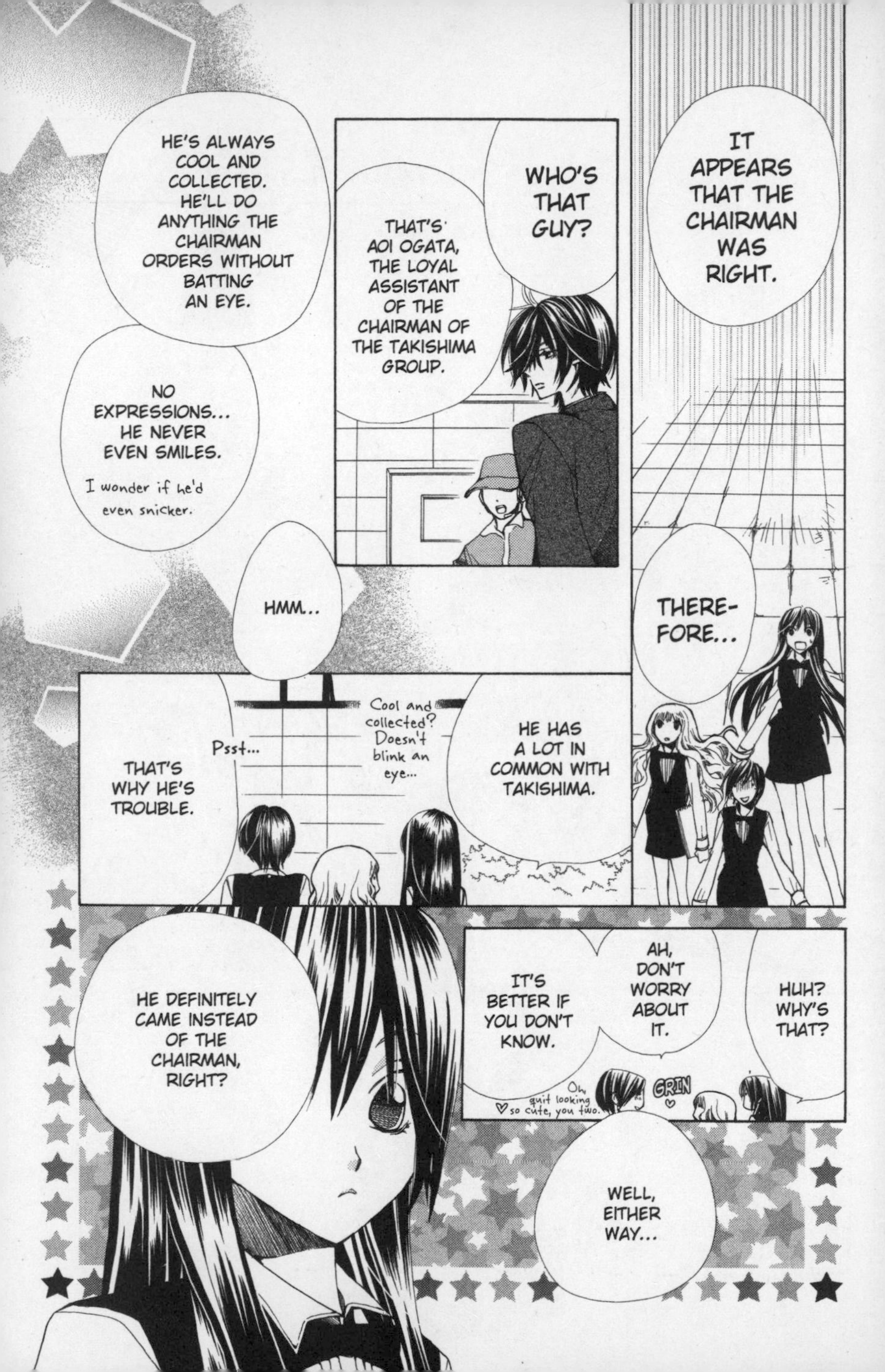
IT APPEARS THAT THE CHAIRMAN WAS RIGHT.
THERE-FORE...
WHO'S THAT GUY?
THAT'S AOI OGATA, THE LOYAL ASSISTANT OF THE CHAIRMAN OF THE TAKISHIMA GROUP.
HE'S ALWAYS COOL AND COLLECTED. HE'LL DO ANYTHING THE CHAIRMAN ORDERS WITHOUT BATTING AN EYE.
NO EXPRESSIONS... HE NEVER EVEN SMILES.
I wonder if he'd even snicker.
HMM...
HE HAS A LOT IN COMMON WITH TAKISHIMA.
Cool and collected? Doesn't blink an eye...
Psst...
THAT'S WHY HE'S TROUBLE.
HUH? WHY'S THAT?
AH, DON'T WORRY ABOUT IT.
IT'S BETTER IF YOU DON'T KNOW.
GRIN
Oh quit looking so cute, you two.
WELL, EITHER WAY...
HE DEFINITELY CAME INSTEAD OF THE CHAIRMAN, RIGHT?

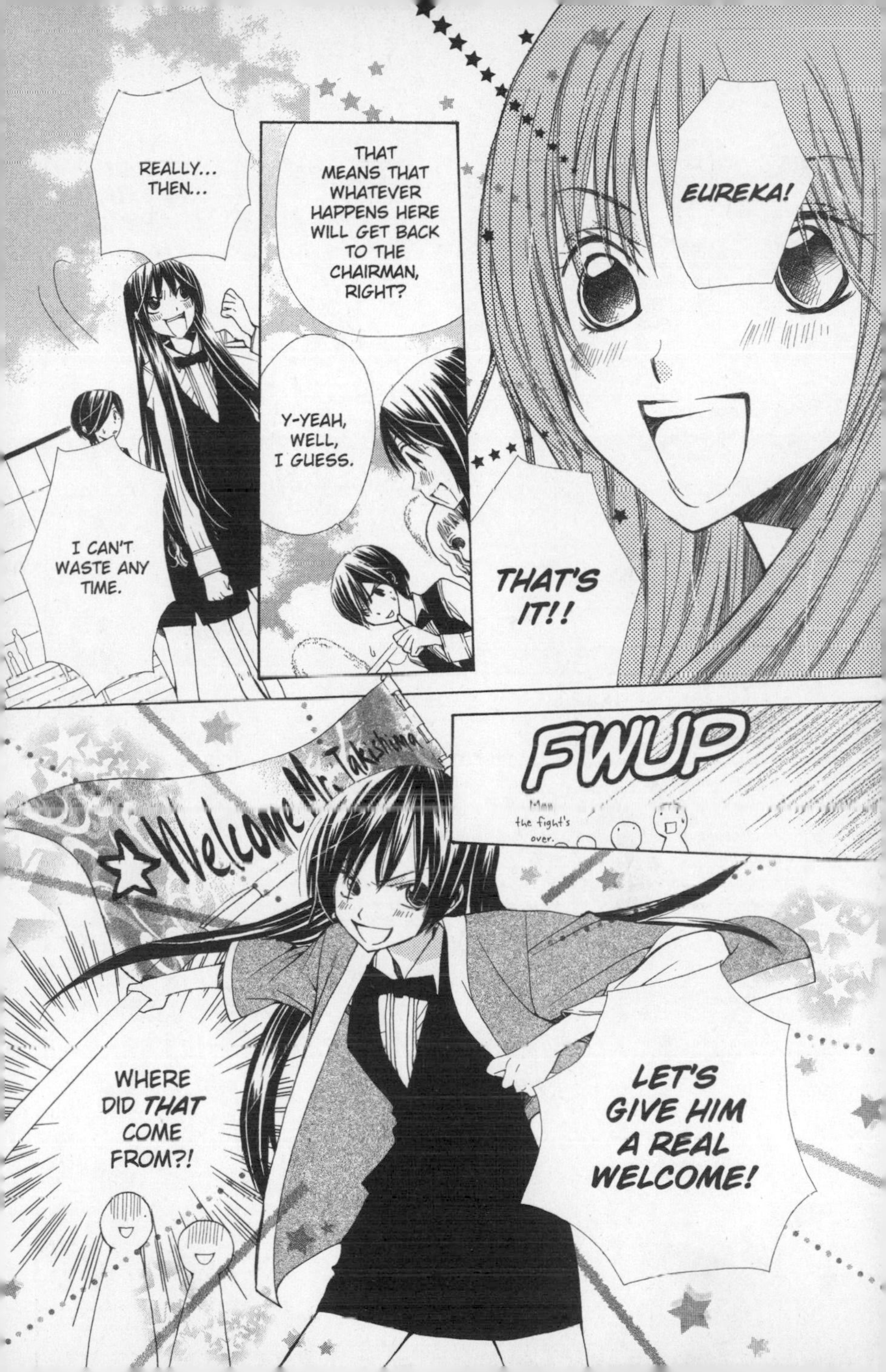
EUREKA!
THAT'S IT!!
THAT MEANS THAT WHATEVER HAPPENS HERE WILL GET BACK TO THE CHAIRMAN, RIGHT?
Y-YEAH, WELL, I GUESS.
REALLY... THEN...
I CAN'T WASTE ANY TIME.
FWUP
Mmm the fight's over.
Welcome Mr. Takishima
LET'S GIVE HIM A REAL WELCOME!
WHERE DID THAT COME FROM?!

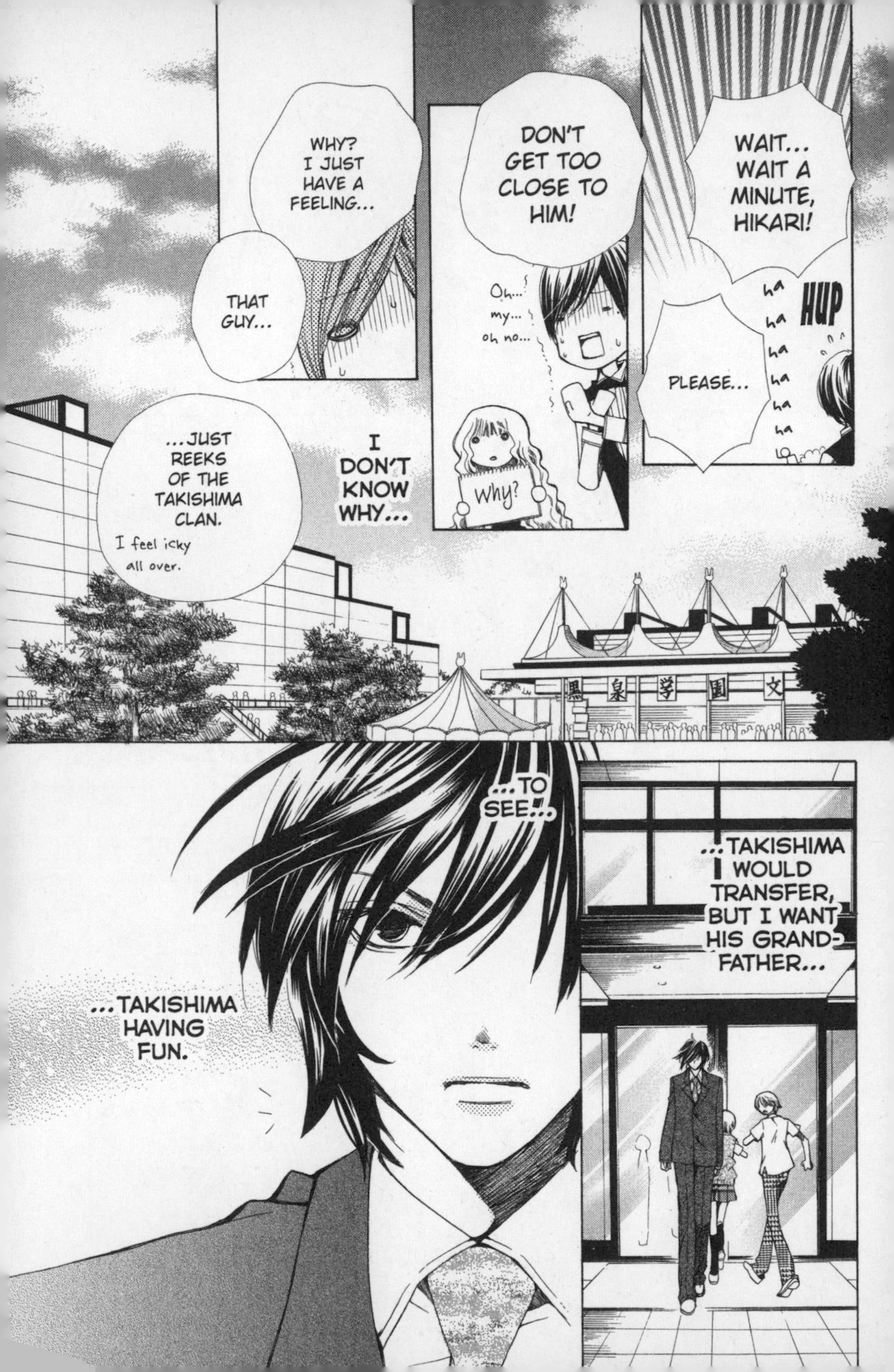
WAIT... WAIT A MINUTE, HIKARI!
HUP
ha ha ha ha ha ha
PLEASE...
DON'T GET TOO CLOSE TO HIM!
Oh... my... oh no...
Why?
WHY? I JUST HAVE A FEELING...
THAT GUY...
...JUST REEKS OF THE TAKISHIMA CLAN.
I feel icky all over.
I DON'T KNOW WHY...
黒泉学園文
...TAKISHIMA WOULD TRANSFER, BUT I WANT HIS GRANDFATHER...
...TO SEE...
...TAKISHIMA HAVING FUN.

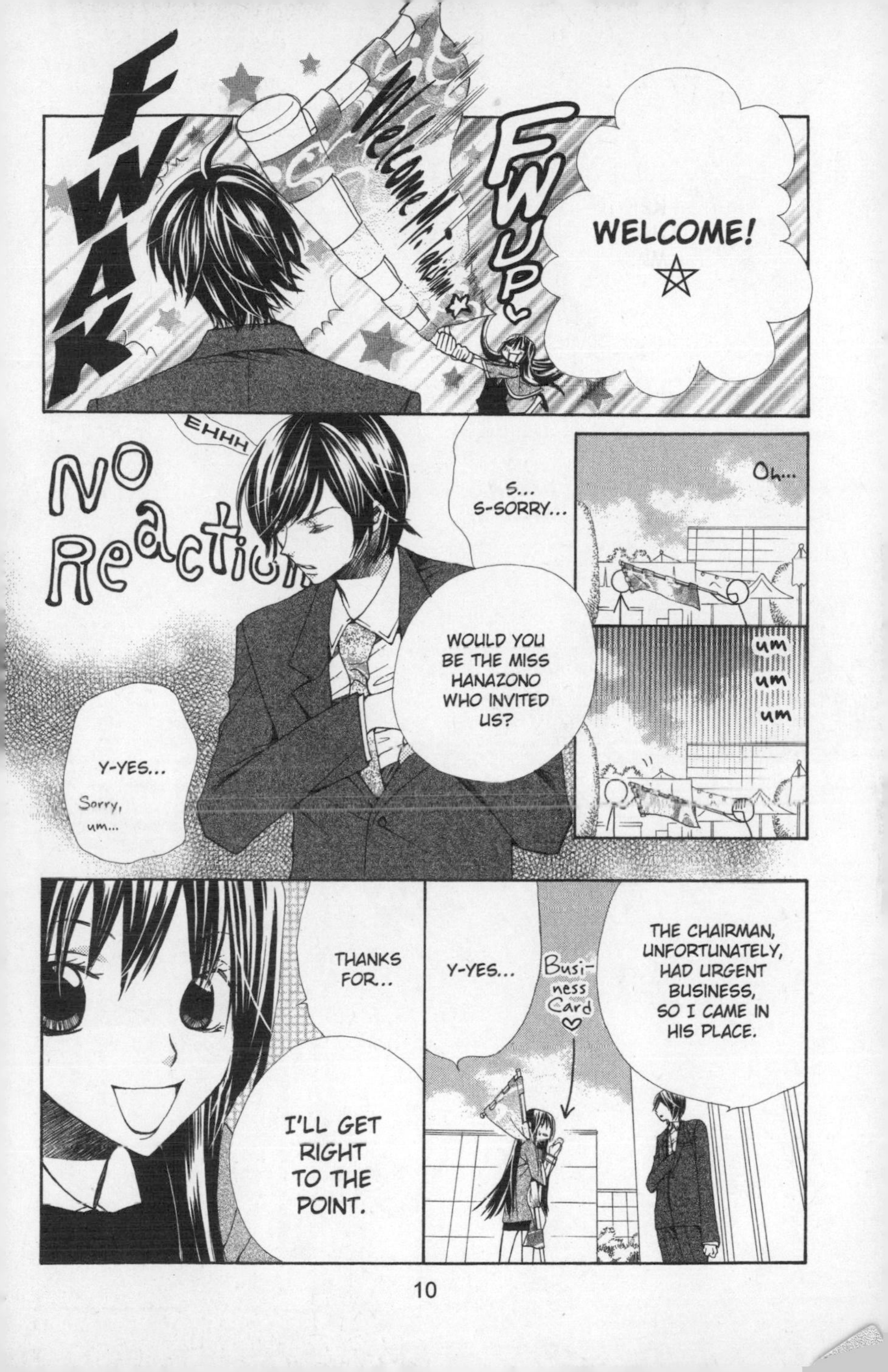
WELCOME! ☆
FWUP
FWAK
Oh...
um um um
S... S-SORRY...
WOULD YOU BE THE MISS HANAZONO WHO INVITED US?
EHHH
NO Reaction
Y-YES...
Sorry, um...
THE CHAIRMAN, UNFORTUNATELY, HAD URGENT BUSINESS, SO I CAME IN HIS PLACE.
Business Card
Y-YES...
THANKS FOR...
I'LL GET RIGHT TO THE POINT.

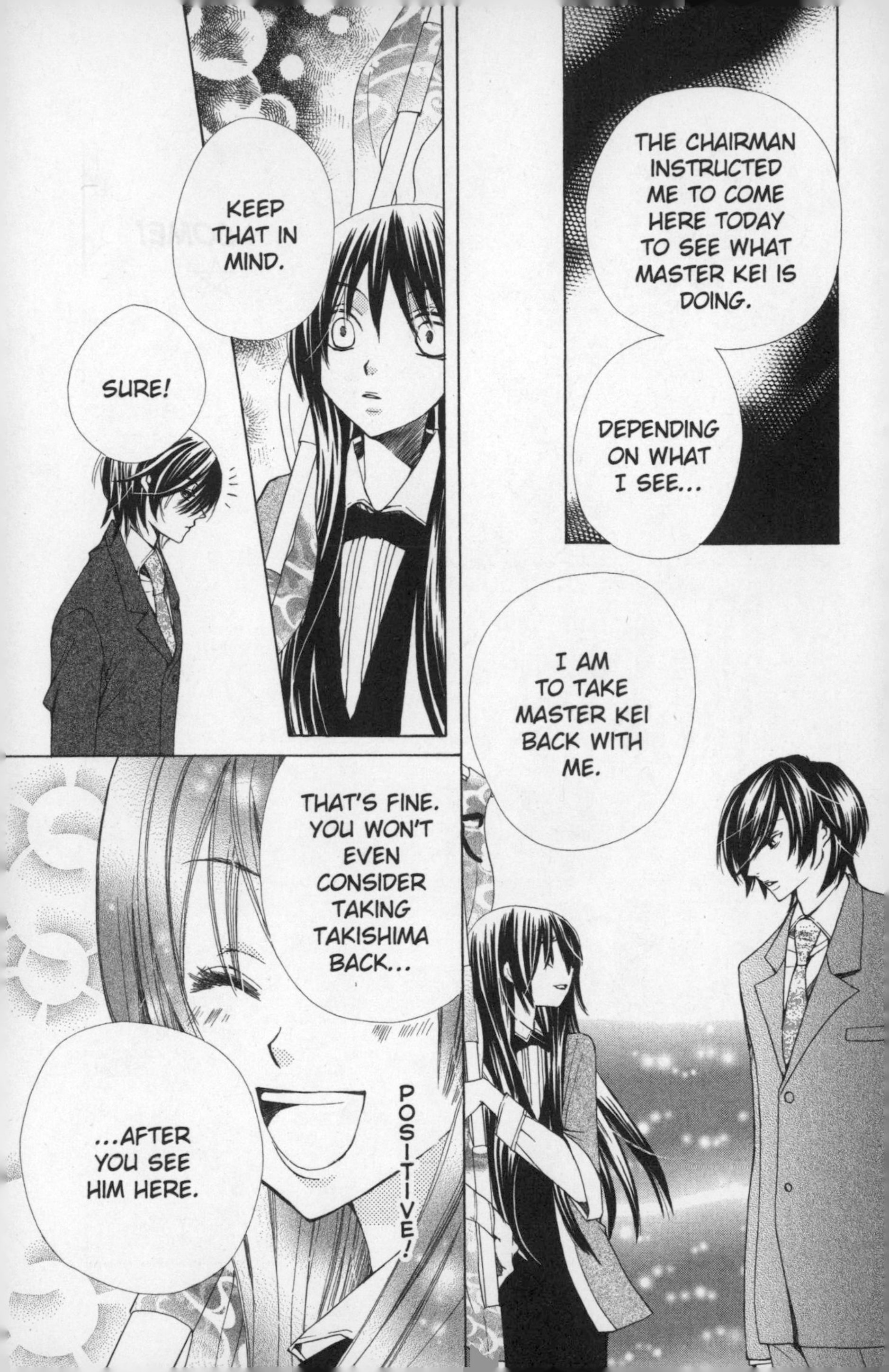
THE CHAIRMAN INSTRUCTED ME TO COME HERE TODAY TO SEE WHAT MASTER KEI IS DOING.
DEPENDING ON WHAT I SEE...
I AM TO TAKE MASTER KEI BACK WITH ME.
KEEP THAT IN MIND.
SURE!
THAT'S FINE. YOU WON'T EVEN CONSIDER TAKING TAKISHIMA BACK...
...AFTER YOU SEE HIM HERE.
POSITIVE!

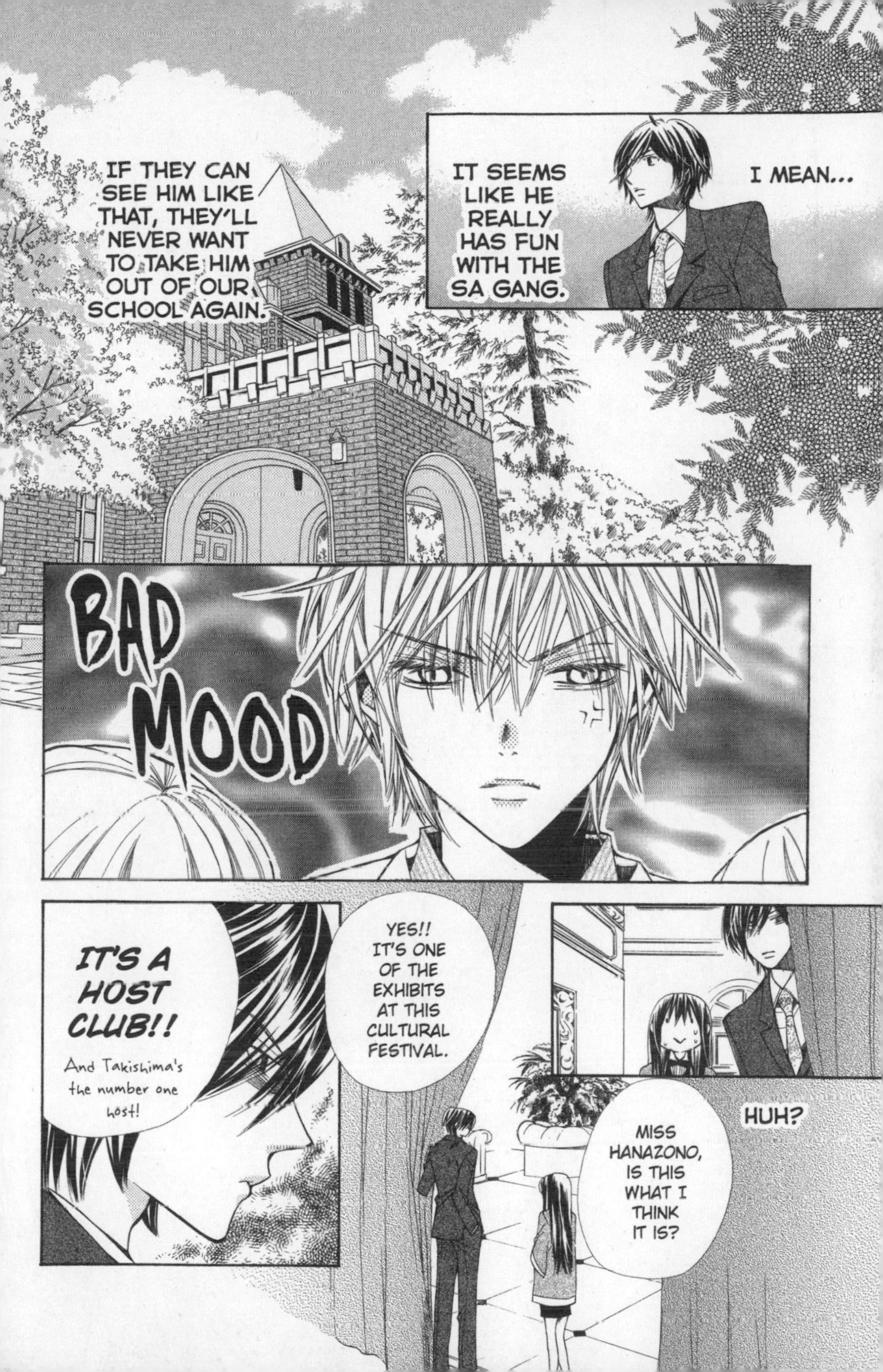
I MEAN...
IT SEEMS LIKE HE REALLY HAS FUN WITH THE SA GANG.
IF THEY CAN SEE HIM LIKE THAT, THEY'LL NEVER WANT TO TAKE HIM OUT OF OUR SCHOOL AGAIN.
BAD MOOD
HUH?
MISS HANAZONO, IS THIS WHAT I THINK IT IS?
YES!! IT'S ONE OF THE EXHIBITS AT THIS CULTURAL FESTIVAL.
IT'S A HOST CLUB!!
And Takishima's the number one host!

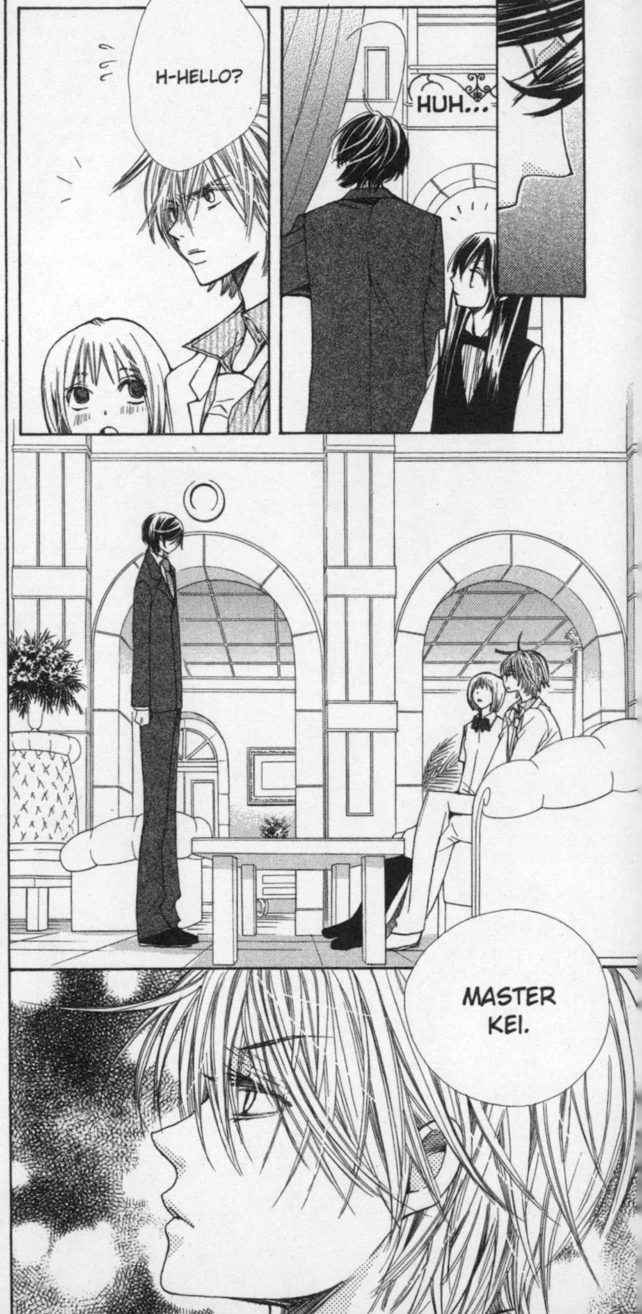
HUH...
H-HELLO?
MASTER KEI.

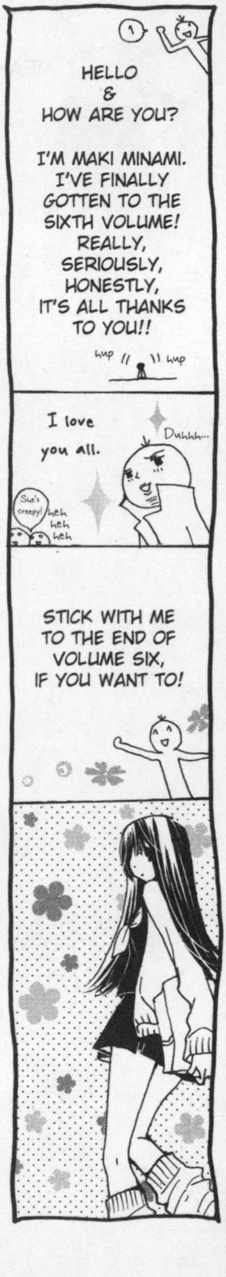
1
HELLO
&
HOW ARE YOU?
I'M MAKI MINAMI.
I'VE FINALLY GOTTEN TO THE SIXTH VOLUME! REALLY, SERIOUSLY, HONESTLY, IT'S ALL THANKS TO YOU!!
hup hup
I love you all.
Duhhh...
She's creepy!
heh heh heh
STICK WITH ME TO THE END OF VOLUME SIX, IF YOU WANT TO!

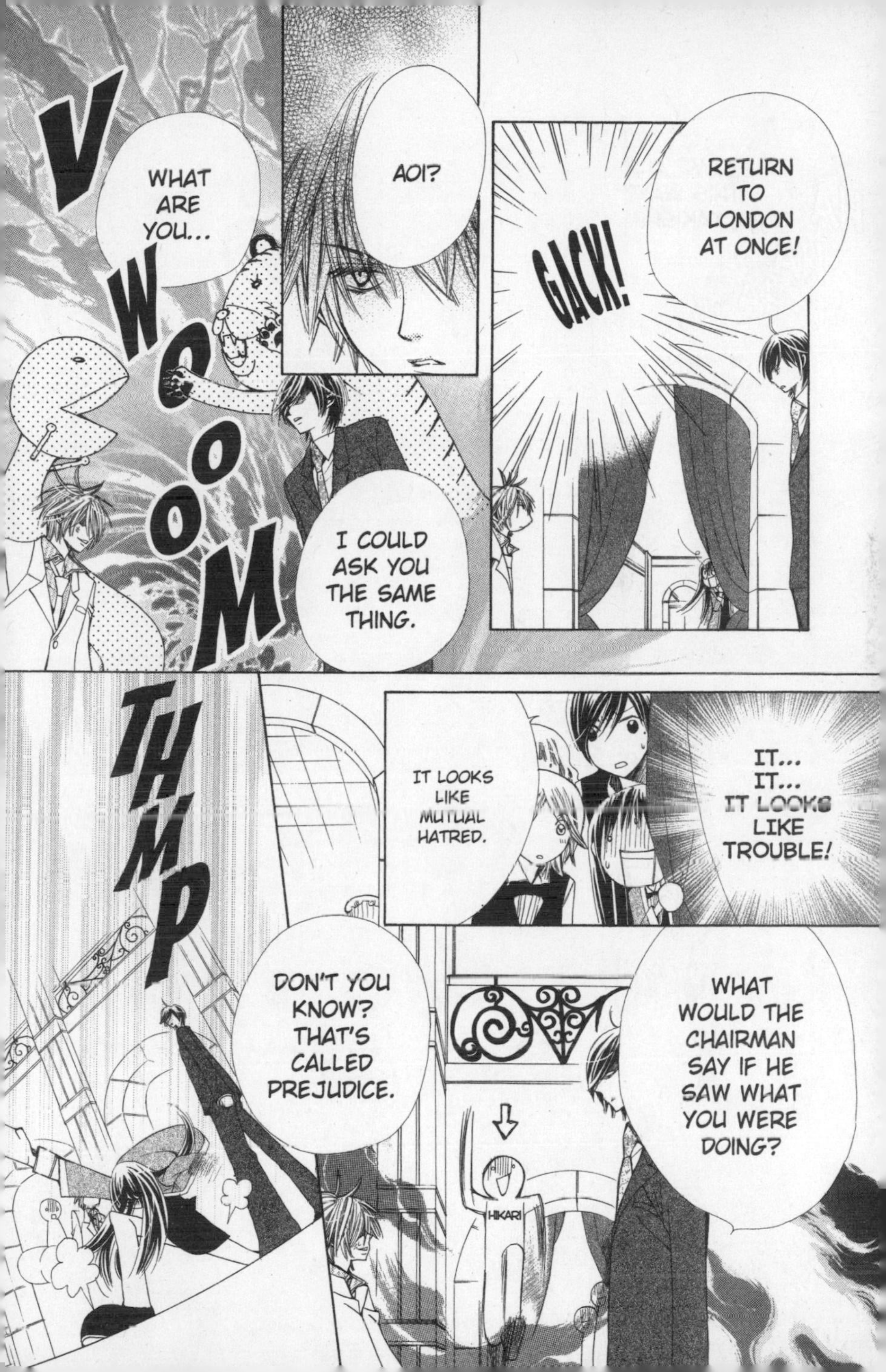
GACK!
RETURN TO LONDON AT ONCE!
AOI?
VWOOOOM
WHAT ARE YOU...
I COULD ASK YOU THE SAME THING.
IT... IT... IT LOOKS LIKE TROUBLE!
IT LOOKS LIKE MUTUAL HATRED.
WHAT WOULD THE CHAIRMAN SAY IF HE SAW WHAT YOU WERE DOING?
HIKARI
DON'T YOU KNOW? THAT'S CALLED PREJUDICE.
THUMP

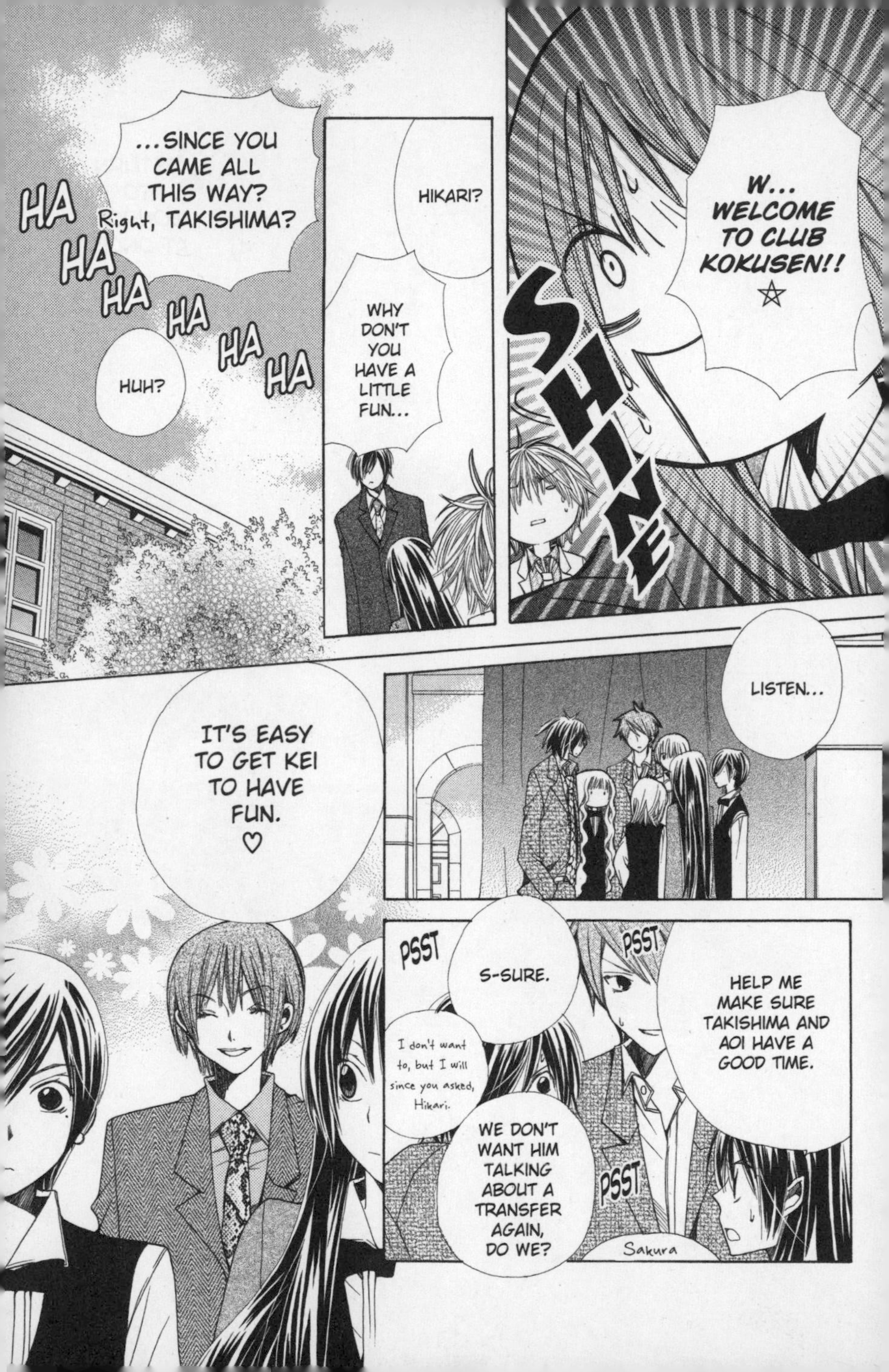
W... WELCOME TO CLUB KOKUSEN!! ☆
SHINE
HIKARI?
WHY DON'T YOU HAVE A LITTLE FUN...
...SINCE YOU CAME ALL THIS WAY? Right, TAKISHIMA?
HA HA HA HA HA HA
HUH?
LISTEN...
PSST
HELP ME MAKE SURE TAKISHIMA AND AOI HAVE A GOOD TIME.
PSST
S-SURE.
I don't want to, but I will since you asked, Hikari.
WE DON'T WANT HIM TALKING ABOUT A TRANSFER AGAIN, DO WE?
PSST
Sakura
IT'S EASY TO GET KEI TO HAVE FUN. ♡

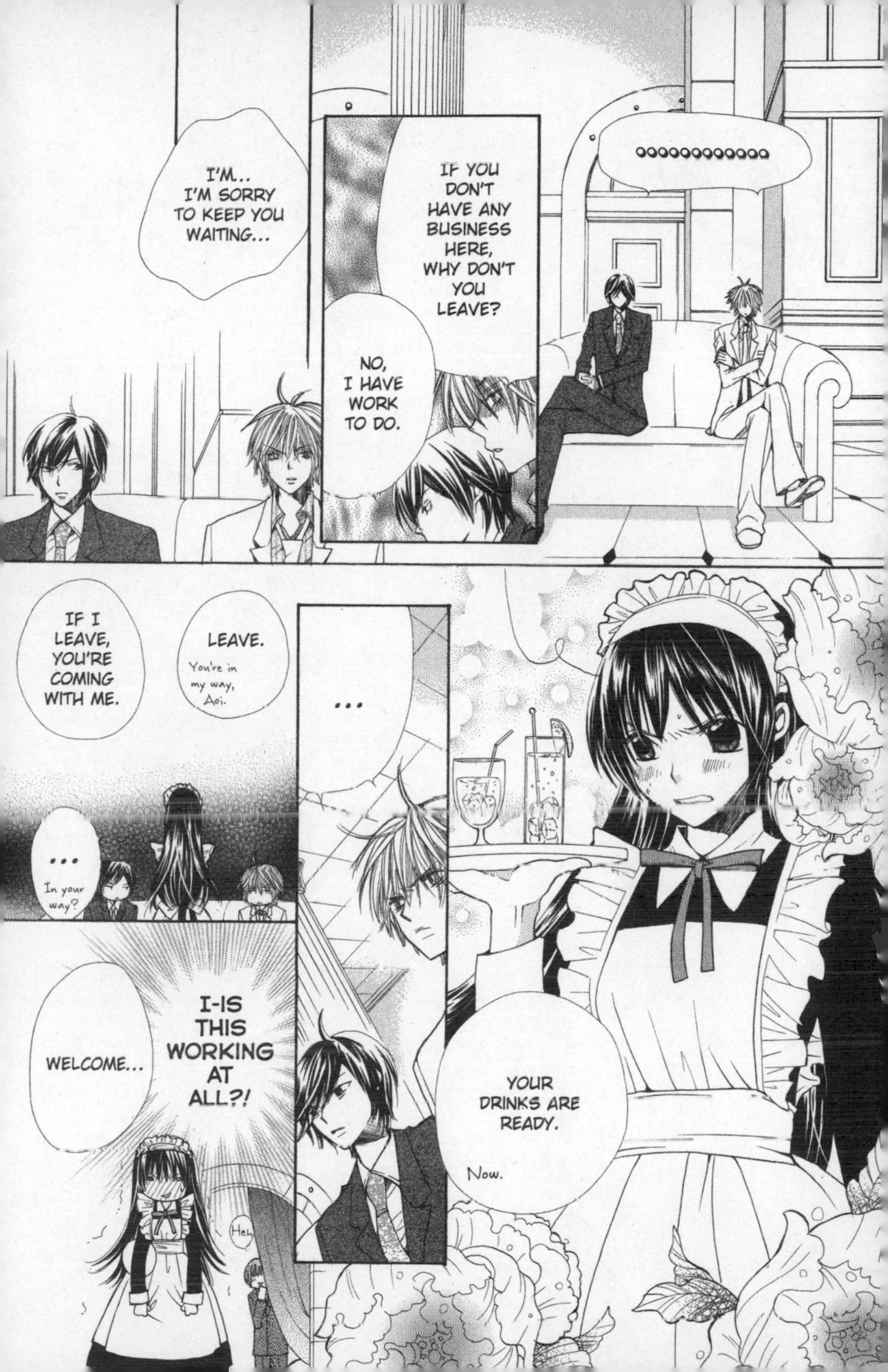
....
IF YOU DON'T HAVE ANY BUSINESS HERE, WHY DON'T YOU LEAVE?
NO, I HAVE WORK TO DO.
I'M... I'M SORRY TO KEEP YOU WAITING...
YOUR DRINKS ARE READY.
Now.
...
LEAVE.
You're in my way, Aoi.
IF I LEAVE, YOU'RE COMING WITH ME.
...
In your way?
I-IS THIS WORKING AT ALL?!
WELCOME...
Heh

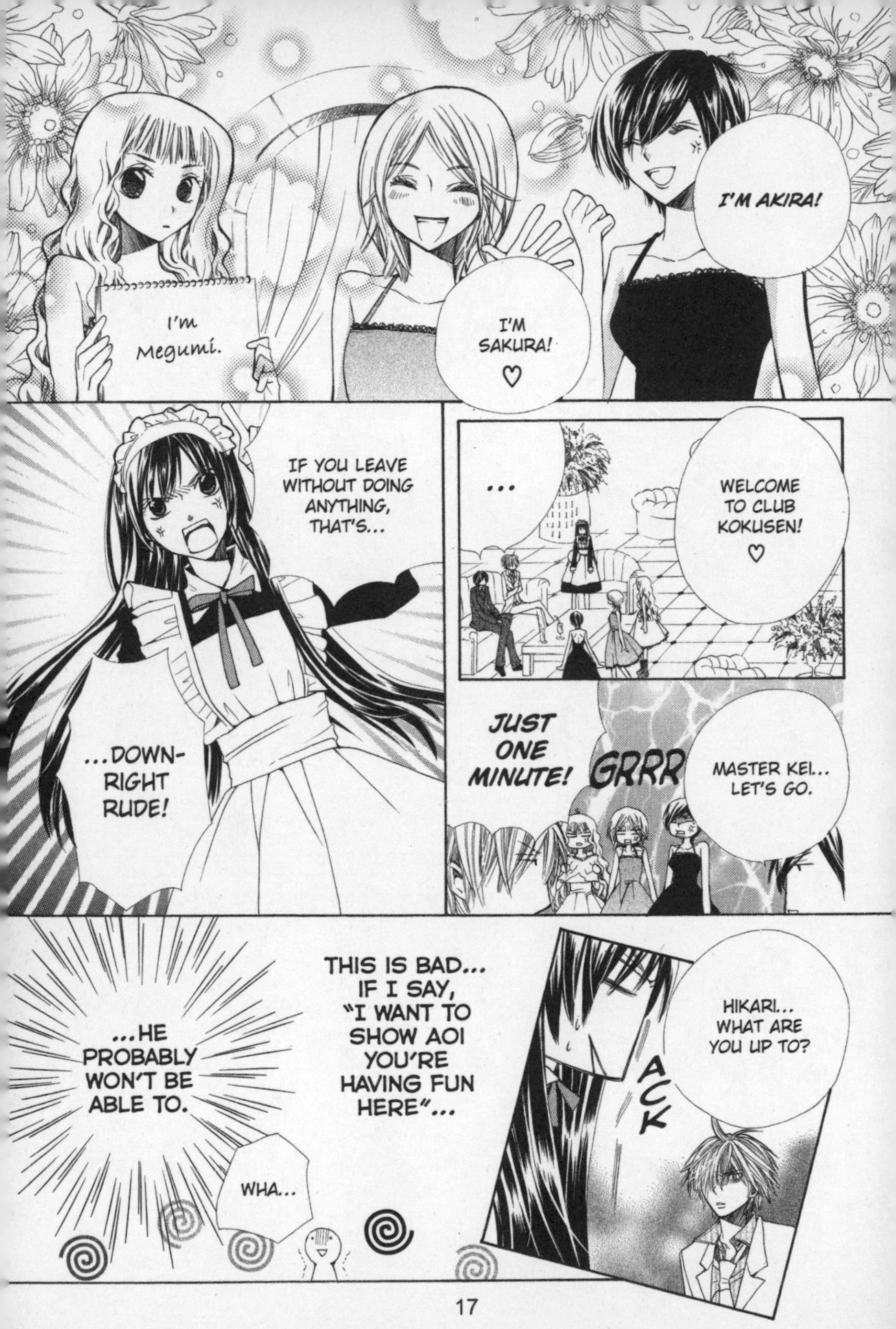
I'M AKIRA!
I'M SAKURA! ♡
I'm Megumi.
WELCOME TO CLUB KOKUSEN! ♡
...
MASTER KEI... LET'S GO.
GRRR
JUST ONE MINUTE!
IF YOU LEAVE WITHOUT DOING ANYTHING, THAT'S...
...DOWN-RIGHT RUDE!
HIKARI... WHAT ARE YOU UP TO?
ACK
THIS IS BAD... IF I SAY, "I WANT TO SHOW AOI YOU'RE HAVING FUN HERE"...
...HE PROBABLY WON'T BE ABLE TO.
WHA...

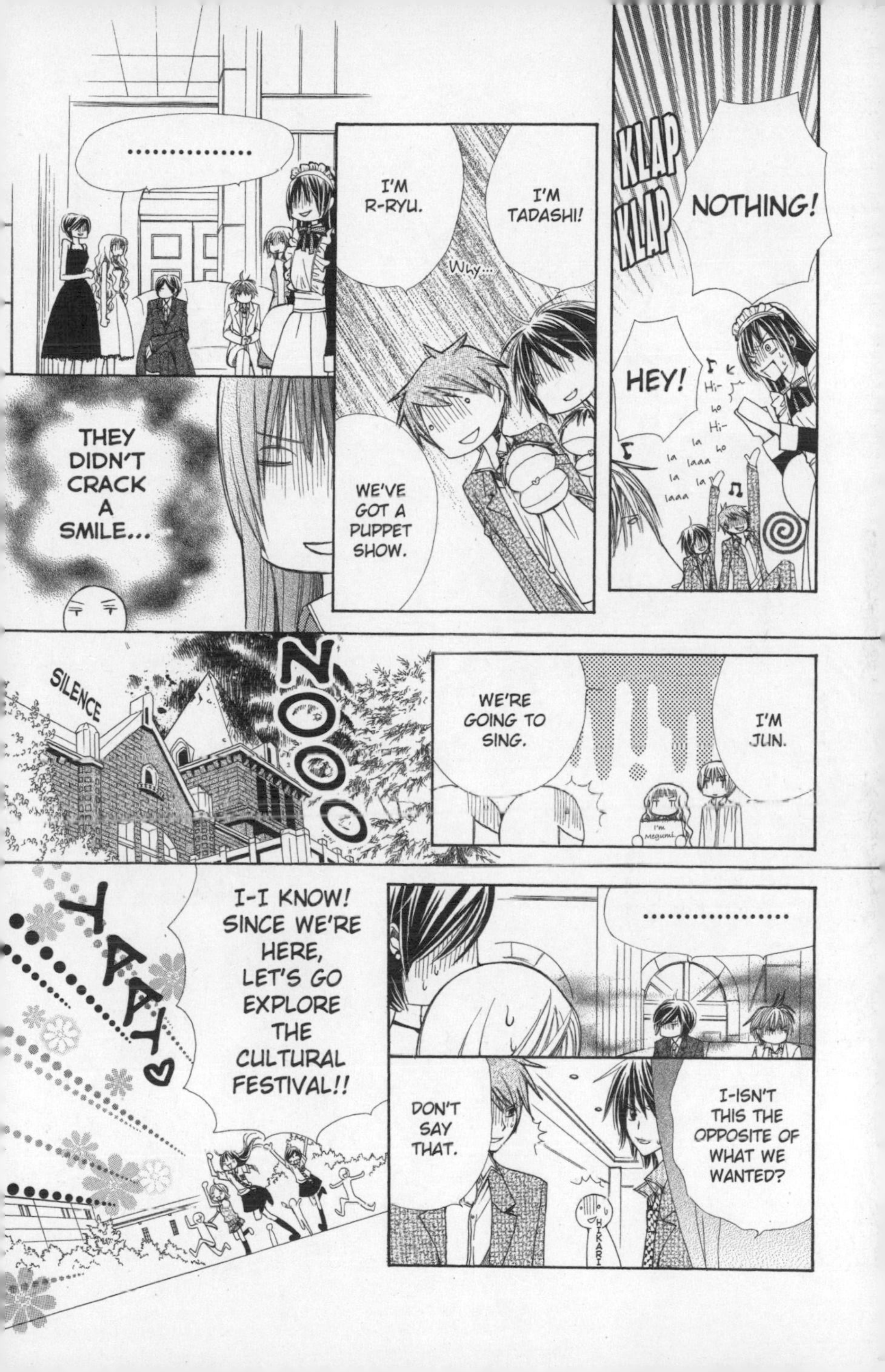
KLAP KLAP
NOTHING!
HEY!
Hi- ho Hi- ho
la laaa la la la laaa
I'M TADASHI!
I'M R-RYU.
Why...
WE'VE GOT A PUPPET SHOW.
....
THEY DIDN'T CRACK A SMILE...
I'M JUN.
WE'RE GOING TO SING.
I'm Megumi.
NOOO
SILENCE
....
I-ISN'T THIS THE OPPOSITE OF WHAT WE WANTED?
DON'T SAY THAT.
HIKARI
TAAT♥
I-I KNOW! SINCE WE'RE HERE, LET'S GO EXPLORE THE CULTURAL FESTIVAL!!

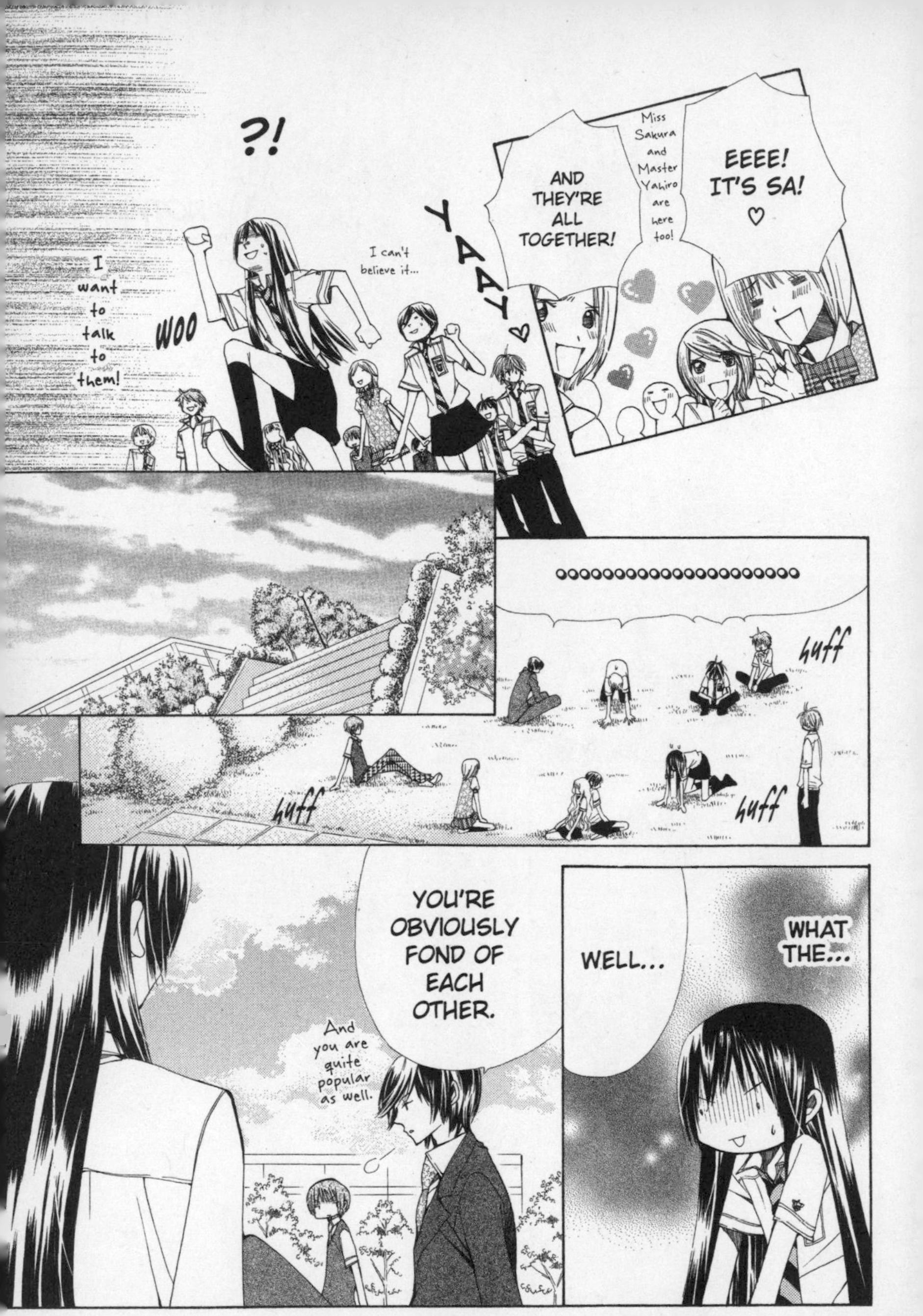

EEEE! IT'S SA! ♡
Miss Sakura and Master Yahiro are here too!
AND THEY'RE ALL TOGETHER!
?!
YAAAY ♡
I can't believe it...
WOO
I want to talk to them!
huff
huff
huff
WHAT THE...
WELL...
YOU'RE OBVIOUSLY FOND OF EACH OTHER.
And you are quite popular as well.

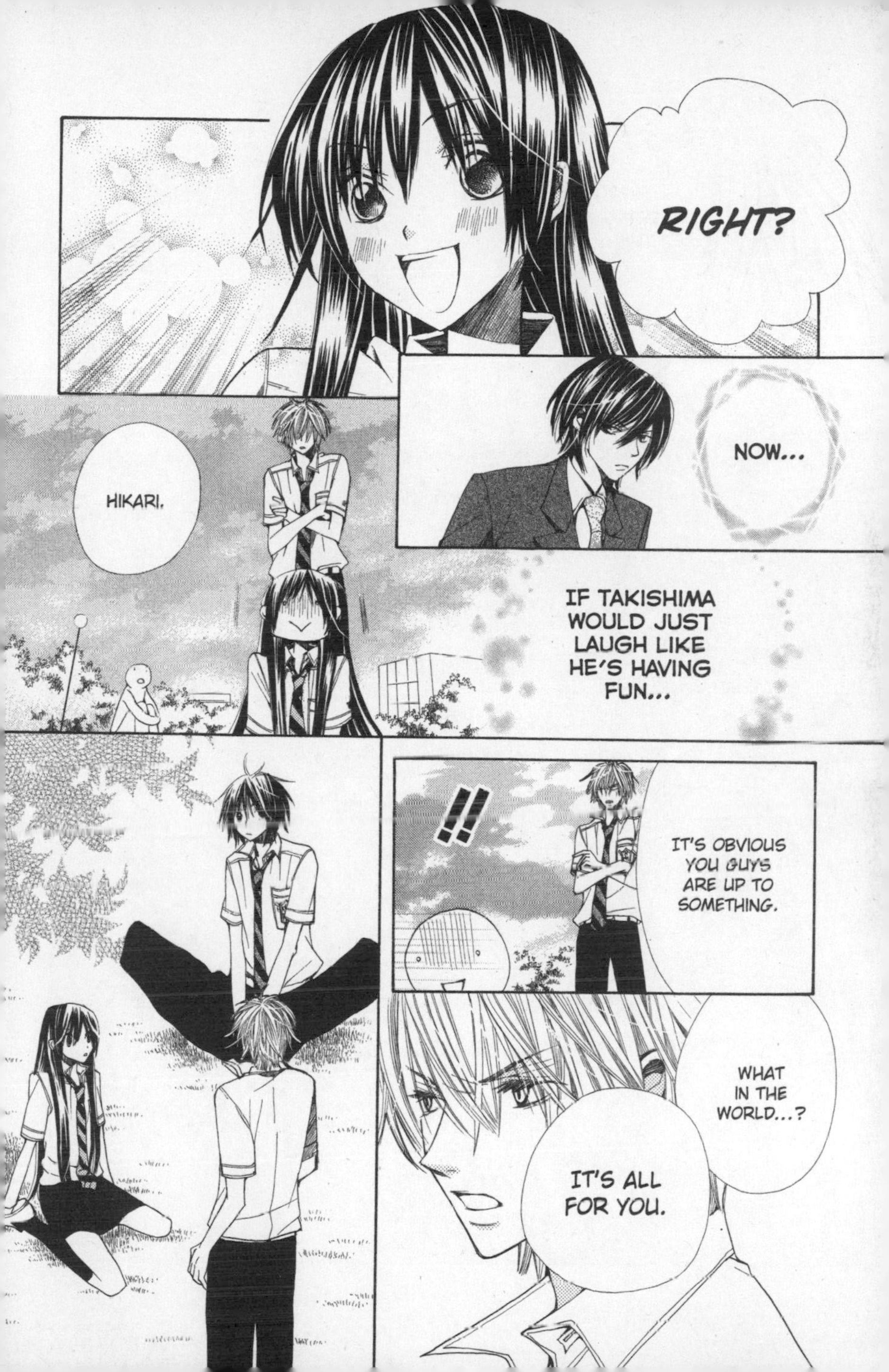

RIGHT?
NOW...
IF TAKISHIMA WOULD JUST LAUGH LIKE HE'S HAVING FUN...
HIKARI.
!!
IT'S OBVIOUS YOU GUYS ARE UP TO SOMETHING.
WHAT IN THE WORLD...?
IT'S ALL FOR YOU.

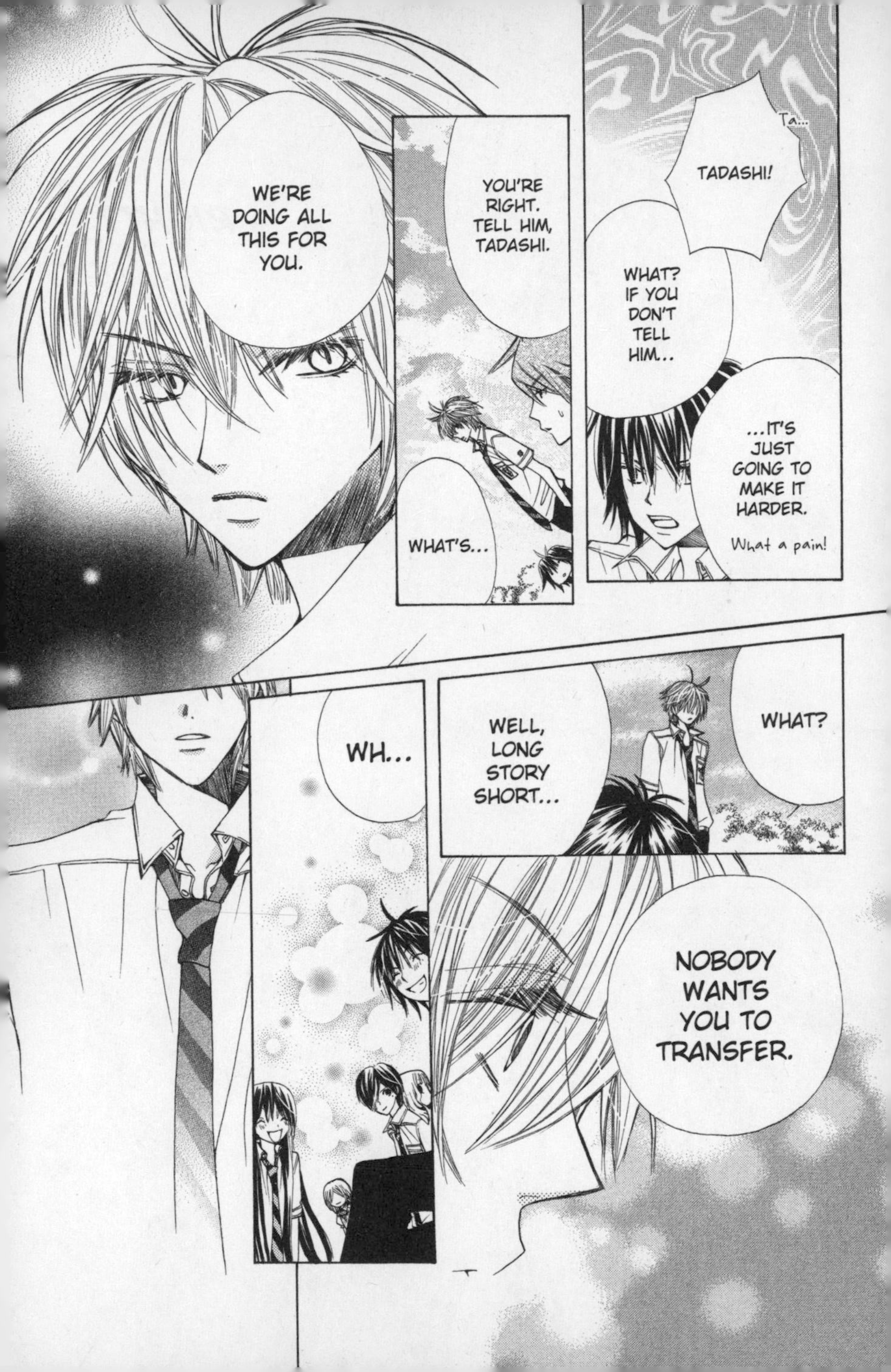
Ta...
TADASHI!
WHAT? IF YOU DON'T TELL HIM...
...IT'S JUST GOING TO MAKE IT HARDER.
What a pain!
YOU'RE RIGHT. TELL HIM, TADASHI.
WHAT'S...
WE'RE DOING ALL THIS FOR YOU.
WHAT?
WELL, LONG STORY SHORT...
NOBODY WANTS YOU TO TRANSFER.
WH...

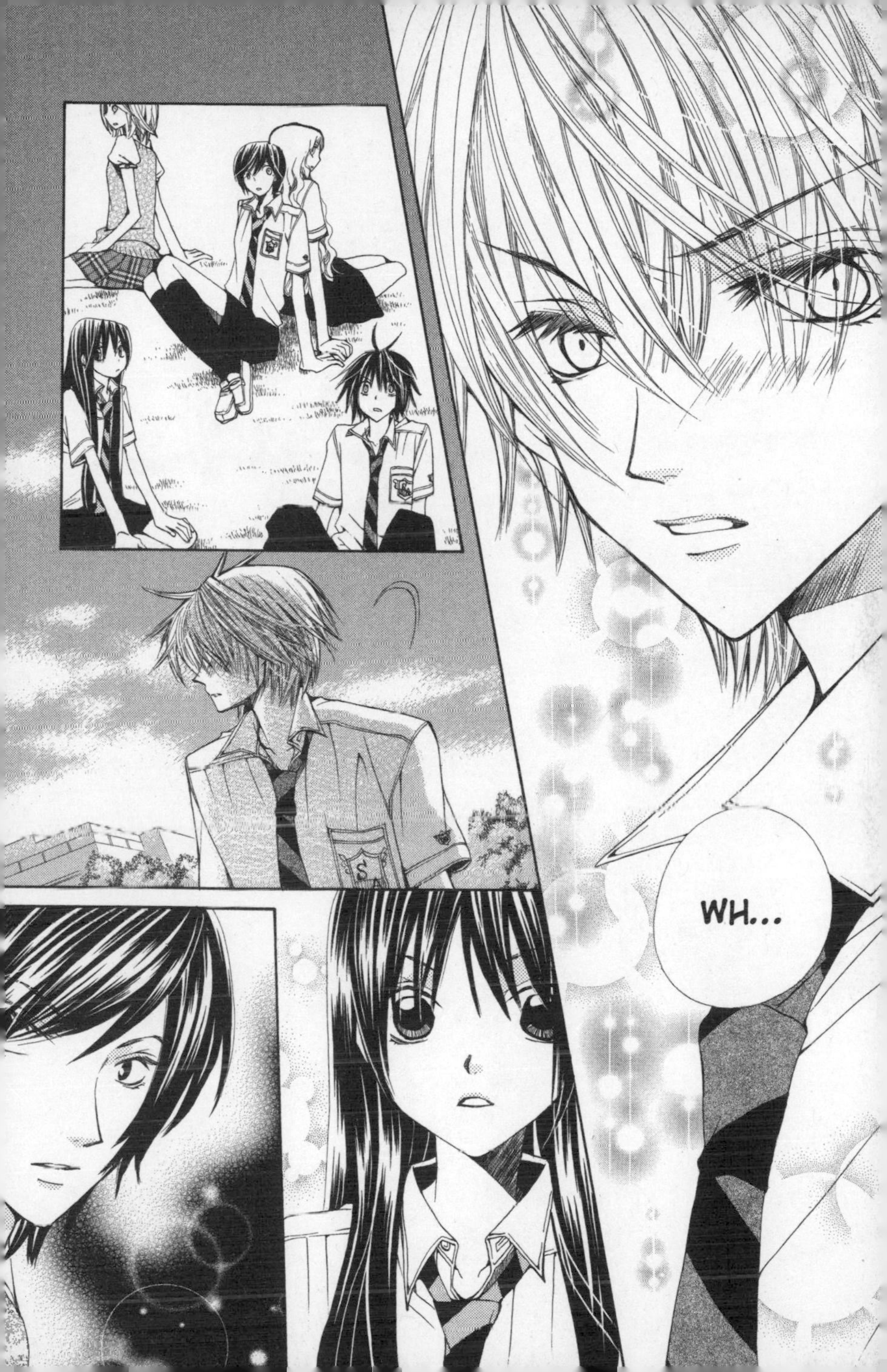
WH...

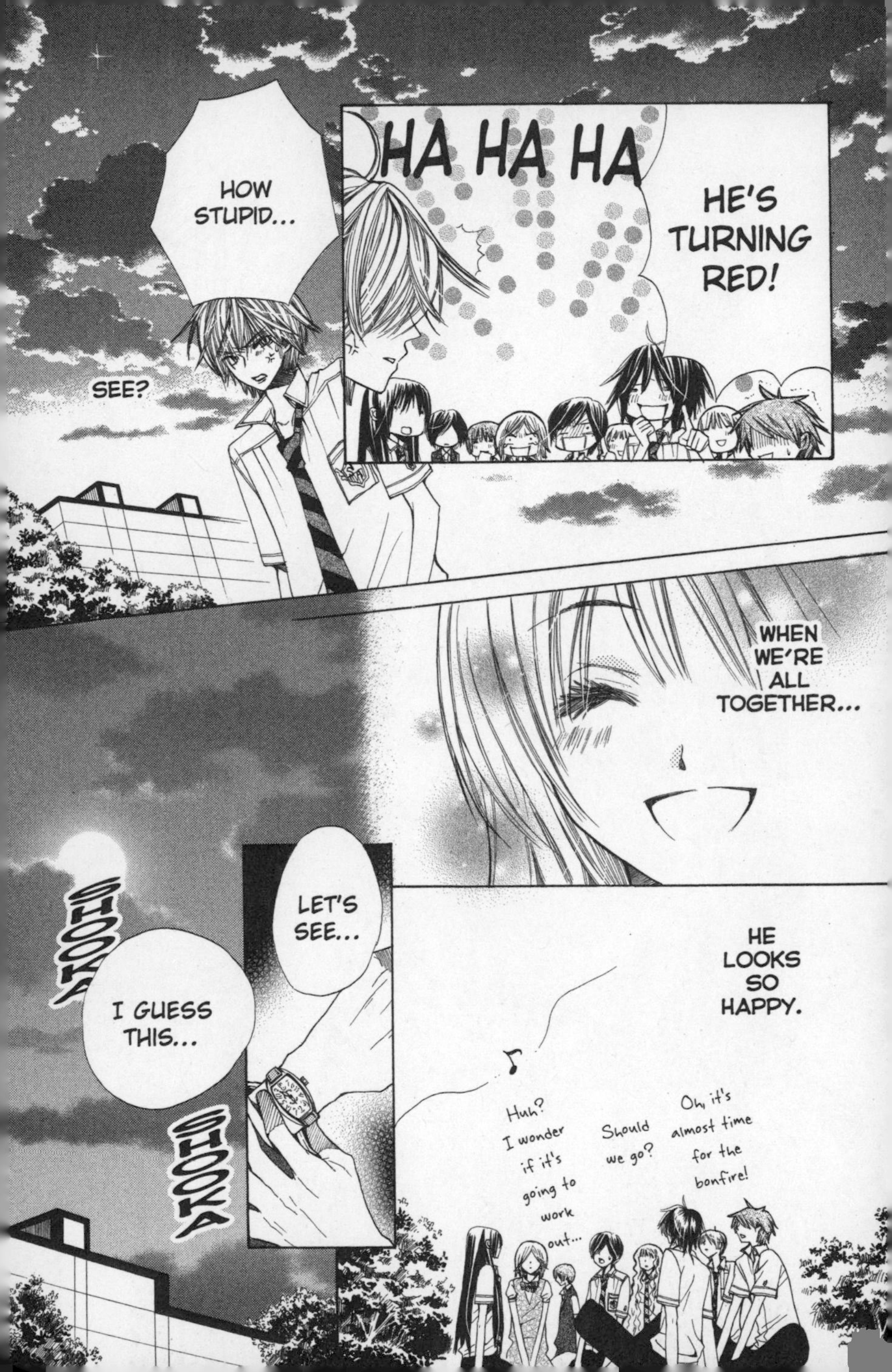
HE'S TURNING RED!
HA HA HA
HOW STUPID...
SEE?
WHEN WE'RE ALL TOGETHER...
HE LOOKS SO HAPPY.
Oh, it's almost time for the bonfire!
Should we go?
Huh? I wonder if it's going to work out...
LET'S SEE...
I GUESS THIS...
SHOOKA
SHOOKA

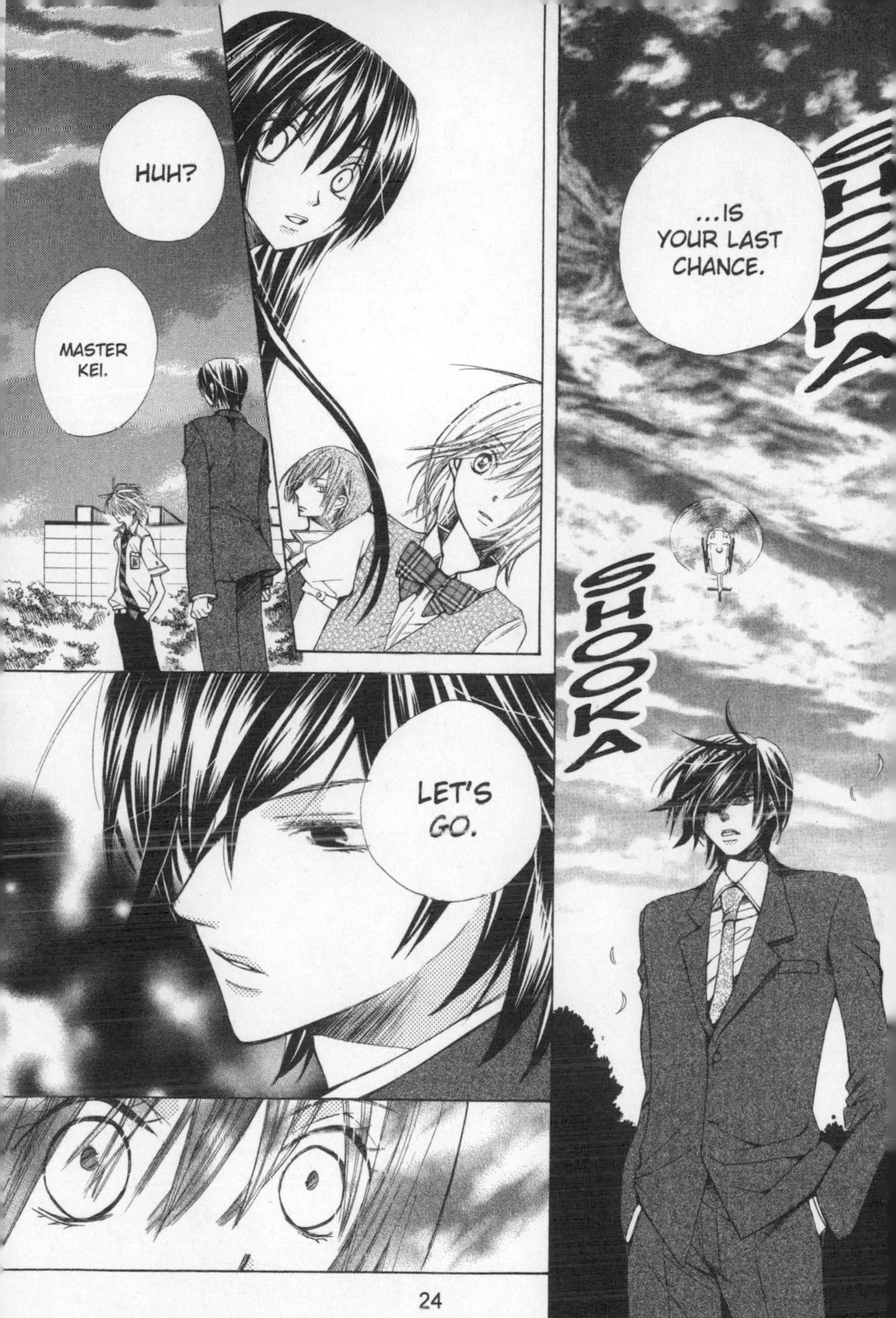
SHOOKA
...IS YOUR LAST CHANCE.
SHOOKA
HUH?
MASTER KEI.
LET'S GO.

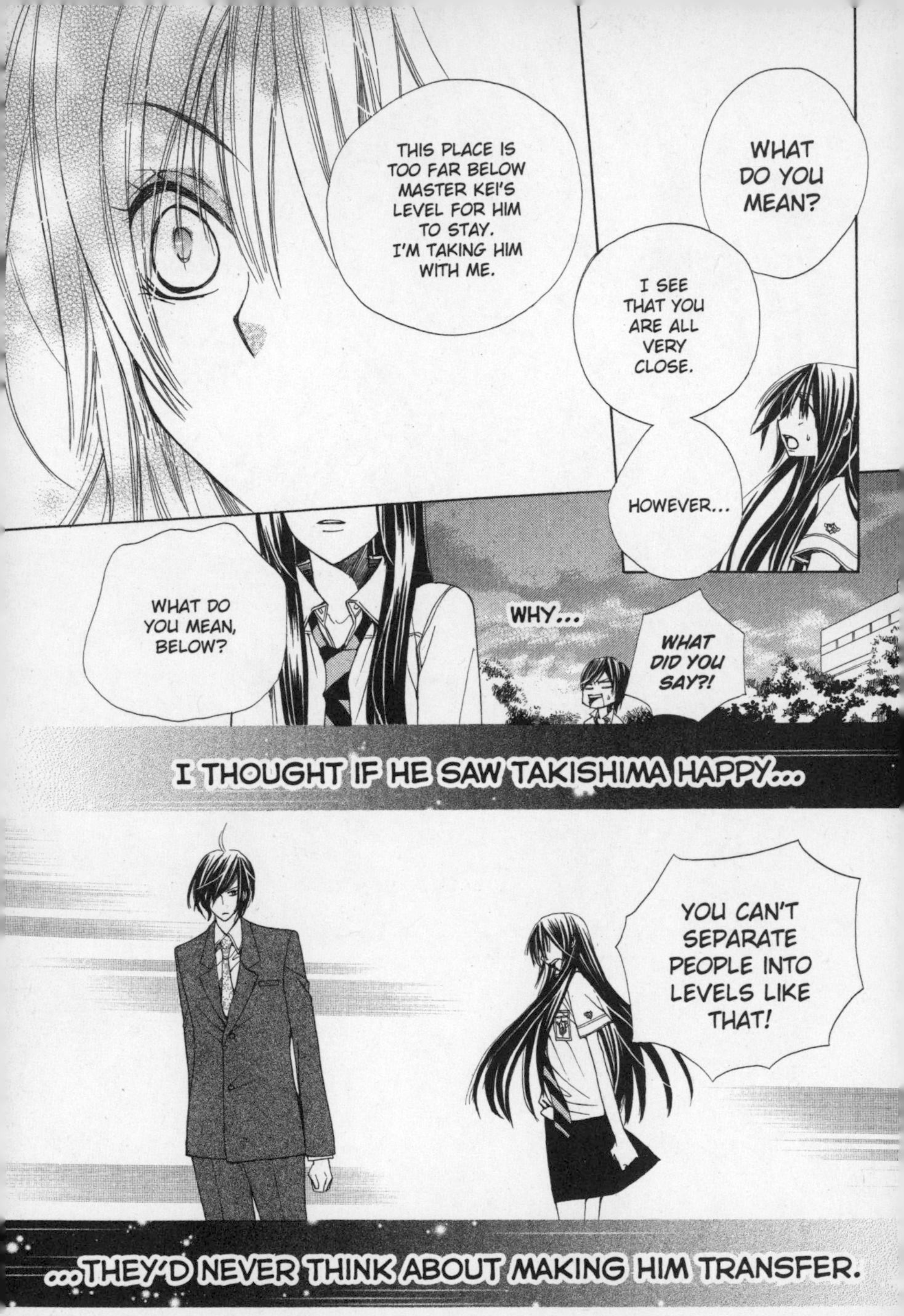
I SEE THAT YOU ARE ALL VERY CLOSE.
HOWEVER...
THIS PLACE IS TOO FAR BELOW MASTER KEI'S LEVEL FOR HIM TO STAY. I'M TAKING HIM WITH ME.
WHAT DO YOU MEAN?
WHY...
WHAT DID YOU SAY?!
WHAT DO YOU MEAN, BELOW?
I THOUGHT IF HE SAW TAKISHIMA HAPPY...
YOU CAN'T SEPARATE PEOPLE INTO LEVELS LIKE THAT!
...THEY'D NEVER THINK ABOUT MAKING HIM TRANSFER.

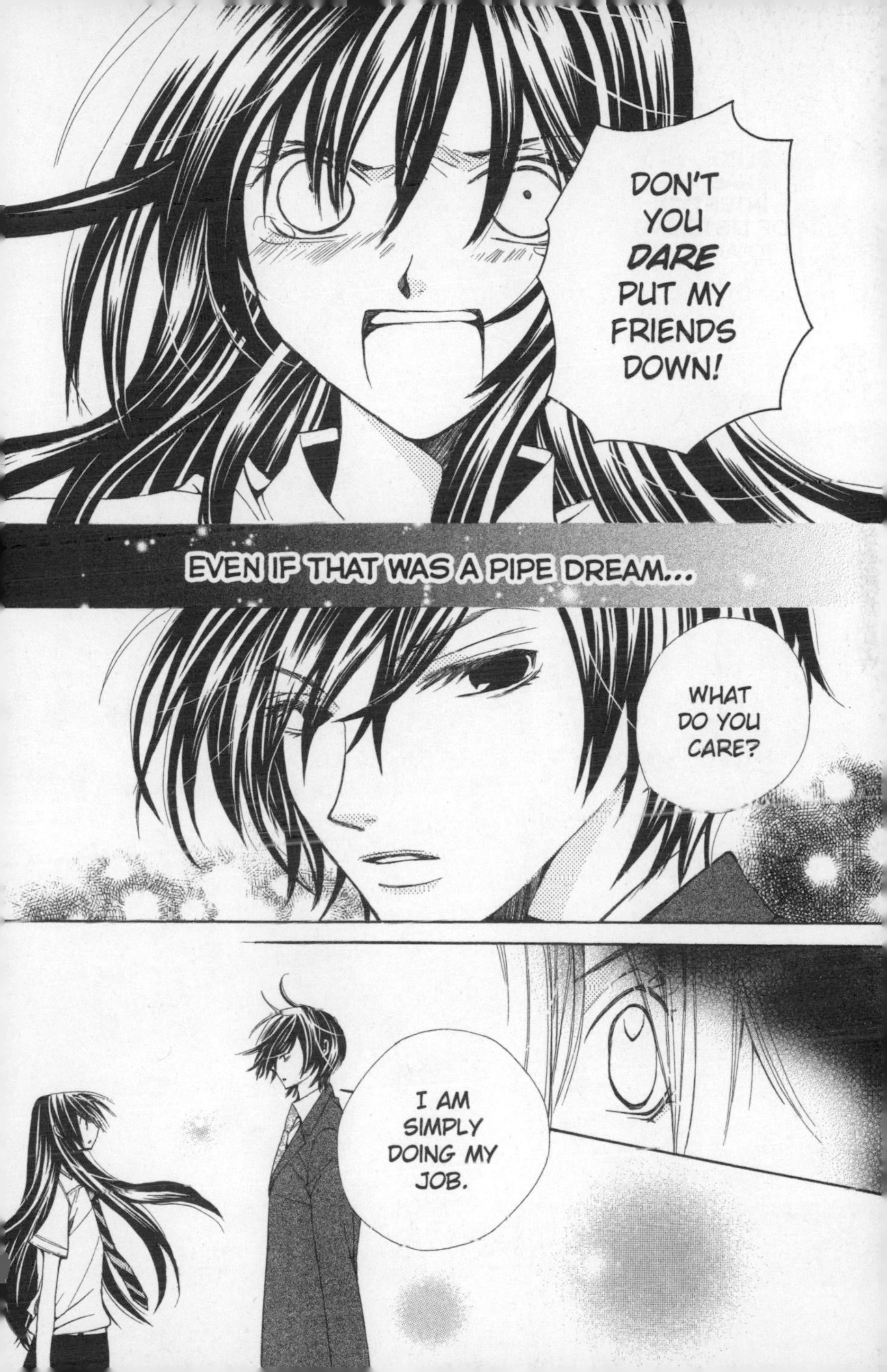
DON'T YOU DARE PUT MY FRIENDS DOWN!
EVEN IF THAT WAS A PIPE DREAM...
WHAT DO YOU CARE?
I AM SIMPLY DOING MY JOB.

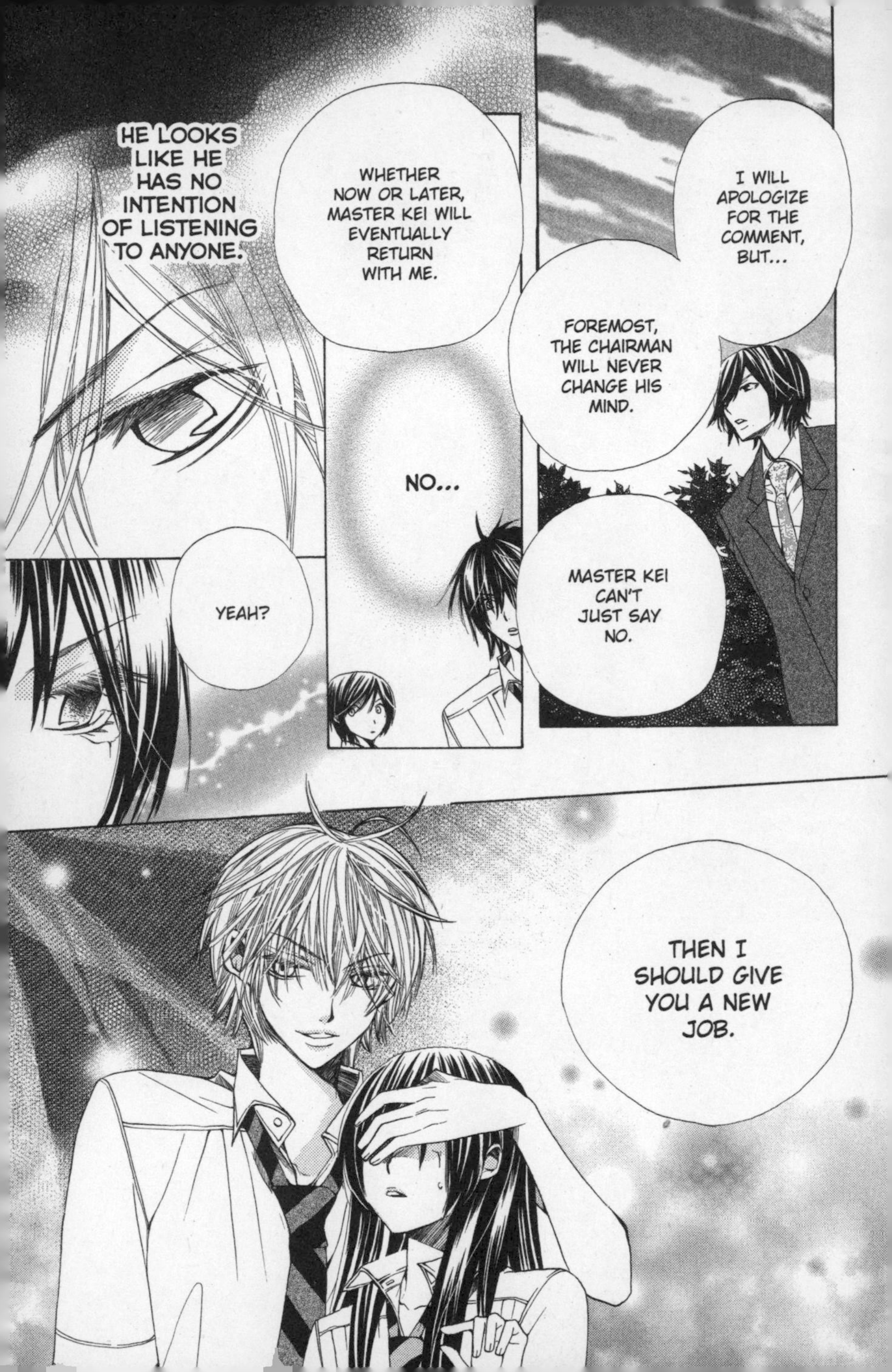
I WILL APOLOGIZE FOR THE COMMENT, BUT...
FOREMOST, THE CHAIRMAN WILL NEVER CHANGE HIS MIND.
MASTER KEI CAN'T JUST SAY NO.
WHETHER NOW OR LATER, MASTER KEI WILL EVENTUALLY RETURN WITH ME.
NO...
HE LOOKS LIKE HE HAS NO INTENTION OF LISTENING TO ANYONE.
YEAH?
THEN I SHOULD GIVE YOU A NEW JOB.

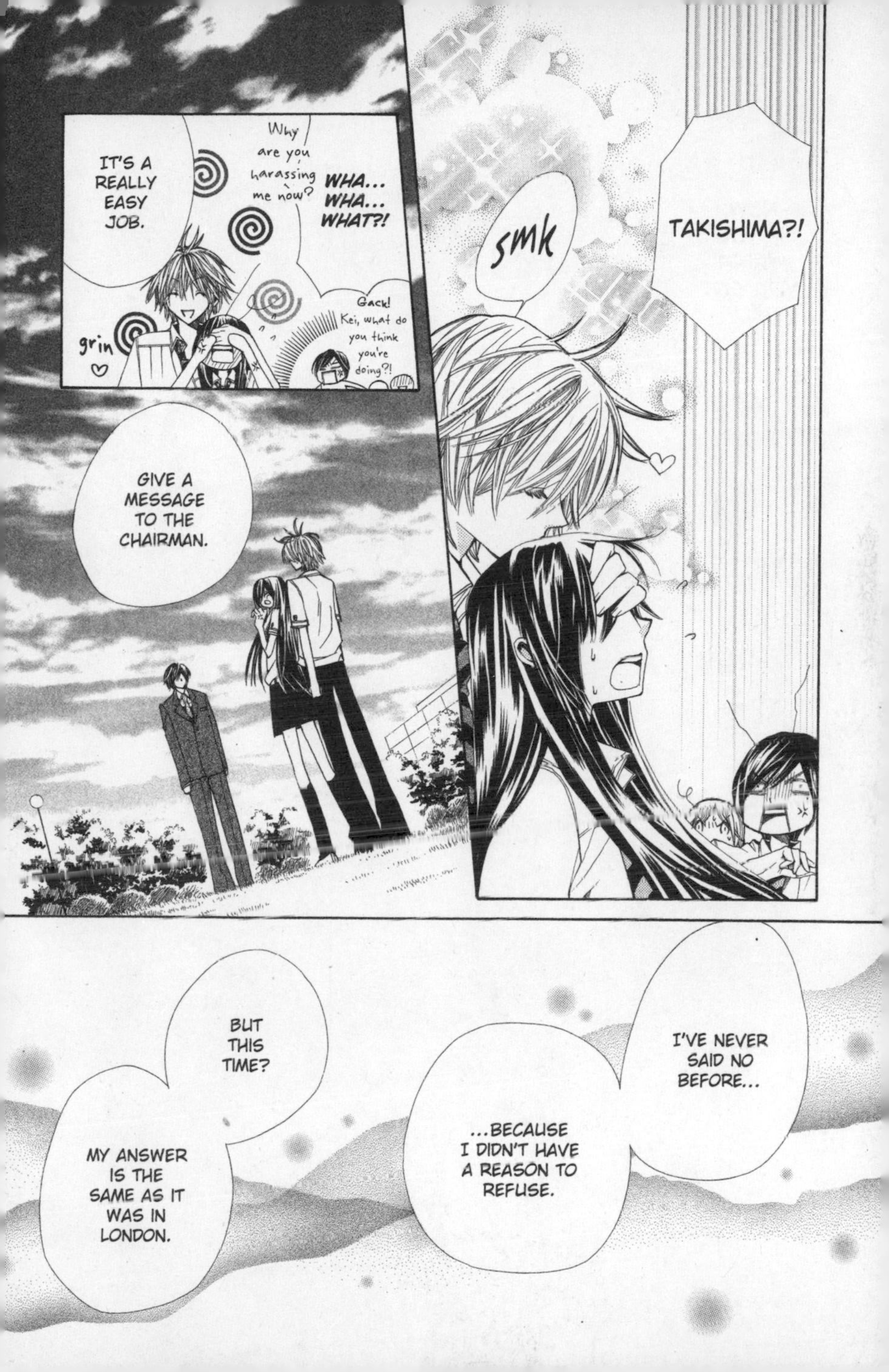
TAKISHIMA?!
smk
WHA... WHA... WHAT?!
Why are you harassing me now?
IT'S A REALLY EASY JOB.
Gack! Kei, what do you think you're doing?!
grin
GIVE A MESSAGE TO THE CHAIRMAN.
I'VE NEVER SAID NO BEFORE...
...BECAUSE I DIDN'T HAVE A REASON TO REFUSE.
BUT THIS TIME?
MY ANSWER IS THE SAME AS IT WAS IN LONDON.

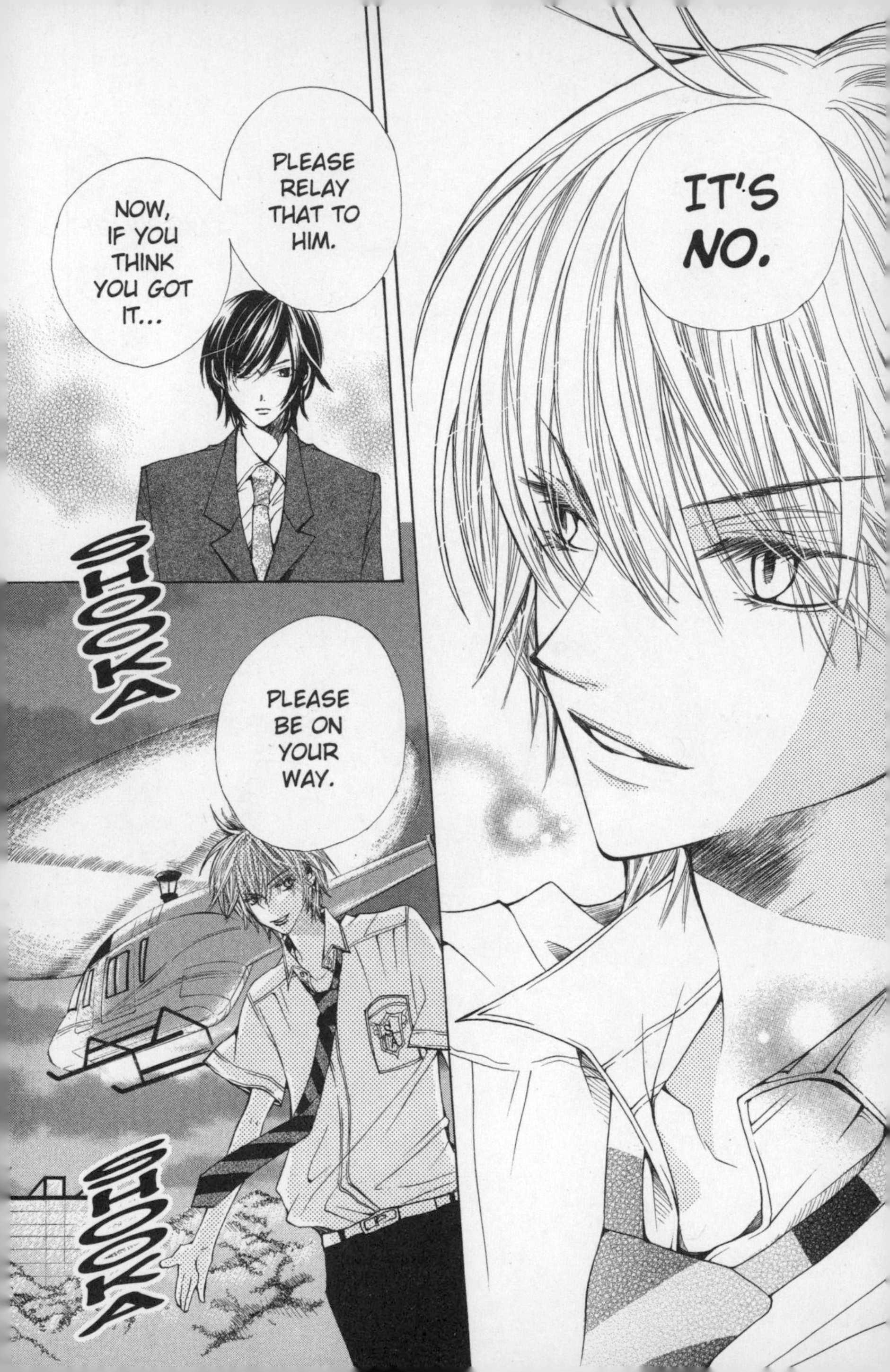
IT'S NO.
PLEASE RELAY THAT TO HIM.
NOW, IF YOU THINK YOU GOT IT...
SHOOKA
PLEASE BE ON YOUR WAY.
SHOOKA

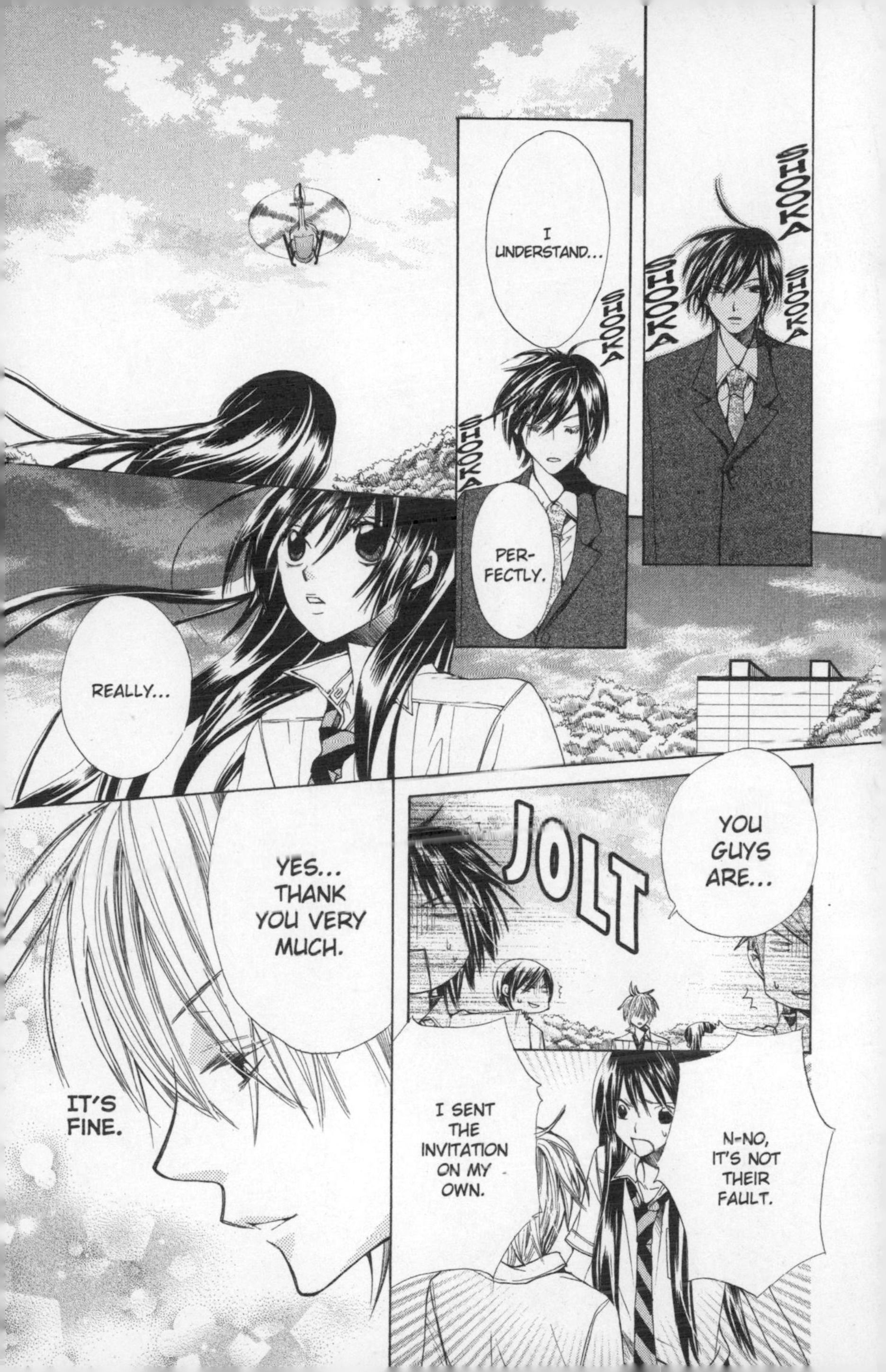
SHOOKA
SHOOKA
SHOOKA
SHOOKA
SHOOKA
I UNDERSTAND...
PER-FECTLY.
REALLY...
YOU GUYS ARE...
JOLT
N-NO, IT'S NOT THEIR FAULT.
I SENT THE INVITATION ON MY OWN.
YES... THANK YOU VERY MUCH.
IT'S FINE.

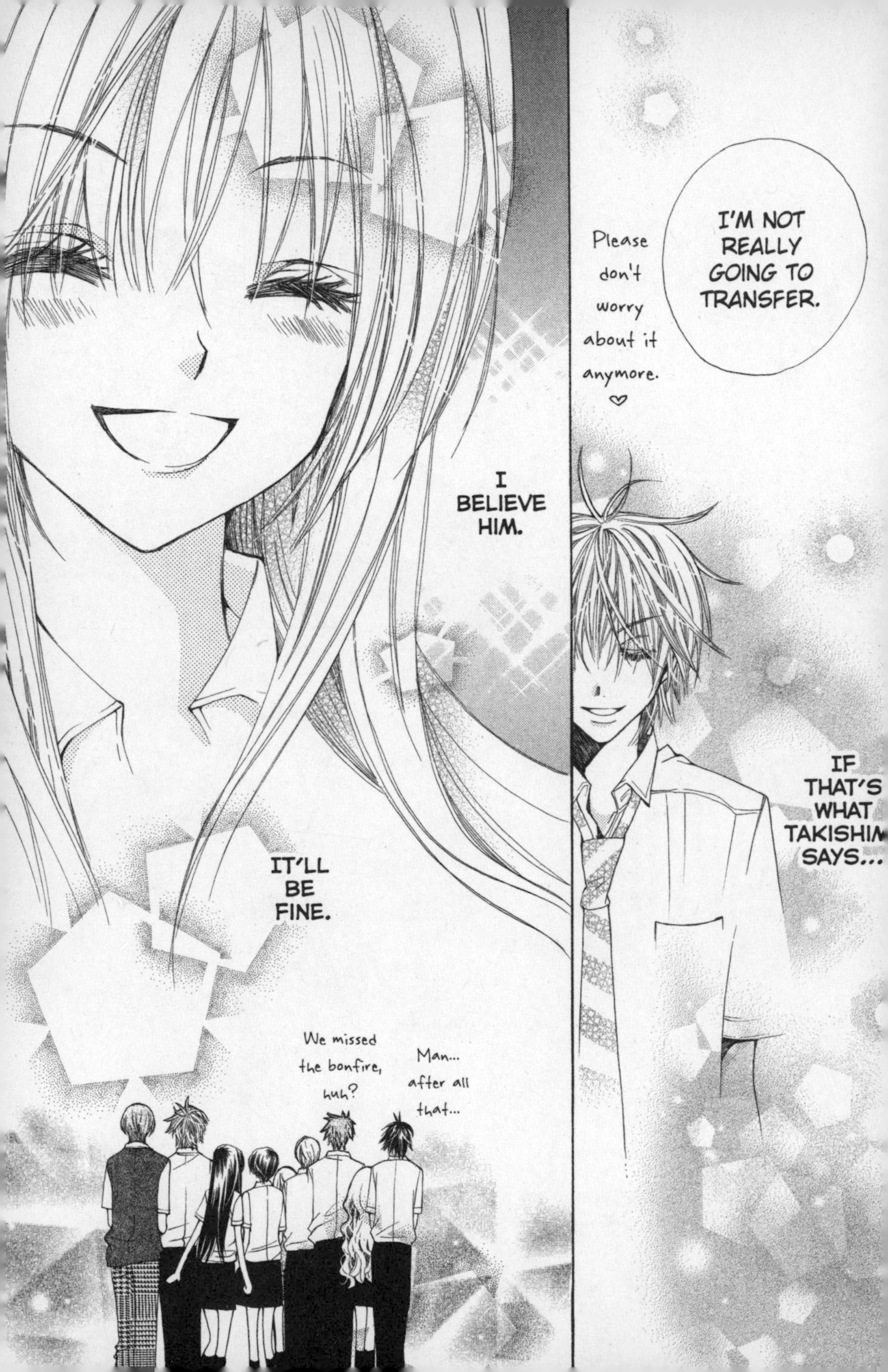
I'M NOT REALLY GOING TO TRANSFER.
Please don't worry about it anymore. ♡
IF THAT'S WHAT TAKISHIM SAYS...
I BELIEVE HIM.
IT'LL BE FINE.
Man... after all that...
We missed the bonfire, huh?

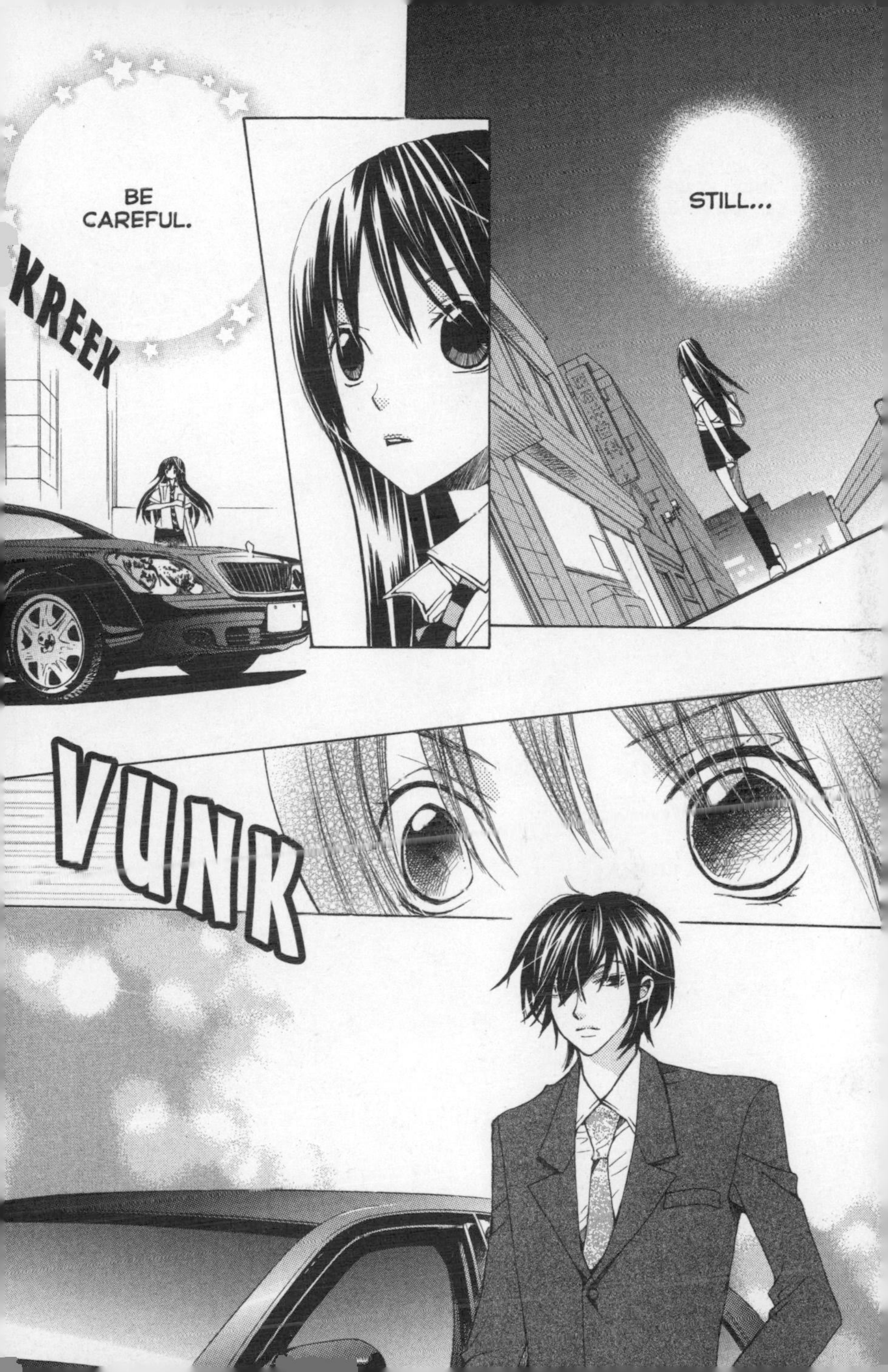
STILL...
BE CAREFUL.
KREEK
VUNK

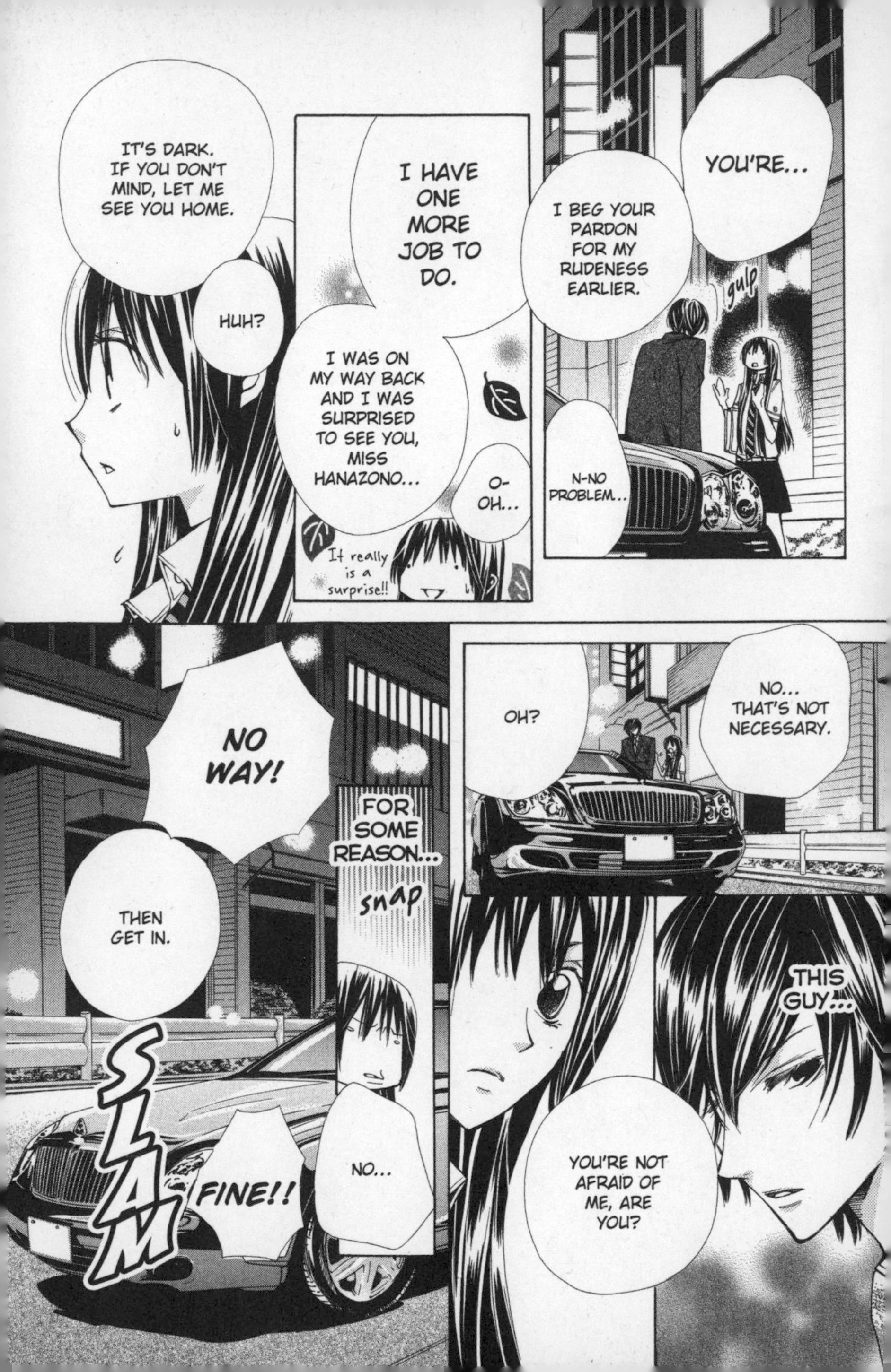
YOU'RE...
gulp
I BEG YOUR PARDON FOR MY RUDENESS EARLIER.
N-NO PROBLEM...
I HAVE ONE MORE JOB TO DO.
I WAS ON MY WAY BACK AND I WAS SURPRISED TO SEE YOU, MISS HANAZONO...
O-OH...
It really is a surprise!!
IT'S DARK. IF YOU DON'T MIND, LET ME SEE YOU HOME.
HUH?
NO... THAT'S NOT NECESSARY.
OH?
THIS GUY...
YOU'RE NOT AFRAID OF ME, ARE YOU?
FOR SOME REASON...
snap
NO WAY!
THEN GET IN.
NO...
FINE!!
SLAM

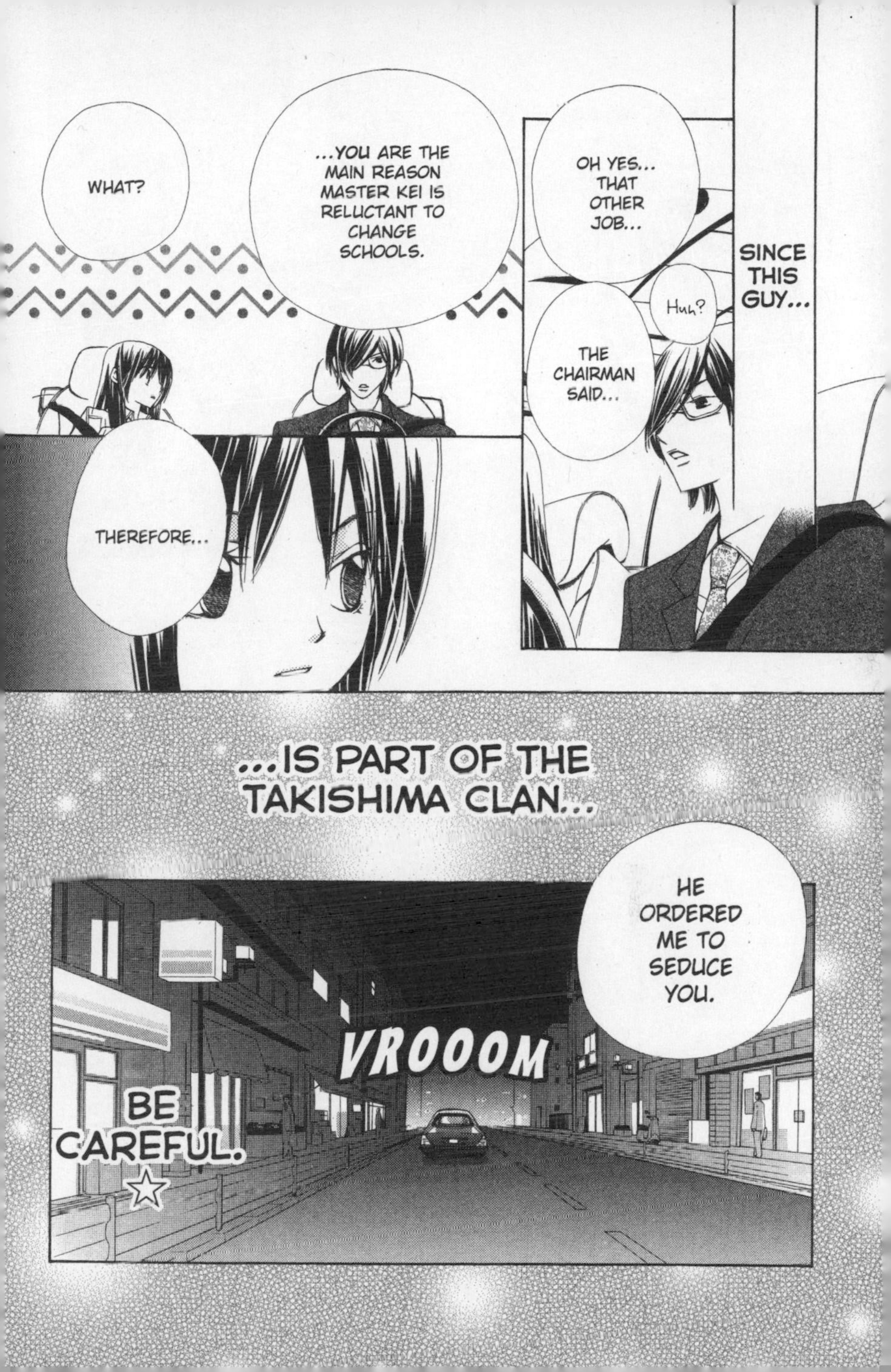
OH YES... THAT OTHER JOB...
Huh?
THE CHAIRMAN SAID...
SINCE THIS GUY...
...YOU ARE THE MAIN REASON MASTER KEI IS RELUCTANT TO CHANGE SCHOOLS.
WHAT?
THEREFORE...
...IS PART OF THE TAKISHIMA CLAN...
HE ORDERED ME TO SEDUCE YOU.
VROOOM
BE CAREFUL. ☆

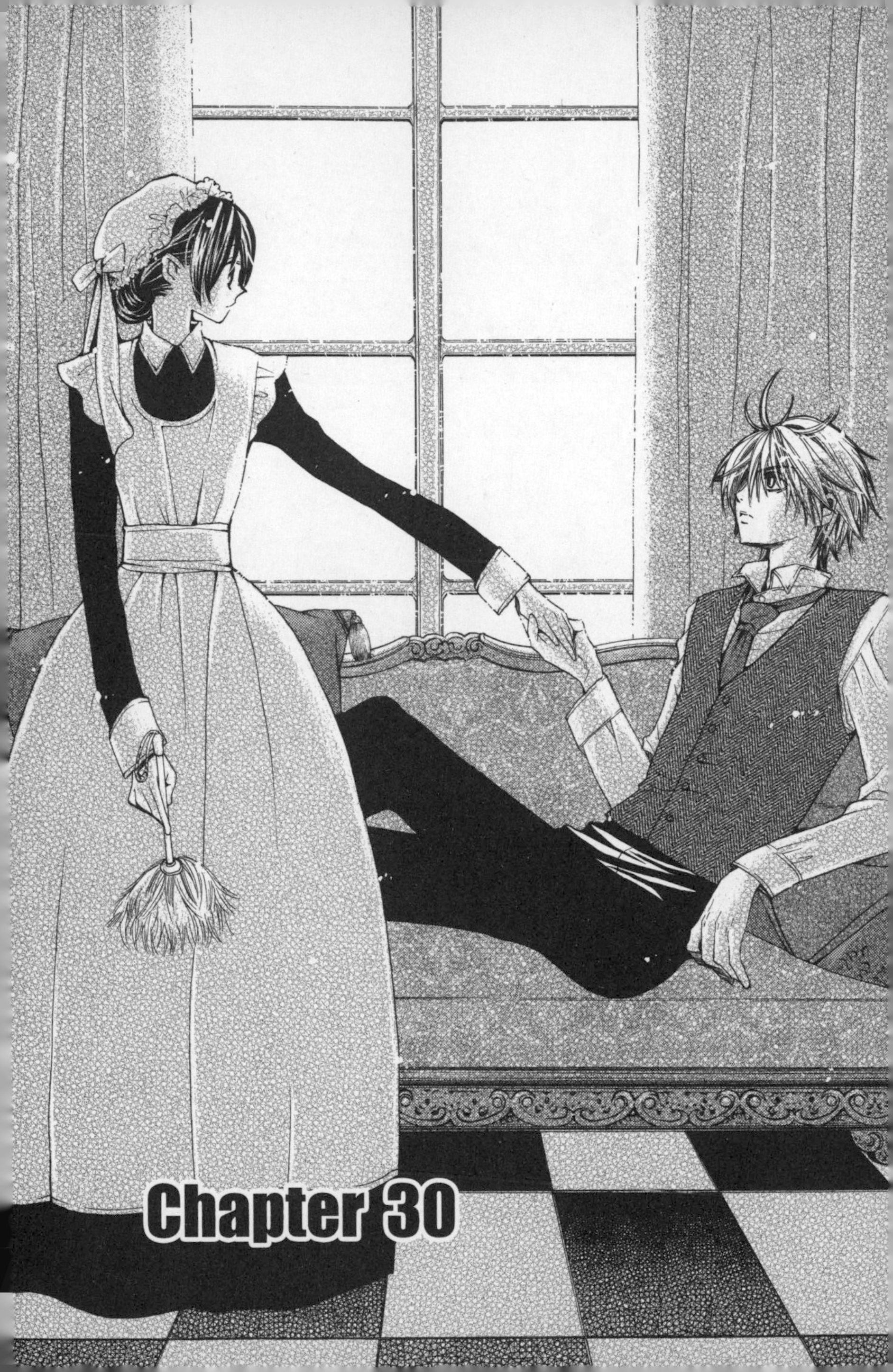
Chapter 30

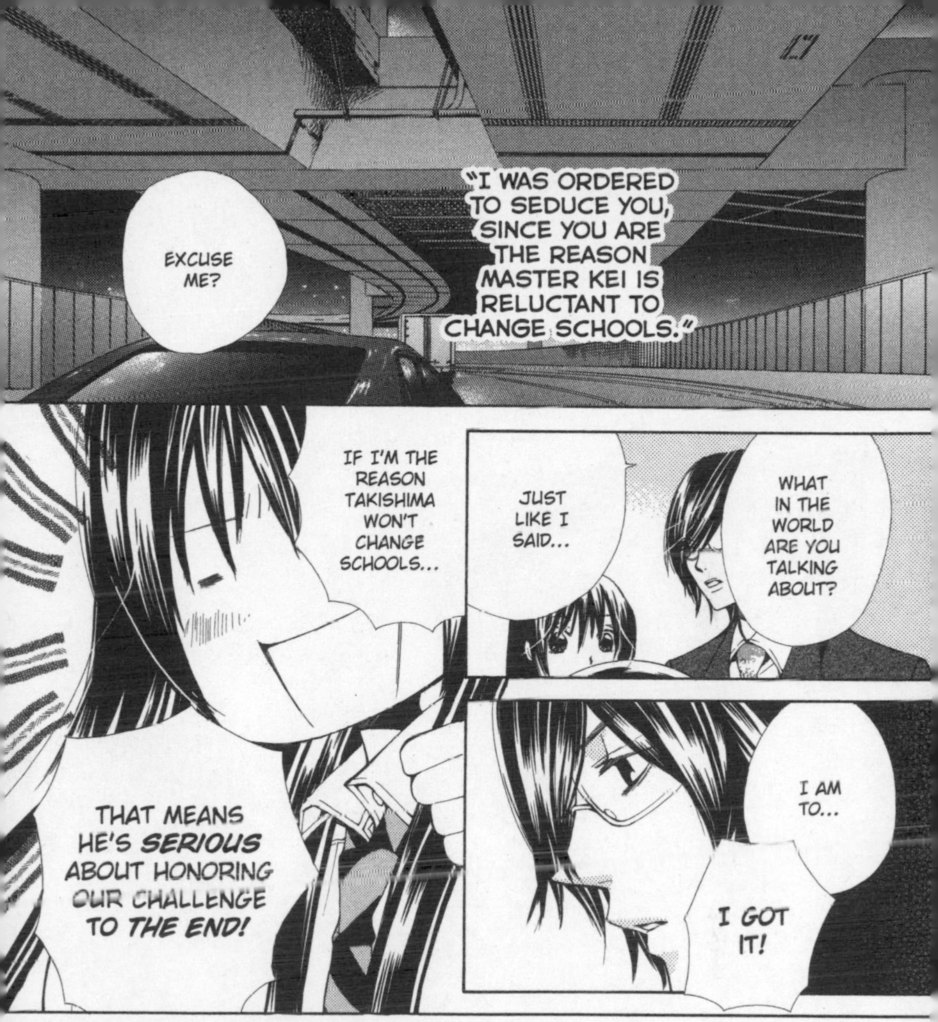
"I WAS ORDERED TO SEDUCE YOU, SINCE YOU ARE THE REASON MASTER KEI IS RELUCTANT TO CHANGE SCHOOLS."
EXCUSE ME?
WHAT IN THE WORLD ARE YOU TALKING ABOUT?
JUST LIKE I SAID...
I AM TO...
I GOT IT!
IF I'M THE REASON TAKISHIMA WON'T CHANGE SCHOOLS...
THAT MEANS HE'S *SERIOUS* ABOUT HONORING OUR CHALLENGE TO *THE END!*

• ARTISTS •

A LOT OF TIMES, YOUR LETTERS COME WITH LITTLE PICTURES. I'M REALLY IMPRESSED WITH YOUR SUPER-CUTE DRAWINGS! THEY REMIND ME OF THE DRAWINGS I USED TO DO WHEN I WAS IN SCHOOL.

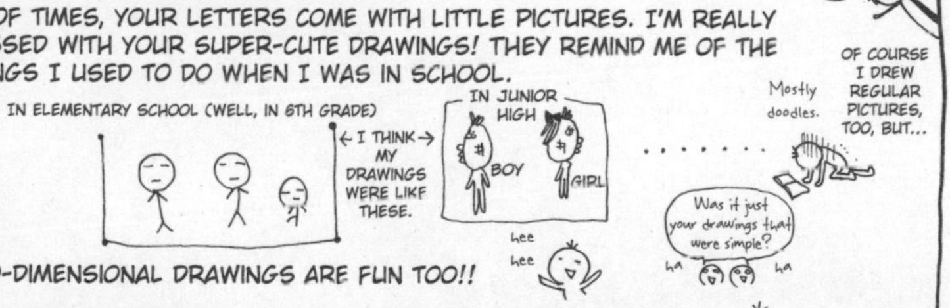
B
OF COURSE I DREW REGULAR PICTURES, TOO, BUT...
Mostly doodles.
IN ELEMENTARY SCHOOL (WELL, IN 6TH GRADE)
← I THINK → MY DRAWINGS WERE LIKE THESE.
IN JUNIOR HIGH
BOY
GIRL
. . . .
Was it just your drawings that were simple?
ha
ha
hee
hee

TWO-DIMENSIONAL DRAWINGS ARE FUN TOO!!

THANK YOU FOR SENDING SO MANY FUNNY AND CUTE DRAWINGS!!

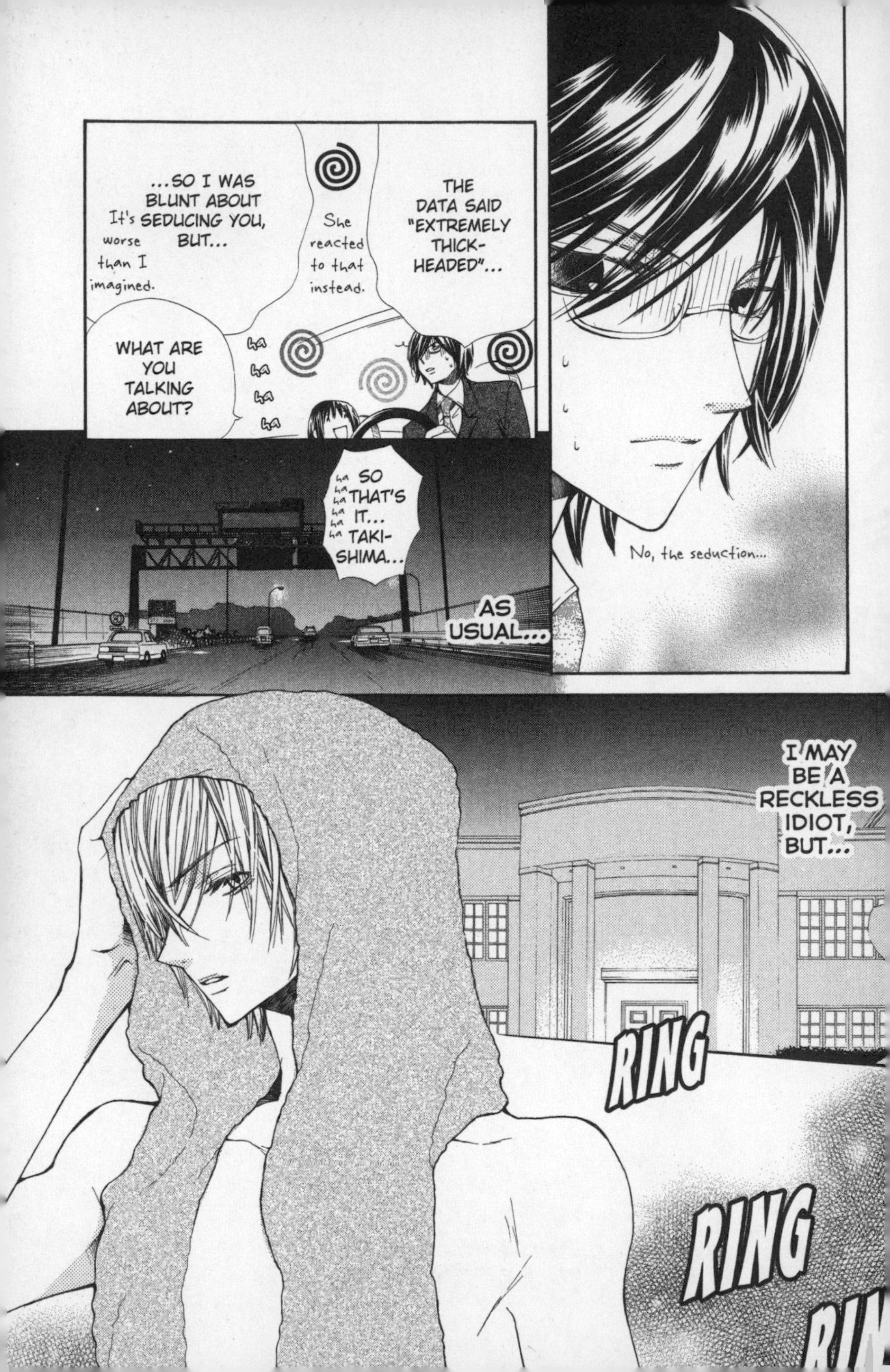

No, the seduction...
THE DATA SAID "EXTREMELY THICK-HEADED"...
She reacted to that instead.
...SO I WAS BLUNT ABOUT SEDUCING YOU, BUT...
It's worse than I imagined.
ha ha ha ha
WHAT ARE YOU TALKING ABOUT?
ha ha ha ha ha ha
SO THAT'S IT... TAKI-SHIMA...
AS USUAL...
I MAY BE A RECKLESS IDIOT, BUT...
RING
RING

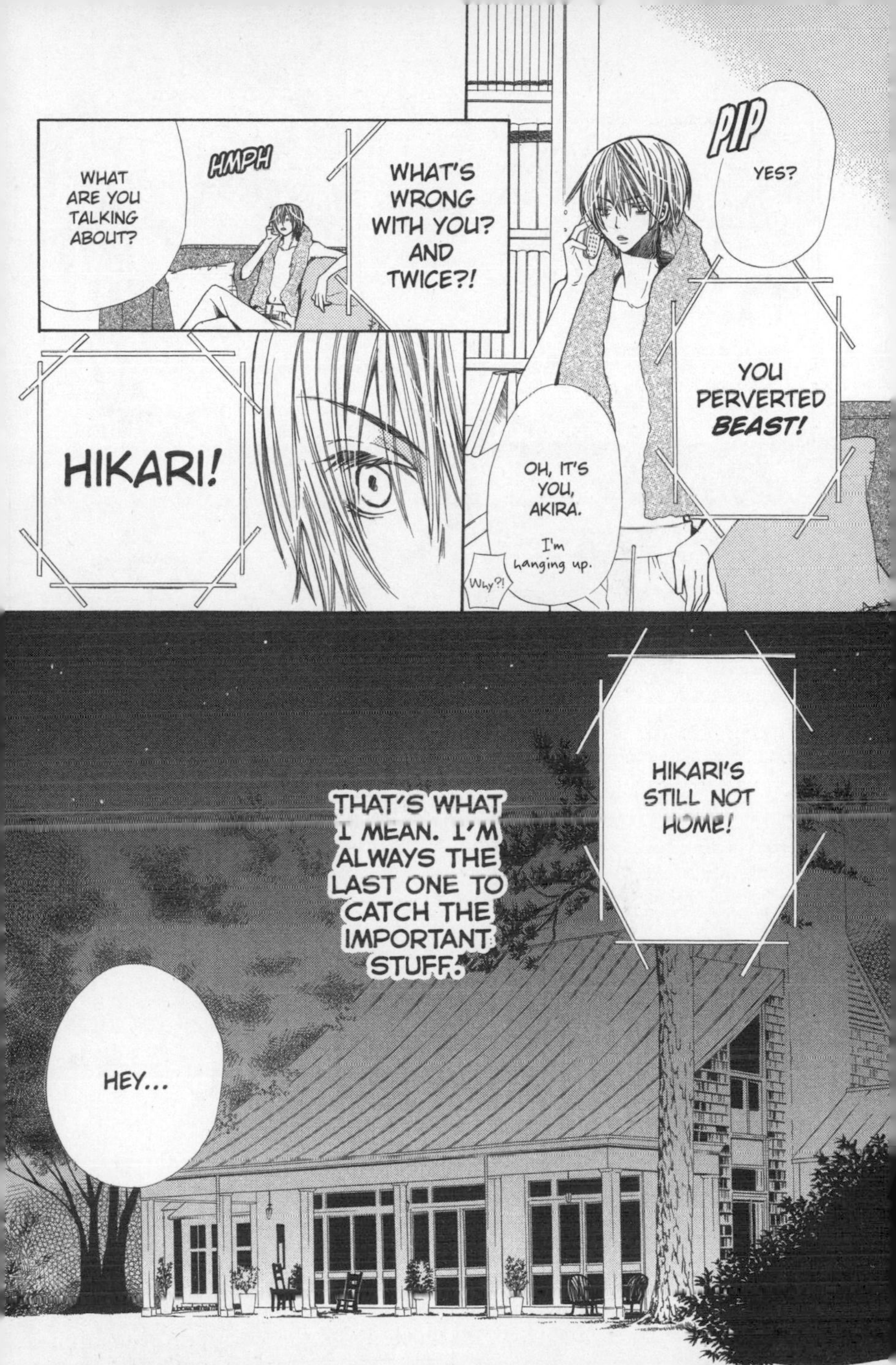
PIP
YES?
YOU PERVERTED BEAST!
OH, IT'S YOU, AKIRA.
I'm hanging up.
Why?!
WHAT'S WRONG WITH YOU? AND TWICE?!
HMPH
WHAT ARE YOU TALKING ABOUT?
HIKARI!
HIKARI'S STILL NOT HOME!
THAT'S WHAT I MEAN. I'M ALWAYS THE LAST ONE TO CATCH THE IMPORTANT STUFF.
HEY...

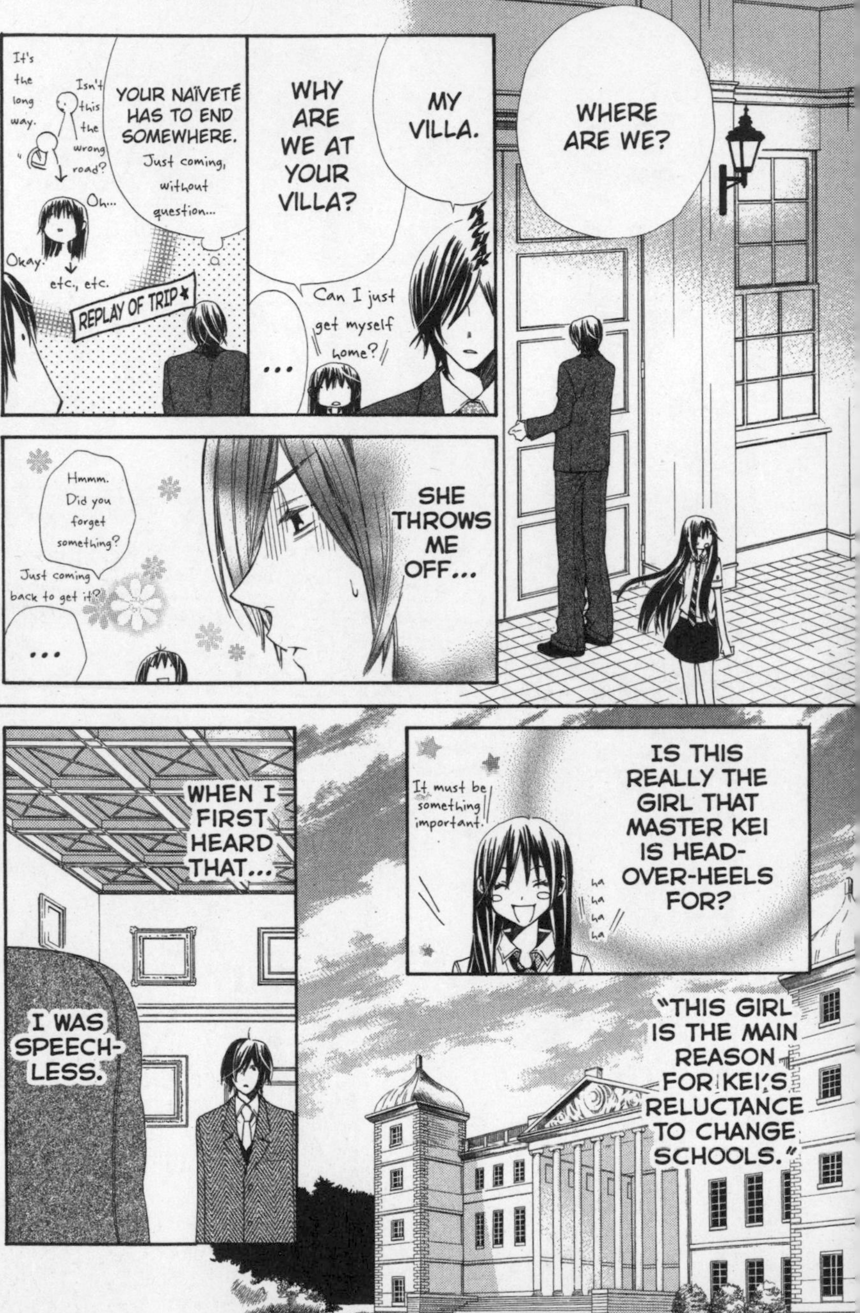
WHERE ARE WE?
MY VILLA.
WHY ARE WE AT YOUR VILLA?
Can I just get myself home?
...
YOUR NAÏVETÉ HAS TO END SOMEWHERE.
Just coming, without question...
It's the long way.
Isn't this the wrong road?
Oh...
Okay.
etc., etc.
REPLAY OF TRIP
SHE THROWS ME OFF...
Hmmm. Did you forget something?
Just coming back to get it?
...
IS THIS REALLY THE GIRL THAT MASTER KEI IS HEAD-OVER-HEELS FOR?
It must be something important.
ha ha ha ha
"THIS GIRL IS THE MAIN REASON FOR KEI'S RELUCTANCE TO CHANGE SCHOOLS."
WHEN I FIRST HEARD THAT...
I WAS SPEECHLESS.

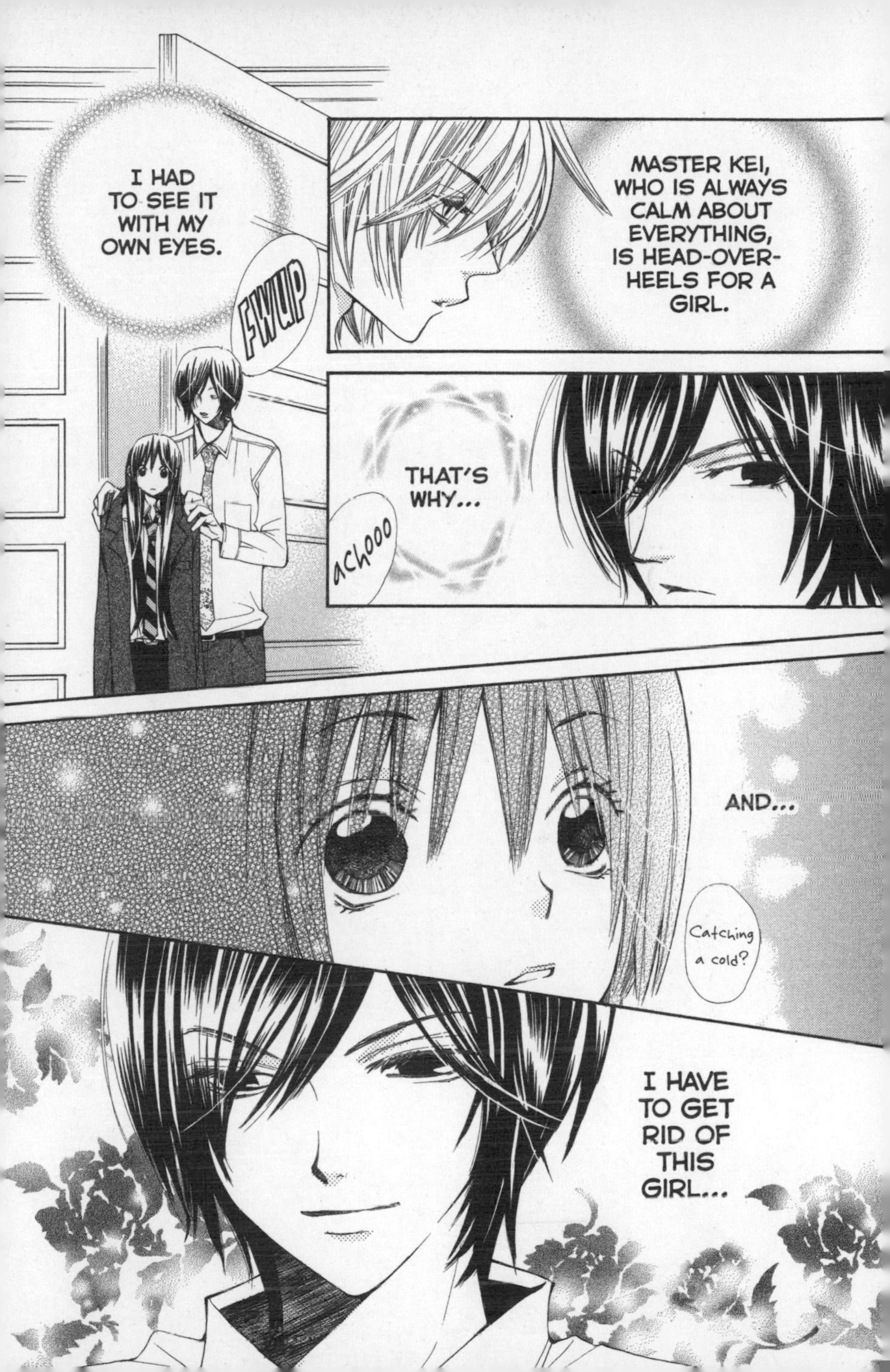
MASTER KEI, WHO IS ALWAYS CALM ABOUT EVERYTHING, IS HEAD-OVER-HEELS FOR A GIRL.
THAT'S WHY...
achooo
I HAD TO SEE IT WITH MY OWN EYES.
FWUP
AND...
Catching a cold?
I HAVE TO GET RID OF THIS GIRL...

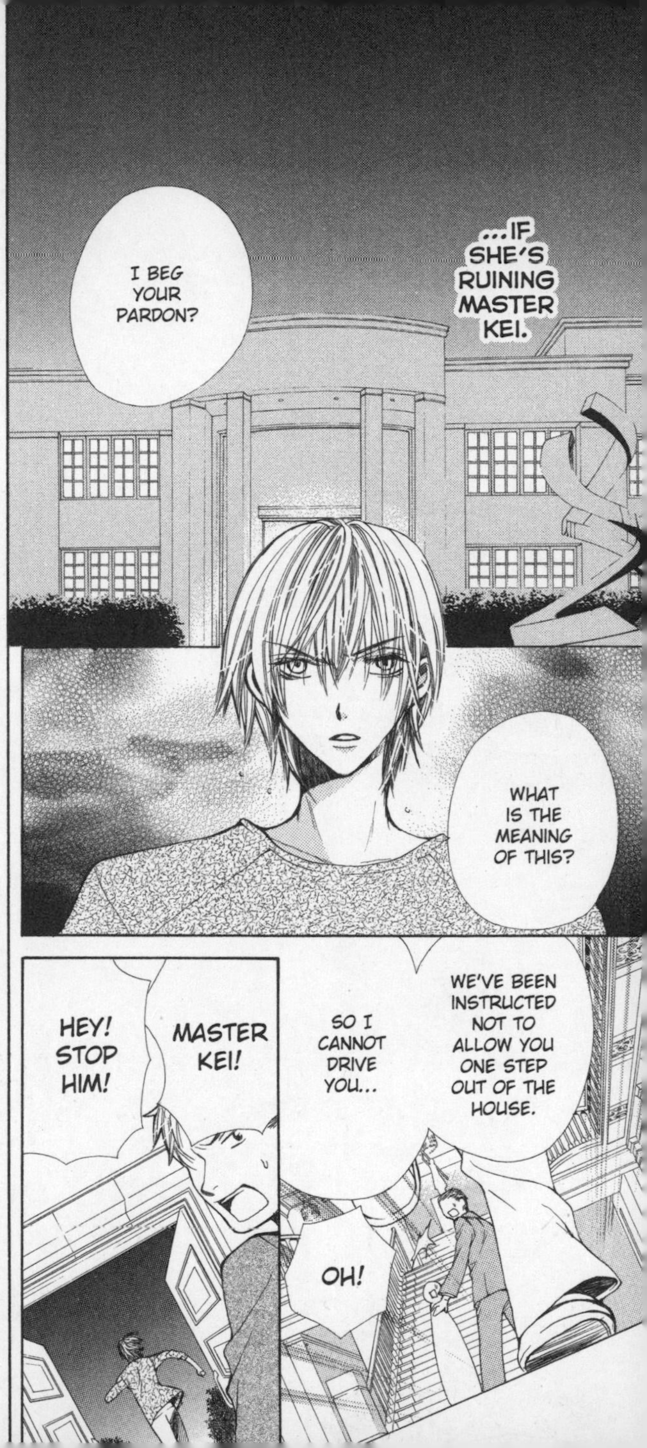
...IF SHE'S RUINING MASTER KEI.
I BEG YOUR PARDON?
WHAT IS THE MEANING OF THIS?
WE'VE BEEN INSTRUCTED NOT TO ALLOW YOU ONE STEP OUT OF THE HOUSE.
SO I CANNOT DRIVE YOU...
OH!
MASTER KEI!
HEY! STOP HIM!

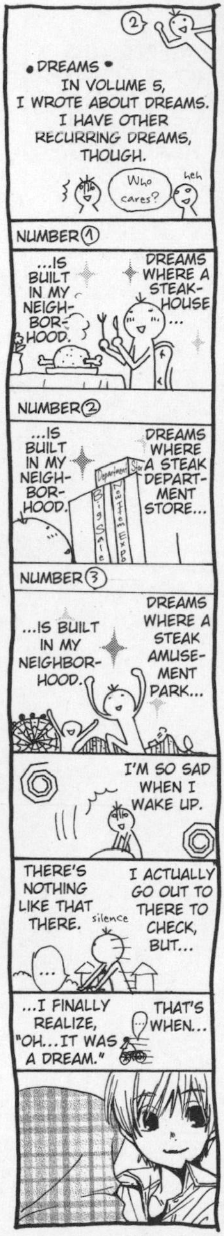
2
• DREAMS •
IN VOLUME 5, I WROTE ABOUT DREAMS. I HAVE OTHER RECURRING DREAMS, THOUGH.
Who cares?
heh
NUMBER 1
DREAMS WHERE A STEAK-HOUSE...
...IS BUILT IN MY NEIGH-BOR-HOOD.
NUMBER 2
DREAMS WHERE A STEAK DEPART-MENT STORE...
...IS BUILT IN MY NEIGH-BOR-HOOD.
Department Store
Big Sale
New Item Expo
NUMBER 3
DREAMS WHERE A STEAK AMUSE-MENT PARK...
...IS BUILT IN MY NEIGHBOR-HOOD.
I'M SO SAD WHEN I WAKE UP.
I ACTUALLY GO OUT TO THERE TO CHECK, BUT...
THERE'S NOTHING LIKE THAT THERE.
silence
...
THAT'S WHEN...
...I FINALLY REALIZE, "OH...IT WAS A DREAM."

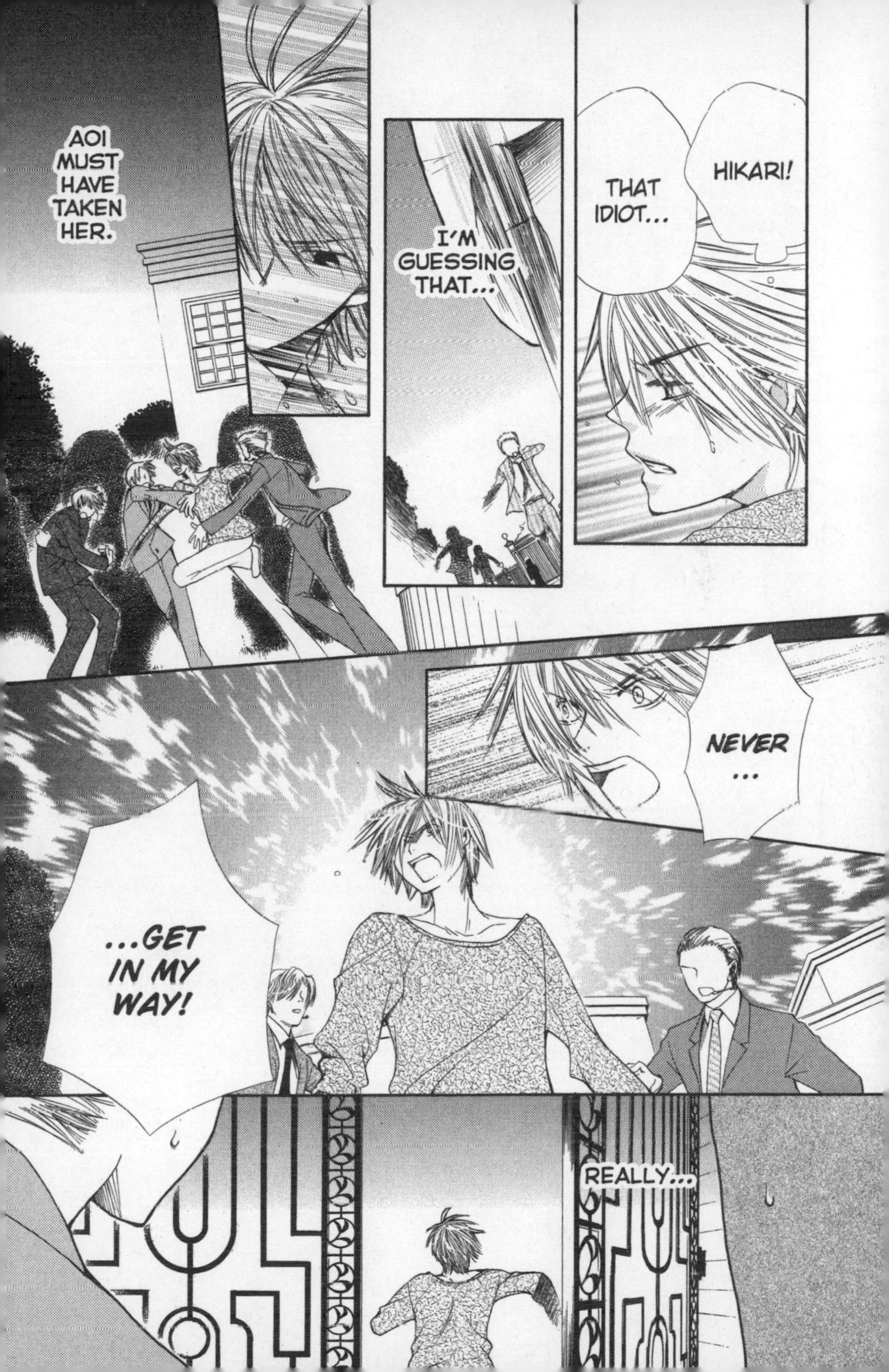
HIKARI!
THAT IDIOT...
I'M GUESSING THAT...
AOI MUST HAVE TAKEN HER.
NEVER ...
...GET IN MY WAY!
REALLY...

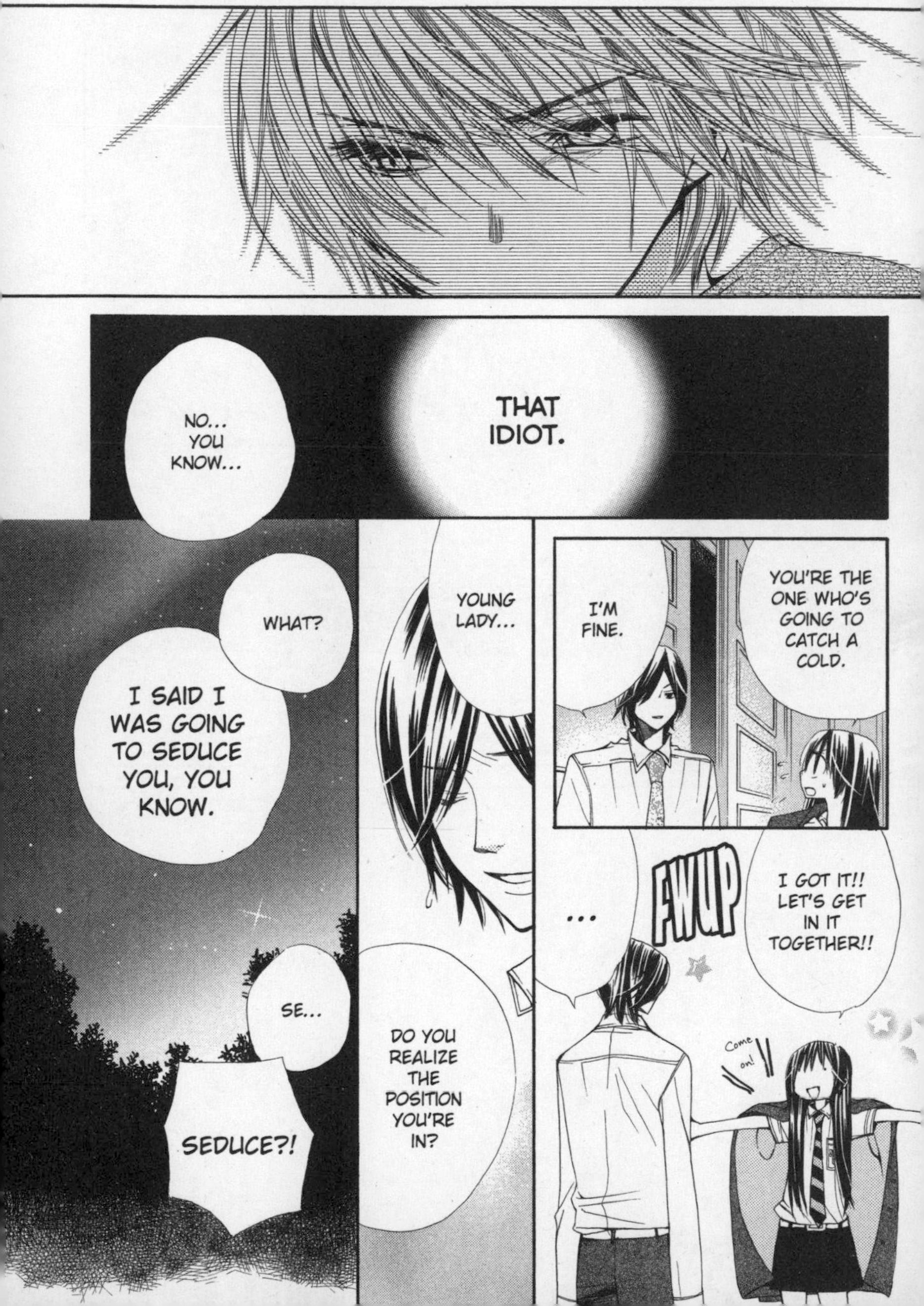
THAT IDIOT.
NO... YOU KNOW...
YOU'RE THE ONE WHO'S GOING TO CATCH A COLD.
I'M FINE.
I GOT IT!! LET'S GET IN IT TOGETHER!!
FWUP
Come on!
...
YOUNG LADY...
DO YOU REALIZE THE POSITION YOU'RE IN?
WHAT?
I SAID I WAS GOING TO SEDUCE YOU, YOU KNOW.
SE...
SEDUCE?!

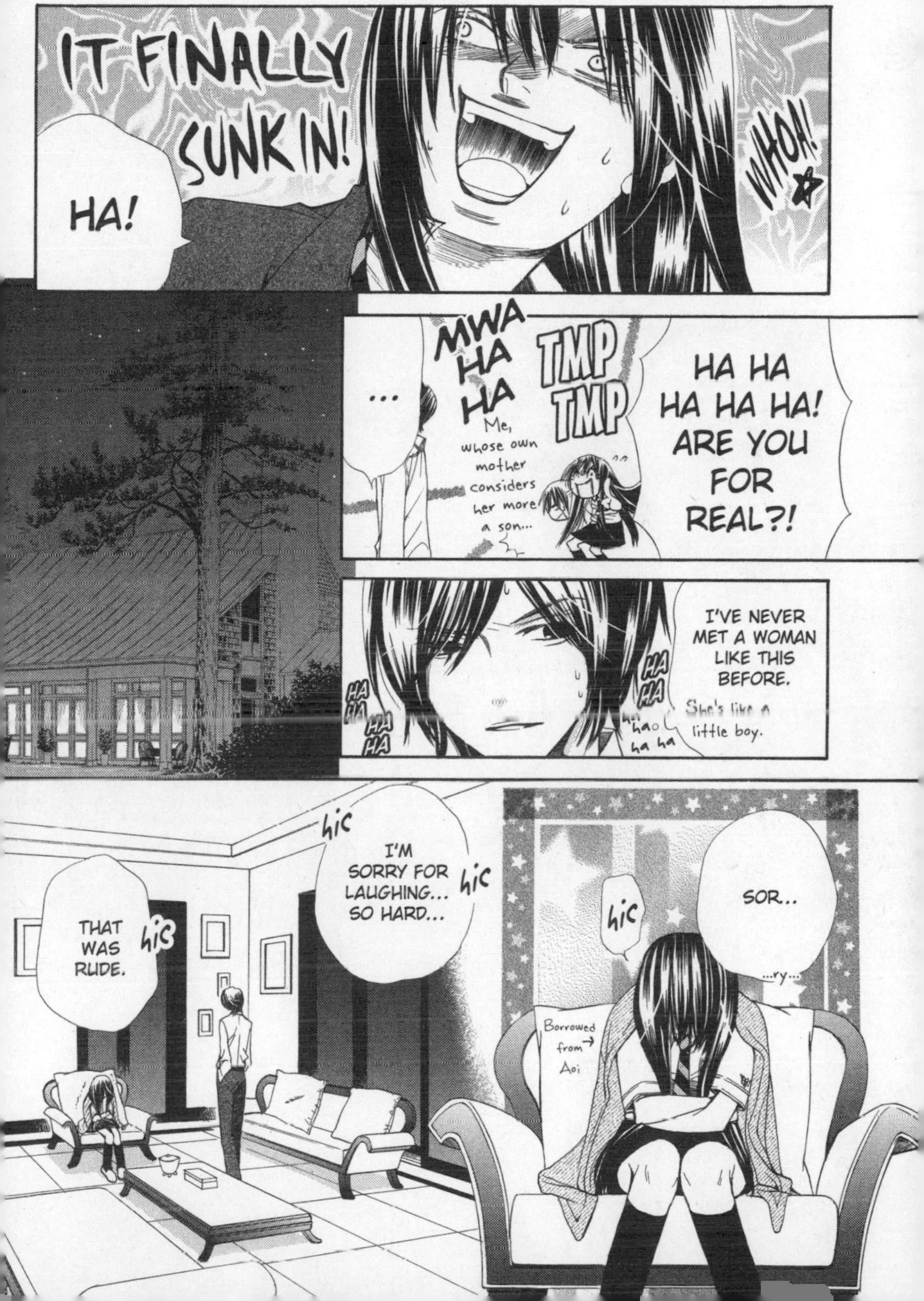
WHOA!
IT FINALLY SUNK IN!
HA!
HA HA HA HA HA! ARE YOU FOR REAL?!
TMP TMP
MWA HA HA
Me, whose own mother considers her more a son...
...
I'VE NEVER MET A WOMAN LIKE THIS BEFORE.
She's like a little boy.
HA HA
hao ha ha
HA HA HA HA
SOR...
hic
...ry...
Borrowed from Aoi
hic
I'M SORRY FOR LAUGHING... SO HARD...
hic
THAT WAS RUDE.
hic

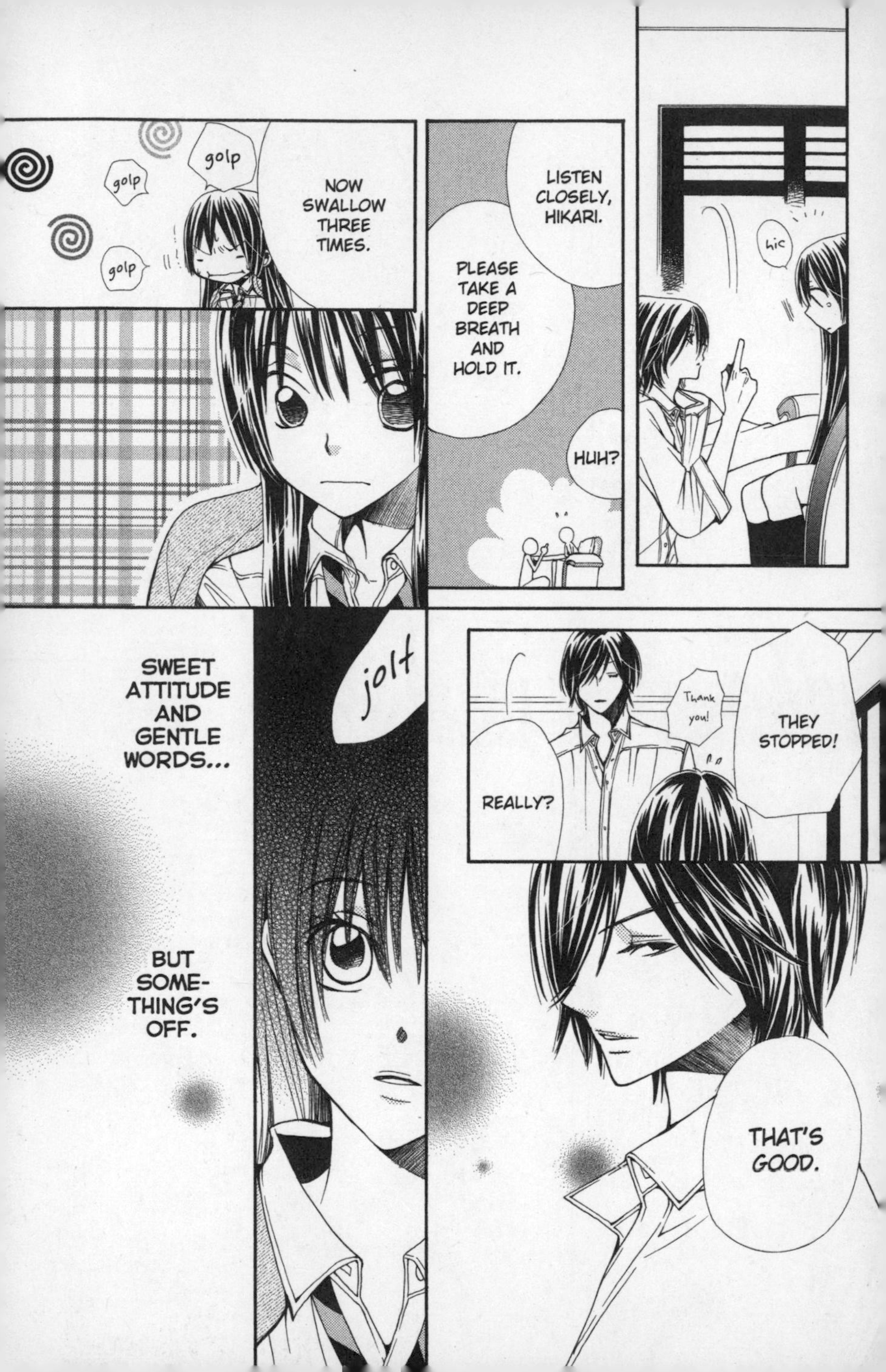
hic
LISTEN CLOSELY, HIKARI.
PLEASE TAKE A DEEP BREATH AND HOLD IT.
HUH?
NOW SWALLOW THREE TIMES.
golp
golp
golp
THEY STOPPED!
Thank you!
REALLY?
THAT'S GOOD.
jolt
SWEET ATTITUDE AND GENTLE WORDS...
BUT SOME-THING'S OFF.

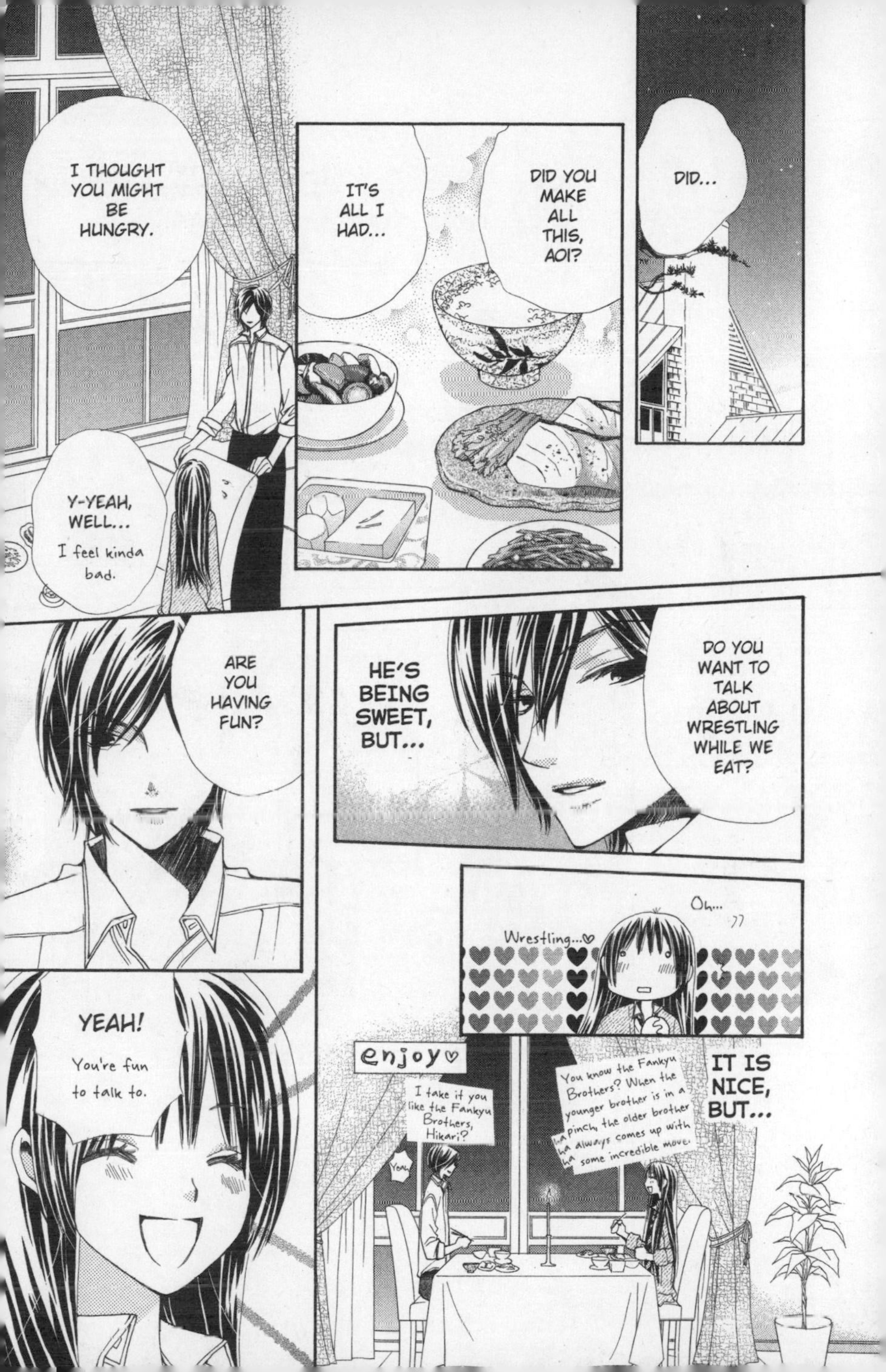
DID...
DID YOU MAKE ALL THIS, AOI?
IT'S ALL I HAD...
I THOUGHT YOU MIGHT BE HUNGRY.
Y-YEAH, WELL... I feel kinda bad.
DO YOU WANT TO TALK ABOUT WRESTLING WHILE WE EAT?
HE'S BEING SWEET, BUT...
Oh...
Wrestling...♡
IT IS NICE, BUT...
You know the Fankyu Brothers? When the younger brother is in a pinch, the older brother always comes up with some incredible move.
ha ha ha
I take it you like the Fankyu Brothers, Hikari?
Yeah
enjoy♡
ARE YOU HAVING FUN?
YEAH! You're fun to talk to.

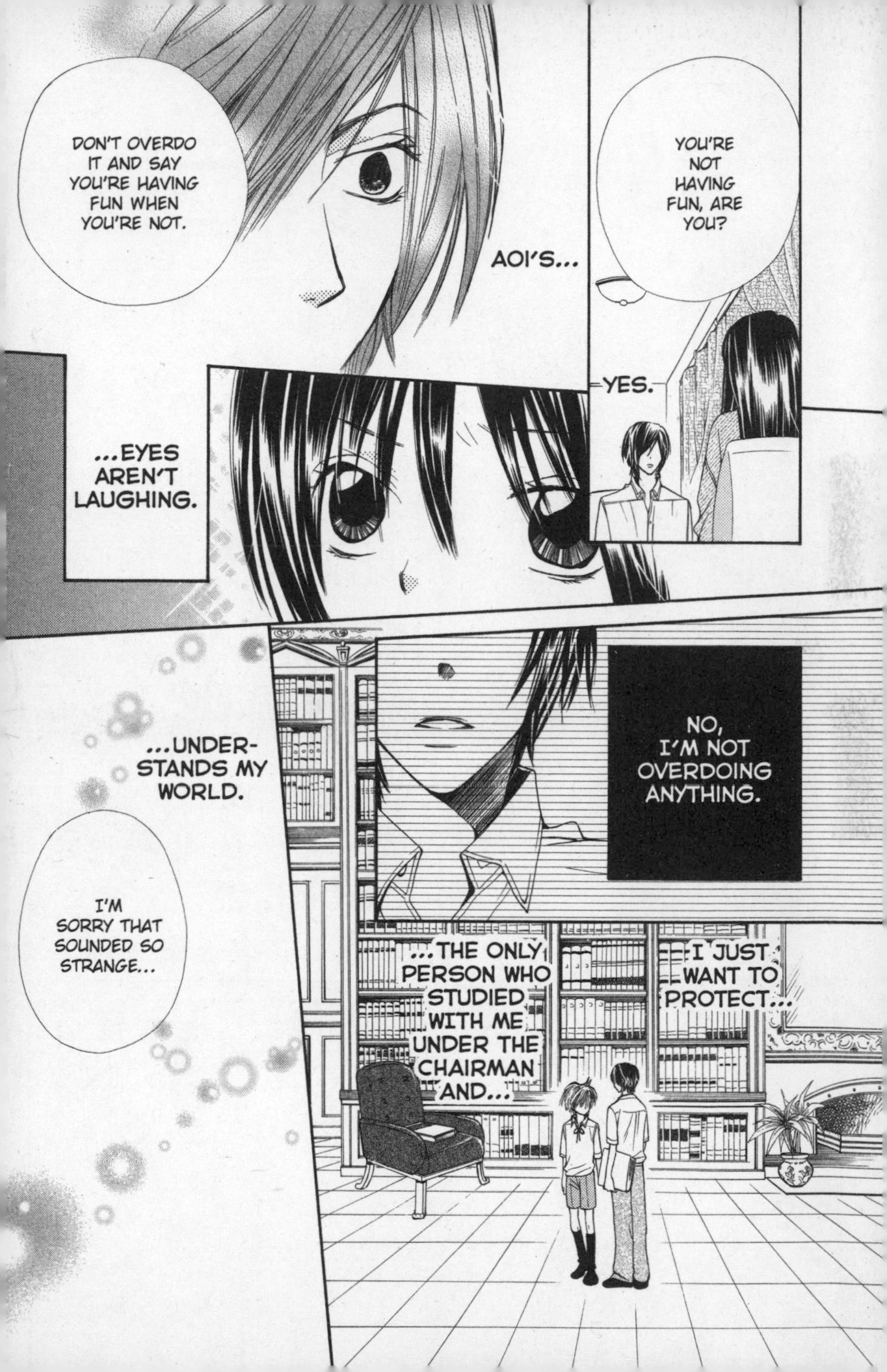
YOU'RE NOT HAVING FUN, ARE YOU?
DON'T OVERDO IT AND SAY YOU'RE HAVING FUN WHEN YOU'RE NOT.
AOI'S...
YES.
...EYES AREN'T LAUGHING.
NO, I'M NOT OVERDOING ANYTHING.
I JUST WANT TO PROTECT...
...THE ONLY PERSON WHO STUDIED WITH ME UNDER THE CHAIRMAN AND...
...UNDER-STANDS MY WORLD.
I'M SORRY THAT SOUNDED SO STRANGE...

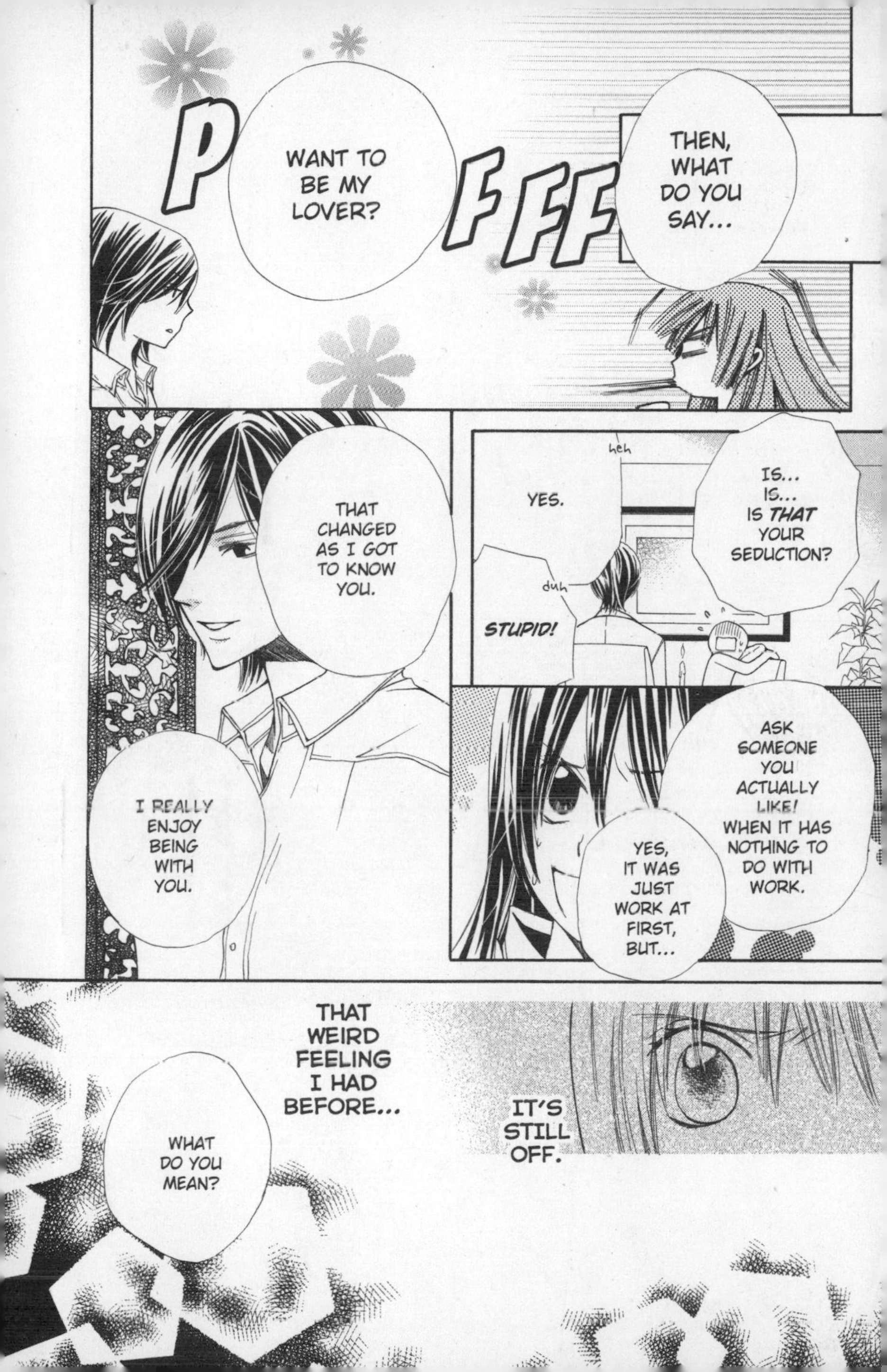
THEN, WHAT DO YOU SAY...
WANT TO BE MY LOVER?
PFFF
IS... IS... IS *THAT* YOUR SEDUCTION?
heh
YES.
duh
STUPID!
ASK SOMEONE YOU ACTUALLY LIKE! WHEN IT HAS NOTHING TO DO WITH WORK.
YES, IT WAS JUST WORK AT FIRST, BUT...
THAT CHANGED AS I GOT TO KNOW YOU.
I REALLY ENJOY BEING WITH YOU.
THAT WEIRD FEELING I HAD BEFORE...
IT'S STILL OFF.
WHAT DO YOU MEAN?

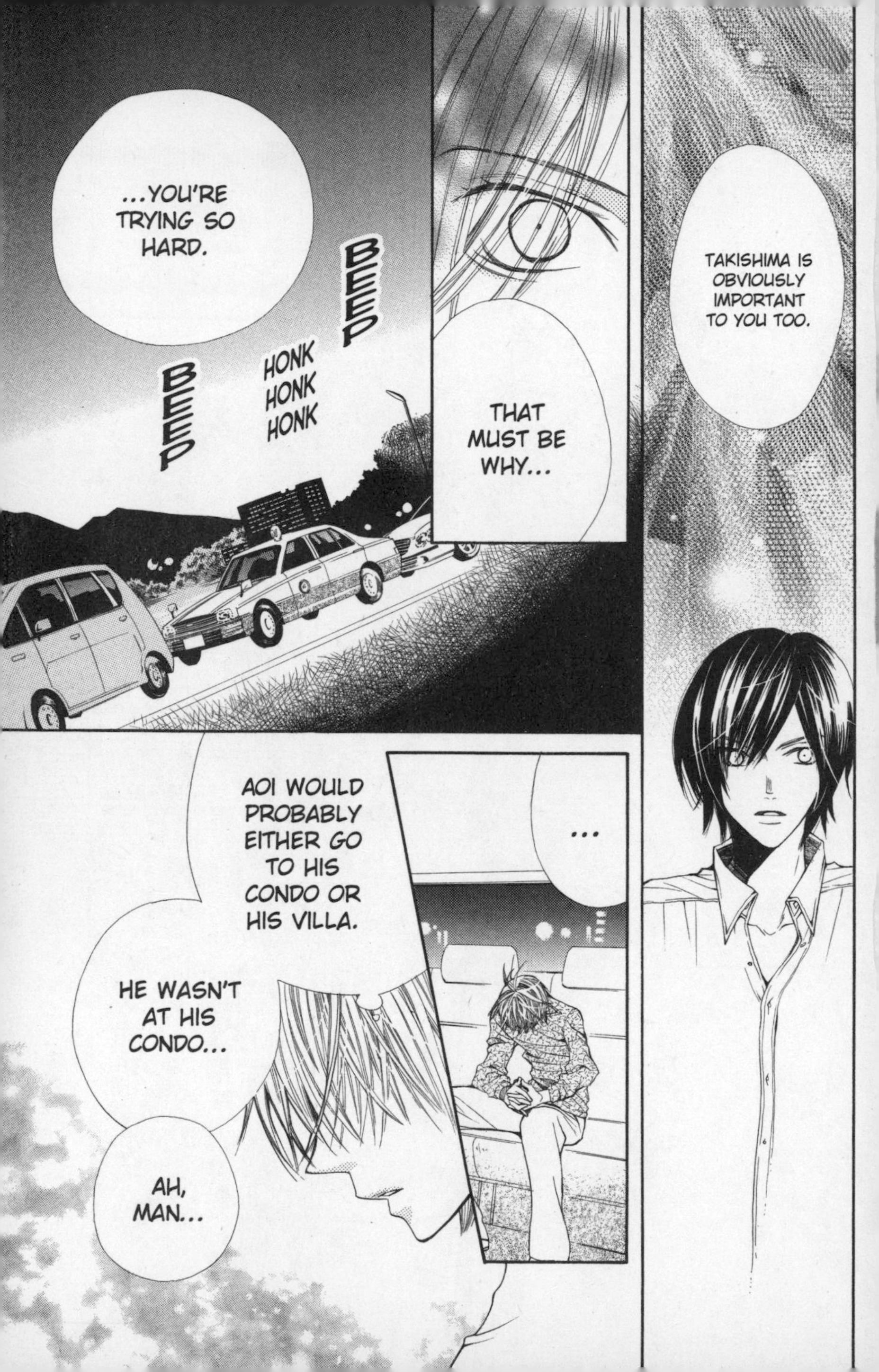
TAKISHIMA IS OBVIOUSLY IMPORTANT TO YOU TOO.
THAT MUST BE WHY...
...YOU'RE TRYING SO HARD.
BEEP
HONK HONK HONK
BEEP
...
AOI WOULD PROBABLY EITHER GO TO HIS CONDO OR HIS VILLA.
HE WASN'T AT HIS CONDO...
AH, MAN...

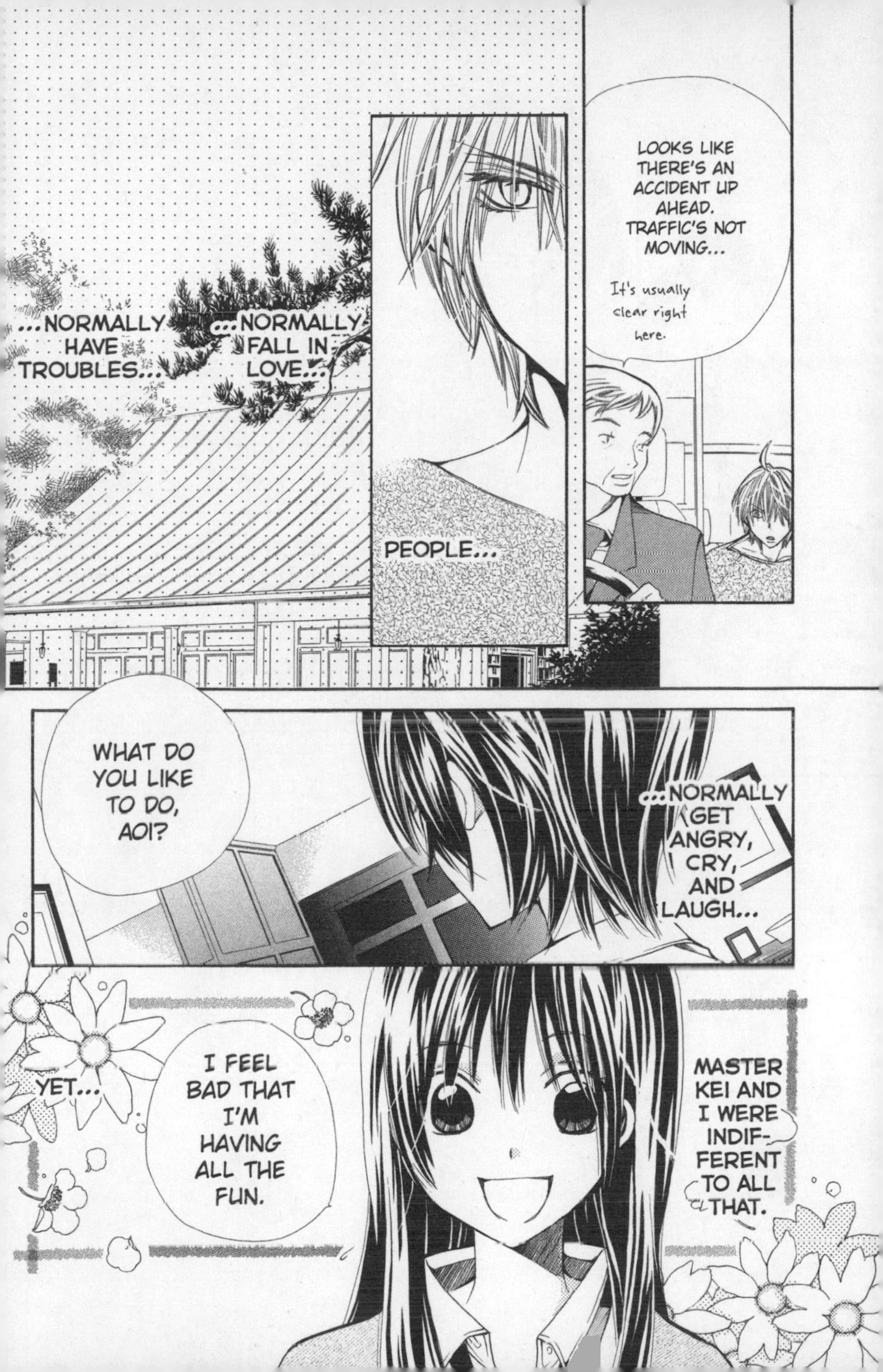
LOOKS LIKE THERE'S AN ACCIDENT UP AHEAD. TRAFFIC'S NOT MOVING...
It's usually clear right here.
PEOPLE...
...NORMALLY FALL IN LOVE...
...NORMALLY HAVE TROUBLES...
...NORMALLY GET ANGRY, CRY, AND LAUGH...
WHAT DO YOU LIKE TO DO, AOI?
MASTER KEI AND I WERE INDIF-FERENT TO ALL THAT.
I FEEL BAD THAT I'M HAVING ALL THE FUN.
YET...

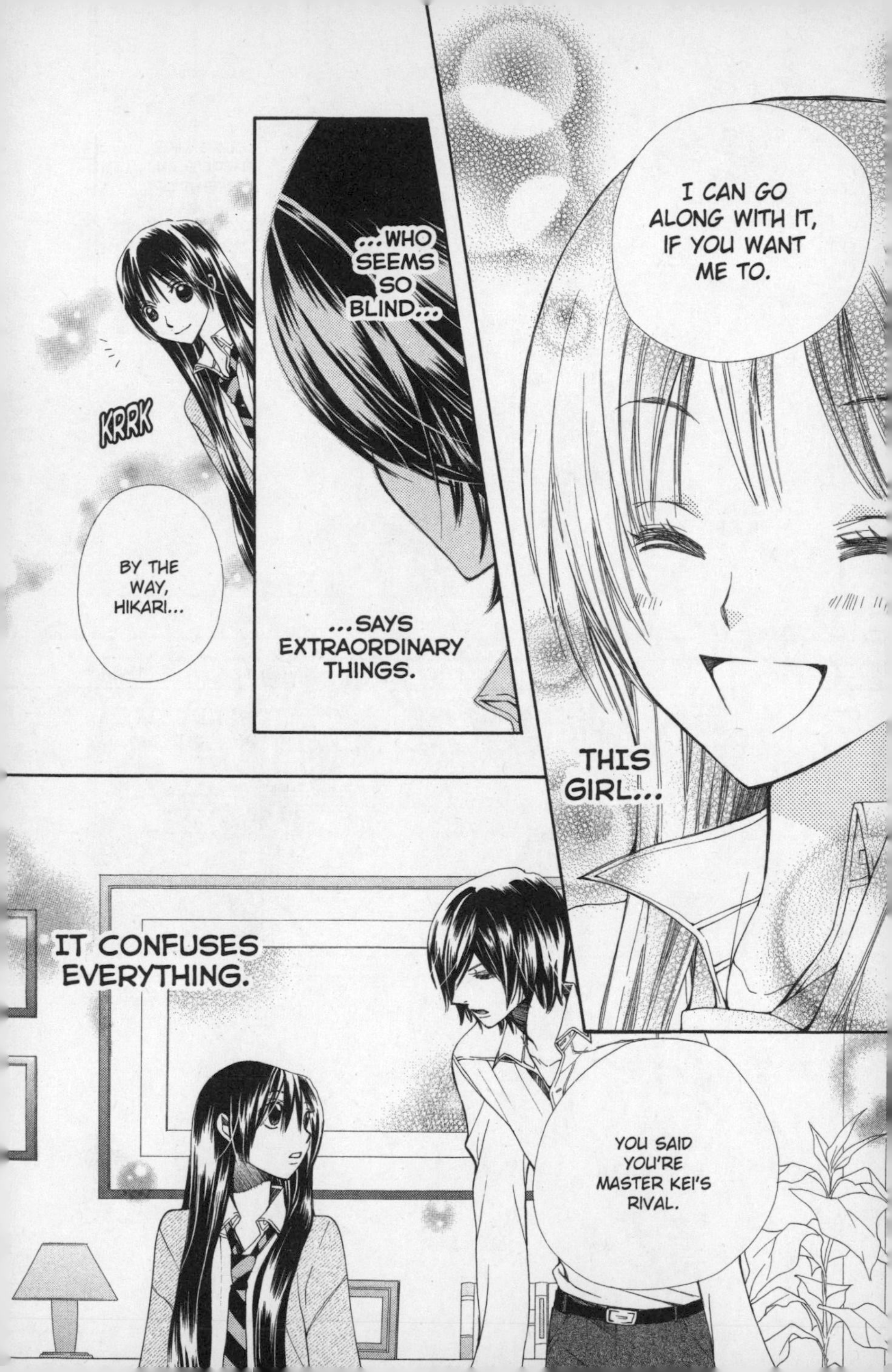
I CAN GO ALONG WITH IT, IF YOU WANT ME TO.
THIS GIRL...
...WHO SEEMS SO BLIND...
...SAYS EXTRAORDINARY THINGS.
KRRK
BY THE WAY, HIKARI...
IT CONFUSES EVERYTHING.
YOU SAID YOU'RE MASTER KEI'S RIVAL.

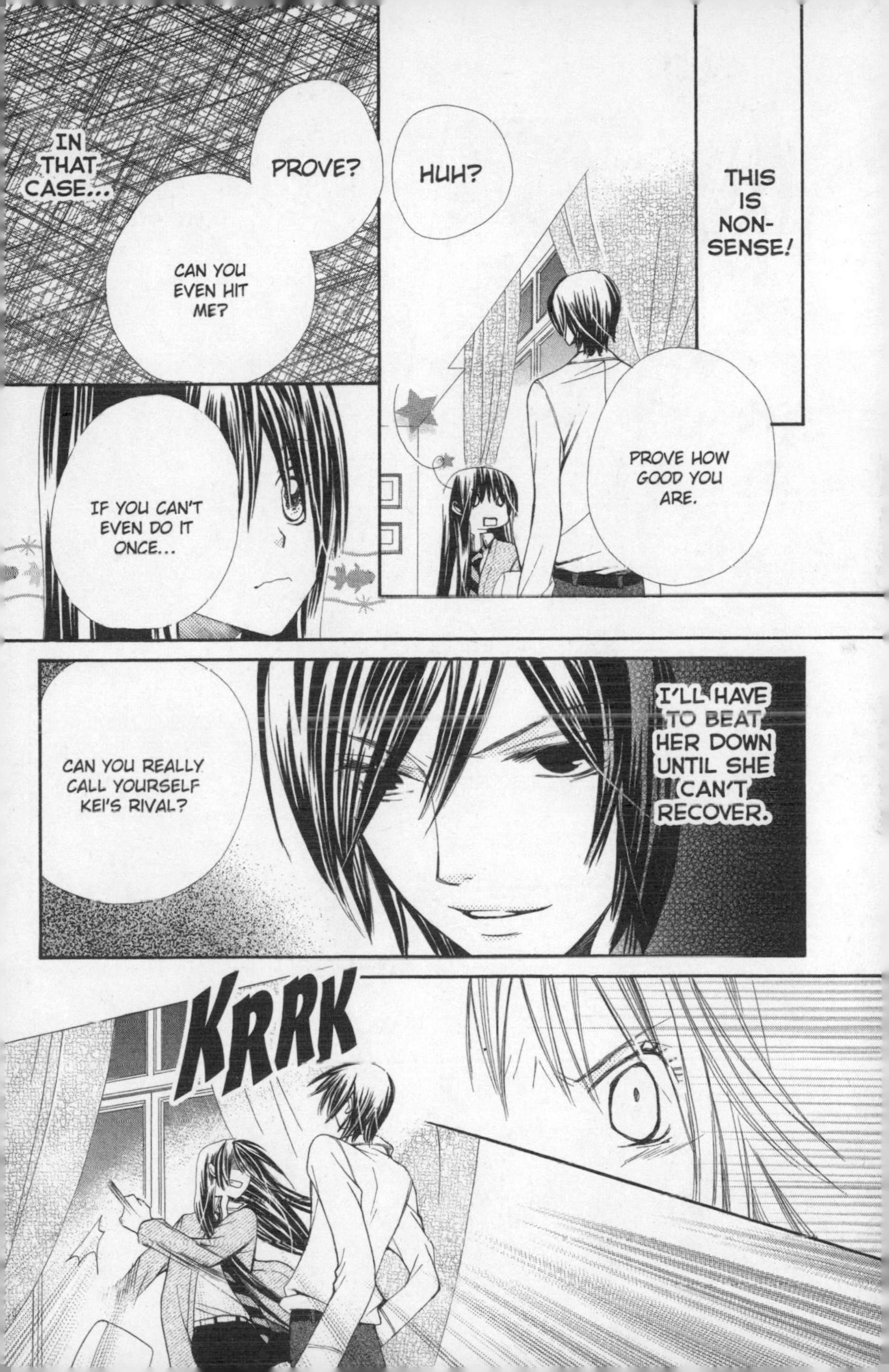
THIS IS NON-SENSE!
HUH?
PROVE HOW GOOD YOU ARE.
PROVE?
IN THAT CASE...
CAN YOU EVEN HIT ME?
IF YOU CAN'T EVEN DO IT ONCE...
I'LL HAVE TO BEAT HER DOWN UNTIL SHE CAN'T RECOVER.
CAN YOU REALLY CALL YOURSELF KEI'S RIVAL?
KRRK

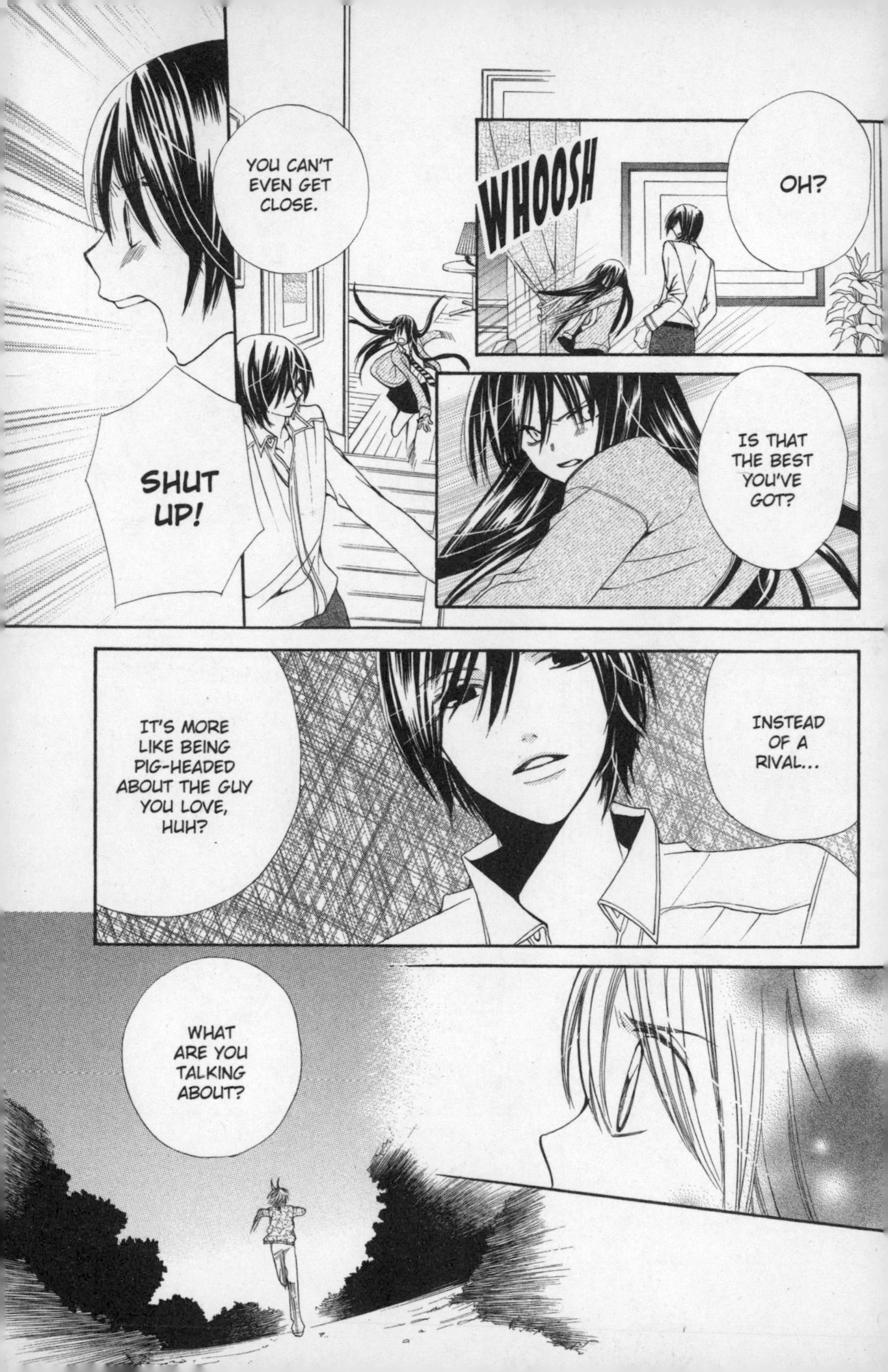
OH?
WHOOSH
IS THAT THE BEST YOU'VE GOT?
YOU CAN'T EVEN GET CLOSE.
SHUT UP!
INSTEAD OF A RIVAL...
IT'S MORE LIKE BEING PIG-HEADED ABOUT THE GUY YOU LOVE, HUH?
WHAT ARE YOU TALKING ABOUT?

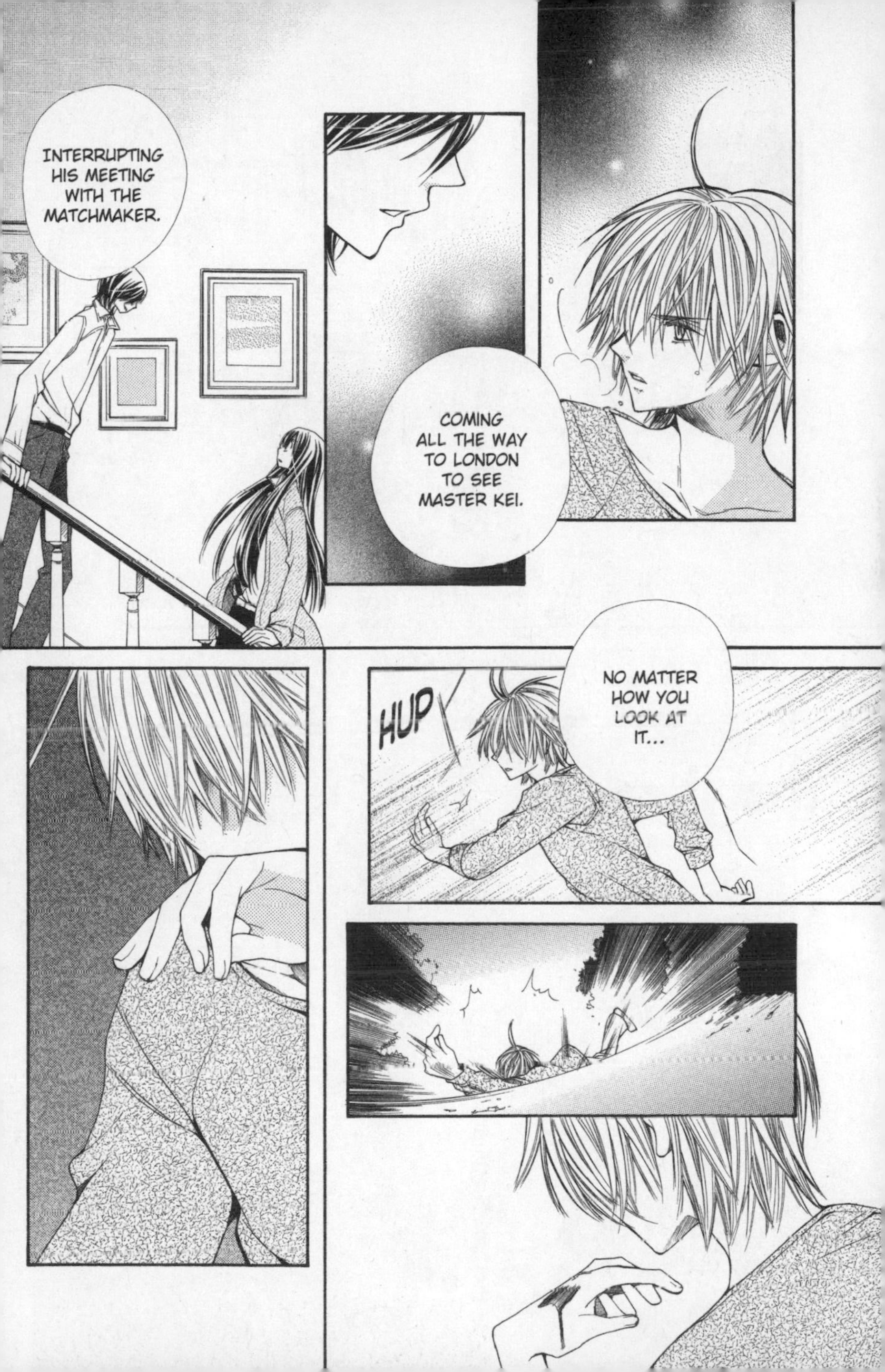
COMING ALL THE WAY TO LONDON TO SEE MASTER KEI.
INTERRUPTING HIS MEETING WITH THE MATCHMAKER.
NO MATTER HOW YOU LOOK AT IT...
HUP

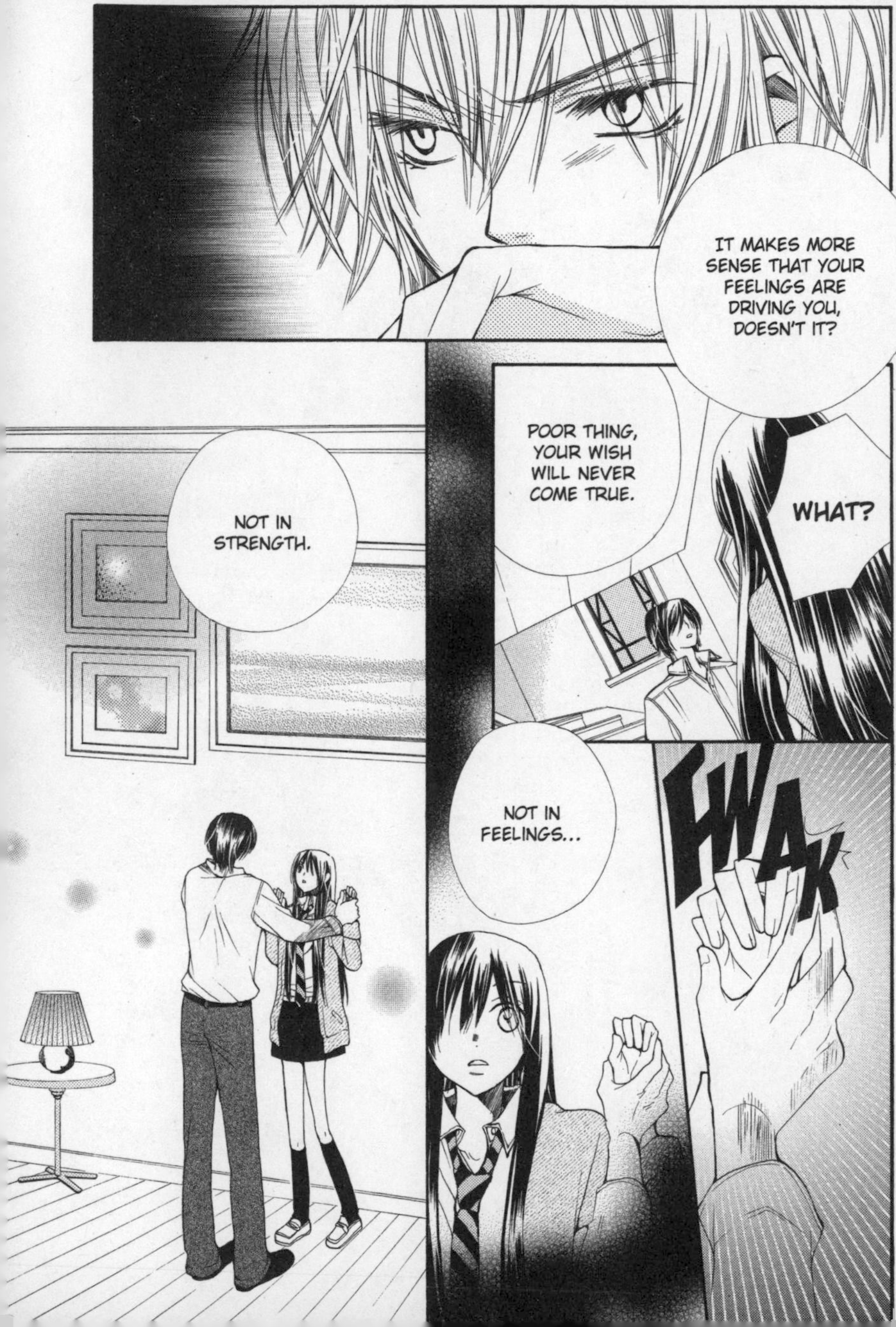
IT MAKES MORE SENSE THAT YOUR FEELINGS ARE DRIVING YOU, DOESN'T IT?
WHAT?
POOR THING, YOUR WISH WILL NEVER COME TRUE.
HWAK
NOT IN FEELINGS...
NOT IN STRENGTH.

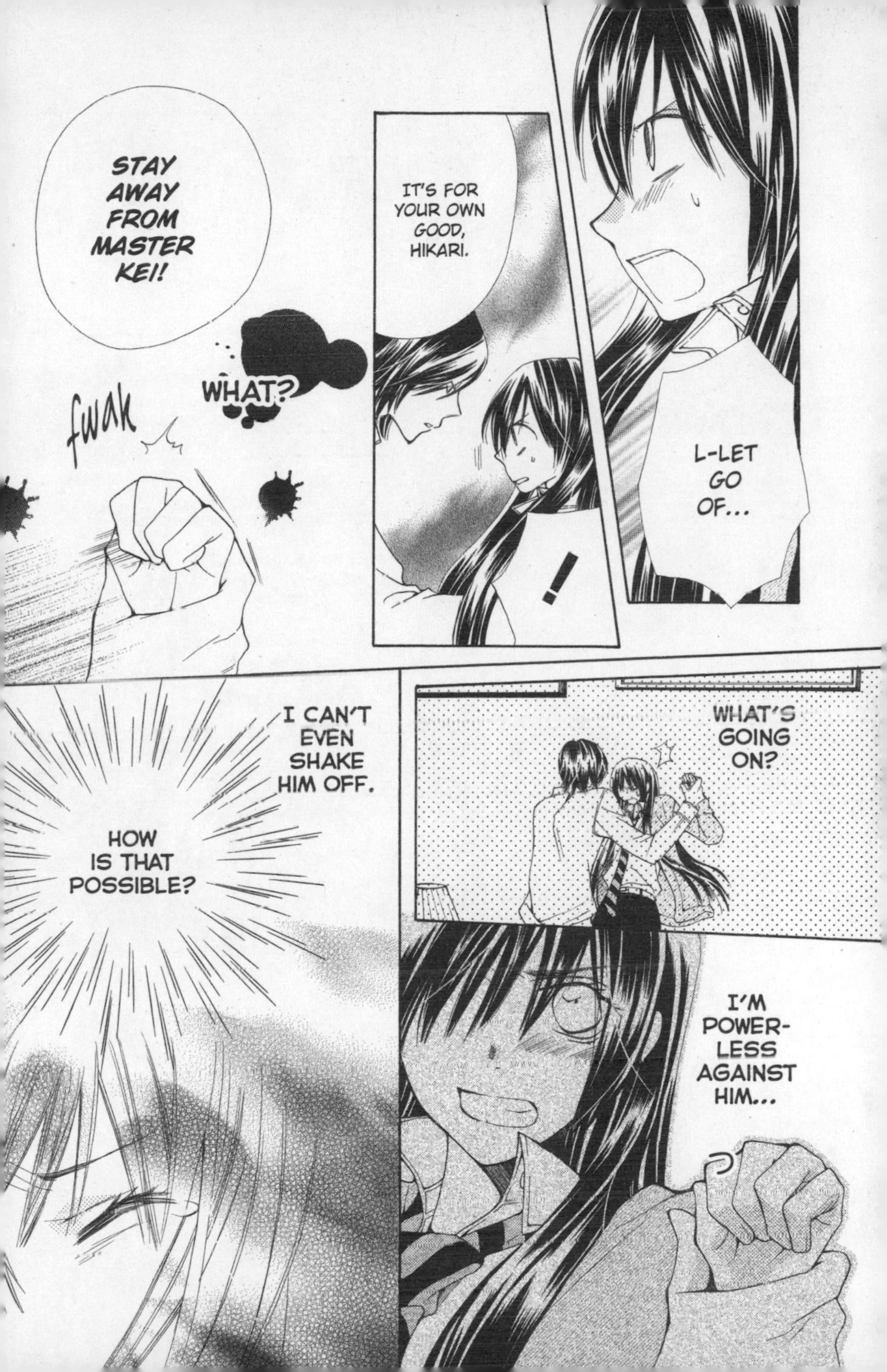
L-LET GO OF...
IT'S FOR YOUR OWN GOOD, HIKARI.
!
STAY AWAY FROM MASTER KEI!
WHAT?
fwak
WHAT'S GOING ON?
I'M POWER-LESS AGAINST HIM...
I CAN'T EVEN SHAKE HIM OFF.
HOW IS THAT POSSIBLE?

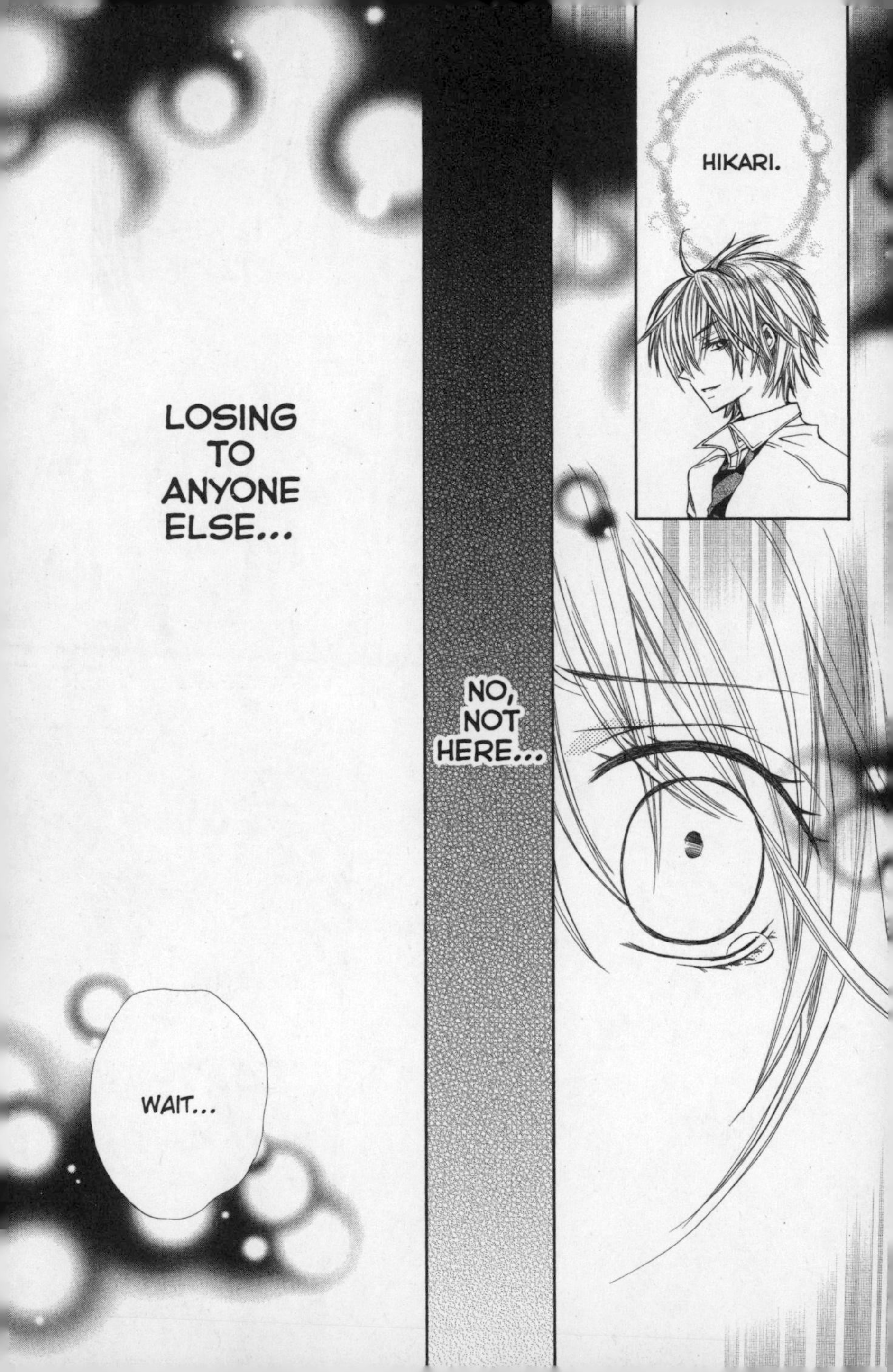
HIKARI.
NO, NOT HERE...
LOSING TO ANYONE ELSE...
WAIT...

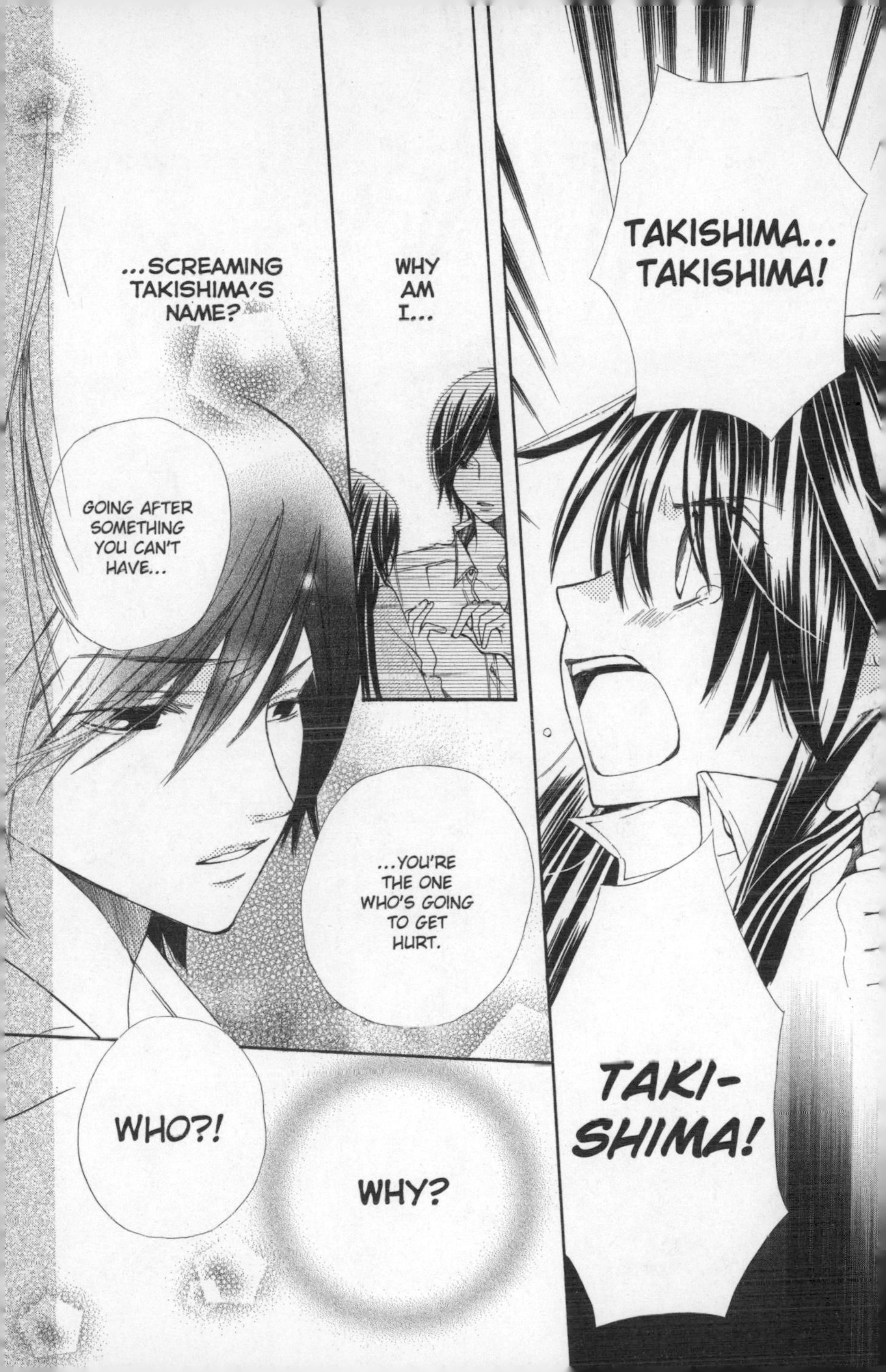
TAKISHIMA... TAKISHIMA!
TAKI-SHIMA!
WHY AM I...
...SCREAMING TAKISHIMA'S NAME?
GOING AFTER SOMETHING YOU CAN'T HAVE...
...YOU'RE THE ONE WHO'S GOING TO GET HURT.
WHO?!
WHY?

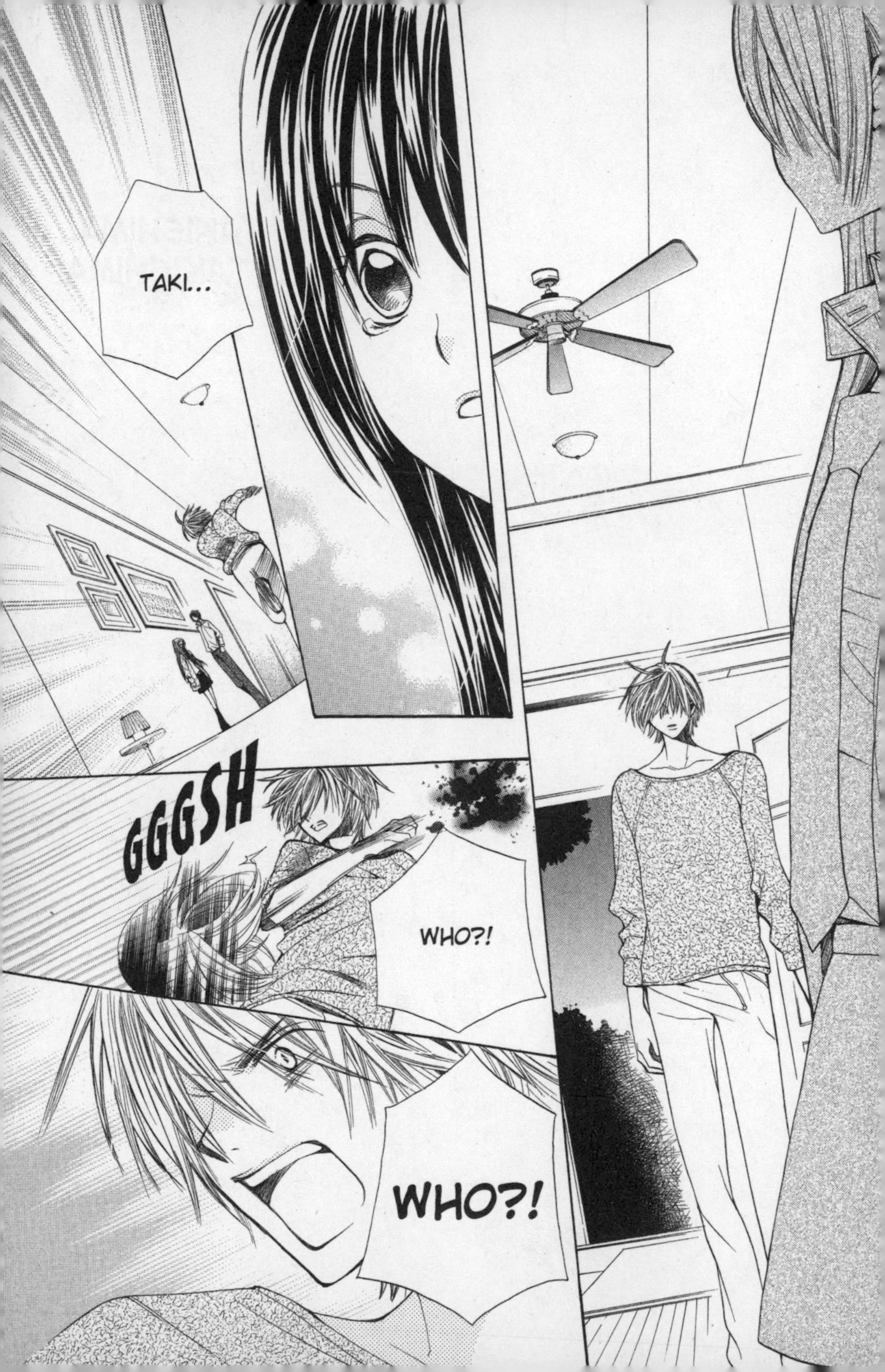
TAKI...
WHO?!
GGGSH
WHO?!

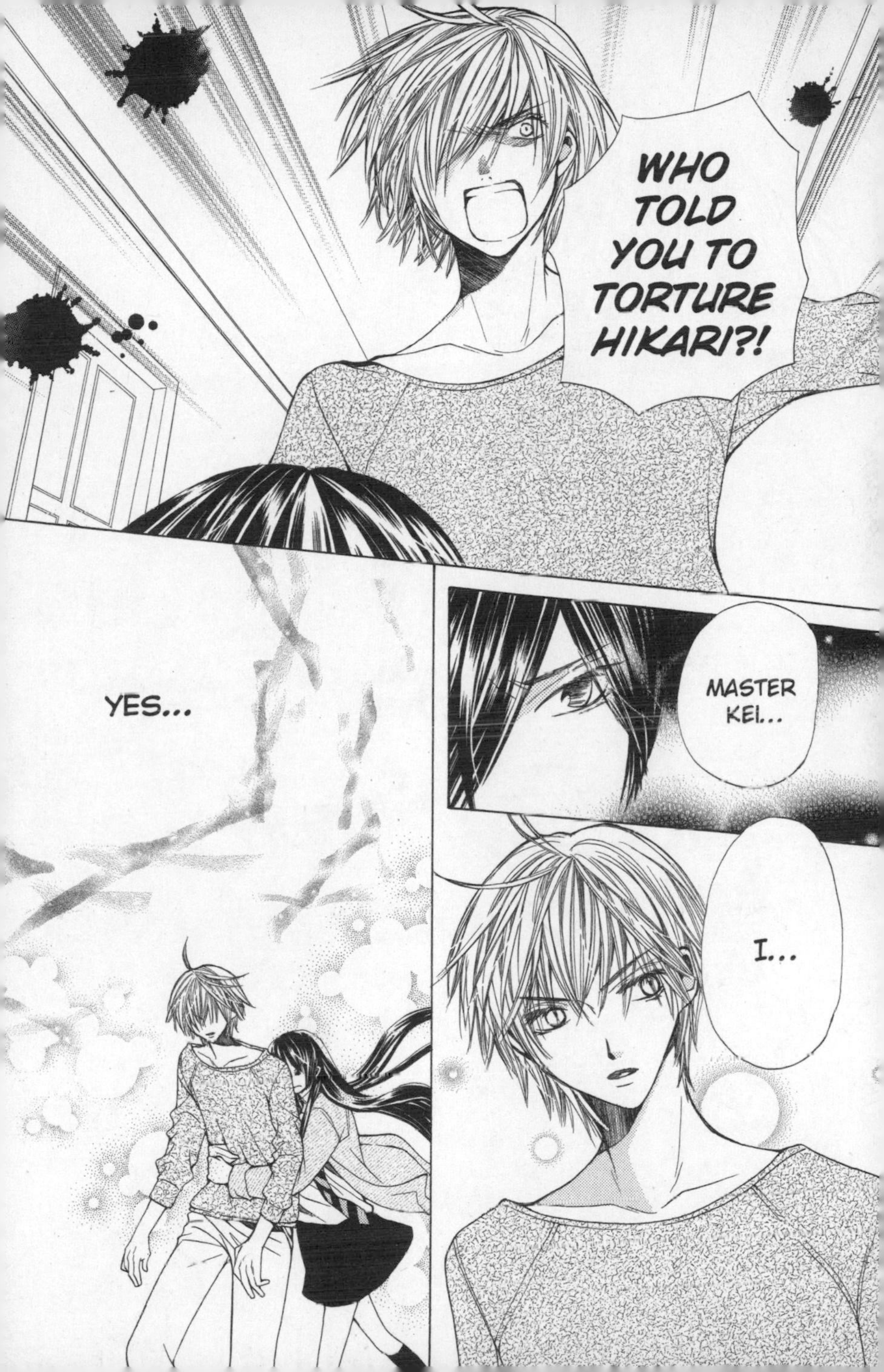
WHO TOLD YOU TO TORTURE HIKARI?!
MASTER KEI...
I...
YES...

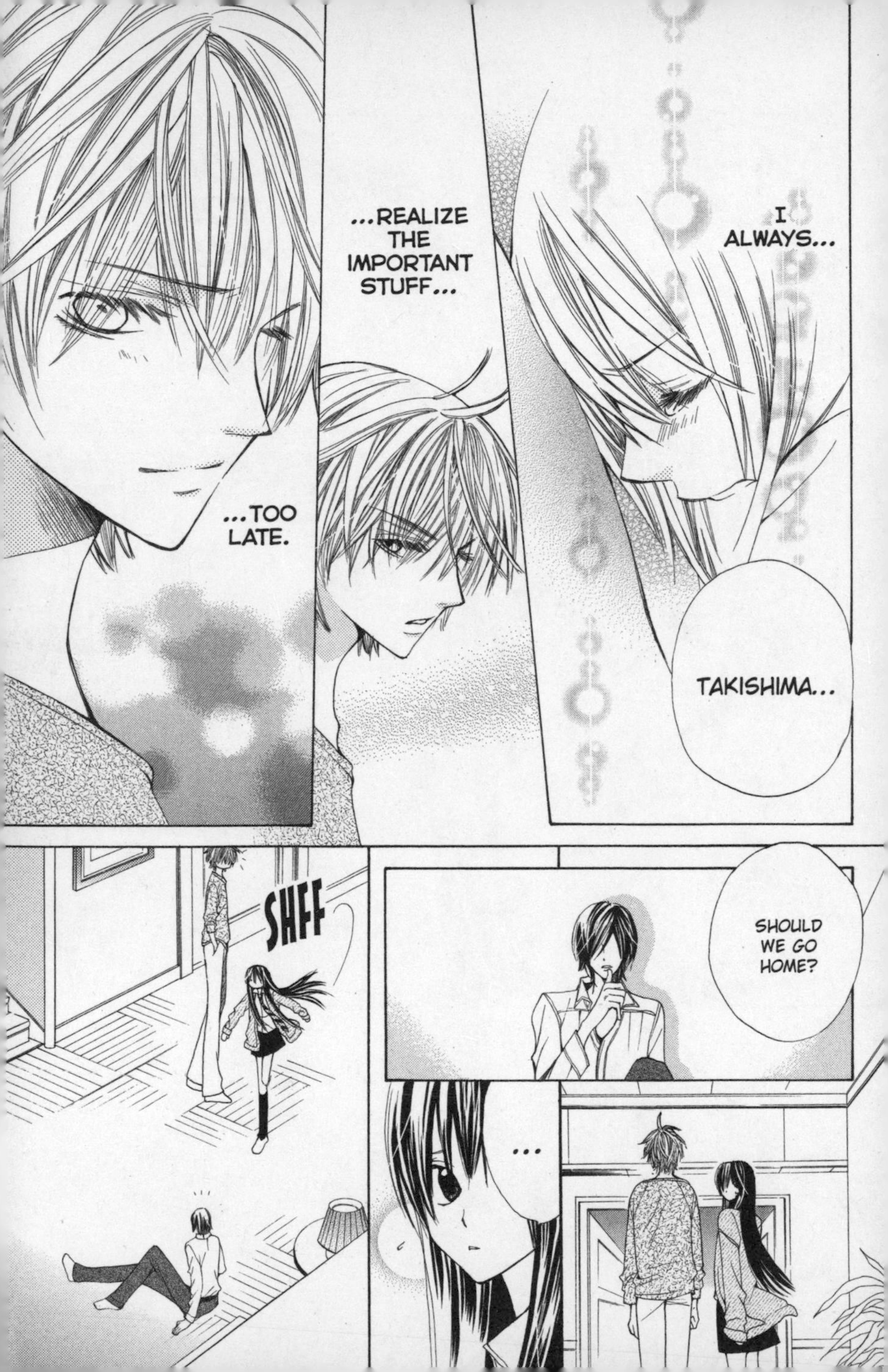
I ALWAYS...
TAKISHIMA...
...REALIZE THE IMPORTANT STUFF...
...TOO LATE.
SHOULD WE GO HOME?
...
SHFF

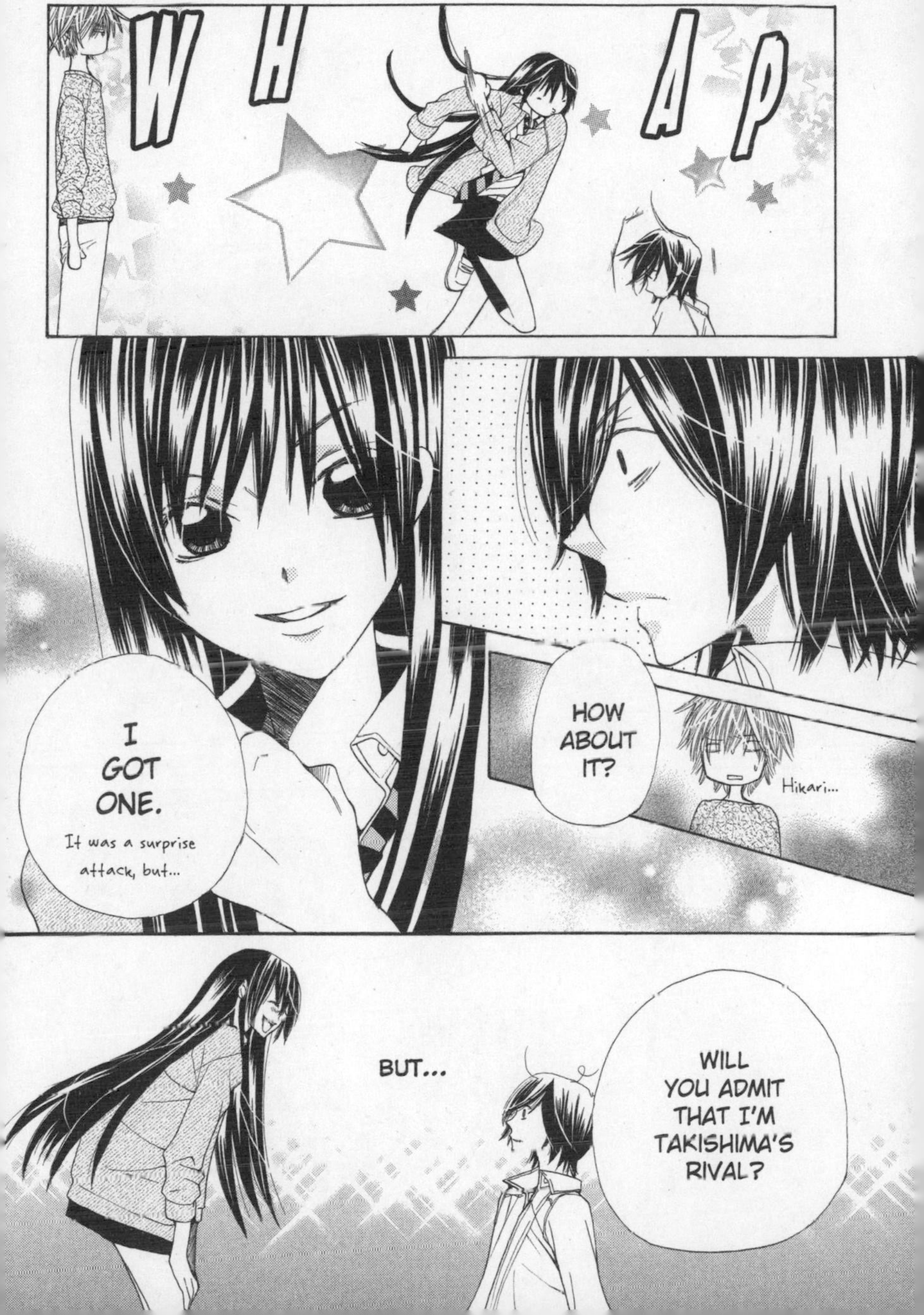
WHAP
HOW ABOUT IT?
Hikari...
I GOT ONE.
It was a surprise attack, but...
BUT...
WILL YOU ADMIT THAT I'M TAKISHIMA'S RIVAL?

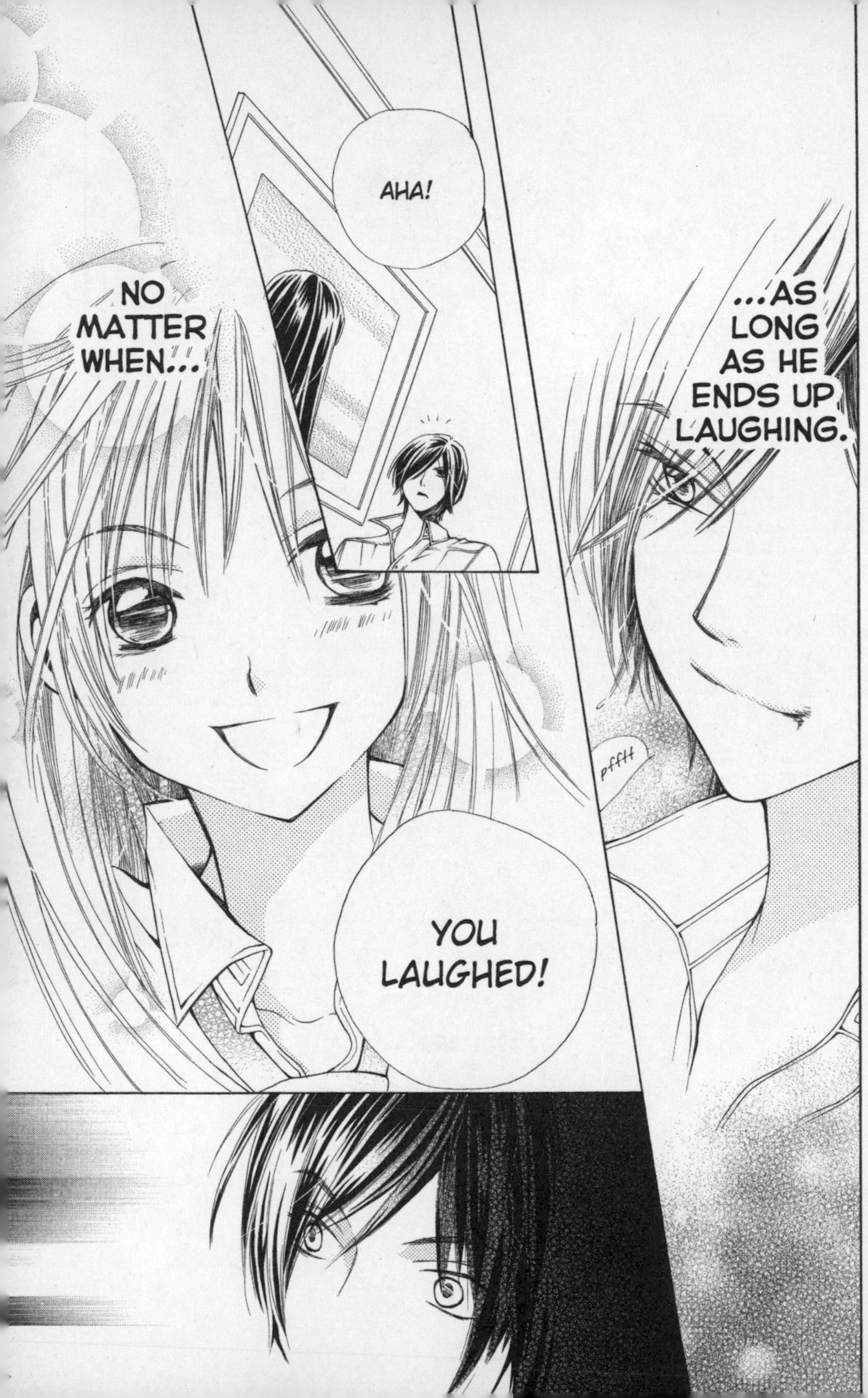
...AS LONG AS HE ENDS UP LAUGHING.
pffft
AHA!
NO MATTER WHEN...
YOU LAUGHED!

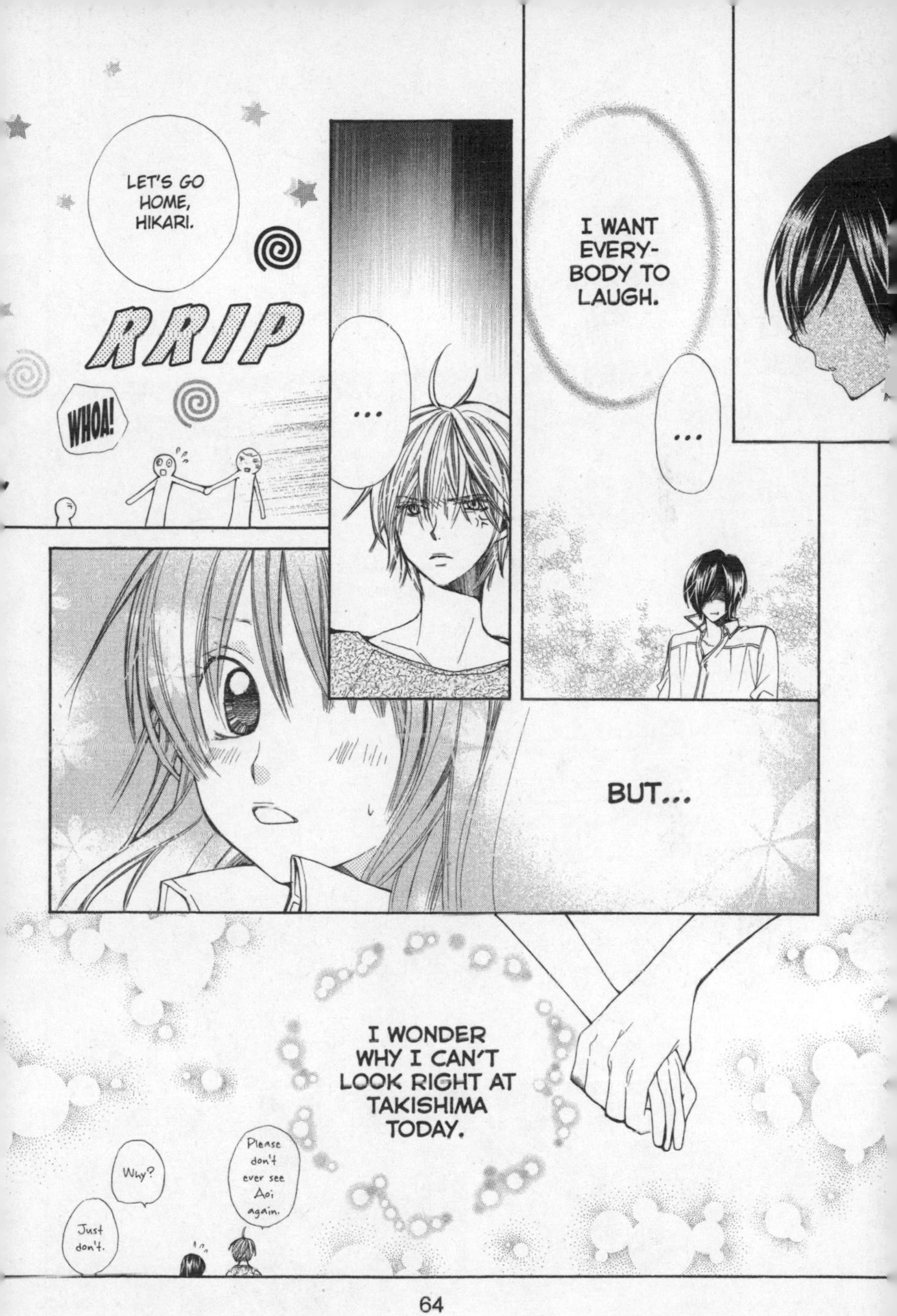
I WANT EVERY-BODY TO LAUGH.
...
...
LET'S GO HOME, HIKARI.
RRIP
WHOA!
BUT...
I WONDER WHY I CAN'T LOOK RIGHT AT TAKISHIMA TODAY.
Please don't ever see Aoi again.
Why?
Just don't.

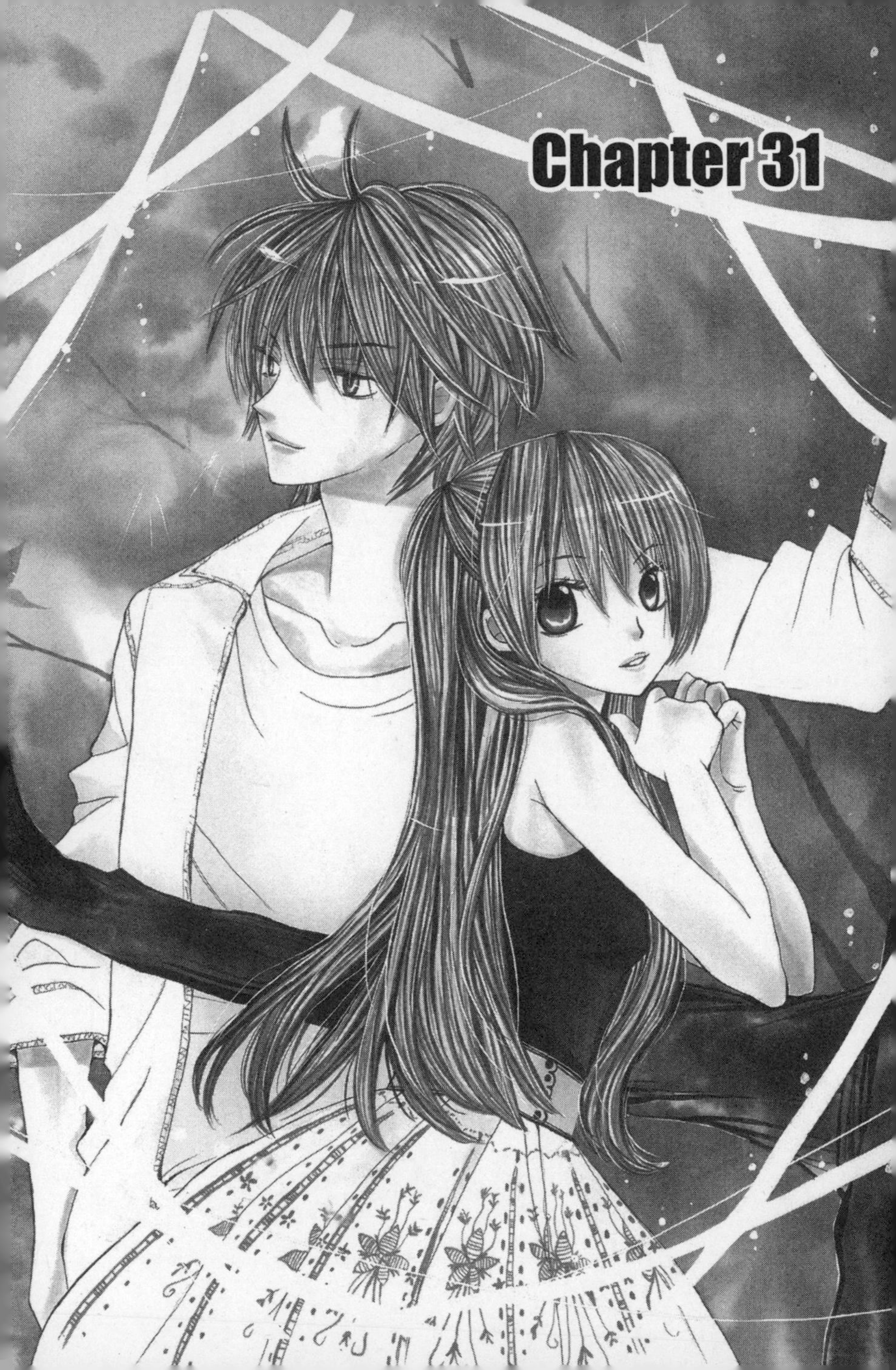
Chapter 31

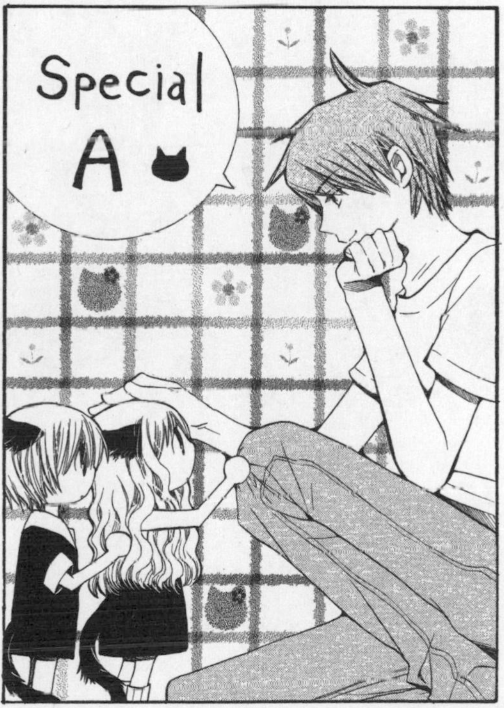
Special
A

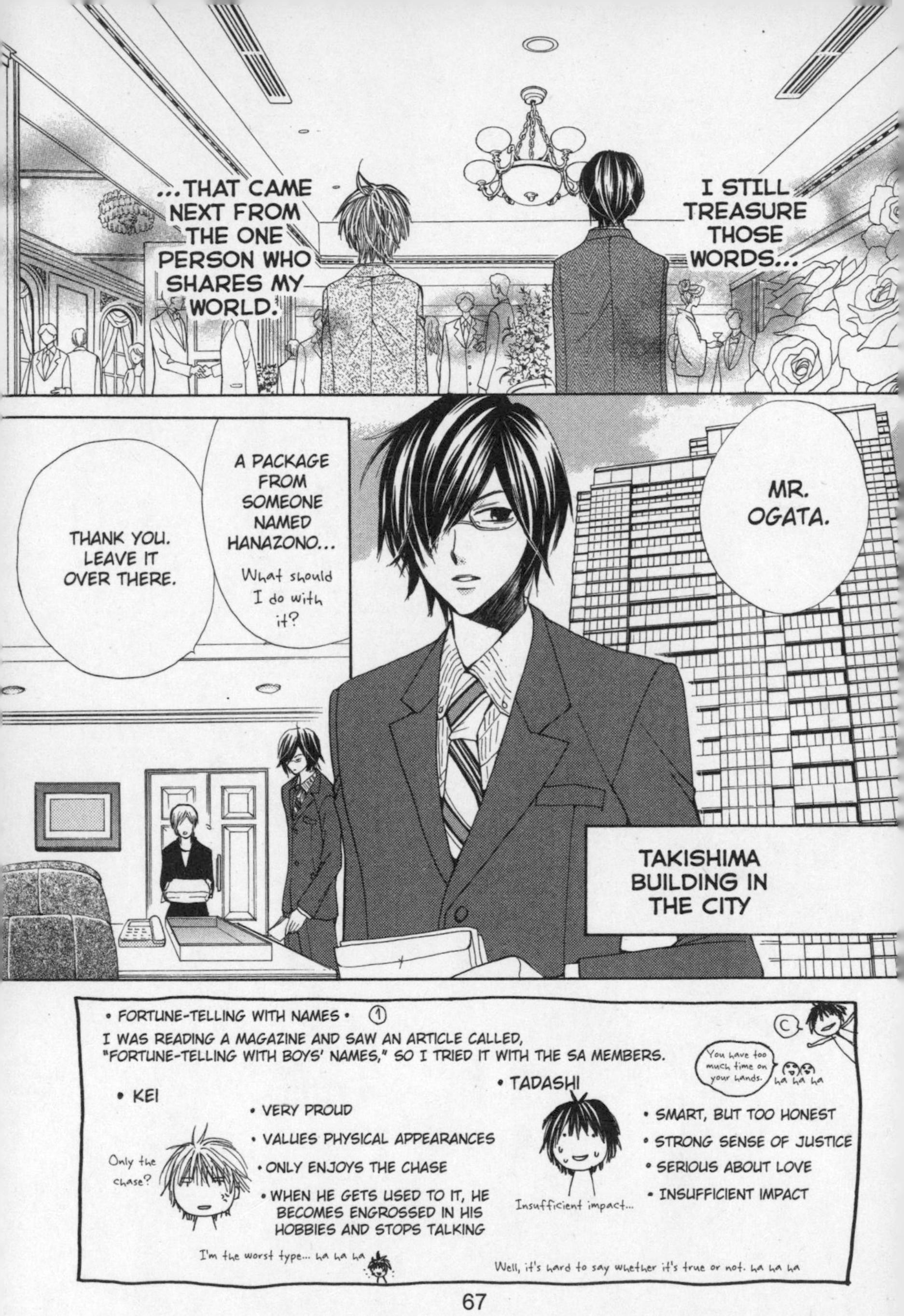
I STILL TREASURE THOSE WORDS...
...THAT CAME NEXT FROM THE ONE PERSON WHO SHARES MY WORLD.
MR. OGATA.
TAKISHIMA BUILDING IN THE CITY
A PACKAGE FROM SOMEONE NAMED HANAZONO...
What should I do with it?
THANK YOU. LEAVE IT OVER THERE.

• FORTUNE-TELLING WITH NAMES • ①

I WAS READING A MAGAZINE AND SAW AN ARTICLE CALLED, "FORTUNE-TELLING WITH BOYS' NAMES," SO I TRIED IT WITH THE SA MEMBERS.

You have too much time on your hands. ha ha ha

• KEI

- VERY PROUD
- VALUES PHYSICAL APPEARANCES
- ONLY ENJOYS THE CHASE
- WHEN HE GETS USED TO IT, HE BECOMES ENGROSSED IN HIS HOBBIES AND STOPS TALKING

Only the chase?

I'm the worst type... ha ha ha

• TADASHI

- SMART, BUT TOO HONEST
- STRONG SENSE OF JUSTICE
- SERIOUS ABOUT LOVE
- INSUFFICIENT IMPACT

Insufficient impact...

Well, it's hard to say whether it's true or not. ha ha ha

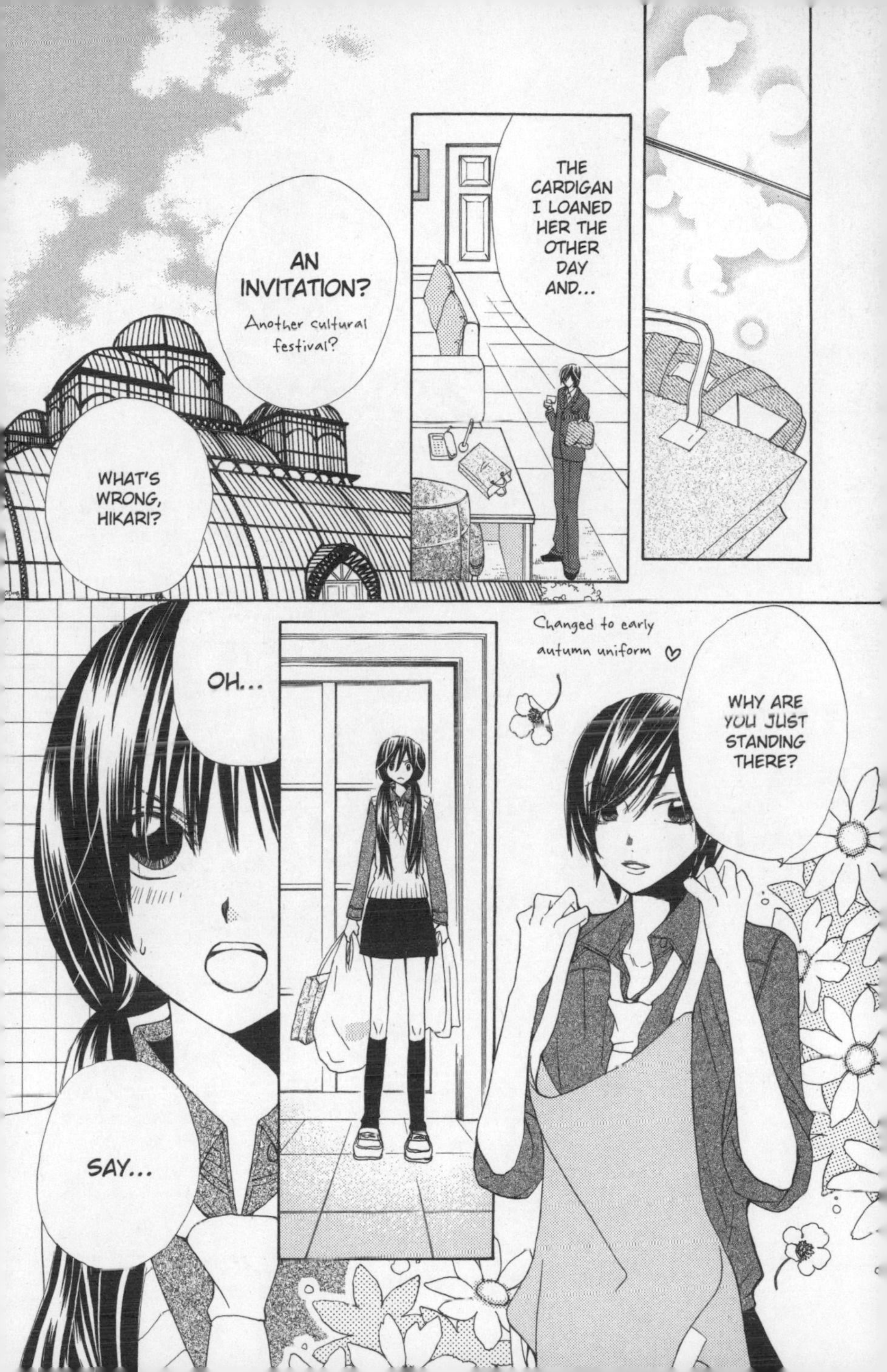
THE CARDIGAN I LOANED HER THE OTHER DAY AND...
AN INVITATION?
Another cultural festival?
WHAT'S WRONG, HIKARI?
WHY ARE YOU JUST STANDING THERE?
Changed to early autumn uniform ♡
OH...
SAY...

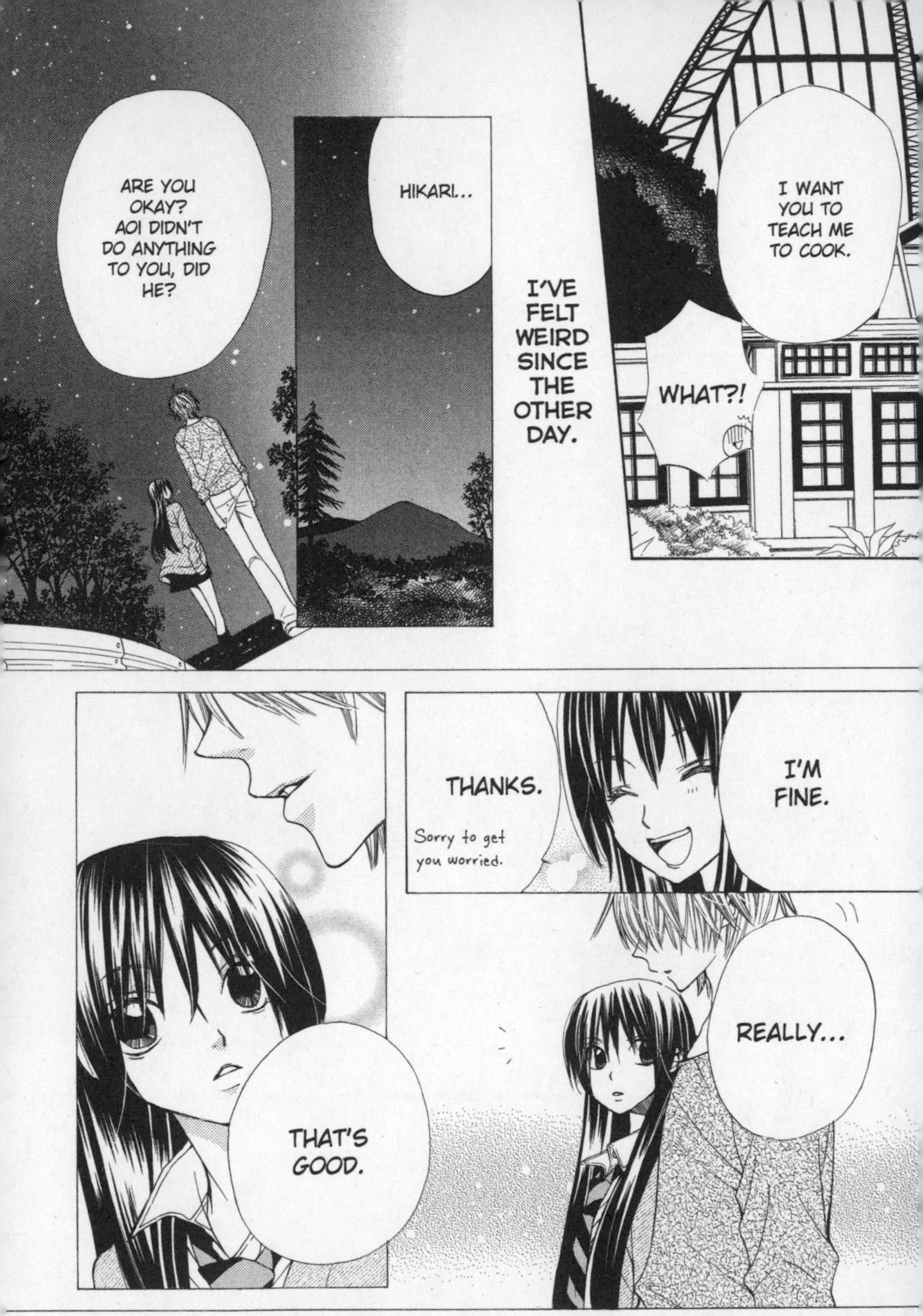
I WANT YOU TO TEACH ME TO COOK.
WHAT?!
I'VE FELT WEIRD SINCE THE OTHER DAY.
HIKARI...
ARE YOU OKAY? AOI DIDN'T DO ANYTHING TO YOU, DID HE?
I'M FINE.
THANKS.
Sorry to get you worried.
REALLY...
THAT'S GOOD.

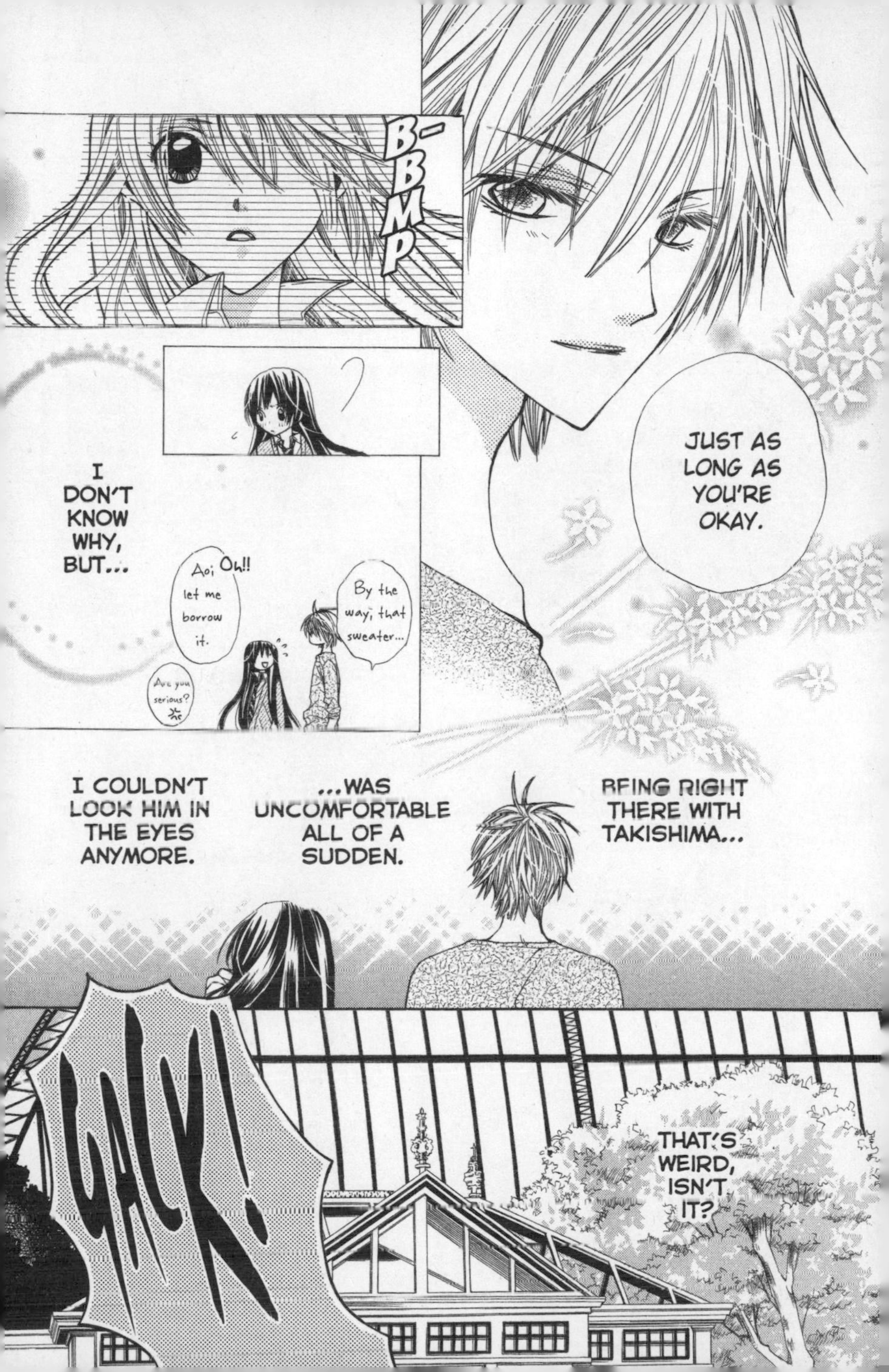
JUST AS LONG AS YOU'RE OKAY.
B-BMP
I DON'T KNOW WHY, BUT...
By the way, that sweater...
Oh!!
Aoi let me borrow it.
Are you serious?
BEING RIGHT THERE WITH TAKISHIMA...
...WAS UNCOMFORTABLE ALL OF A SUDDEN.
I COULDN'T LOOK HIM IN THE EYES ANYMORE.
THAT'S WEIRD, ISN'T IT?
GACK!

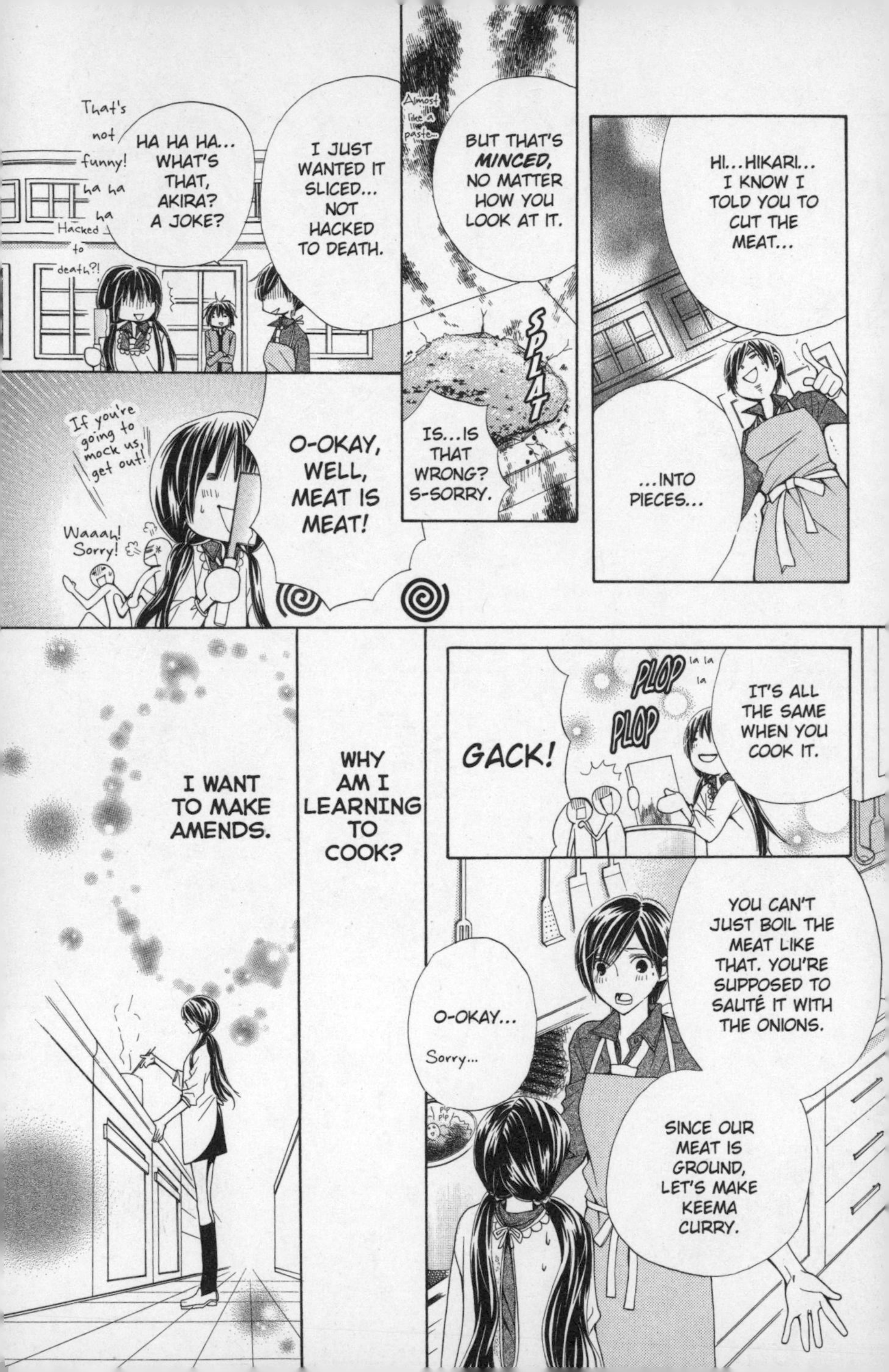
HI...HIKARI... I KNOW I TOLD YOU TO CUT THE MEAT...
...INTO PIECES...
BUT THAT'S *MINCED,* NO MATTER HOW YOU LOOK AT IT.
Almost like a paste...
SPLAT
IS...IS THAT WRONG? S-SORRY.
I JUST WANTED IT SLICED... NOT HACKED TO DEATH.
HA HA HA... WHAT'S THAT, AKIRA? A JOKE?
That's not funny!
ha ha ha
Hacked to death?!
O-OKAY, WELL, MEAT IS MEAT!
If you're going to mock us, get out!
Waaah! Sorry!
IT'S ALL THE SAME WHEN YOU COOK IT.
la la la
PLOP
PLOP
GACK!
YOU CAN'T JUST BOIL THE MEAT LIKE THAT. YOU'RE SUPPOSED TO SAUTÉ IT WITH THE ONIONS.
O-OKAY...
Sorry...
SINCE OUR MEAT IS GROUND, LET'S MAKE KEEMA CURRY.
WHY AM I LEARNING TO COOK?
I WANT TO MAKE AMENDS.

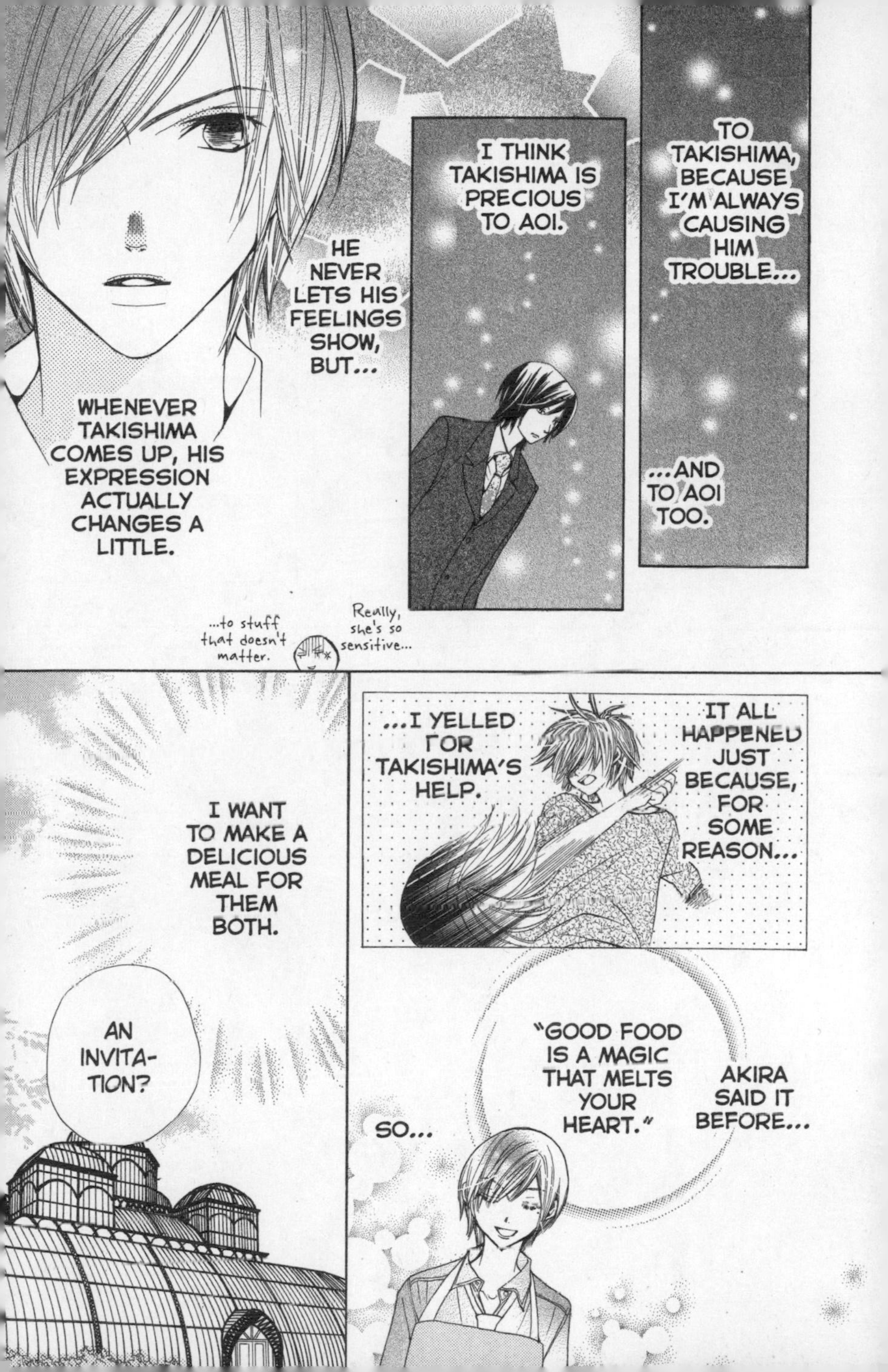
TO TAKISHIMA, BECAUSE I'M ALWAYS CAUSING HIM TROUBLE...
...AND TO AOI TOO.
I THINK TAKISHIMA IS PRECIOUS TO AOI.
HE NEVER LETS HIS FEELINGS SHOW, BUT...
WHENEVER TAKISHIMA COMES UP, HIS EXPRESSION ACTUALLY CHANGES A LITTLE.
Really, she's so sensitive...
...to stuff that doesn't matter.
IT ALL HAPPENED JUST BECAUSE, FOR SOME REASON...
...I YELLED FOR TAKISHIMA'S HELP.
AKIRA SAID IT BEFORE...
"GOOD FOOD IS A MAGIC THAT MELTS YOUR HEART."
SO...
I WANT TO MAKE A DELICIOUS MEAL FOR THEM BOTH.
AN INVITATION?

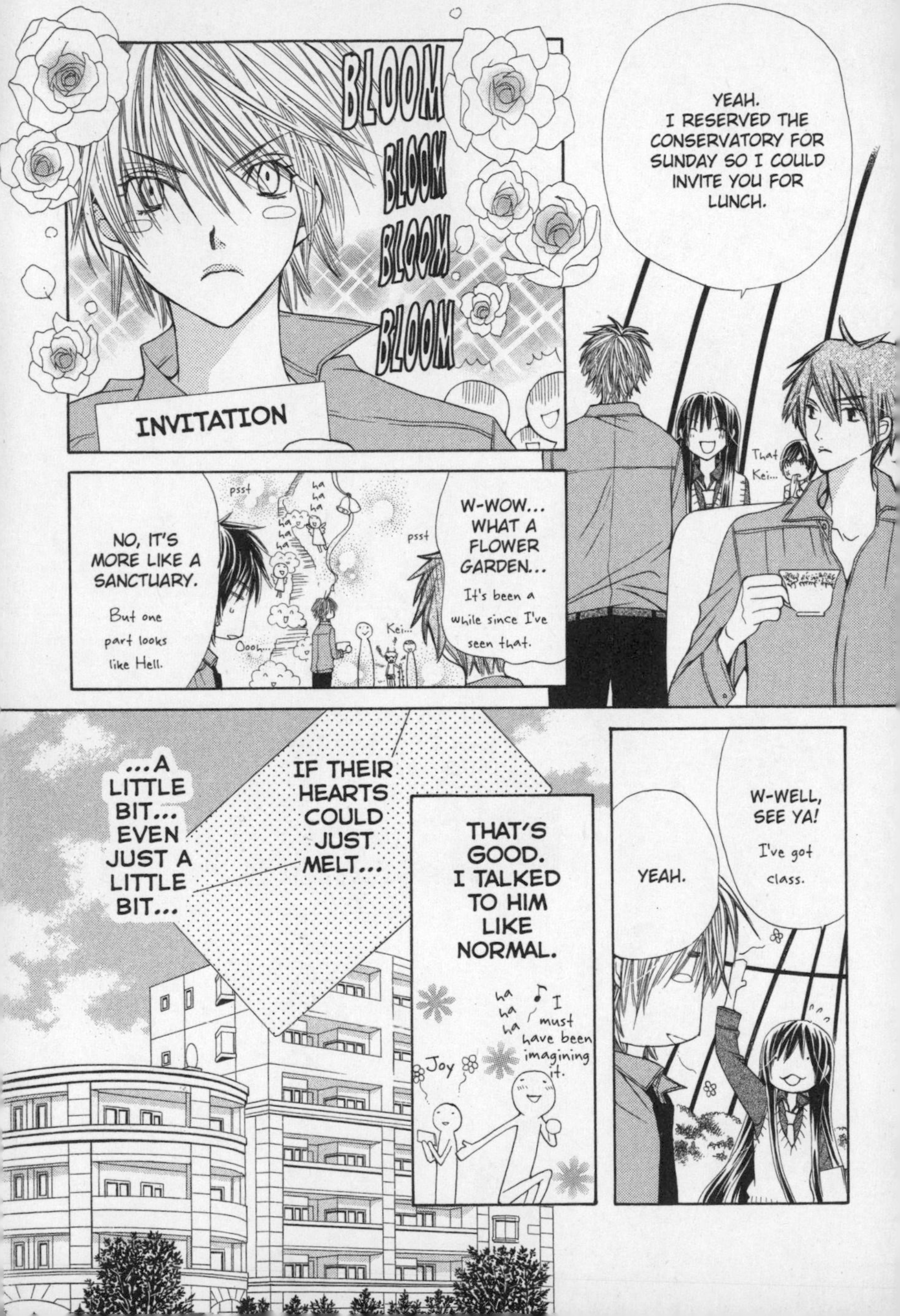
YEAH. I RESERVED THE CONSERVATORY FOR SUNDAY SO I COULD INVITE YOU FOR LUNCH.
That Kei...
BLOOM BLOOM BLOOM BLOOM
INVITATION
W-WOW... WHAT A FLOWER GARDEN...
It's been a while since I've seen that.
psst
psst
NO, IT'S MORE LIKE A SANCTUARY.
But one part looks like Hell.
ha ha ha
ha ha ha
Kei...
Oooh...
W-WELL, SEE YA!
I've got class.
YEAH.
THAT'S GOOD. I TALKED TO HIM LIKE NORMAL.
ha ha ha I must have been imagining it.
Joy
IF THEIR HEARTS COULD JUST MELT...
...A LITTLE BIT... EVEN JUST A LITTLE BIT...

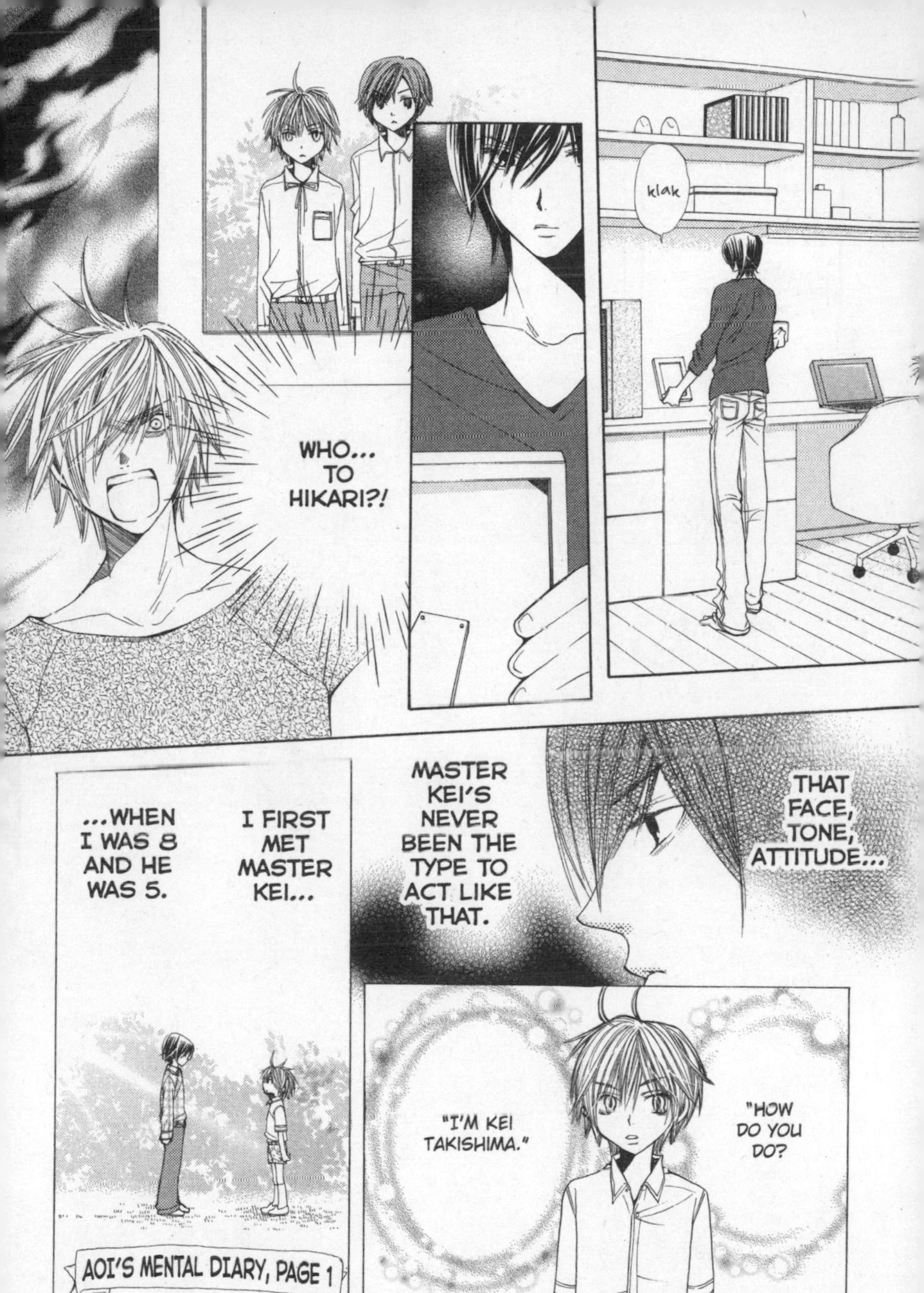
klak
WHO... TO HIKARI?!
THAT FACE, TONE, ATTITUDE...
MASTER KEI'S NEVER BEEN THE TYPE TO ACT LIKE THAT.
"HOW DO YOU DO?
"I'M KEI TAKISHIMA."
I FIRST MET MASTER KEI...
...WHEN I WAS 8 AND HE WAS 5.
AOI'S MENTAL DIARY, PAGE 1

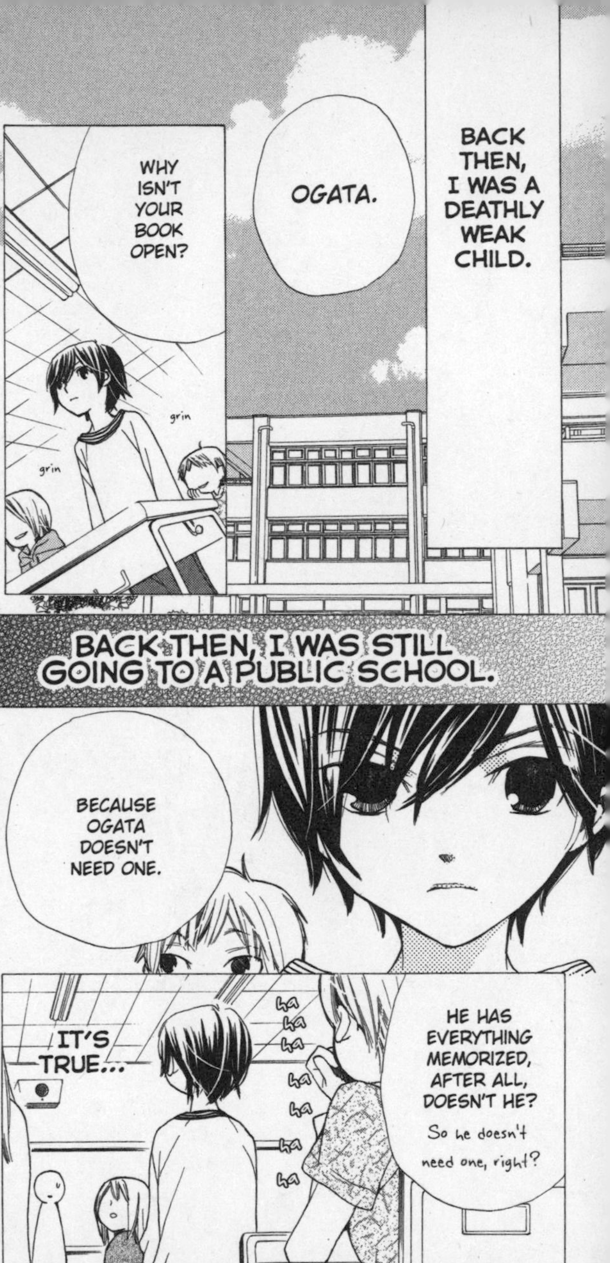
BACK THEN, I WAS A DEATHLY WEAK CHILD.
OGATA.
WHY ISN'T YOUR BOOK OPEN?
grin
grin
BACK THEN, I WAS STILL GOING TO A PUBLIC SCHOOL.
BECAUSE OGATA DOESN'T NEED ONE.
HE HAS EVERYTHING MEMORIZED, AFTER ALL, DOESN'T HE?
So he doesn't need one, right?
ha ha ha ha ha ha ha ha
IT'S TRUE...

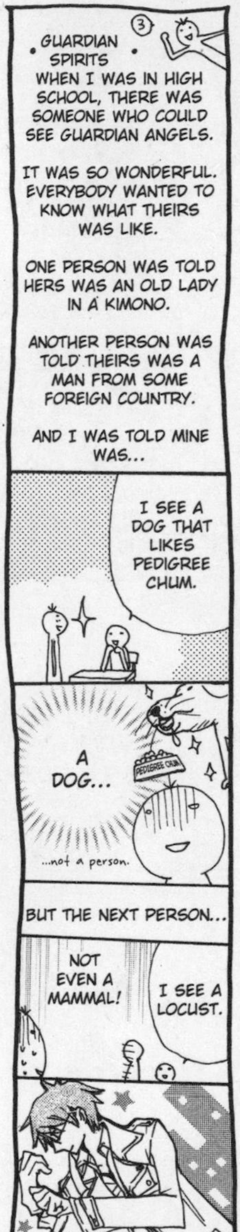
3
• GUARDIAN SPIRITS •
WHEN I WAS IN HIGH SCHOOL, THERE WAS SOMEONE WHO COULD SEE GUARDIAN ANGELS.
IT WAS SO WONDERFUL. EVERYBODY WANTED TO KNOW WHAT THEIRS WAS LIKE.
ONE PERSON WAS TOLD HERS WAS AN OLD LADY IN A KIMONO.
ANOTHER PERSON WAS TOLD THEIRS WAS A MAN FROM SOME FOREIGN COUNTRY.
AND I WAS TOLD MINE WAS...
I SEE A DOG THAT LIKES PEDIGREE CHUM.
A DOG...
PEDIGREE CHUM
...not a person.
BUT THE NEXT PERSON...
I SEE A LOCUST.
NOT EVEN A MAMMAL!

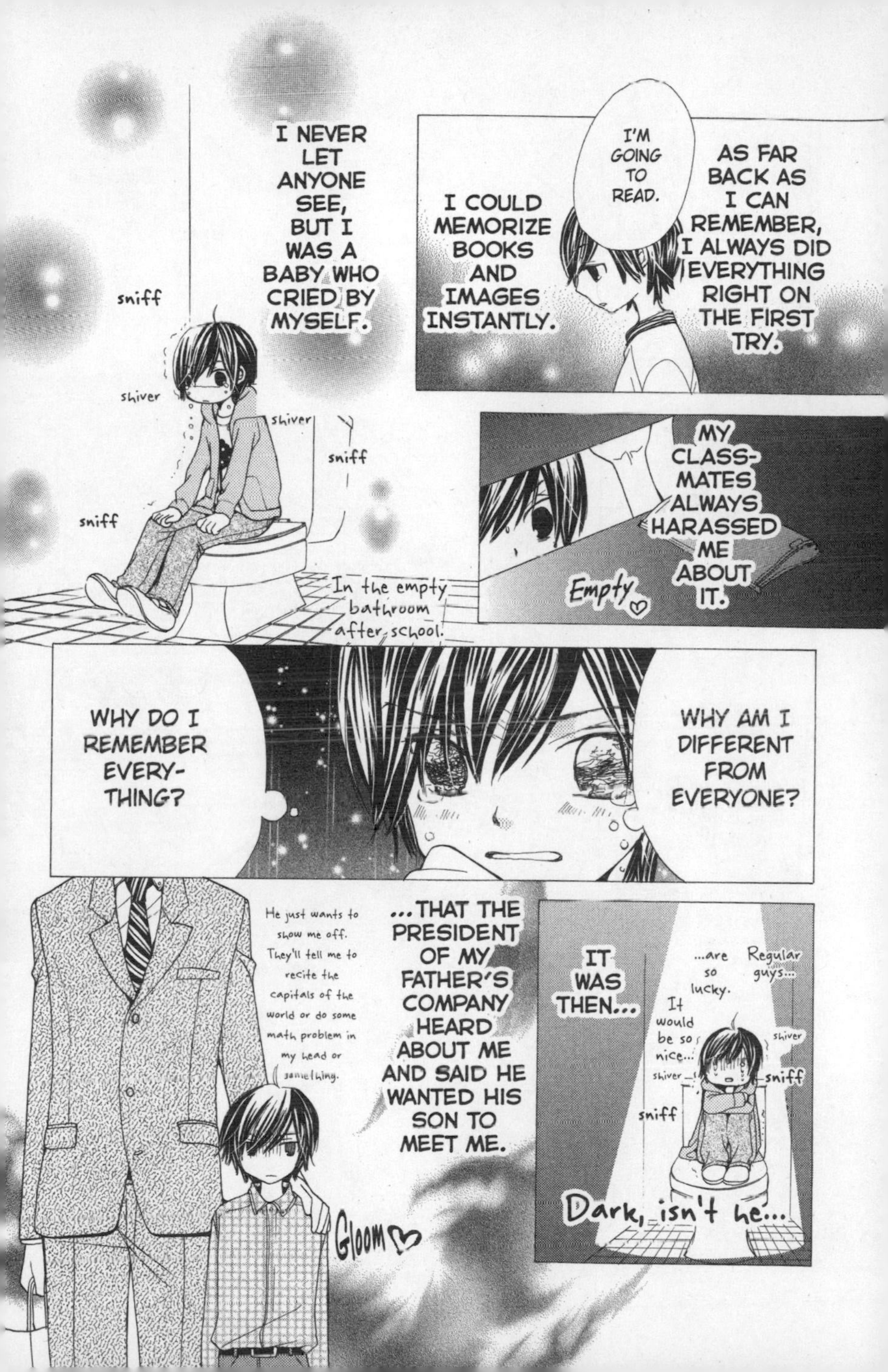
AS FAR BACK AS I CAN REMEMBER, I ALWAYS DID EVERYTHING RIGHT ON THE FIRST TRY.
I'M GOING TO READ.
I COULD MEMORIZE BOOKS AND IMAGES INSTANTLY.
MY CLASSMATES ALWAYS HARASSED ME ABOUT IT.
Empty
I NEVER LET ANYONE SEE, BUT I WAS A BABY WHO CRIED BY MYSELF.
sniff
shiver
shiver
sniff
sniff
In the empty bathroom after school.
WHY AM I DIFFERENT FROM EVERYONE?
WHY DO I REMEMBER EVERY-THING?
IT WAS THEN...
Regular guys...
...are so lucky.
It would be so nice...
shiver
shiver
sniff
sniff
Dark, isn't he...
...THAT THE PRESIDENT OF MY FATHER'S COMPANY HEARD ABOUT ME AND SAID HE WANTED HIS SON TO MEET ME.
He just wants to show me off. They'll tell me to recite the capitals of the world or do some math problem in my head or something.
Gloom

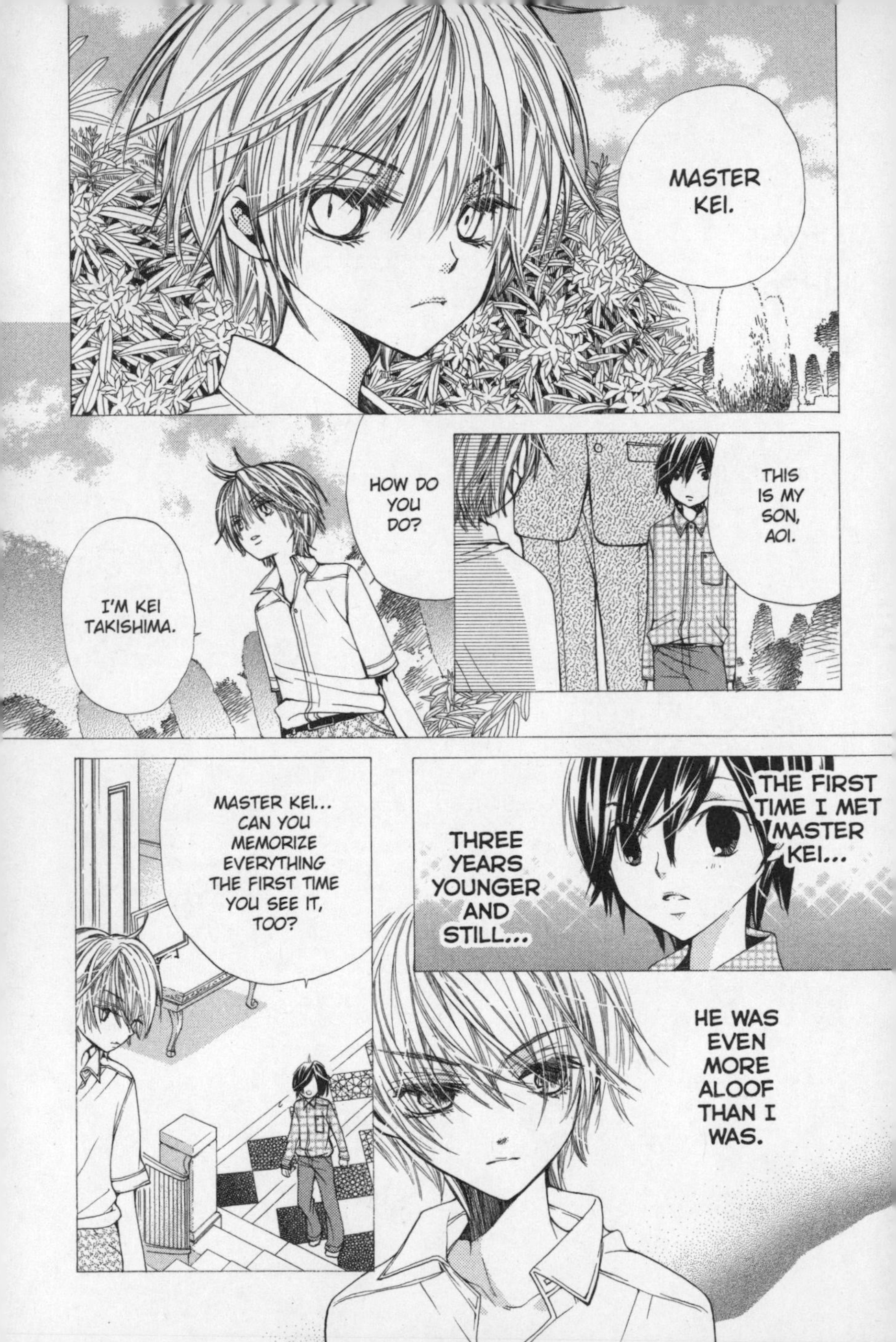
MASTER KEI.
THIS IS MY SON, AOI.
HOW DO YOU DO?
I'M KEI TAKISHIMA.
THE FIRST TIME I MET MASTER KEI...
THREE YEARS YOUNGER AND STILL...
HE WAS EVEN MORE ALOOF THAN I WAS.
MASTER KEI... CAN YOU MEMORIZE EVERYTHING THE FIRST TIME YOU SEE IT, TOO?

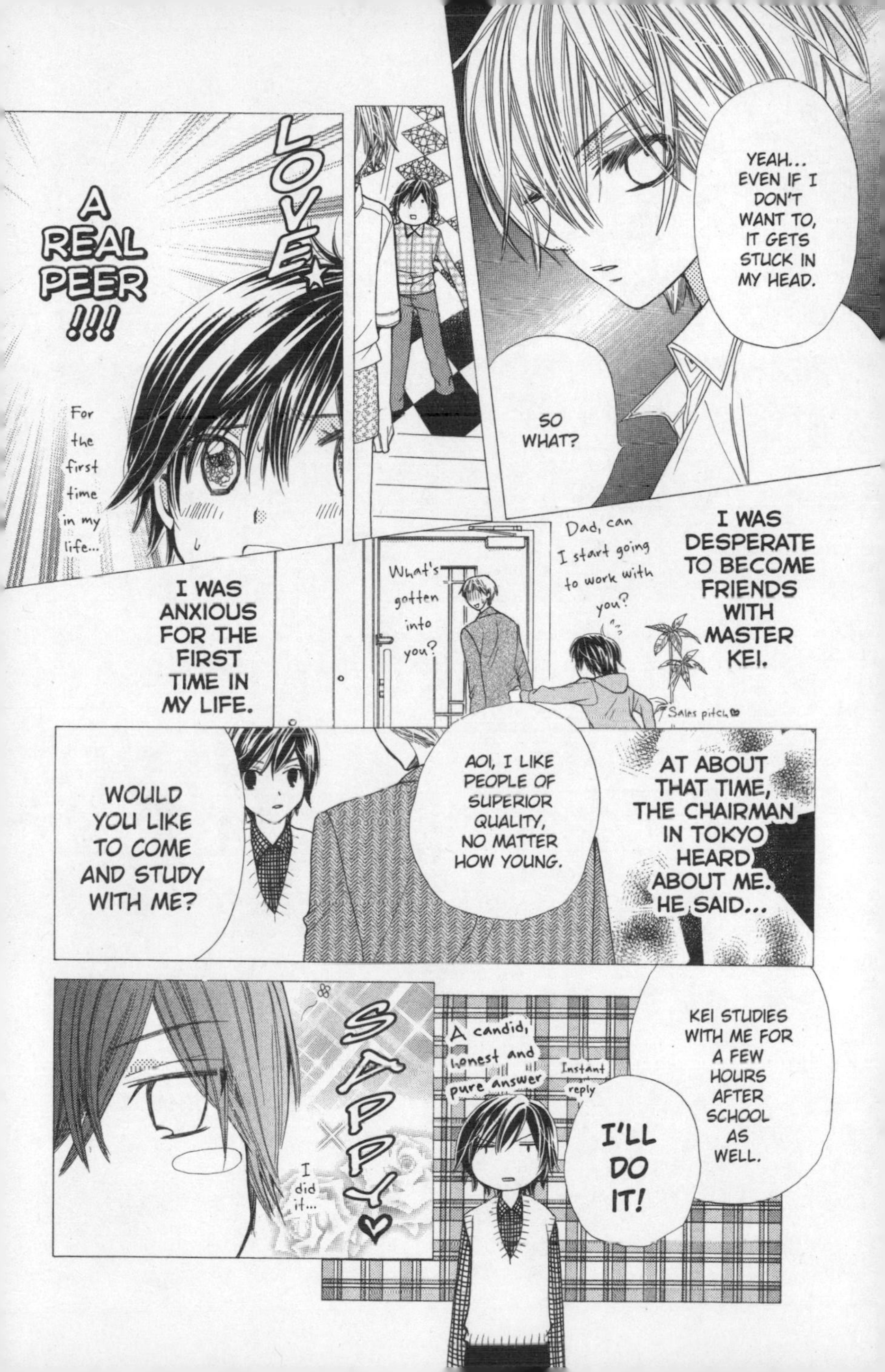
YEAH... EVEN IF I DON'T WANT TO, IT GETS STUCK IN MY HEAD.
SO WHAT?
LOVE★
A REAL PEER!!!
For the first time in my life...
I WAS DESPERATE TO BECOME FRIENDS WITH MASTER KEI.
Dad, can I start going to work with you?
What's gotten into you?
Sales pitch
I WAS ANXIOUS FOR THE FIRST TIME IN MY LIFE.
AT ABOUT THAT TIME, THE CHAIRMAN IN TOKYO HEARD ABOUT ME. HE SAID...
AOI, I LIKE PEOPLE OF SUPERIOR QUALITY, NO MATTER HOW YOUNG.
WOULD YOU LIKE TO COME AND STUDY WITH ME?
KEI STUDIES WITH ME FOR A FEW HOURS AFTER SCHOOL AS WELL.
I'LL DO IT!
Instant reply
A candid, honest and pure answer
SAPPY
I did it...

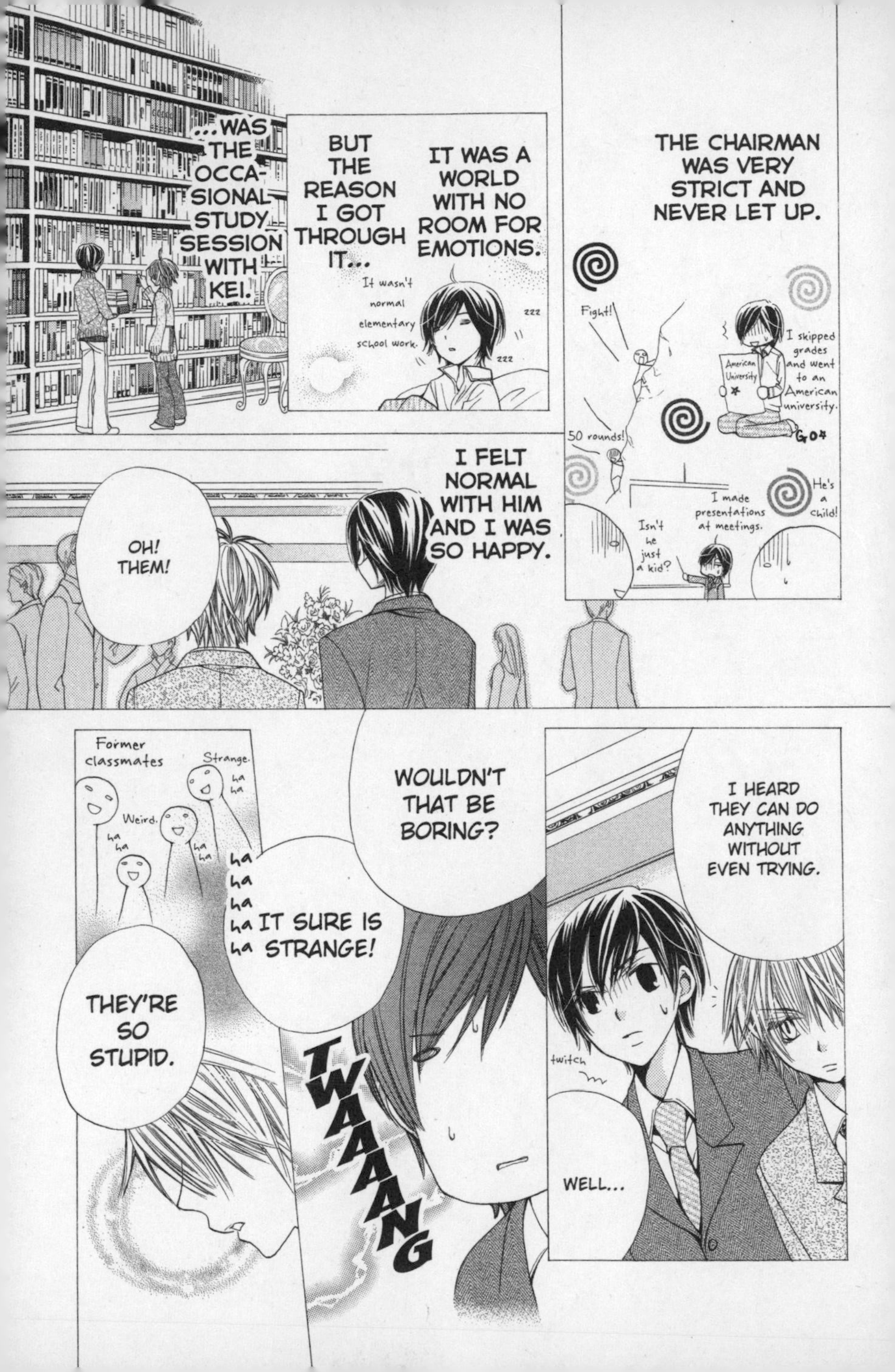
THE CHAIRMAN WAS VERY STRICT AND NEVER LET UP.
I skipped grades and went to an American university.
American University
GO☆
Fight!
50 rounds!
He's a child!
I made presentations at meetings.
Isn't he just a kid?
IT WAS A WORLD WITH NO ROOM FOR EMOTIONS.
BUT THE REASON I GOT THROUGH IT...
zzz
zzz
It wasn't normal elementary school work.
...WAS THE OCCASIONAL STUDY SESSION WITH KEI.
I FELT NORMAL WITH HIM AND I WAS SO HAPPY.
OH! THEM!
I HEARD THEY CAN DO ANYTHING WITHOUT EVEN TRYING.
twitch
WELL...
WOULDN'T THAT BE BORING?
Former classmates
Strange.
ha ha
Weird.
ha ha
ha ha
ha ha ha ha ha
IT SURE IS STRANGE!
THEY'RE SO STUPID.
TWAAAANG

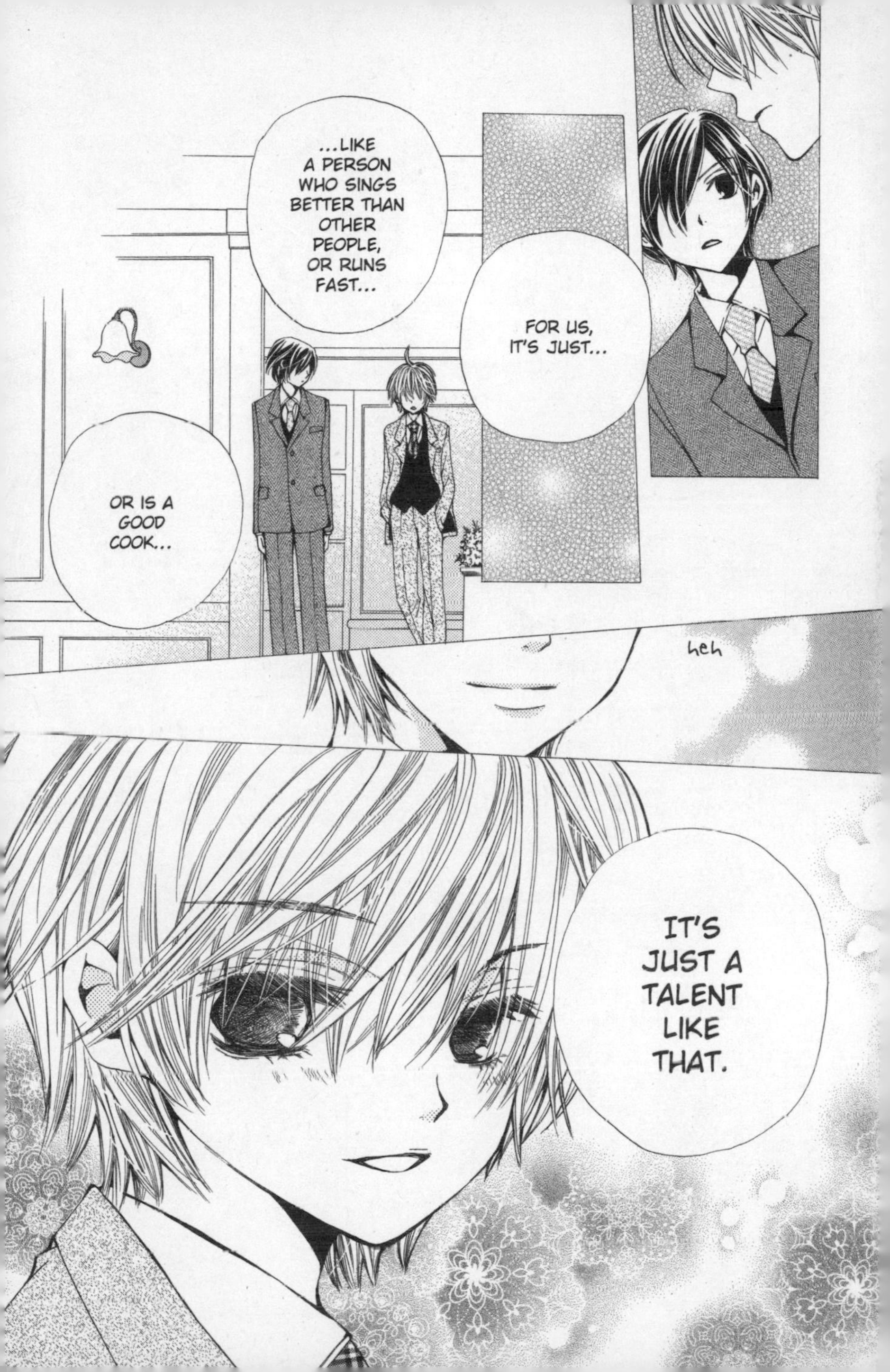
FOR US, IT'S JUST...
...LIKE A PERSON WHO SINGS BETTER THAN OTHER PEOPLE, OR RUNS FAST...
OR IS A GOOD COOK...
heh
IT'S JUST A TALENT LIKE THAT.

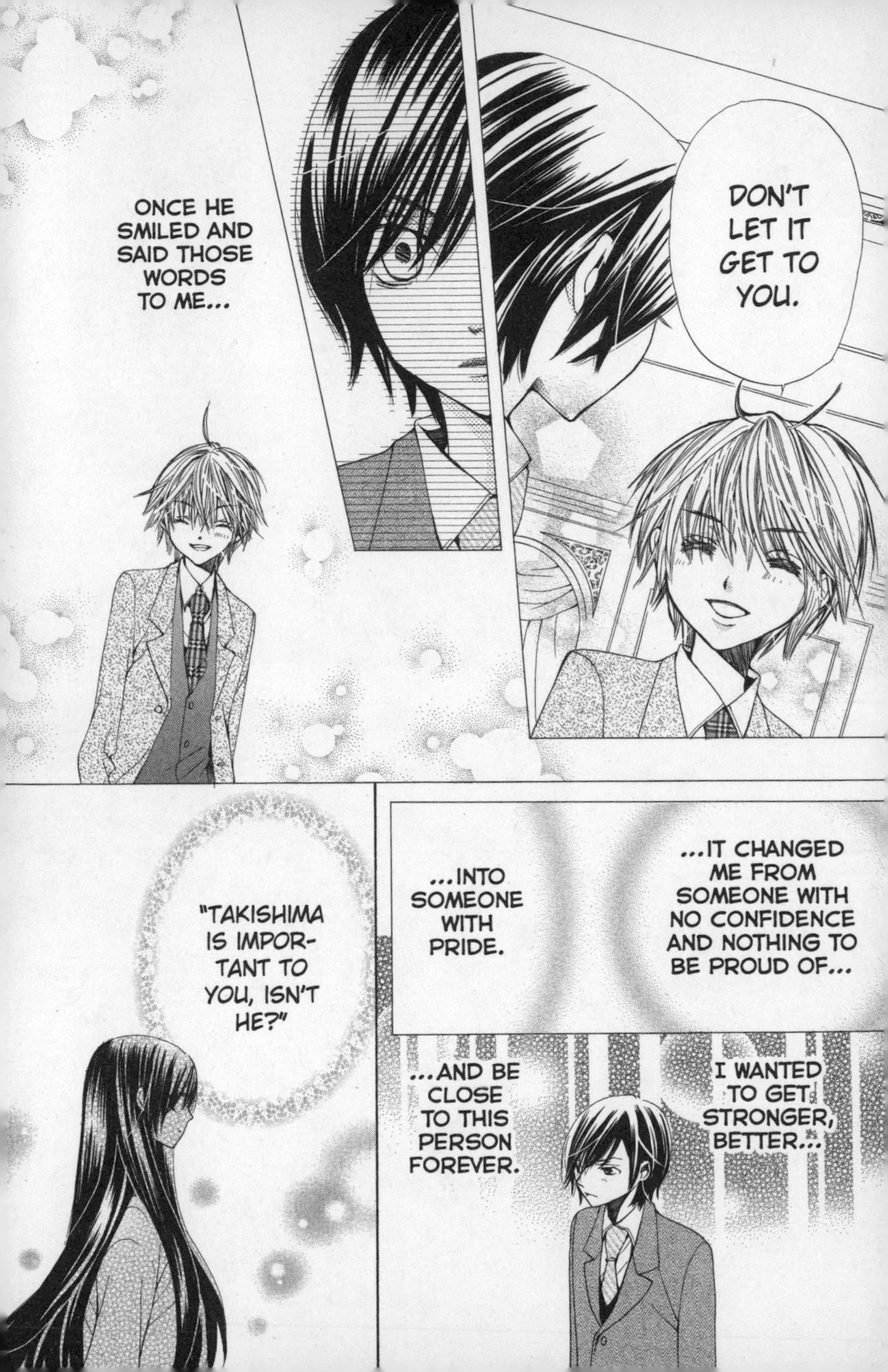
DON'T LET IT GET TO YOU.
ONCE HE SMILED AND SAID THOSE WORDS TO ME...
...IT CHANGED ME FROM SOMEONE WITH NO CONFIDENCE AND NOTHING TO BE PROUD OF...
...INTO SOMEONE WITH PRIDE.
I WANTED TO GET STRONGER, BETTER...
...AND BE CLOSE TO THIS PERSON FOREVER.
"TAKISHIMA IS IMPOR-TANT TO YOU, ISN'T HE?"

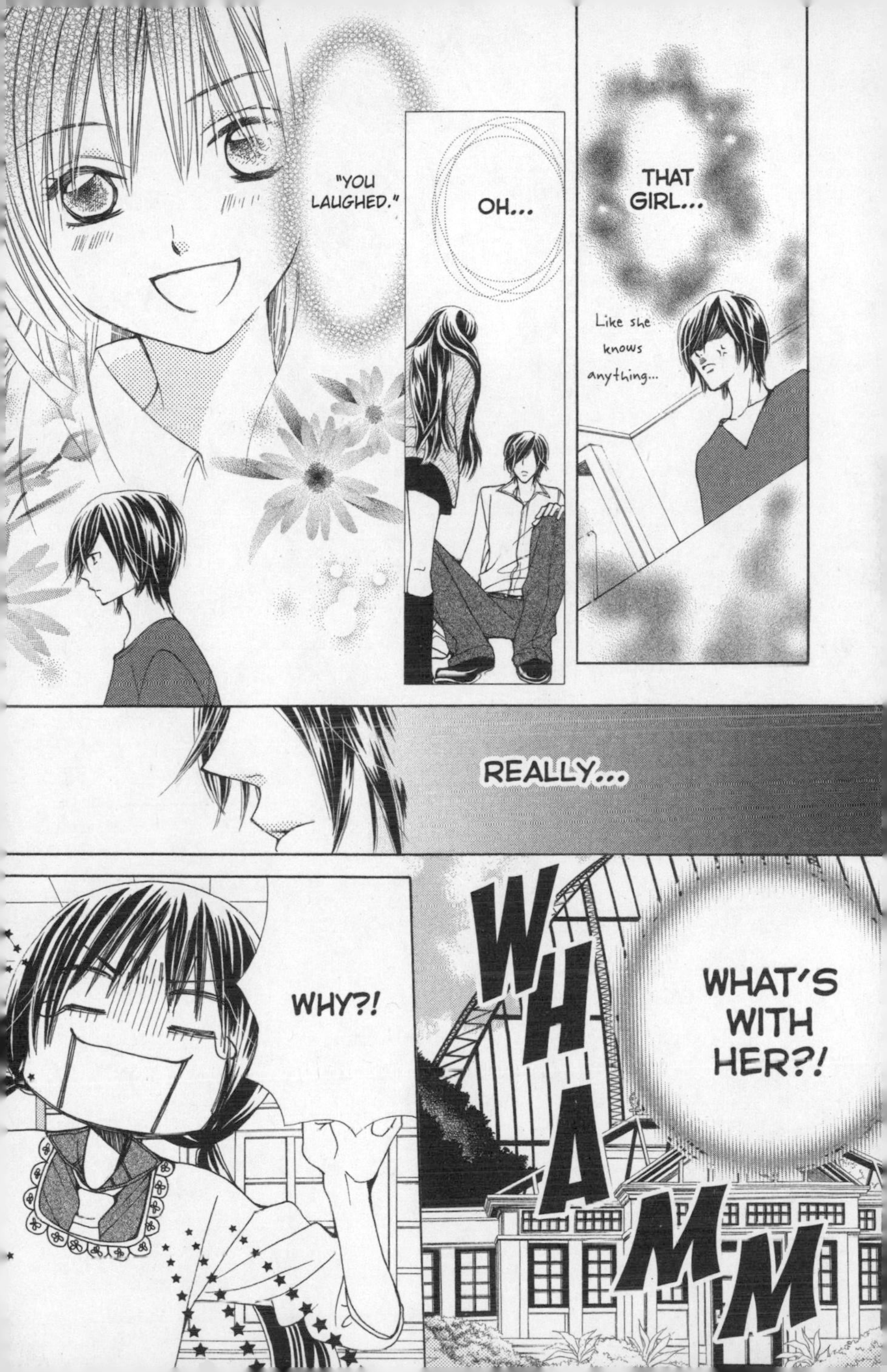
THAT GIRL...
Like she knows anything...
OH...
"YOU LAUGHED."
REALLY...
WHAMM
WHAT'S WITH HER?!
WHY?!

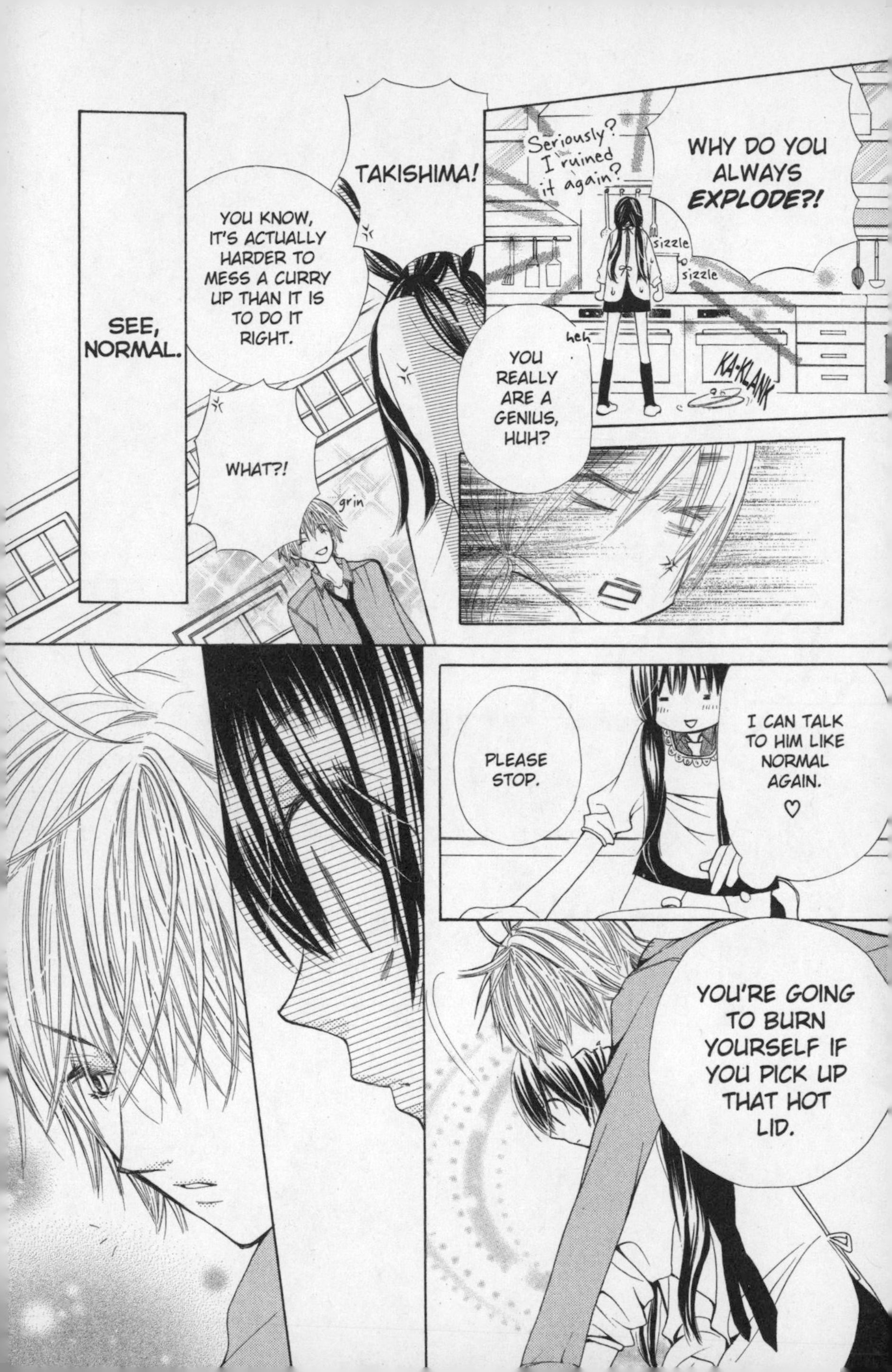
WHY DO YOU ALWAYS EXPLODE?!
Seriously? I ruined it again?
sizzle
sizzle
KA-KLANK
heh
YOU REALLY ARE A GENIUS, HUH?
TAKISHIMA!
YOU KNOW, IT'S ACTUALLY HARDER TO MESS A CURRY UP THAN IT IS TO DO IT RIGHT.
WHAT?!
grin
SEE, NORMAL.
I CAN TALK TO HIM LIKE NORMAL AGAIN. ♡
PLEASE STOP.
YOU'RE GOING TO BURN YOURSELF IF YOU PICK UP THAT HOT LID.

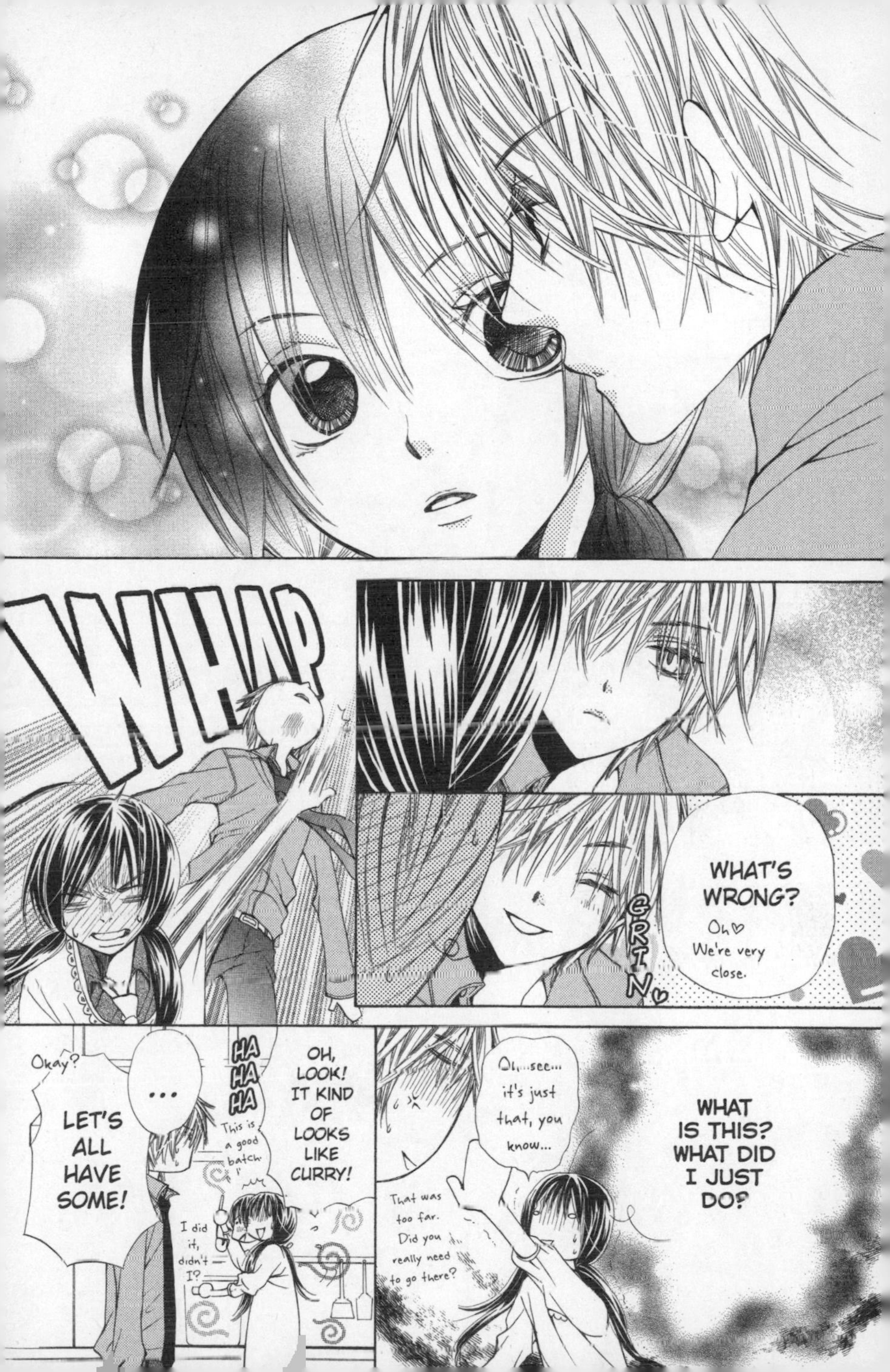
WHAT'S WRONG?
Oh♡ We're very close.
GRIN♡
WHAP
WHAT IS THIS? WHAT DID I JUST DO?
Oh...see... it's just that, you know...
That was too far. Did you really need to go there?
OH, LOOK! IT KIND OF LOOKS LIKE CURRY!
HA HA HA
This is a good batch!
...
Okay?
LET'S ALL HAVE SOME!
I did it, didn't I?

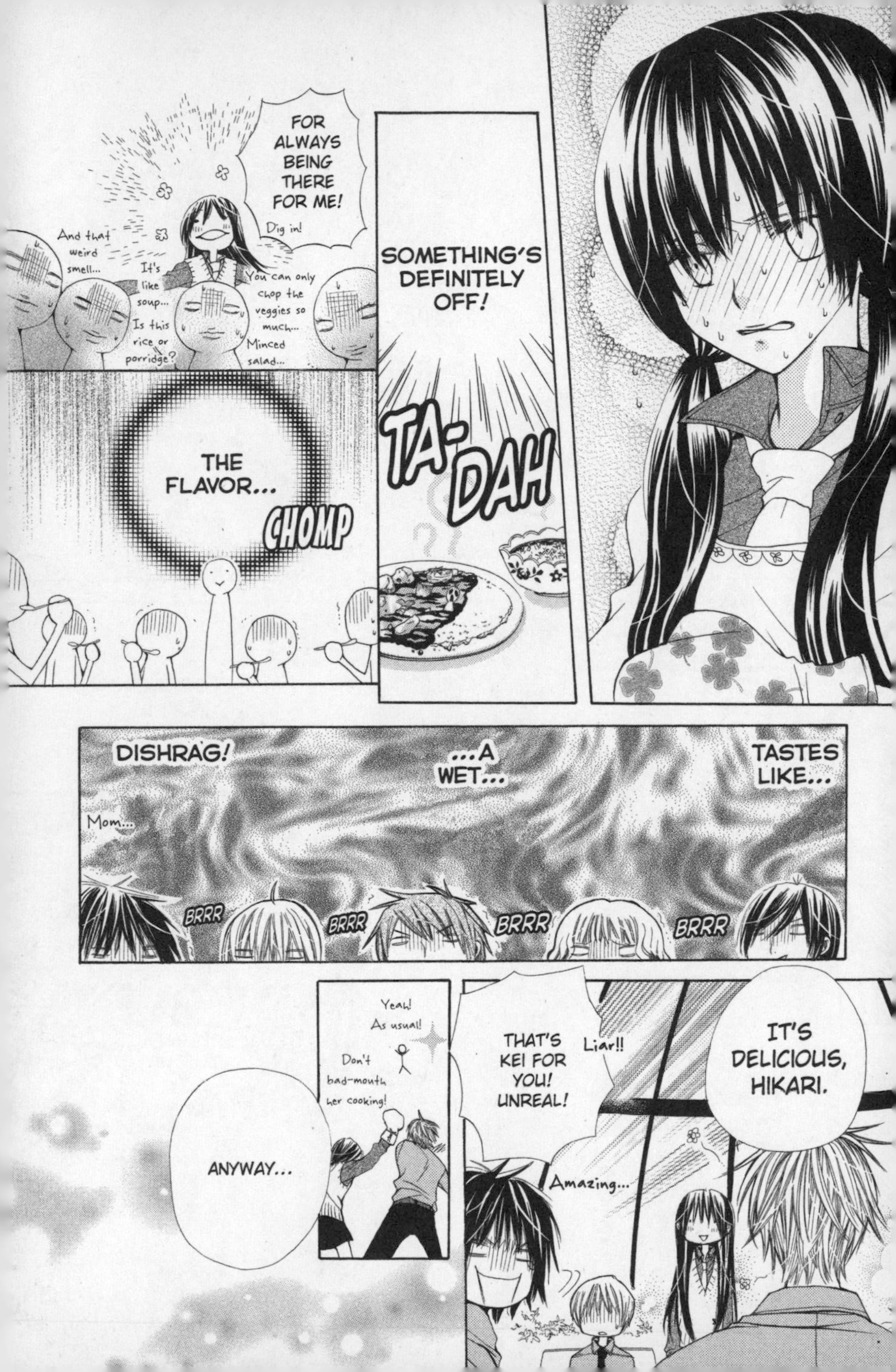
SOMETHING'S DEFINITELY OFF!
TA-DAH
FOR ALWAYS BEING THERE FOR ME!
Dig in!
You can only chop the veggies so much...
Minced salad...
It's like soup...
Is this rice or porridge?
And that weird smell...
THE FLAVOR...
CHOMP
TASTES LIKE...
...A WET...
DISHRAG!
Mom...
BRRR
BRRR
BRRR
BRRR
IT'S DELICIOUS, HIKARI.
Liar!!
THAT'S KEI FOR YOU! UNREAL!
Amazing...
Yeah! As usual!
Don't bad-mouth her cooking!
ANYWAY...

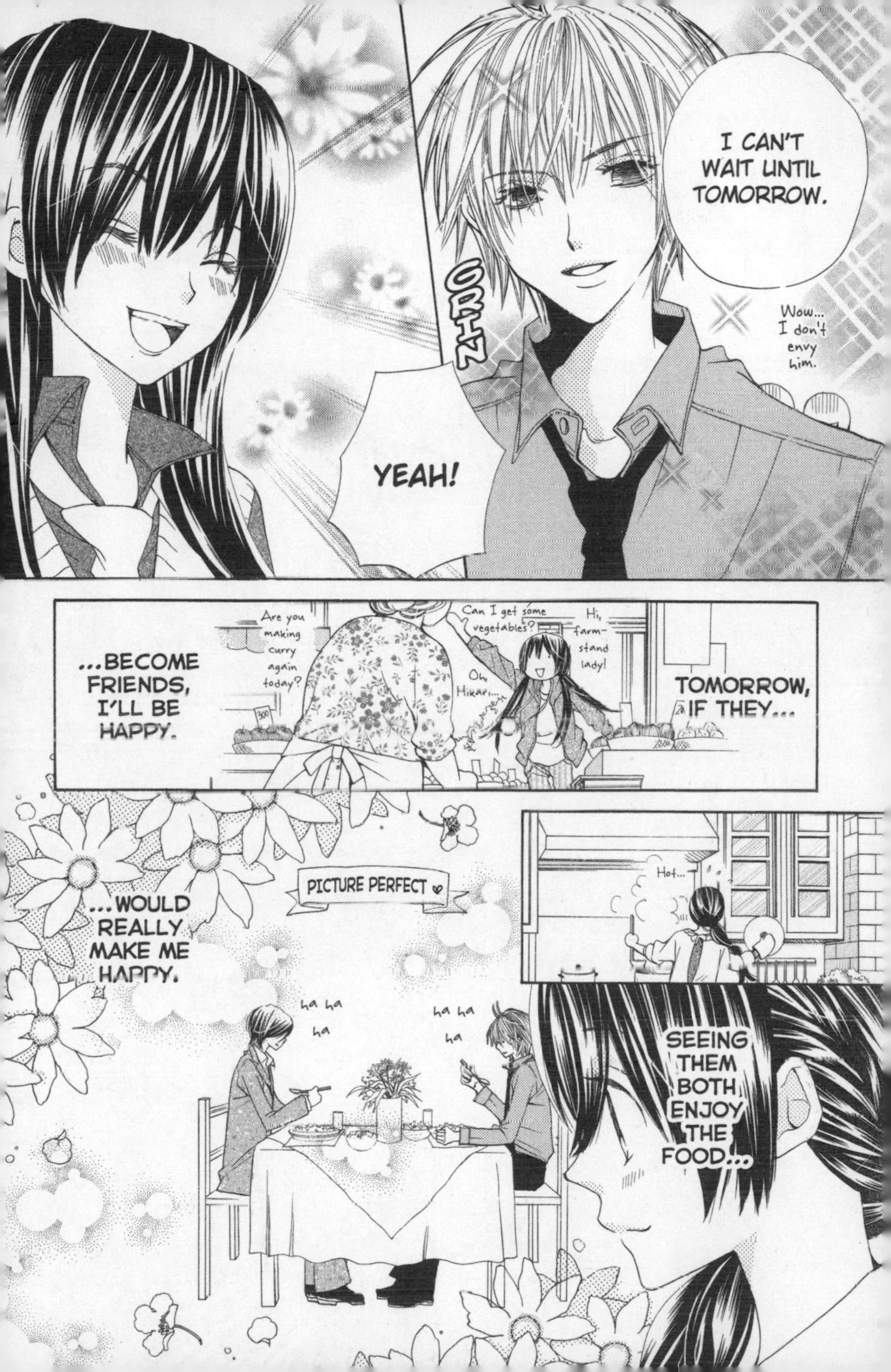
I CAN'T WAIT UNTIL TOMORROW.
GRIN
Wow... I don't envy him.
YEAH!
TOMORROW, IF THEY...
Hi, farm-stand lady!
Can I get some vegetables?
Oh Hikari...
Are you making curry again today?
...BECOME FRIENDS, I'LL BE HAPPY.
Hot...
SEEING THEM BOTH ENJOY THE FOOD...
ha ha ha
ha ha ha
...WOULD REALLY MAKE ME HAPPY.
PICTURE PERFECT

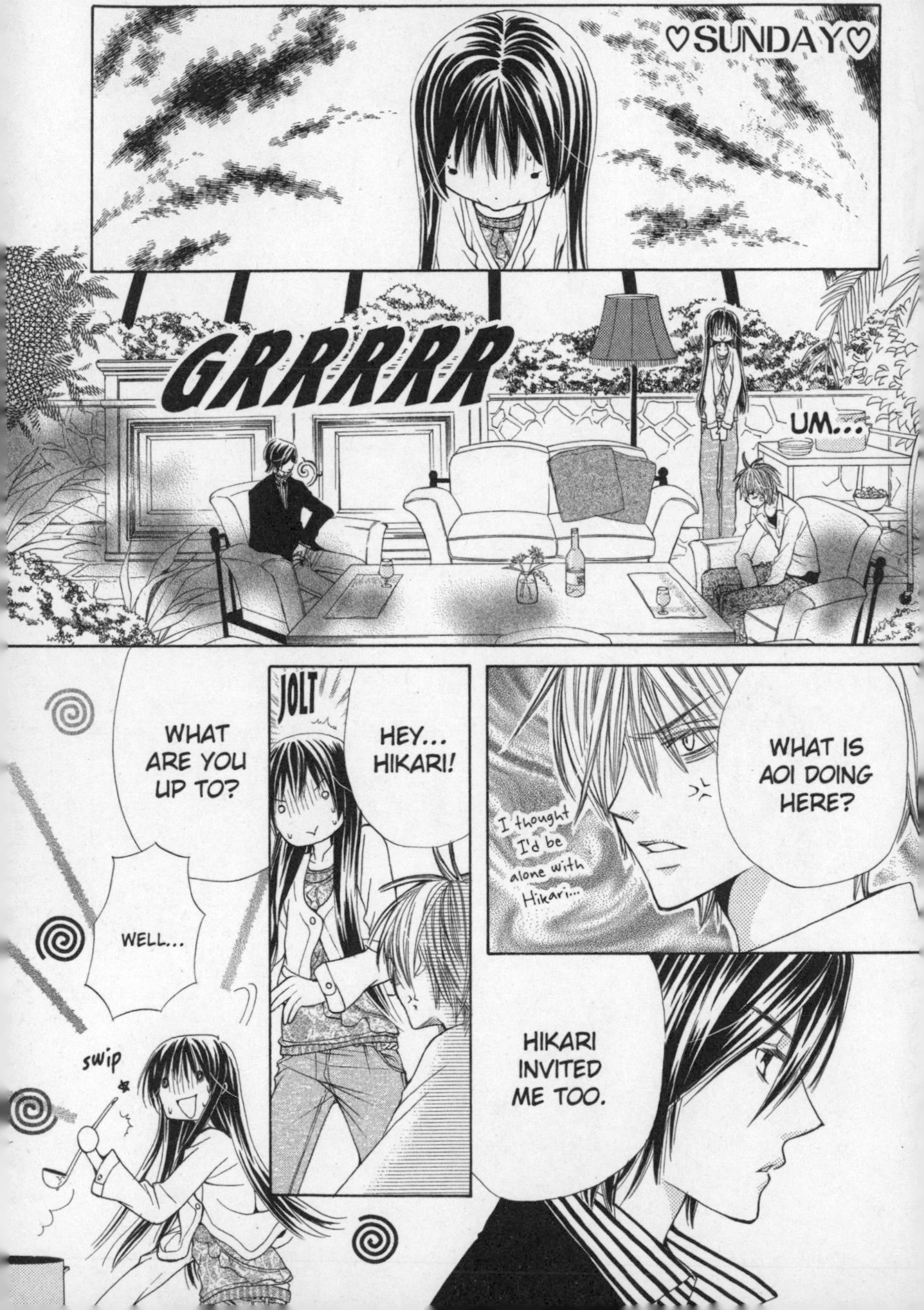
♡SUNDAY♡
GRRRRR
UM...
WHAT IS AOI DOING HERE?
I thought I'd be alone with Hikari...
JOLT
HEY... HIKARI!
WHAT ARE YOU UP TO?
HIKARI INVITED ME TOO.
WELL...
swip

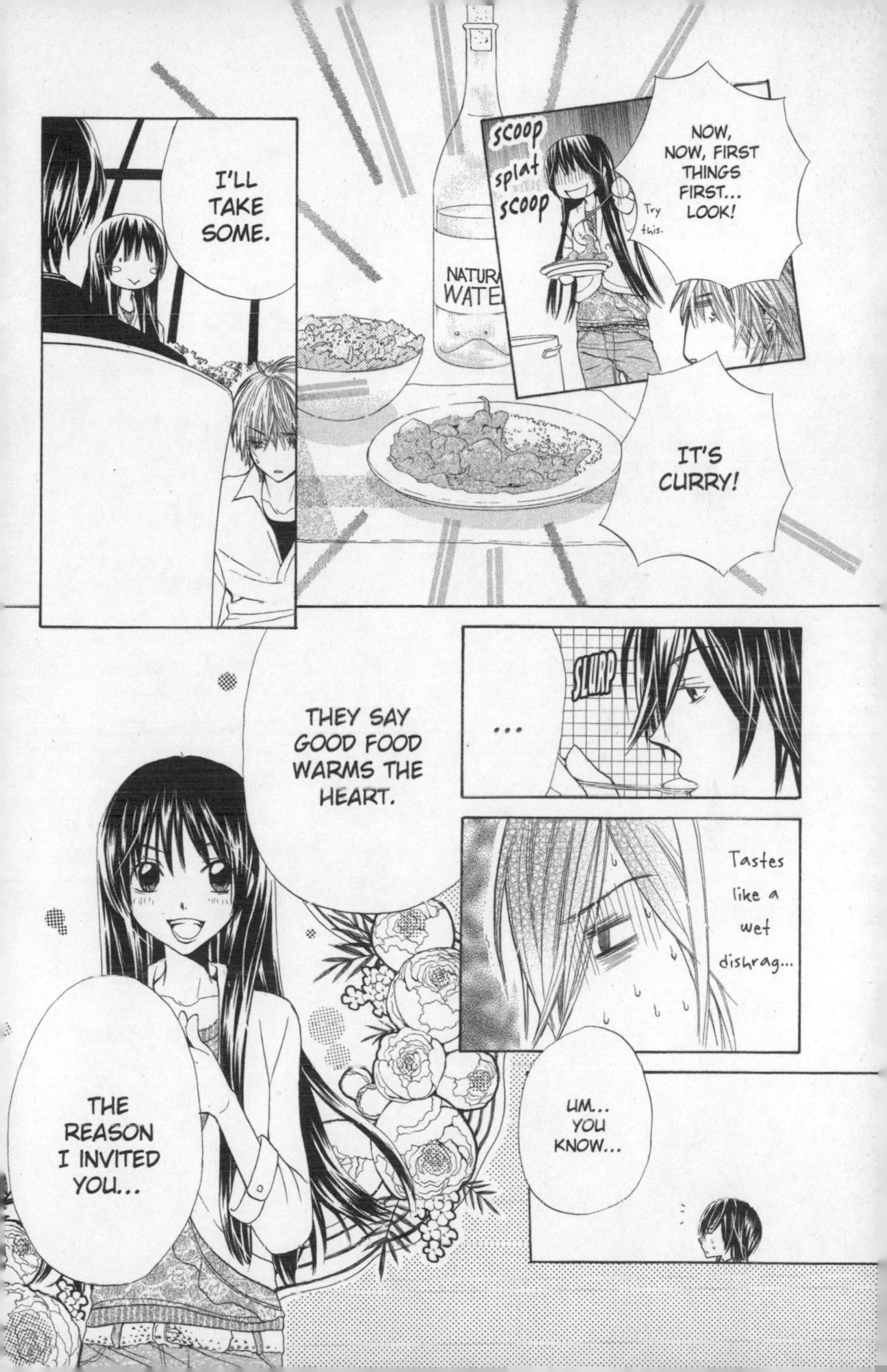
NOW, NOW, FIRST THINGS FIRST... LOOK!
scoop splat scoop
Try this.
IT'S CURRY!
I'LL TAKE SOME.
SLURP
...
Tastes like a wet dishrag...
UM... YOU KNOW...
THEY SAY GOOD FOOD WARMS THE HEART.
THE REASON I INVITED YOU...

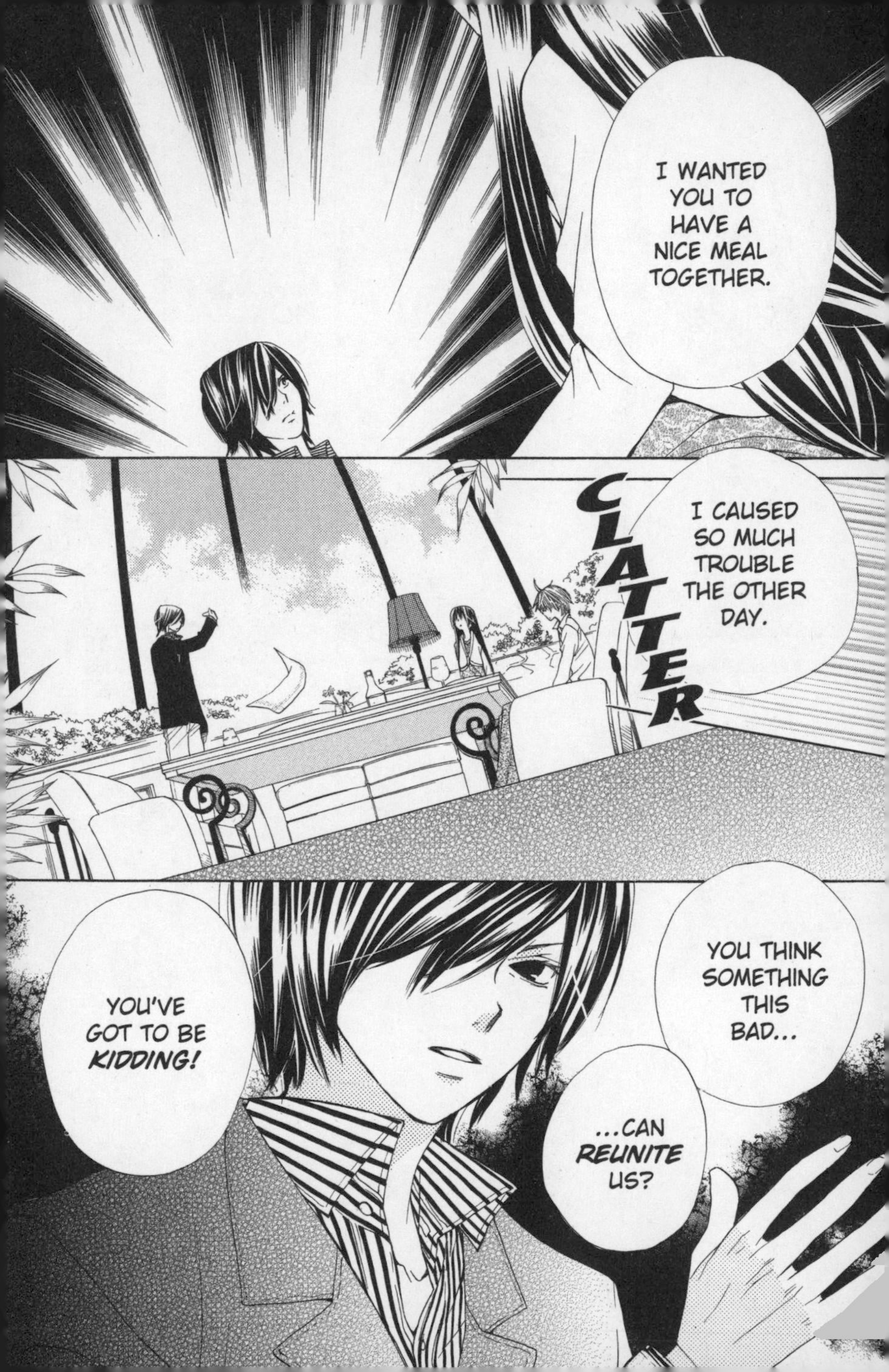
I WANTED YOU TO HAVE A NICE MEAL TOGETHER.
I CAUSED SO MUCH TROUBLE THE OTHER DAY.
CLATTER
YOU THINK SOMETHING THIS BAD...
...CAN REUNITE US?
YOU'VE GOT TO BE KIDDING!

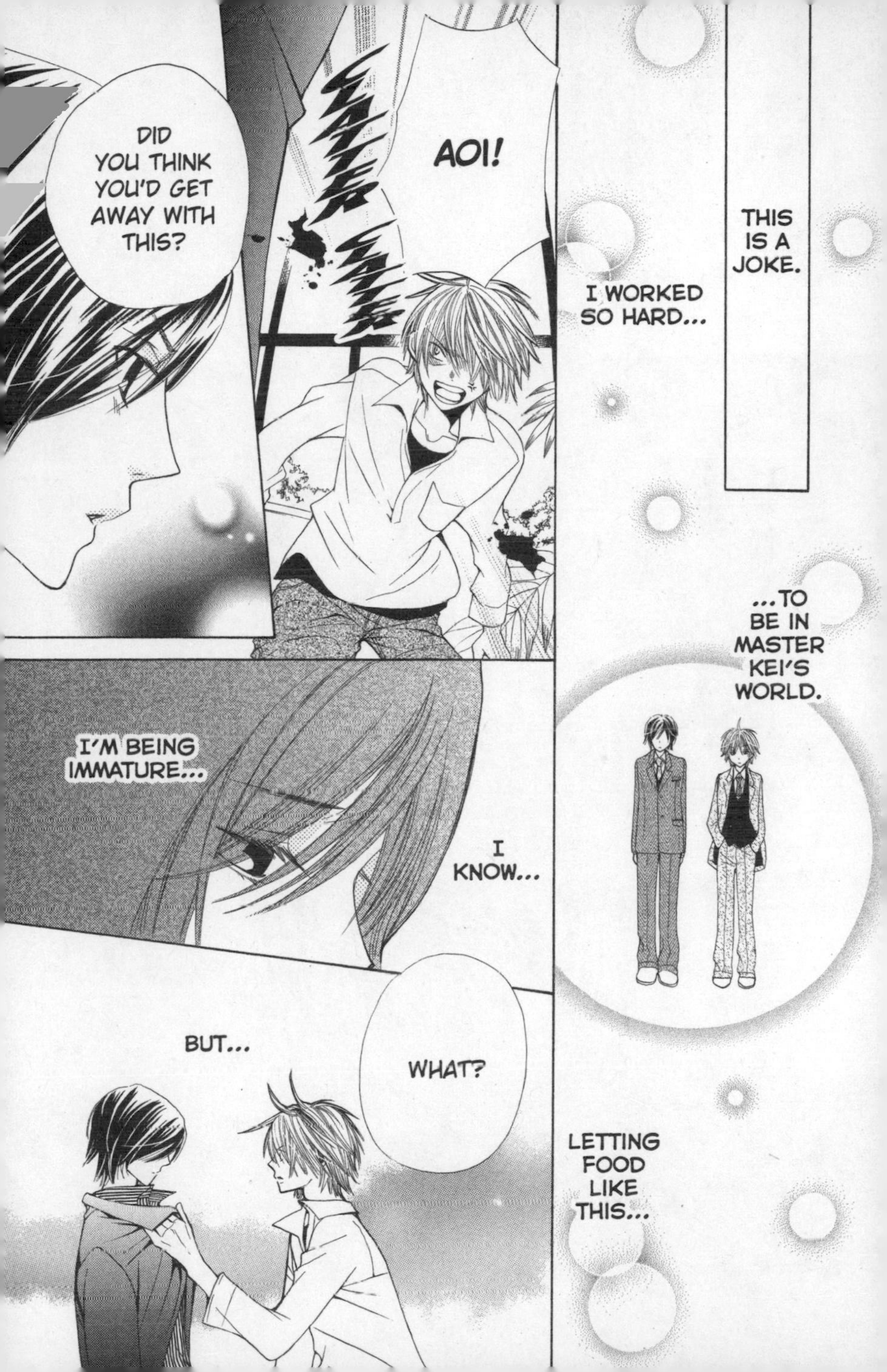
THIS IS A JOKE.
I WORKED SO HARD...
...TO BE IN MASTER KEI'S WORLD.
LETTING FOOD LIKE THIS...
AOI!
DID YOU THINK YOU'D GET AWAY WITH THIS?
I'M BEING IMMATURE...
I KNOW...
BUT...
WHAT?

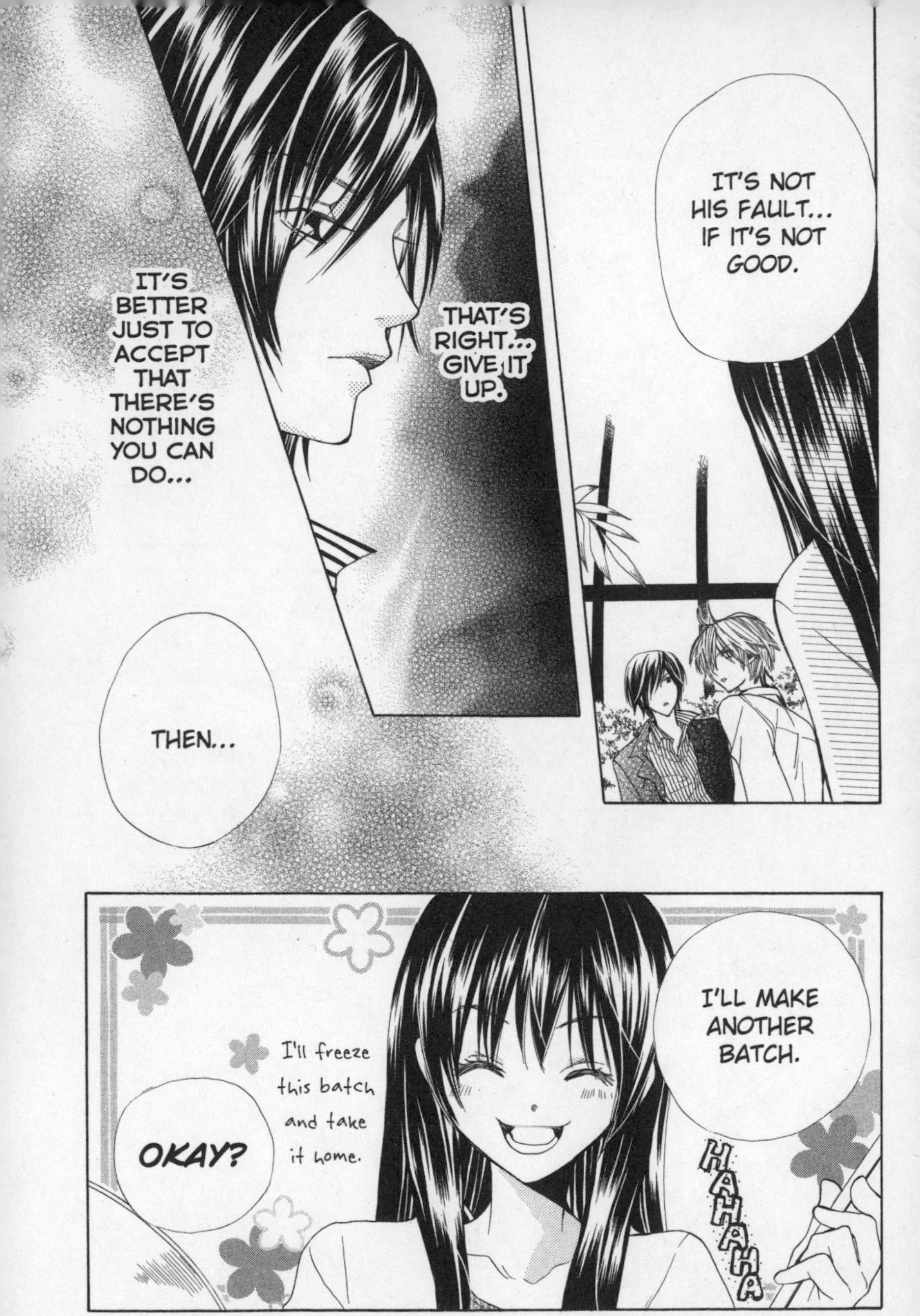
IT'S NOT HIS FAULT... IF IT'S NOT GOOD.
THAT'S RIGHT... GIVE IT UP.
IT'S BETTER JUST TO ACCEPT THAT THERE'S NOTHING YOU CAN DO...
THEN...
I'LL MAKE ANOTHER BATCH.
HAHAHA
I'll freeze this batch and take it home.
OKAY?

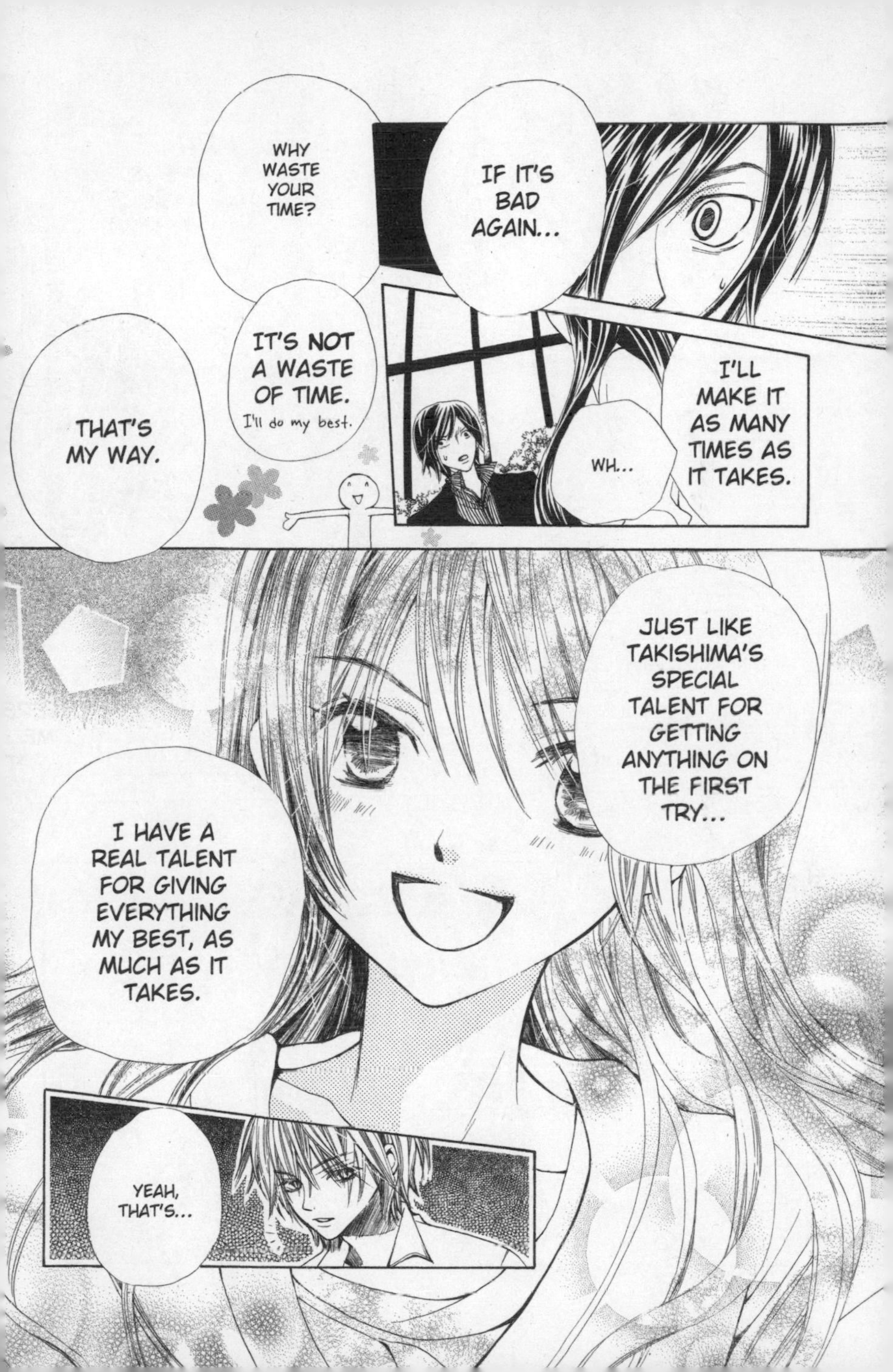
IF IT'S BAD AGAIN...
WHY WASTE YOUR TIME?
I'LL MAKE IT AS MANY TIMES AS IT TAKES.
WH...
IT'S NOT A WASTE OF TIME.
I'll do my best.
THAT'S MY WAY.
JUST LIKE TAKISHIMA'S SPECIAL TALENT FOR GETTING ANYTHING ON THE FIRST TRY...
I HAVE A REAL TALENT FOR GIVING EVERYTHING MY BEST, AS MUCH AS IT TAKES.
YEAH, THAT'S...

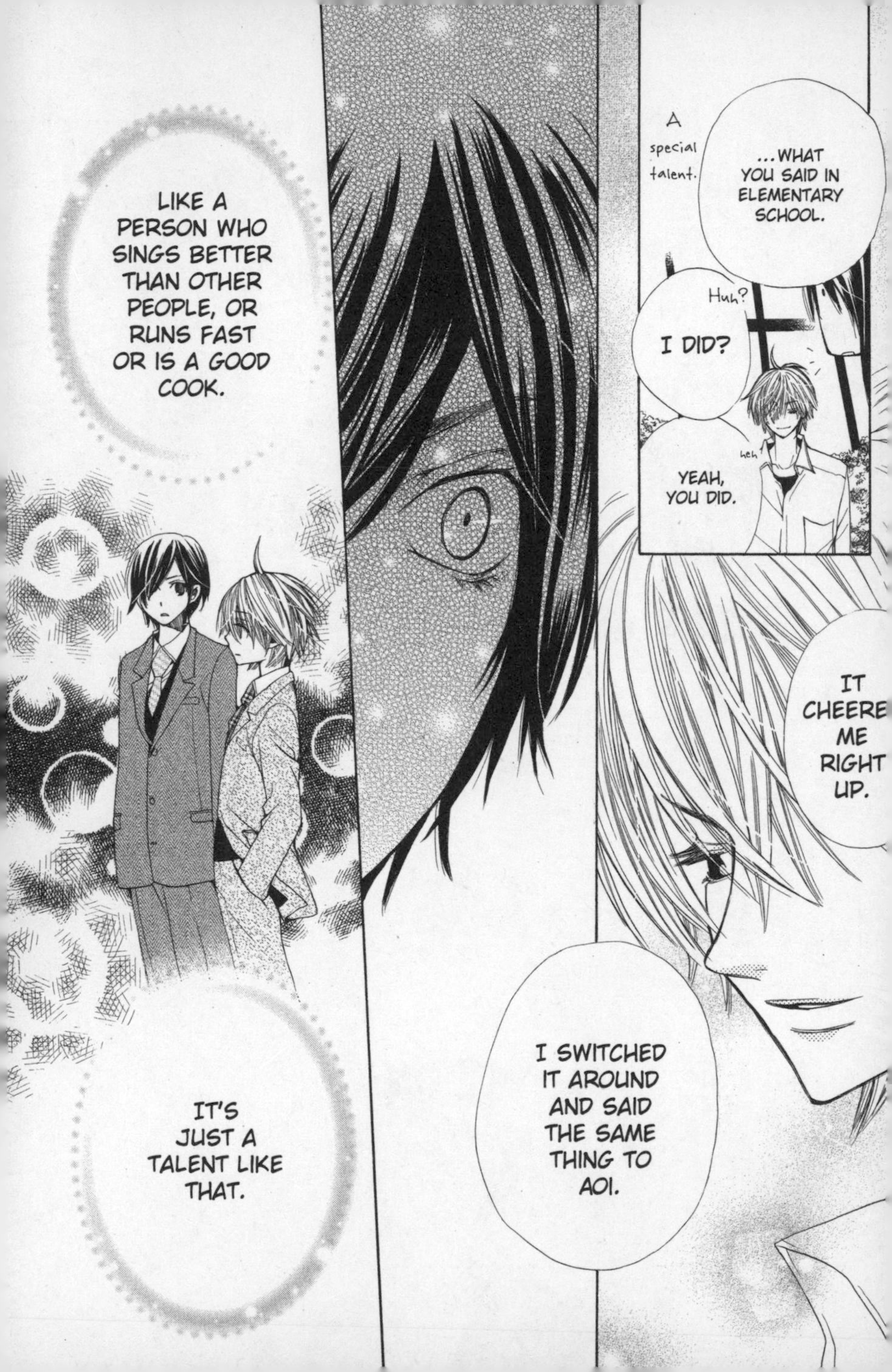
A special talent.
...WHAT YOU SAID IN ELEMENTARY SCHOOL.
Huh?
I DID?
heh
YEAH, YOU DID.
IT CHEERE ME RIGHT UP.
I SWITCHED IT AROUND AND SAID THE SAME THING TO AOI.
LIKE A PERSON WHO SINGS BETTER THAN OTHER PEOPLE, OR RUNS FAST OR IS A GOOD COOK.
IT'S JUST A TALENT LIKE THAT.

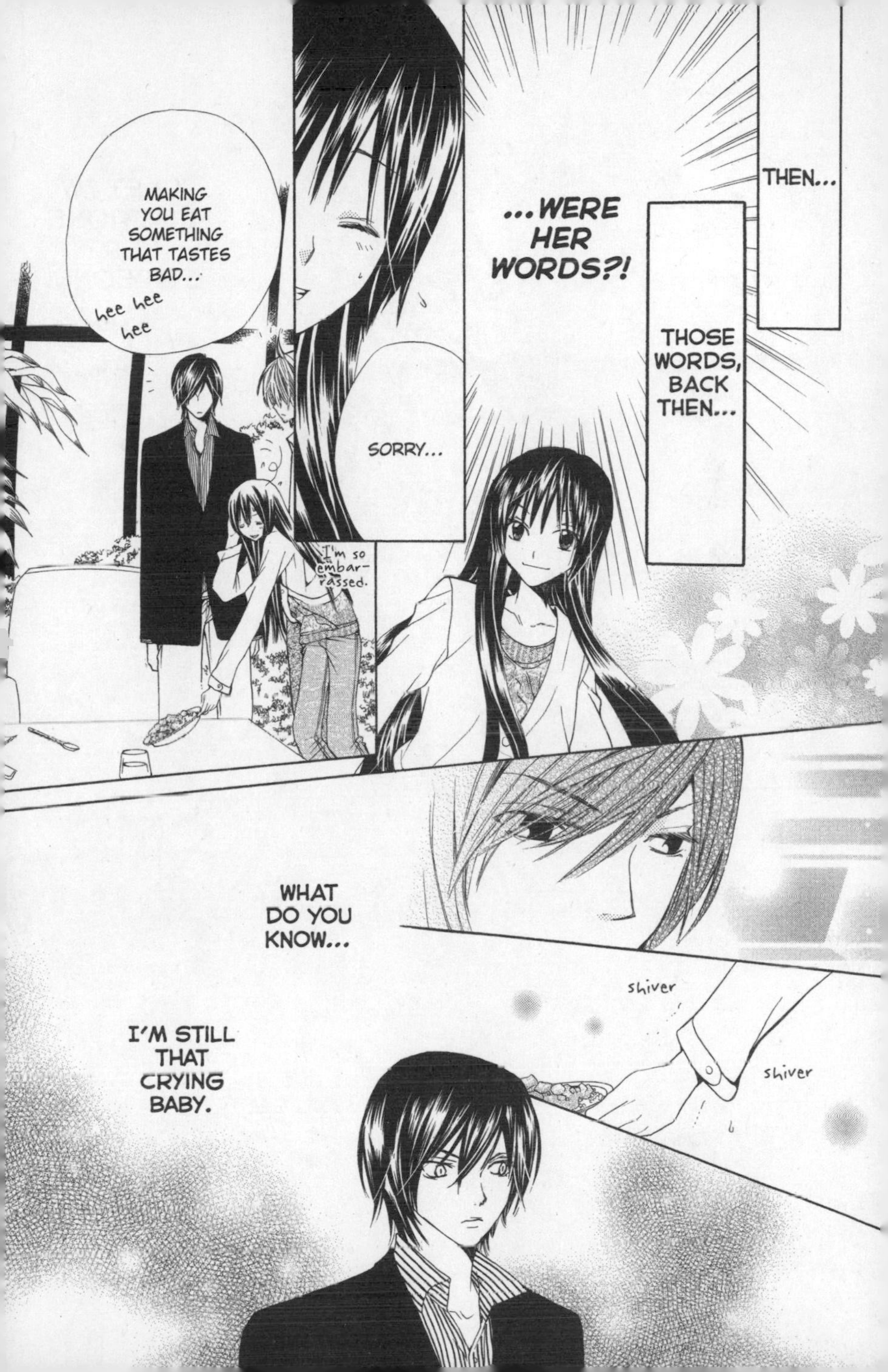
THEN...
THOSE WORDS, BACK THEN...
...WERE HER WORDS?!
SORRY...
MAKING YOU EAT SOMETHING THAT TASTES BAD...
hee hee hee
I'm so embarrassed.
WHAT DO YOU KNOW...
shiver
shiver
I'M STILL THAT CRYING BABY.

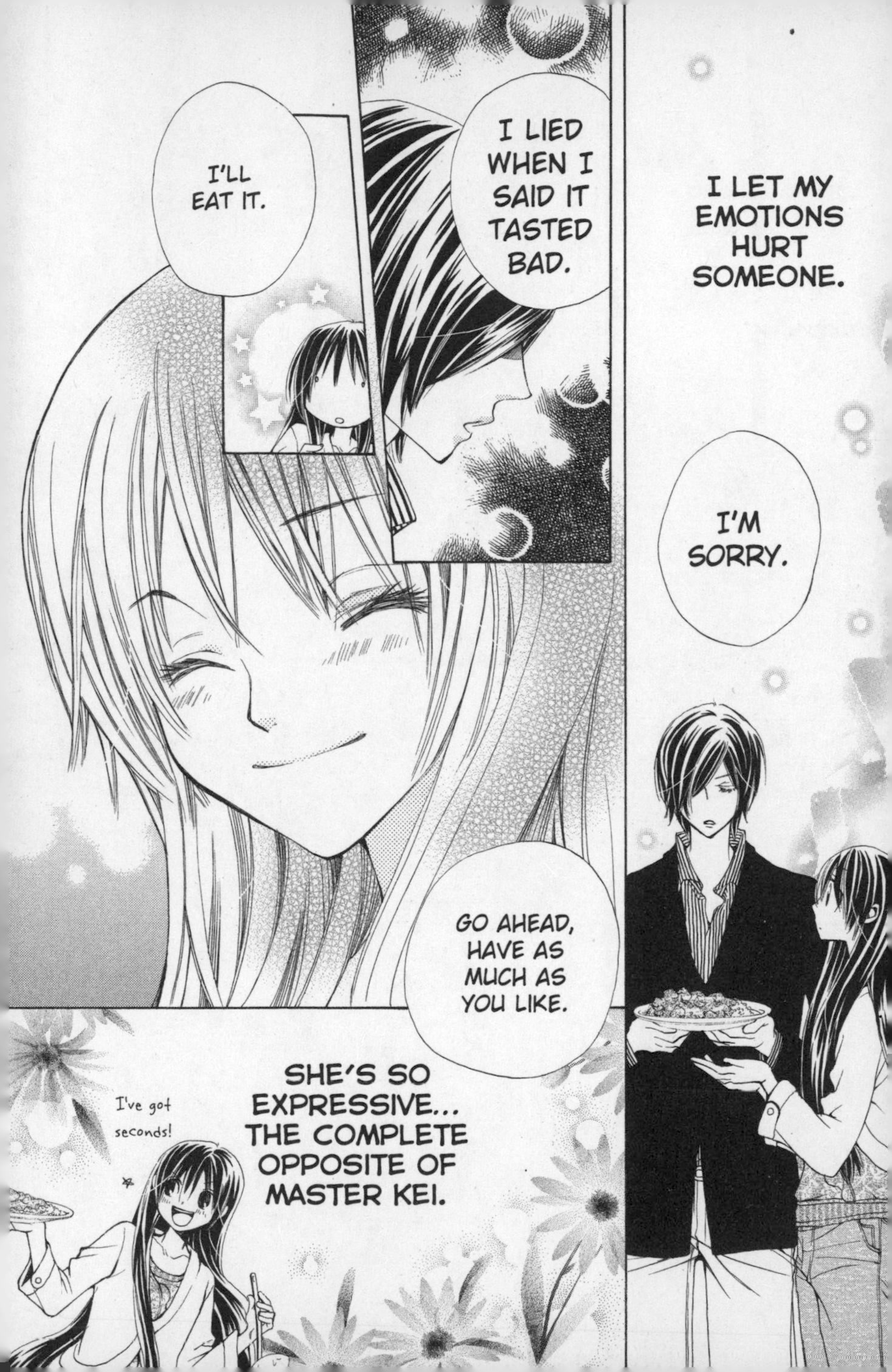
I LET MY EMOTIONS HURT SOMEONE.
I'M SORRY.
I LIED WHEN I SAID IT TASTED BAD.
I'LL EAT IT.
GO AHEAD, HAVE AS MUCH AS YOU LIKE.
SHE'S SO EXPRESSIVE... THE COMPLETE OPPOSITE OF MASTER KEI.
I've got seconds!

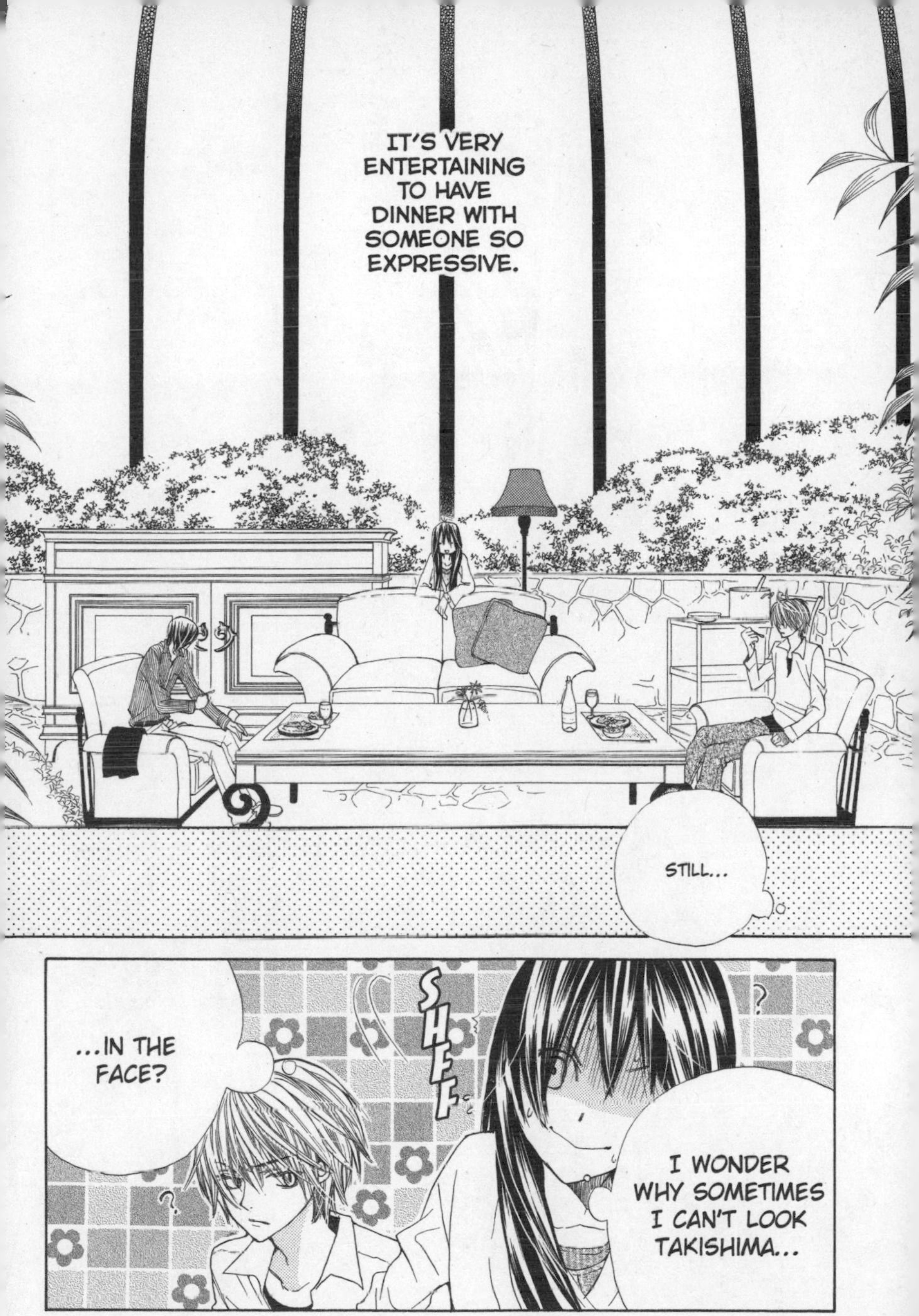
IT'S VERY ENTERTAINING TO HAVE DINNER WITH SOMEONE SO EXPRESSIVE.
STILL...
I WONDER WHY SOMETIMES I CAN'T LOOK TAKISHIMA...
SHFF
...IN THE FACE?

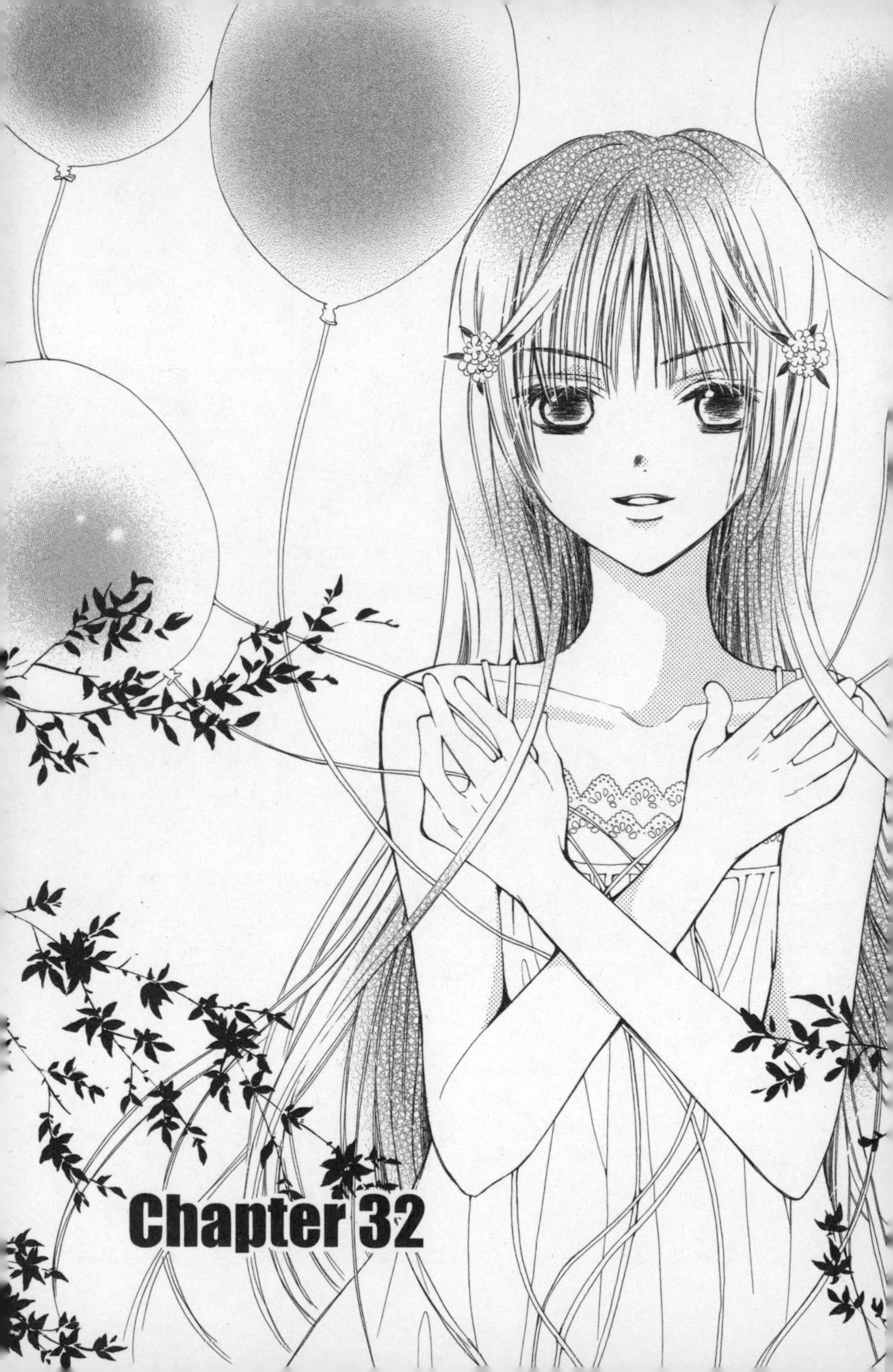
Chapter 32

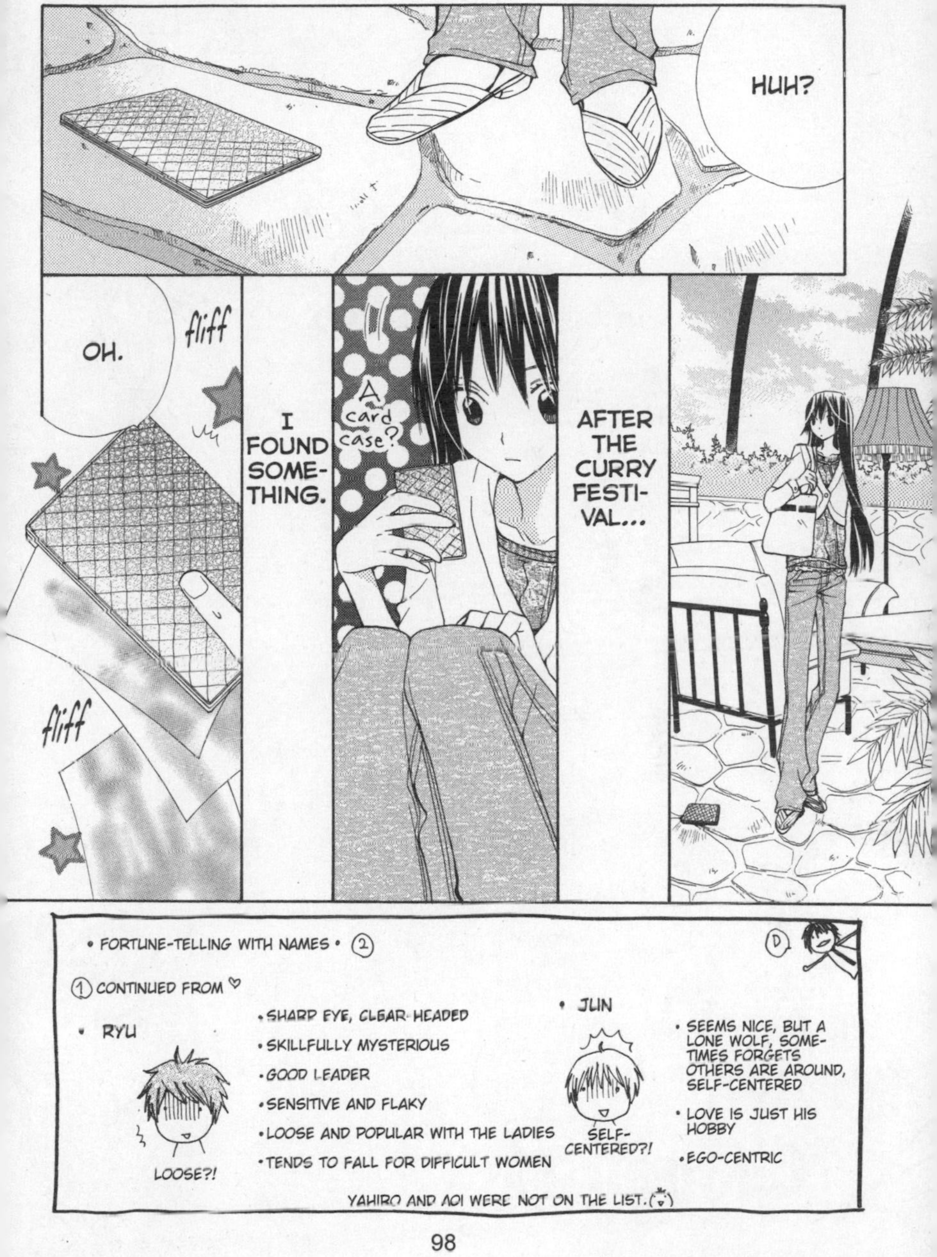
HUH?
AFTER THE CURRY FESTIVAL...
A card case?
I FOUND SOMETHING.
OH.
fliff
fliff

• FORTUNE-TELLING WITH NAMES • ②

① CONTINUED FROM ♡

• RYU

- SHARP EYE, CLEAR-HEADED
- SKILLFULLY MYSTERIOUS
- GOOD LEADER
- SENSITIVE AND FLAKY
- LOOSE AND POPULAR WITH THE LADIES
- TENDS TO FALL FOR DIFFICULT WOMEN

LOOSE?!

• JUN

- SEEMS NICE, BUT A LONE WOLF, SOMETIMES FORGETS OTHERS ARE AROUND, SELF-CENTERED
- LOVE IS JUST HIS HOBBY
- EGO-CENTRIC

SELF-CENTERED?!

YAHIRO AND AOI WERE NOT ON THE LIST.

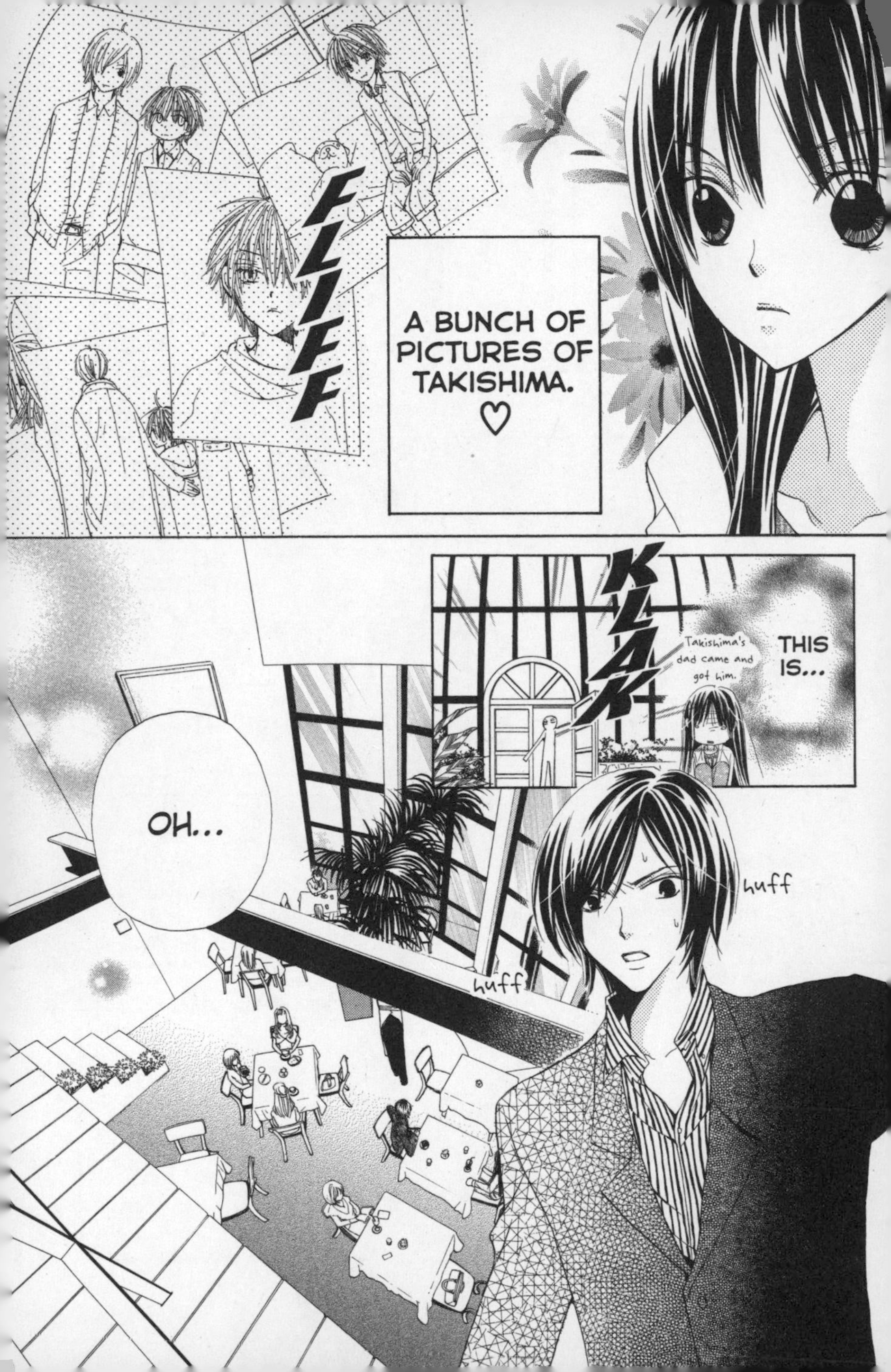
A BUNCH OF PICTURES OF TAKISHIMA. ♡
FLIFF
THIS IS...
Takishima's dad came and got him.
KLAK
huff
huff
OH...

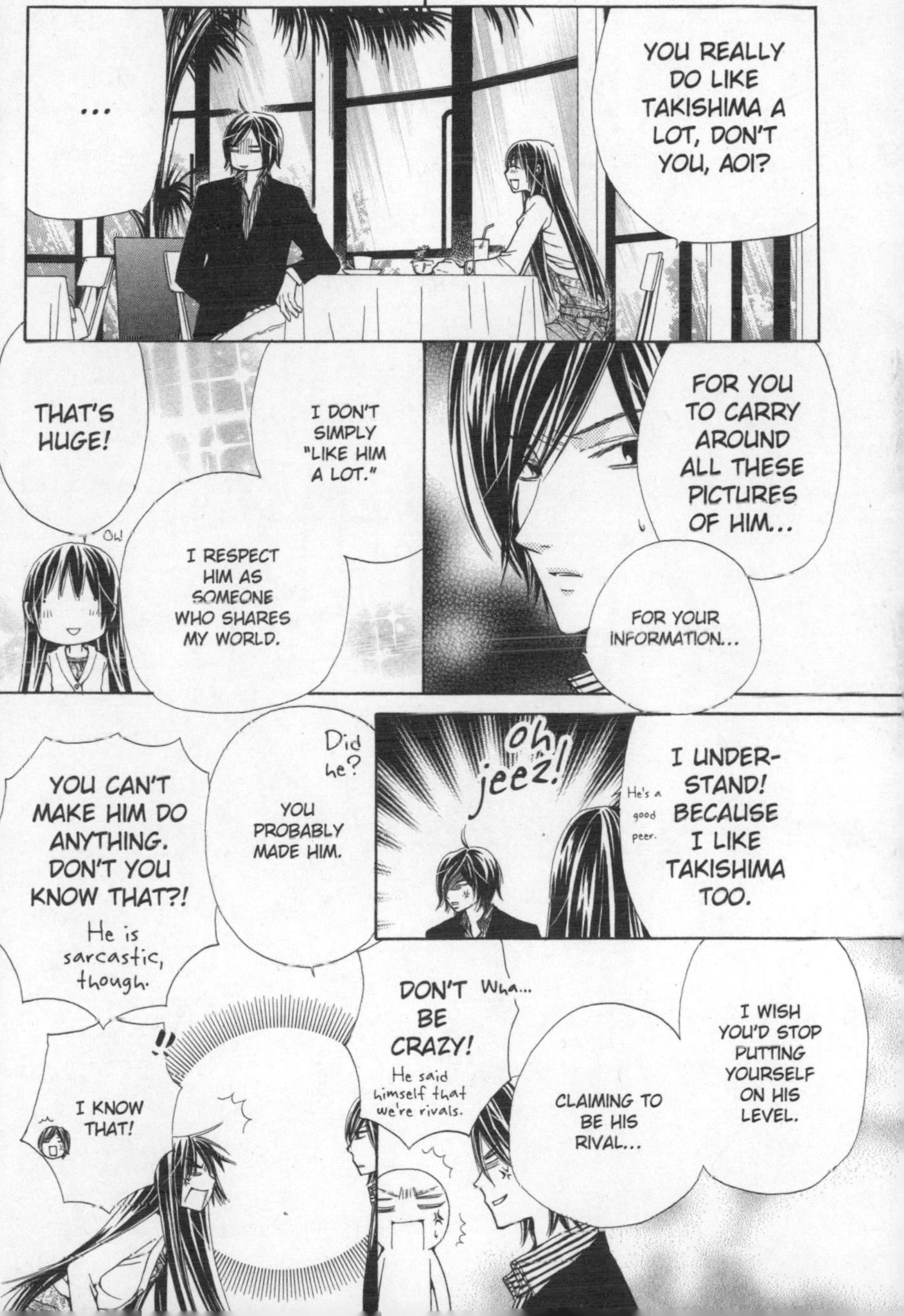
YOU REALLY DO LIKE TAKISHIMA A LOT, DON'T YOU, AOI?
...
FOR YOU TO CARRY AROUND ALL THESE PICTURES OF HIM...
FOR YOUR INFORMATION...
I DON'T SIMPLY "LIKE HIM A LOT."
I RESPECT HIM AS SOMEONE WHO SHARES MY WORLD.
THAT'S HUGE!
Oh!
I UNDER-STAND! BECAUSE I LIKE TAKISHIMA TOO.
He's a good peer.
oh jeez!
Did he?
YOU PROBABLY MADE HIM.
YOU CAN'T MAKE HIM DO ANYTHING. DON'T YOU KNOW THAT?!
He is sarcastic, though.
I WISH YOU'D STOP PUTTING YOURSELF ON HIS LEVEL.
CLAIMING TO BE HIS RIVAL...
Wha...
DON'T BE CRAZY!
He said himself that we're rivals.
!!
I KNOW THAT!

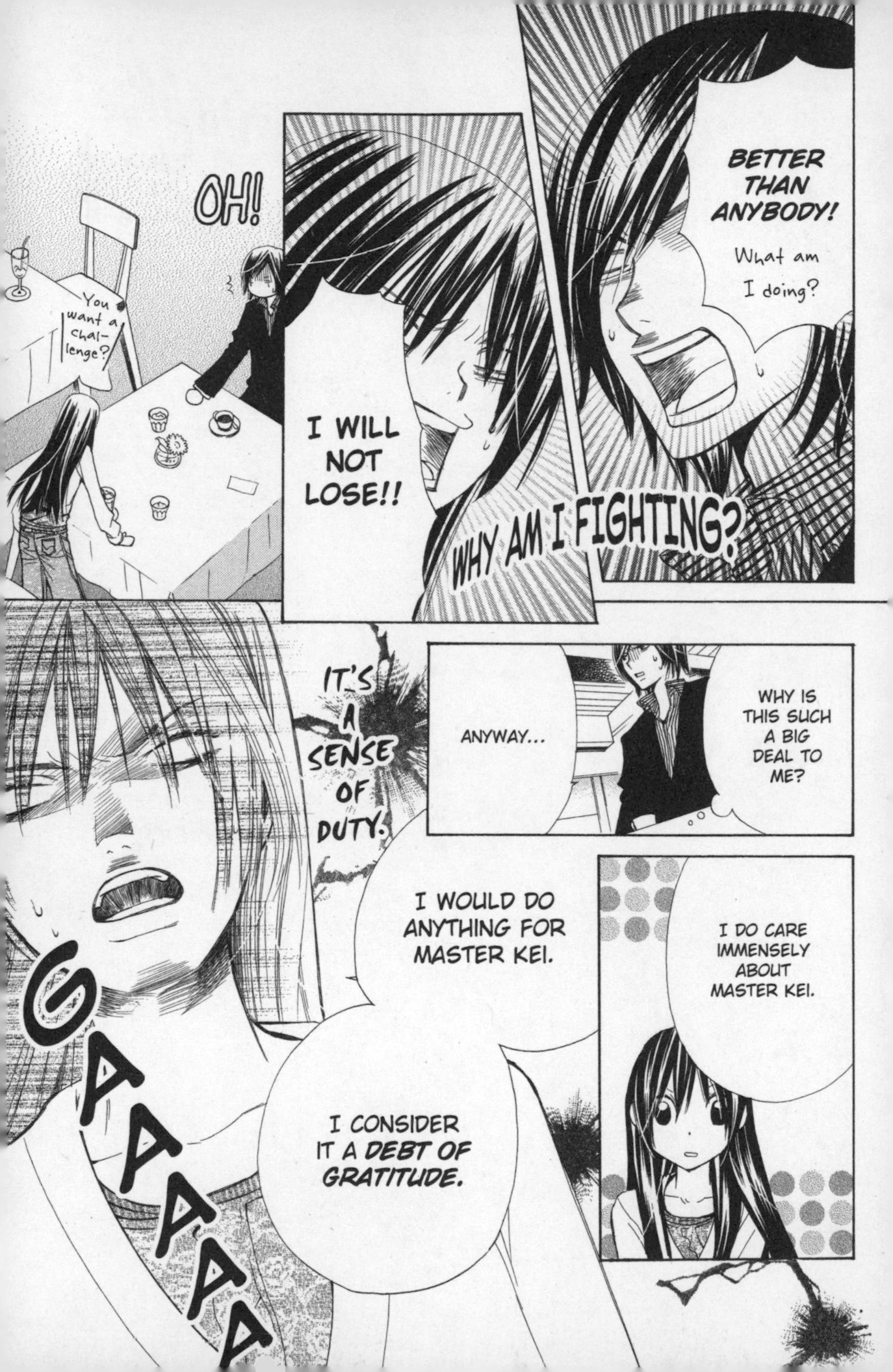
BETTER THAN ANYBODY!
What am I doing?
WHY AM I FIGHTING?
I WILL NOT LOSE!!
OH!
You want a challenge?
WHY IS THIS SUCH A BIG DEAL TO ME?
ANYWAY...
I DO CARE IMMENSELY ABOUT MASTER KEI.
IT'S A SENSE OF DUTY.
I WOULD DO ANYTHING FOR MASTER KEI.
I CONSIDER IT A DEBT OF GRATITUDE.
GAAAAA

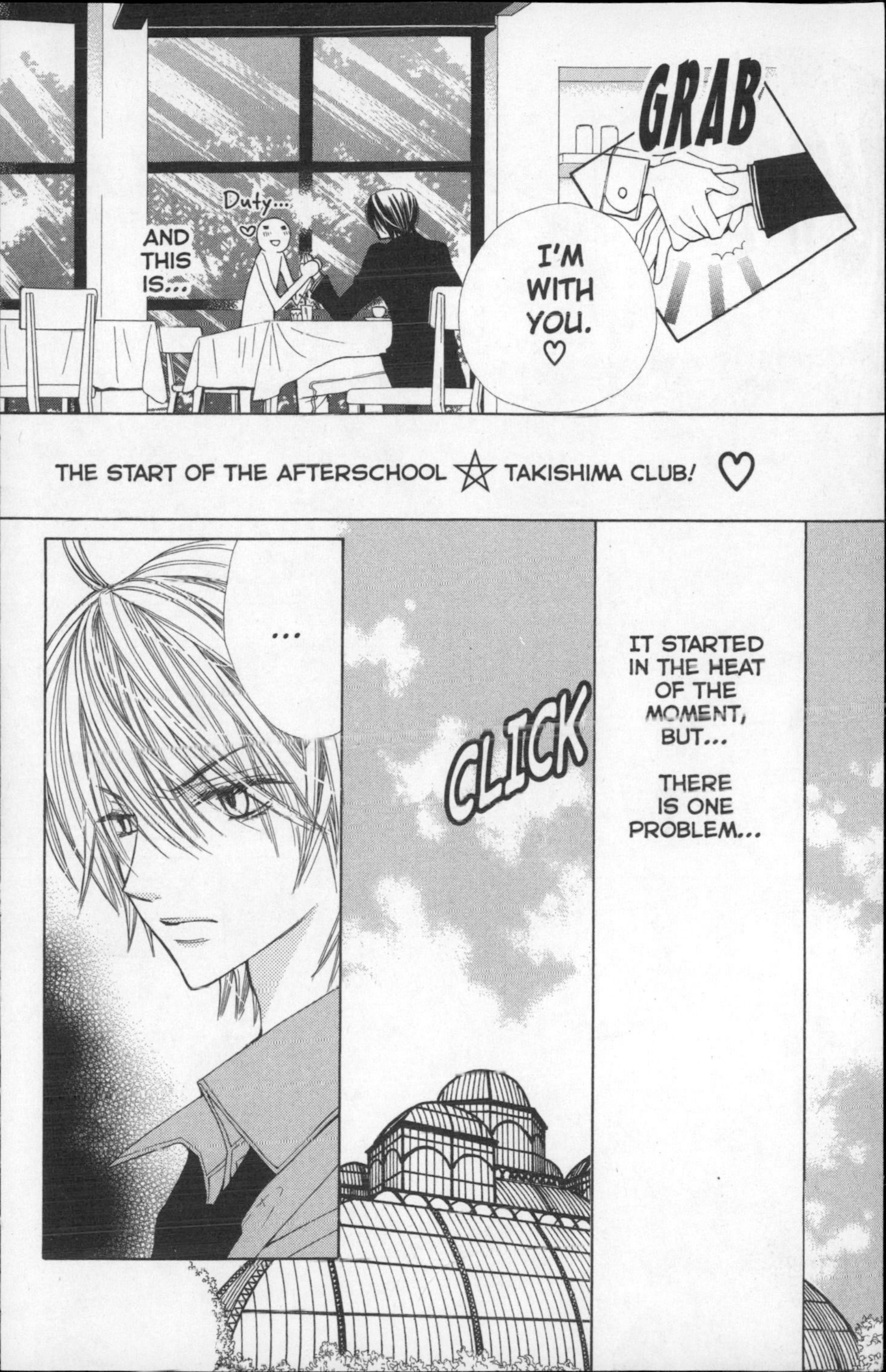
GRAB
I'M WITH YOU. ♡
AND THIS IS...
Duty... ♡
THE START OF THE AFTERSCHOOL ☆ TAKISHIMA CLUB! ♡
IT STARTED IN THE HEAT OF THE MOMENT, BUT...
THERE IS ONE PROBLEM...
CLICK
...

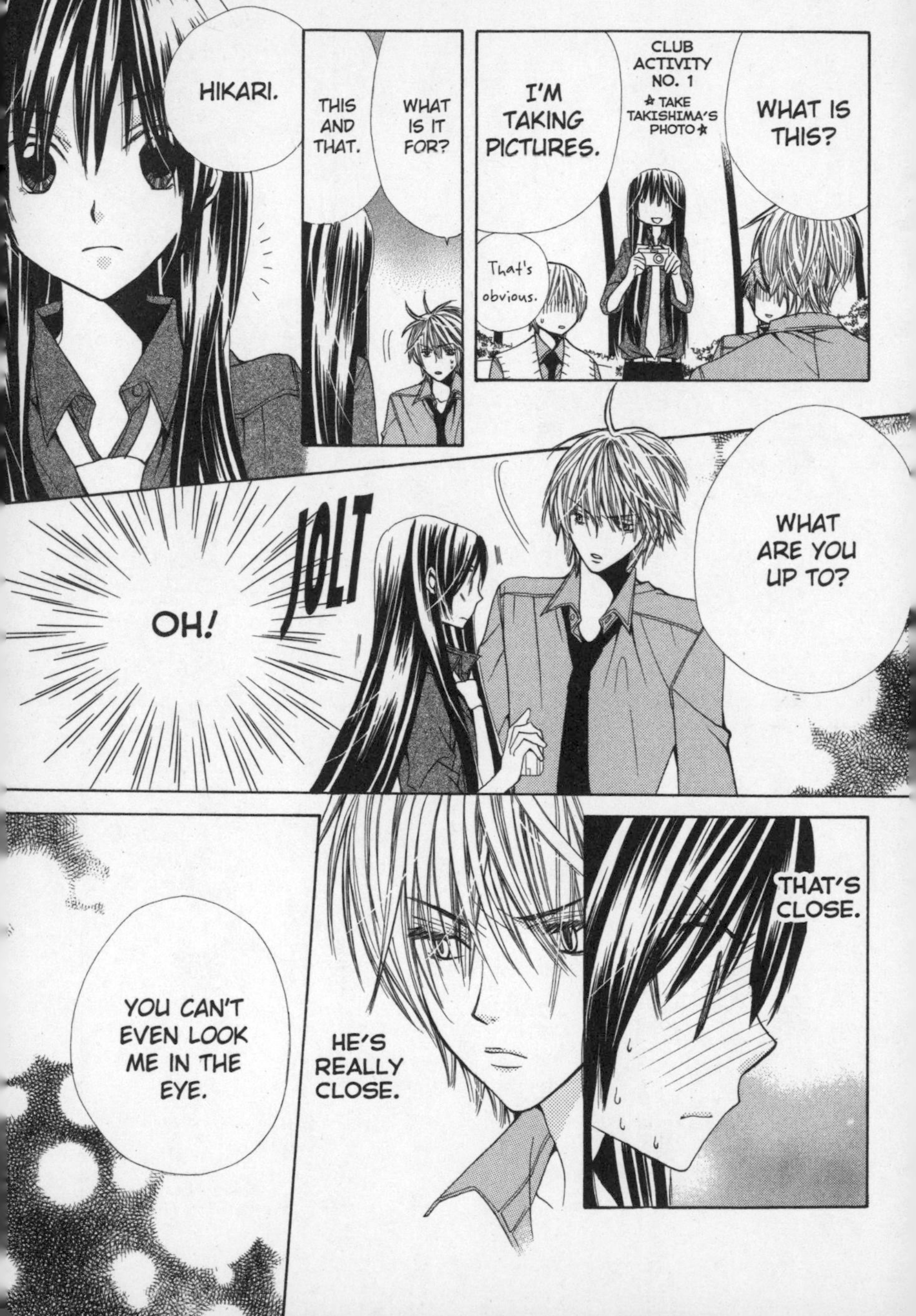
WHAT IS THIS?
CLUB ACTIVITY NO. 1
☆ TAKE TAKISHIMA'S PHOTO ☆
I'M TAKING PICTURES.
That's obvious.
WHAT IS IT FOR?
THIS AND THAT.
HIKARI.
WHAT ARE YOU UP TO?
JOLT
OH!
THAT'S CLOSE.
HE'S REALLY CLOSE.
YOU CAN'T EVEN LOOK ME IN THE EYE.

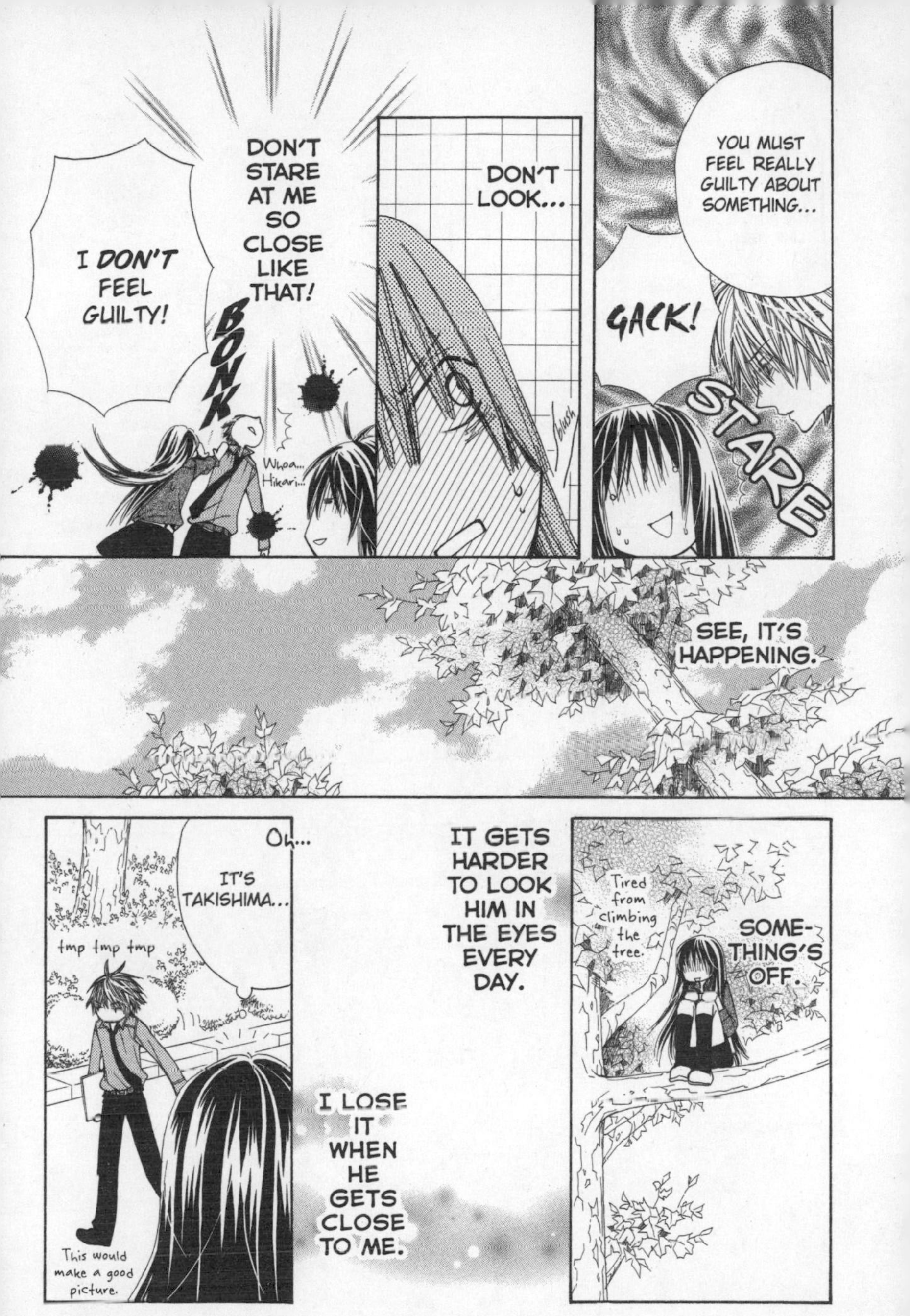
YOU MUST FEEL REALLY GUILTY ABOUT SOMETHING...
GACK!
STARE
DON'T LOOK...
blush
DON'T STARE AT ME SO CLOSE LIKE THAT!
I DON'T FEEL GUILTY!
BONK
Whoa... Hikari...
SEE, IT'S HAPPENING.
Tired from climbing the tree.
SOME-THING'S OFF.
IT GETS HARDER TO LOOK HIM IN THE EYES EVERY DAY.
I LOSE IT WHEN HE GETS CLOSE TO ME.
Oh...
IT'S TAKISHIMA...
tmp tmp tmp
This would make a good picture.

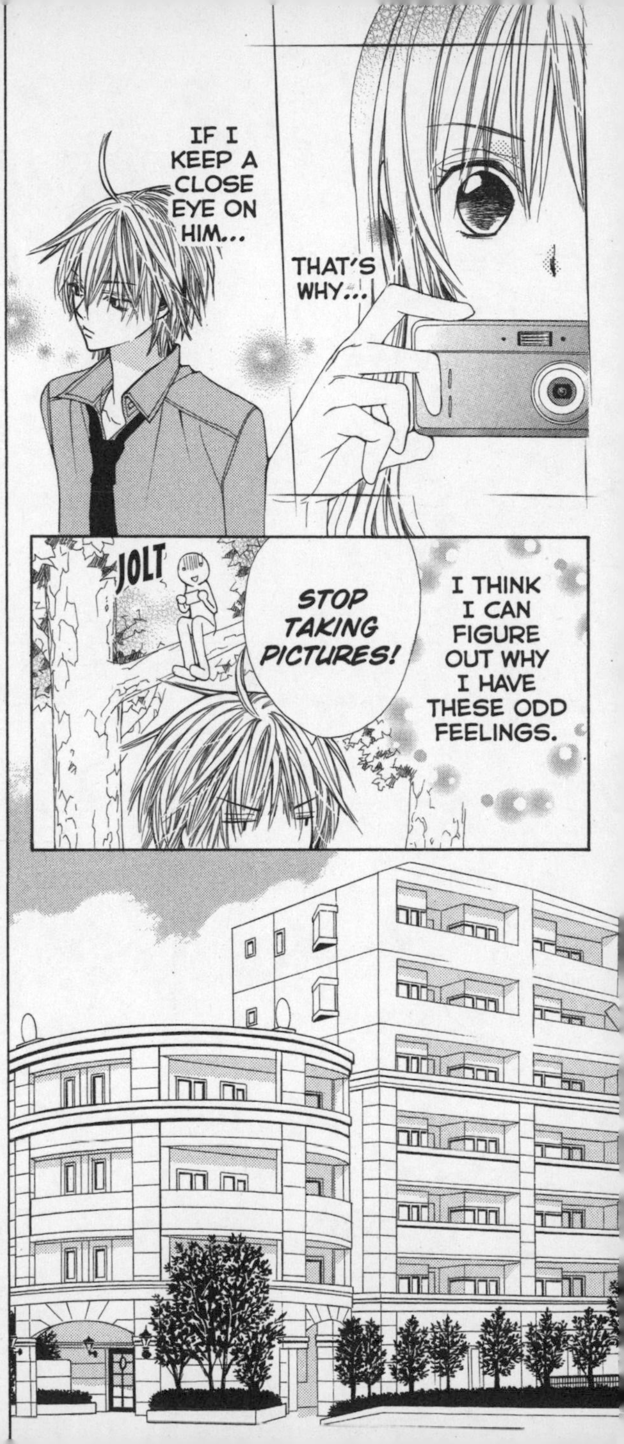
THAT'S WHY...
IF I KEEP A CLOSE EYE ON HIM...
I THINK I CAN FIGURE OUT WHY I HAVE THESE ODD FEELINGS.
STOP TAKING PICTURES!
JOLT

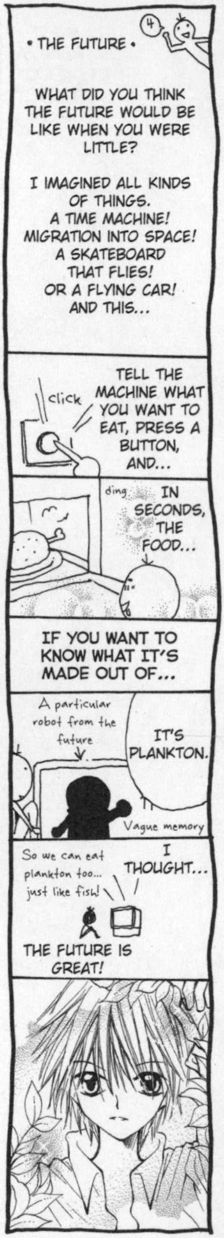
• THE FUTURE •
4
WHAT DID YOU THINK THE FUTURE WOULD BE LIKE WHEN YOU WERE LITTLE?
I IMAGINED ALL KINDS OF THINGS.
A TIME MACHINE!
MIGRATION INTO SPACE!
A SKATEBOARD THAT FLIES!
OR A FLYING CAR!
AND THIS...
TELL THE MACHINE WHAT YOU WANT TO EAT, PRESS A BUTTON, AND...
click
IN SECONDS, THE FOOD...
ding
IF YOU WANT TO KNOW WHAT IT'S MADE OUT OF...
A particular robot from the future
IT'S PLANKTON.
Vague memory
I THOUGHT...
So we can eat plankton too... just like fish!
THE FUTURE IS GREAT!

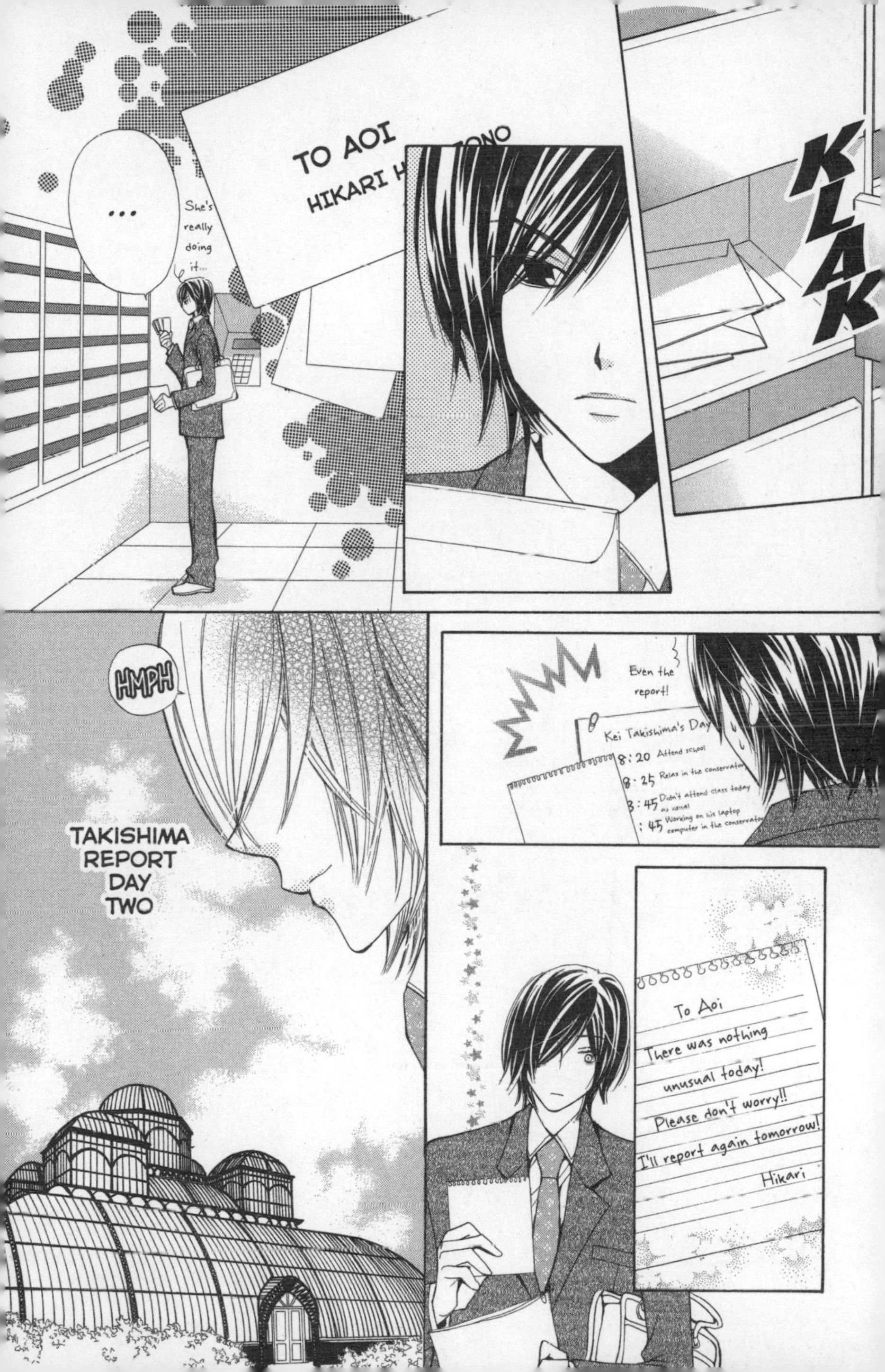
KLAK
TO AOI
HIKARI H ZONO
...
She's really doing it...
Even the report!
Kei Takishima's Day
8:20 Attend school
8:25 Relax in the conservator
8:45 Didn't attend class today as usual
:45 Working on his laptop computer in the conservato
To Aoi
There was nothing unusual today!
Please don't worry!!
I'll report again tomorrow!
Hikari
HMPH
TAKISHIMA REPORT DAY TWO

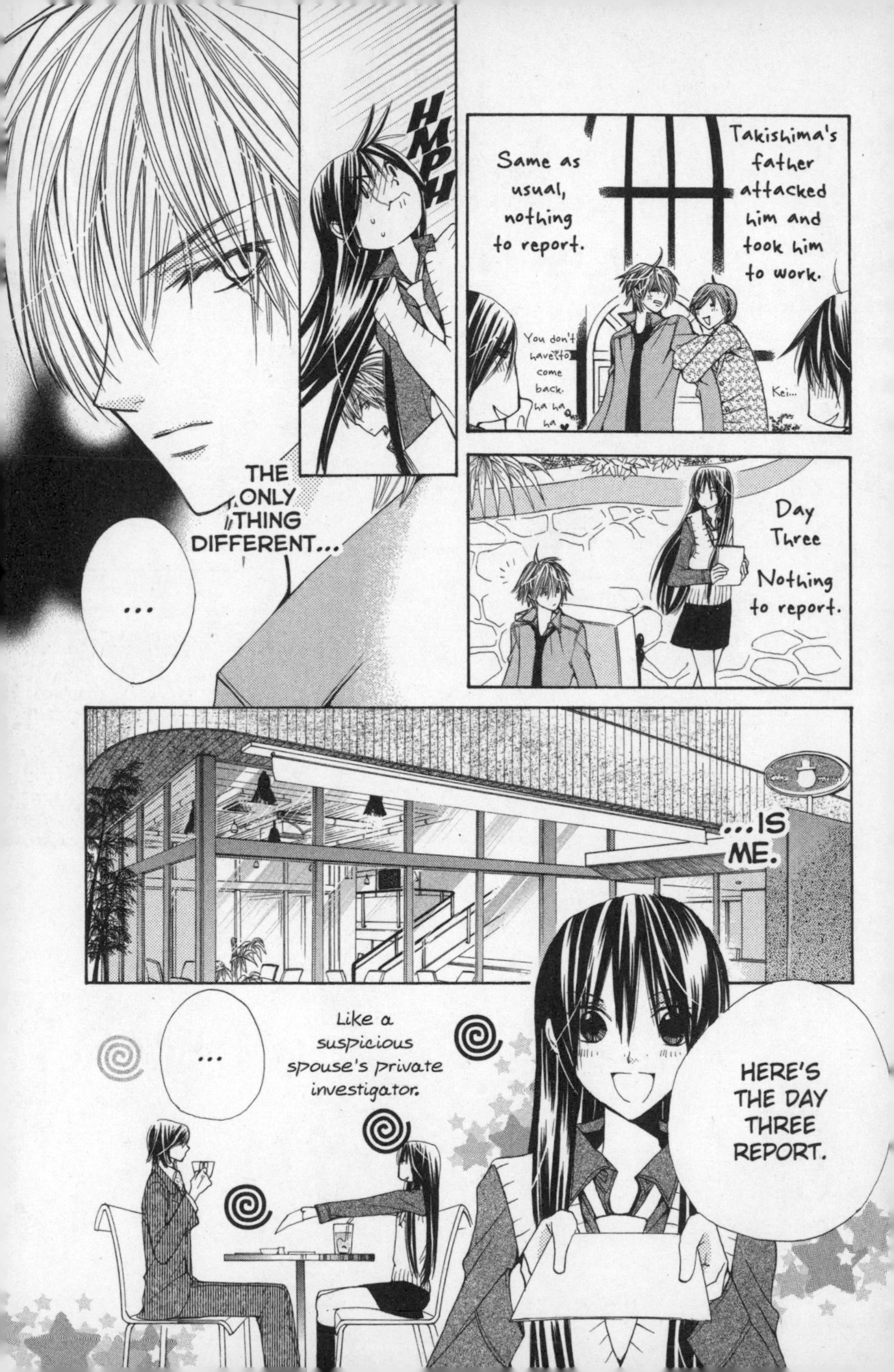
Takishima's father attacked him and took him to work.
Same as usual, nothing to report.
Kei...
You don't have to come back. ha ha ha
Day Three
Nothing to report.
HMPH
THE ONLY THING DIFFERENT...
...
...IS ME.
HERE'S THE DAY THREE REPORT.
Like a suspicious spouse's private investigator.
...

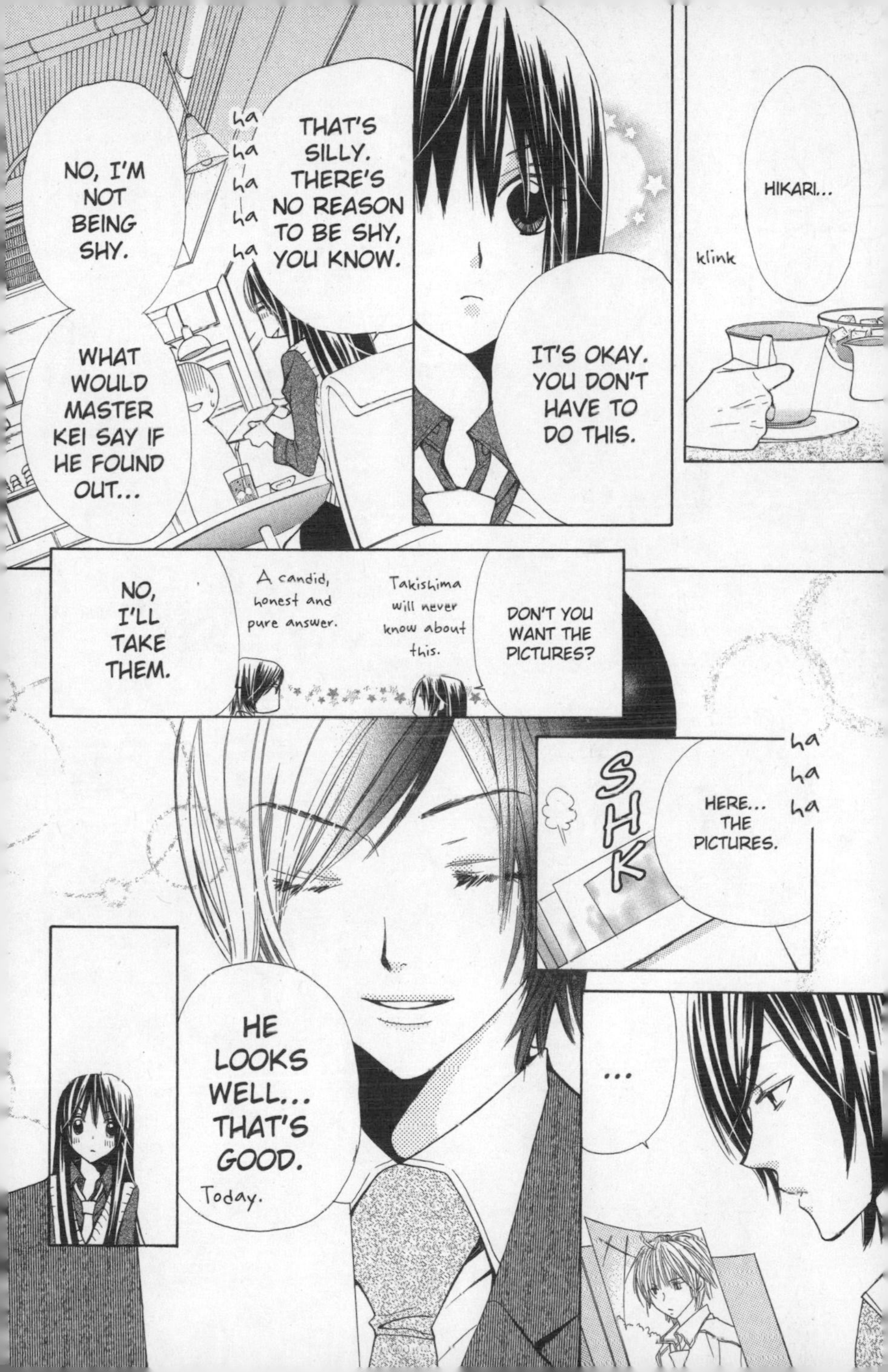
klink
HIKARI...
IT'S OKAY. YOU DON'T HAVE TO DO THIS.
ha ha ha ha ha
THAT'S SILLY. THERE'S NO REASON TO BE SHY, YOU KNOW.
NO, I'M NOT BEING SHY.
WHAT WOULD MASTER KEI SAY IF HE FOUND OUT...
DON'T YOU WANT THE PICTURES?
Takishima will never know about this.
A candid, honest and pure answer.
NO, I'LL TAKE THEM.
ha ha ha
HERE... THE PICTURES.
SHK
...
HE LOOKS WELL... THAT'S GOOD.
Today.

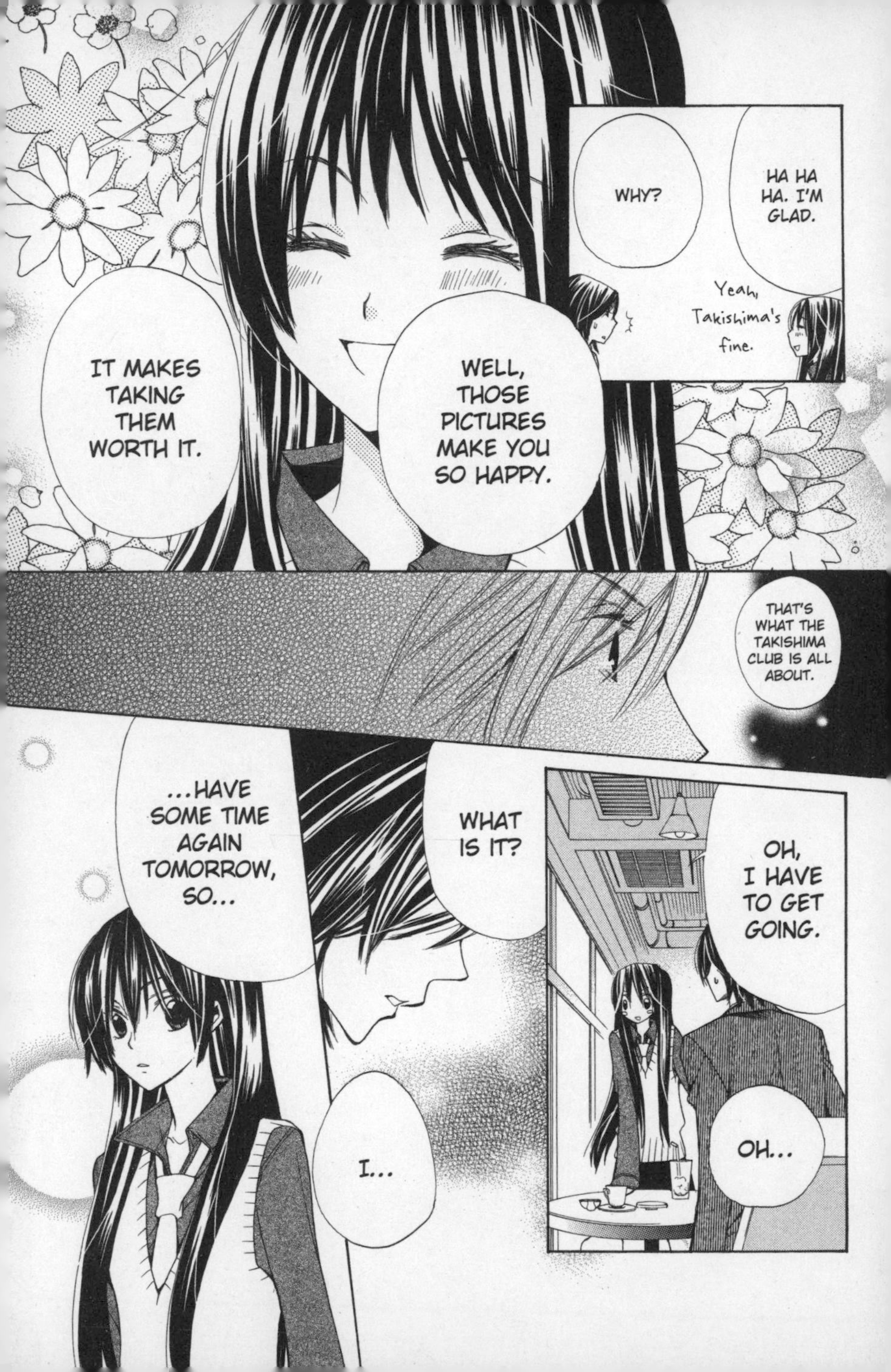
HA HA HA. I'M GLAD.
WHY?
Yeah, Takishima's fine.
WELL, THOSE PICTURES MAKE YOU SO HAPPY.
IT MAKES TAKING THEM WORTH IT.
THAT'S WHAT THE TAKISHIMA CLUB IS ALL ABOUT.
OH, I HAVE TO GET GOING.
OH...
WHAT IS IT?
I...
...HAVE SOME TIME AGAIN TOMORROW, SO...

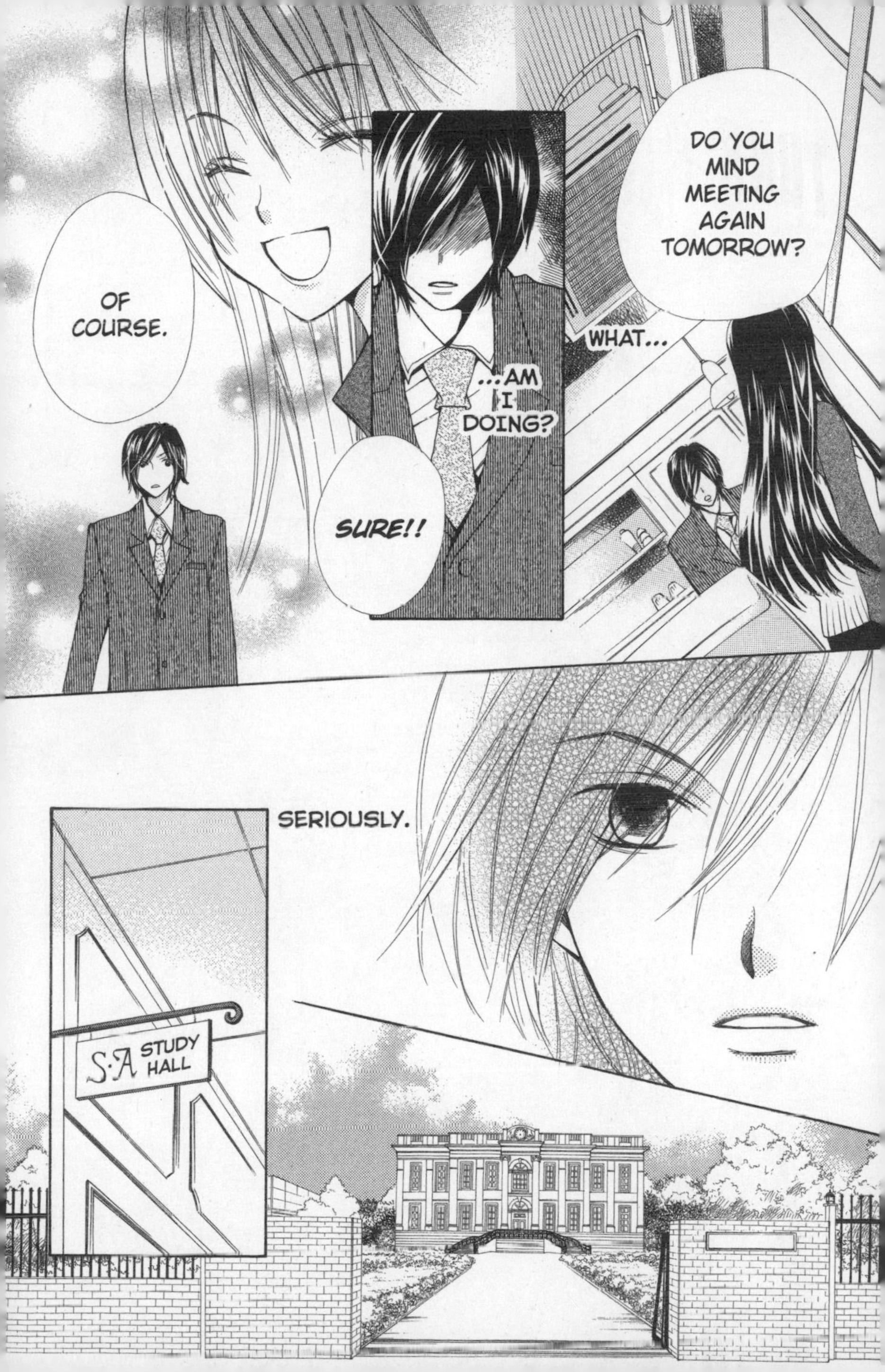
DO YOU MIND MEETING AGAIN TOMORROW?
WHAT...
...AM I DOING?
SURE!!
OF COURSE.
SERIOUSLY.
S·A STUDY HALL

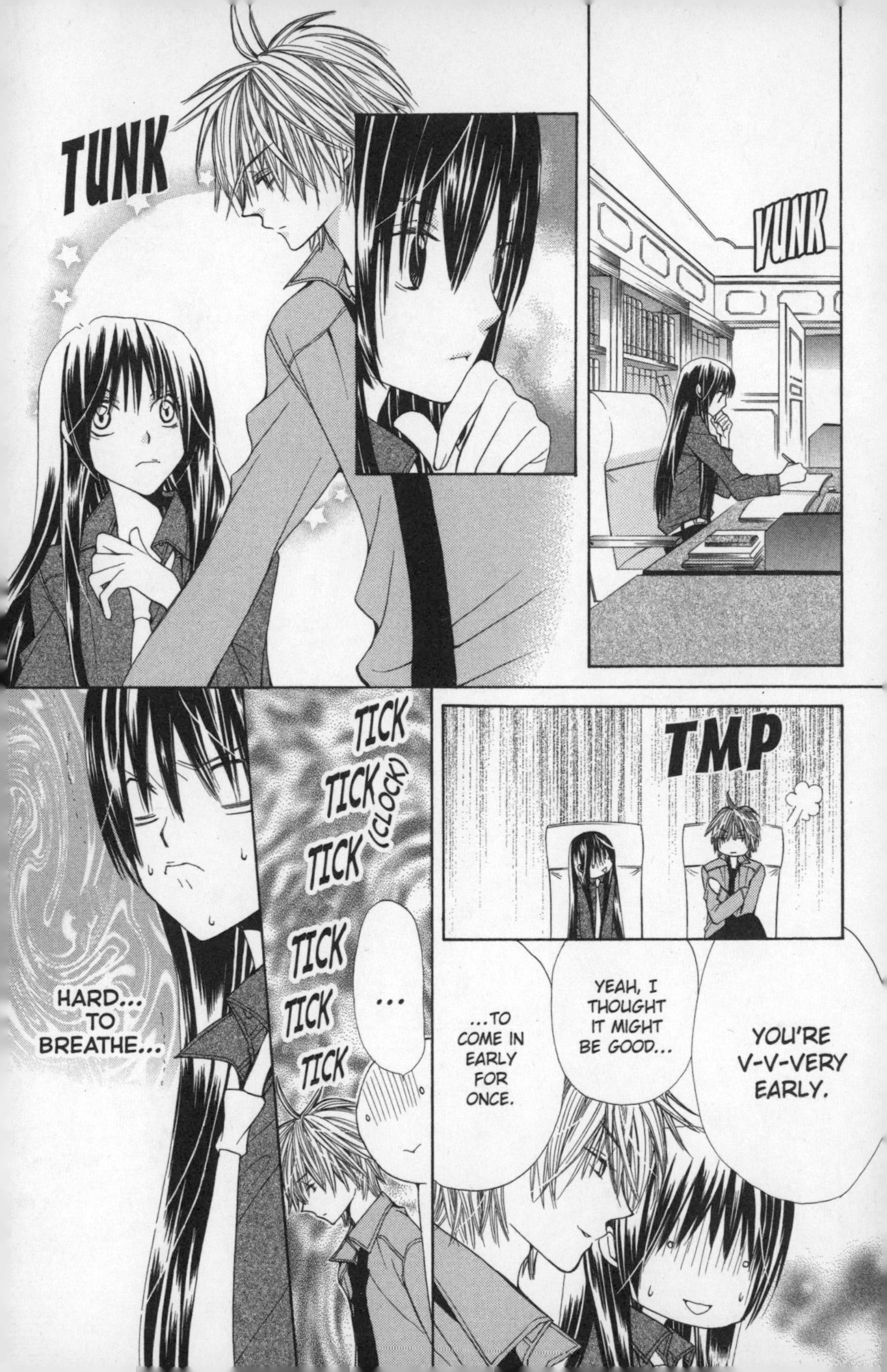
VUNK
TUNK
TMP
YOU'RE V-V-VERY EARLY.
YEAH, I THOUGHT IT MIGHT BE GOOD...
...TO COME IN EARLY FOR ONCE.
...
TICK TICK TICK (CLOCK)
TICK TICK TICK
HARD... TO BREATHE...

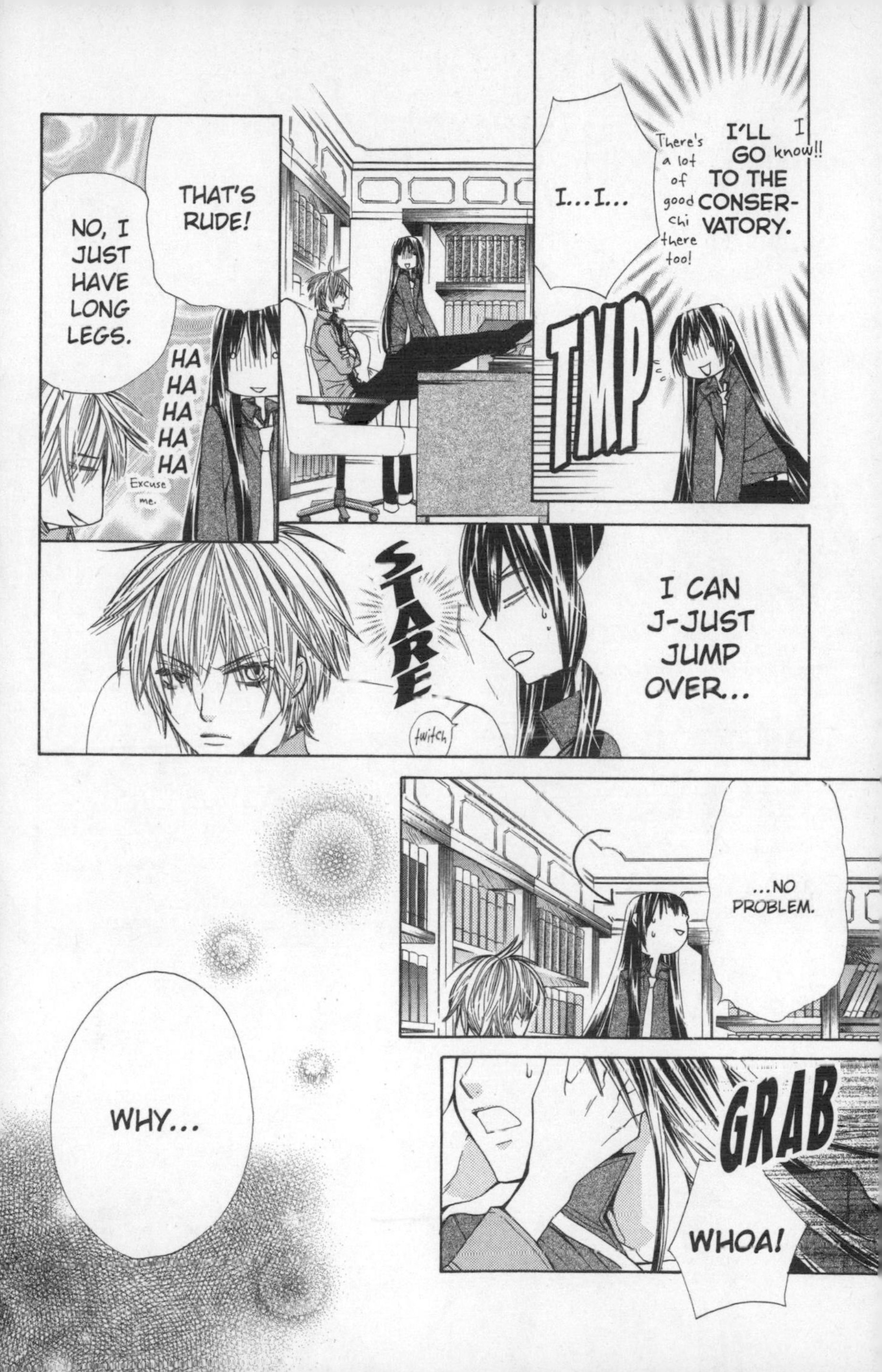
I know!!
I'LL GO TO THE CONSERVATORY.
There's a lot of good chi there too!
I...I...
TMP
THAT'S RUDE!
NO, I JUST HAVE LONG LEGS.
HA HA HA HA HA
Excuse me.
I CAN J-JUST JUMP OVER...
STARE
twitch
...NO PROBLEM.
GRAB
WHOA!
WHY...

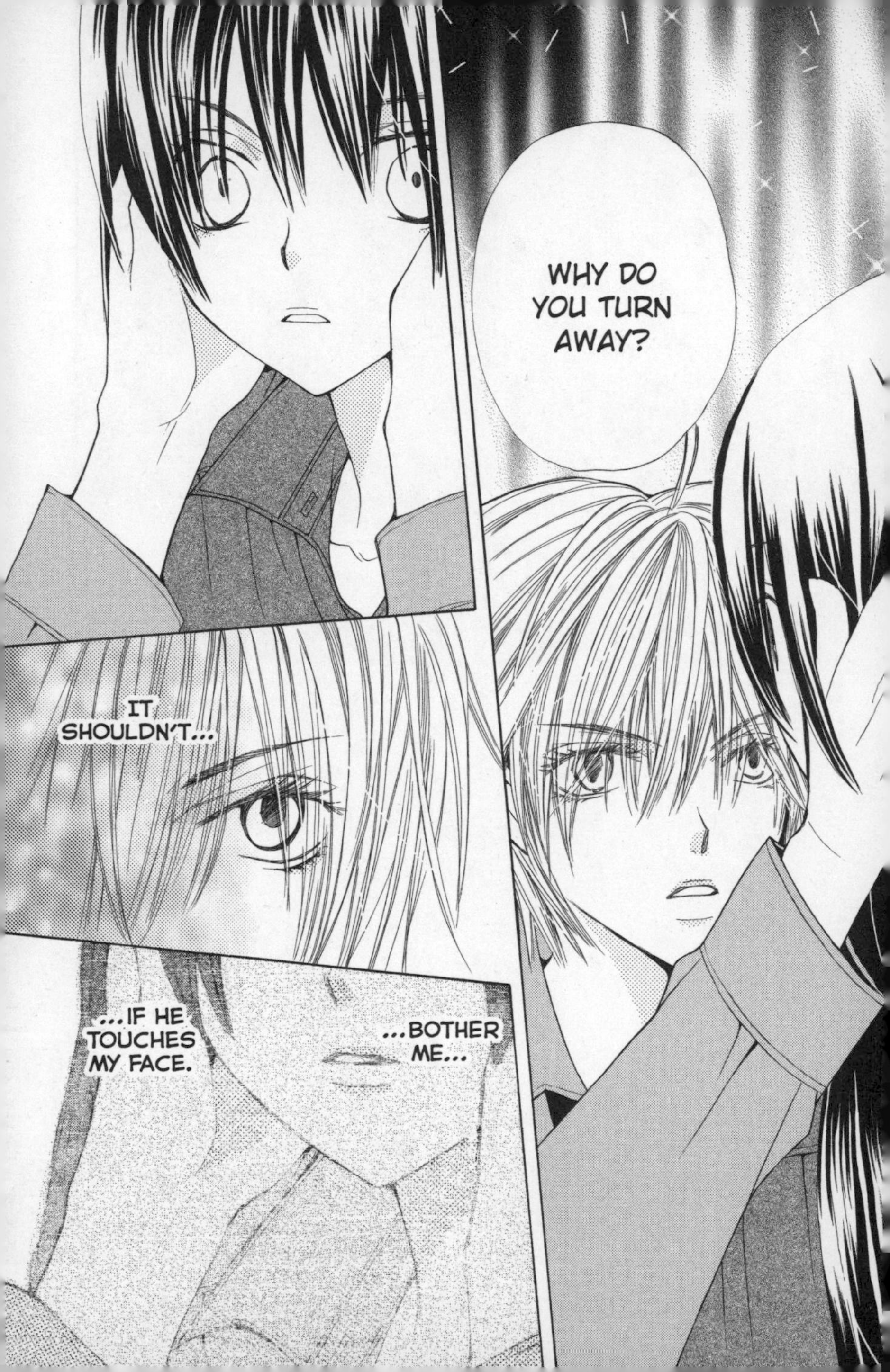
WHY DO YOU TURN AWAY?
IT SHOULDN'T...
...BOTHER ME...
...IF HE TOUCHES MY FACE.

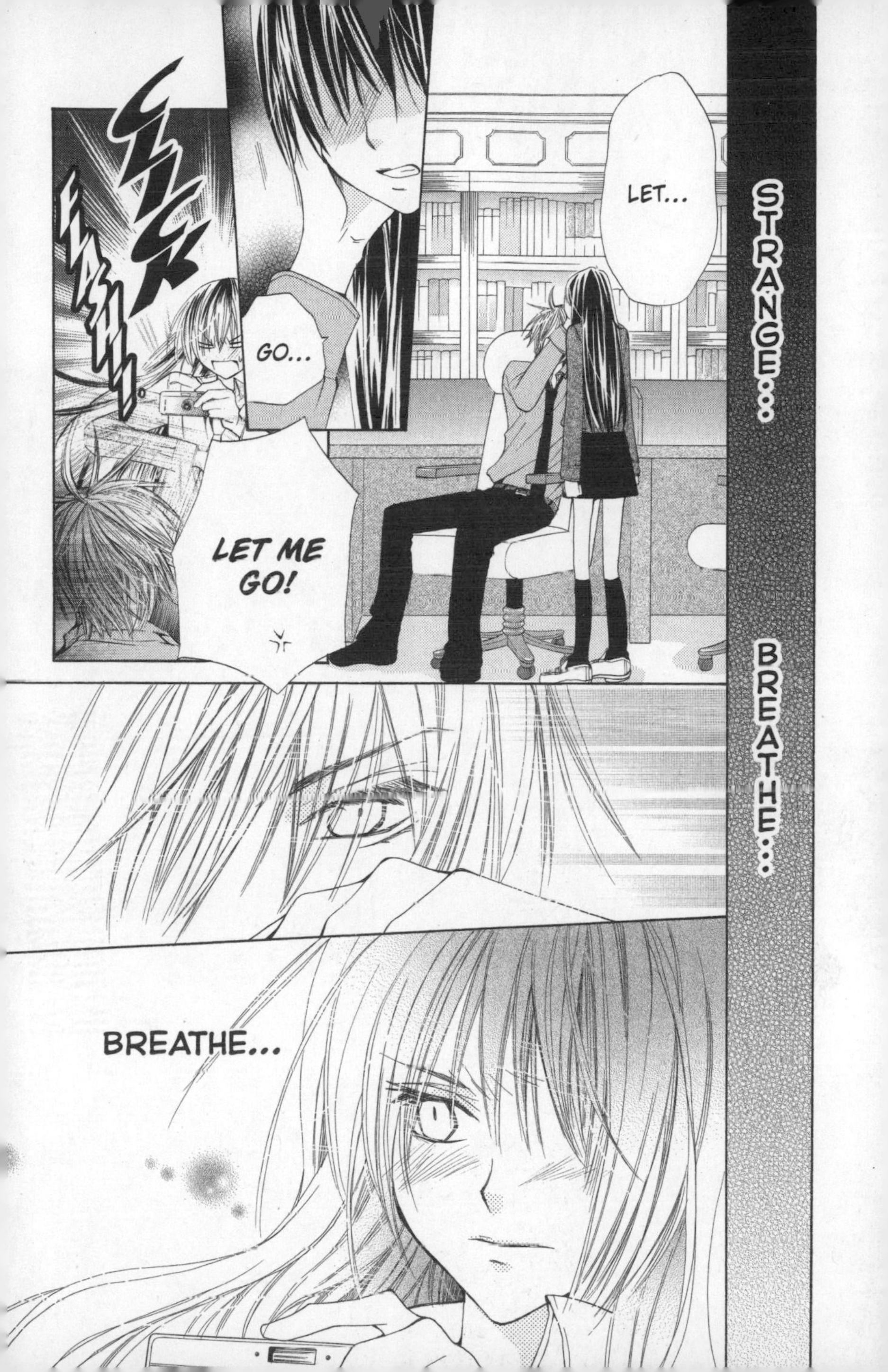
STRANGE...
BREATHE...
LET...
GO...
CLICK
FLASH!!
LET ME GO!
BREATHE...

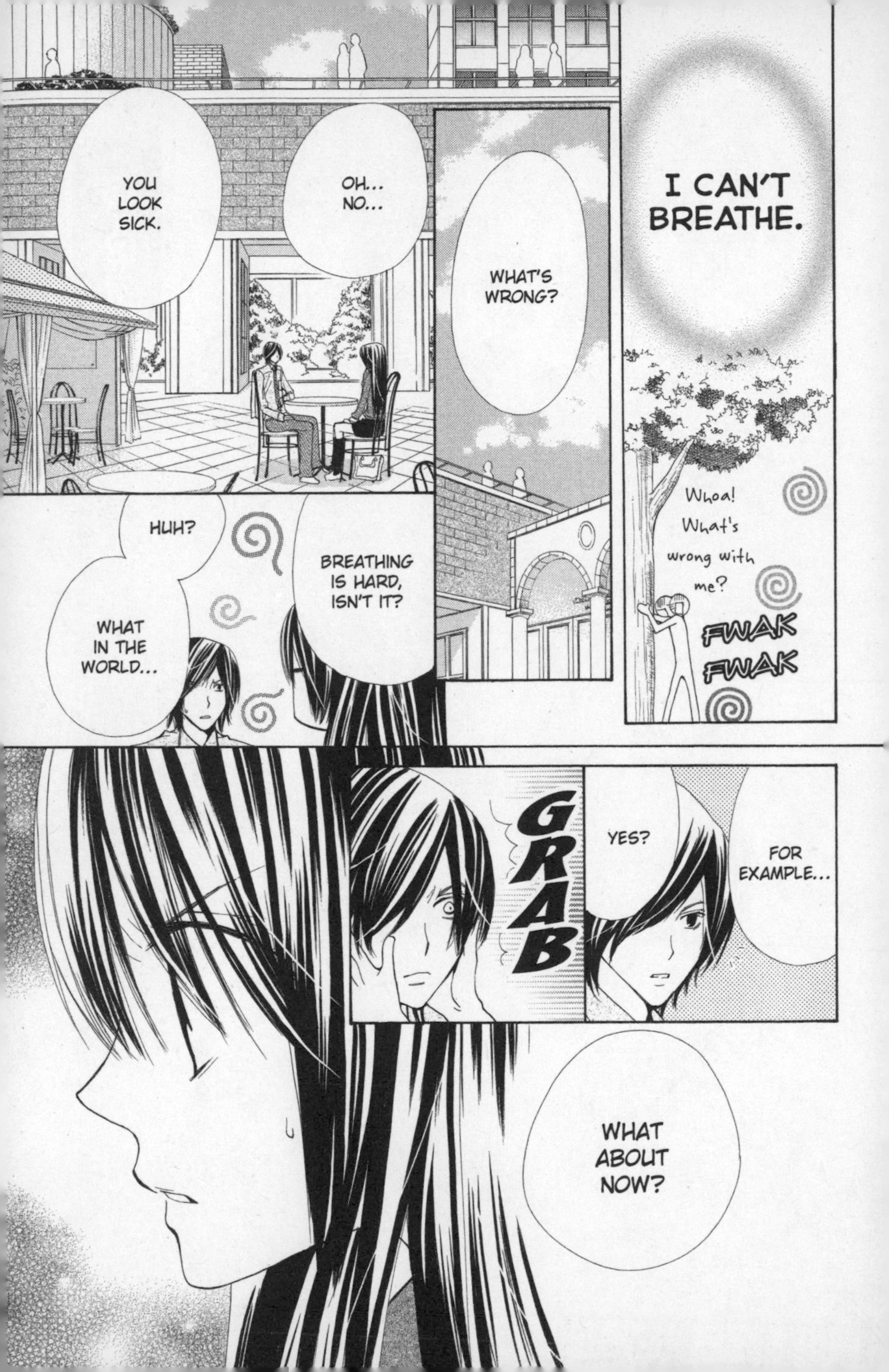
I CAN'T BREATHE.
Whoa! What's wrong with me?
FWAK FWAK
WHAT'S WRONG?
OH... NO...
YOU LOOK SICK.
BREATHING IS HARD, ISN'T IT?
HUH?
WHAT IN THE WORLD...
FOR EXAMPLE...
YES?
GRAB
WHAT ABOUT NOW?

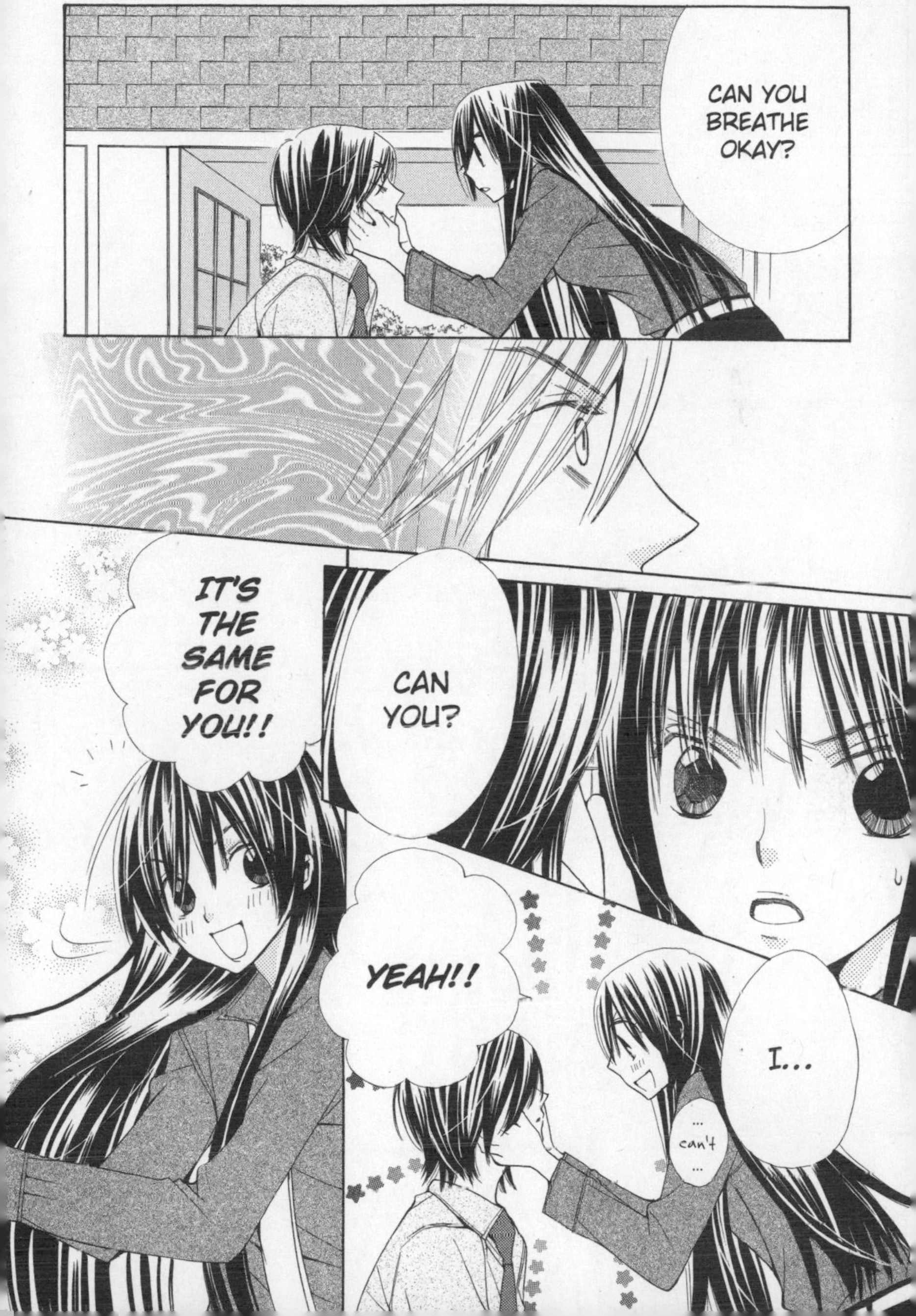
CAN YOU BREATHE OKAY?
CAN YOU?
I...
...can't...
YEAH!!
IT'S THE SAME FOR YOU!!

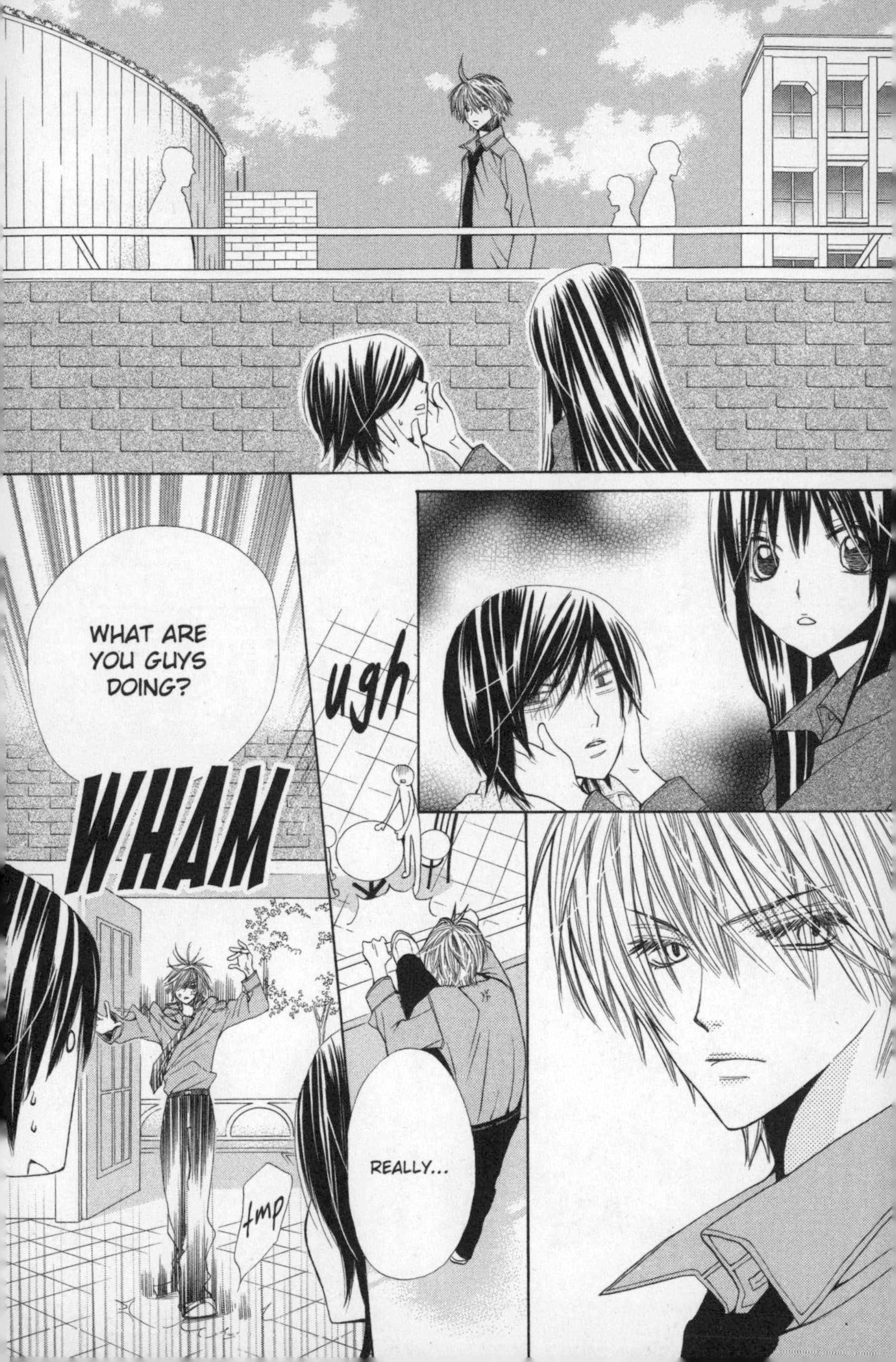
ugh
REALLY...
WHAT ARE YOU GUYS DOING?
WHAM
tmp

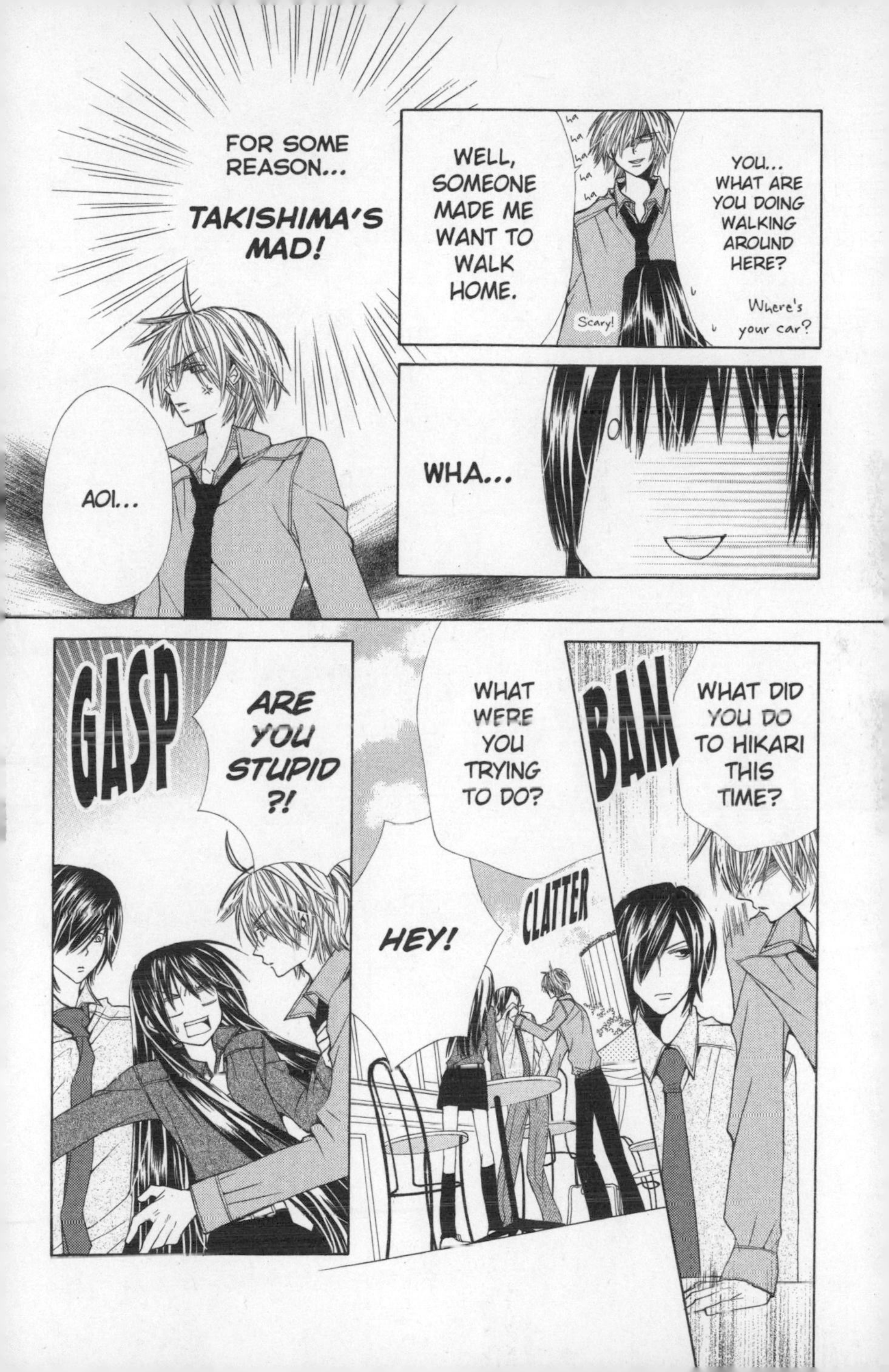
YOU... WHAT ARE YOU DOING WALKING AROUND HERE?
Where's your car?
WELL, SOMEONE MADE ME WANT TO WALK HOME.
ha ha ha ha ha
Scary!
WHA...
FOR SOME REASON...
TAKISHIMA'S MAD!
AOI...
BAM
WHAT DID YOU DO TO HIKARI THIS TIME?
WHAT WERE YOU TRYING TO DO?
CLATTER
HEY!
GASP
ARE YOU STUPID ?!

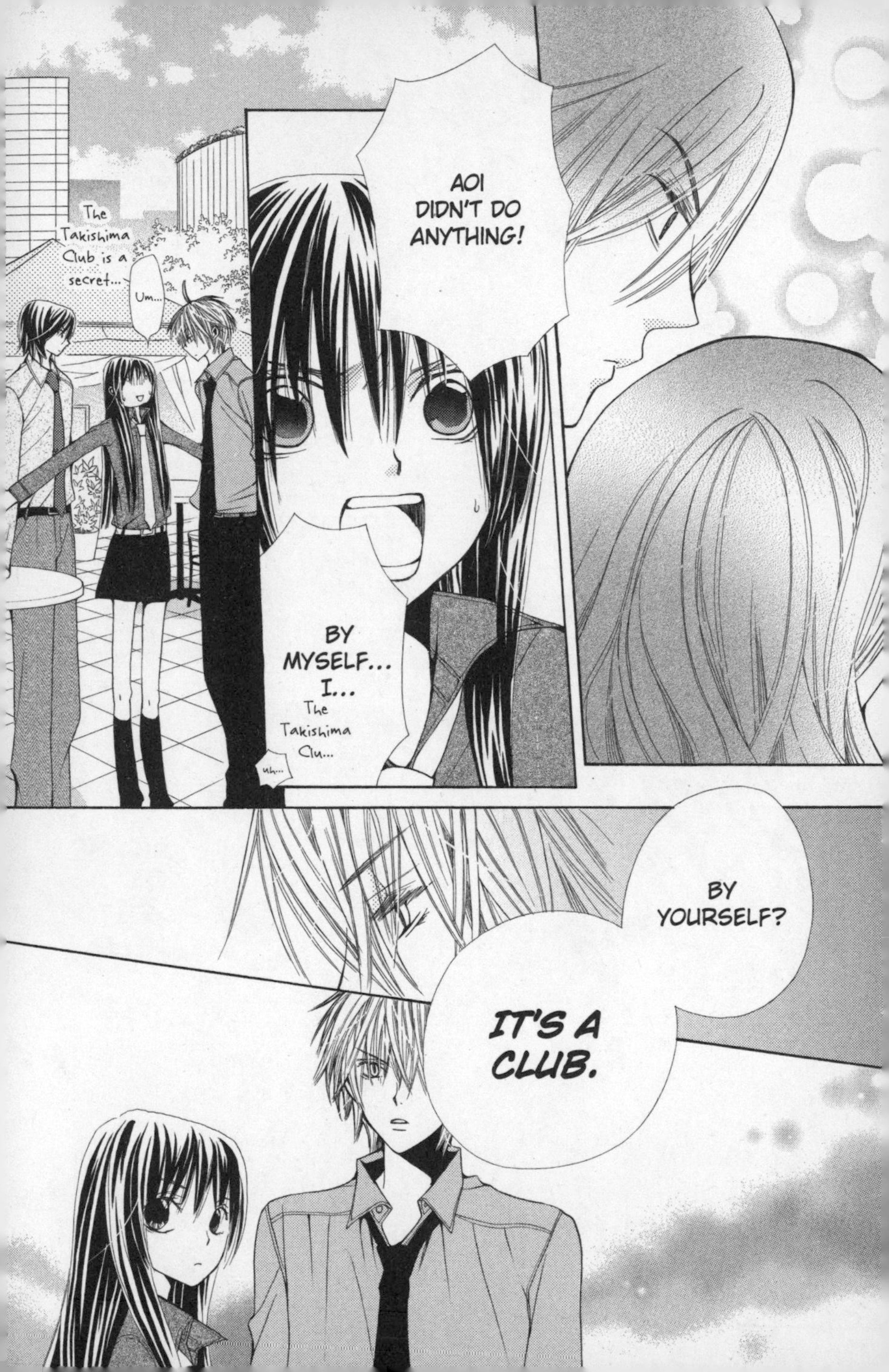
AOI DIDN'T DO ANYTHING!
BY MYSELF... I...
The Takishima Clu...
uh...
The Takishima Club is a secret...
Um...
BY YOURSELF?
IT'S A CLUB.

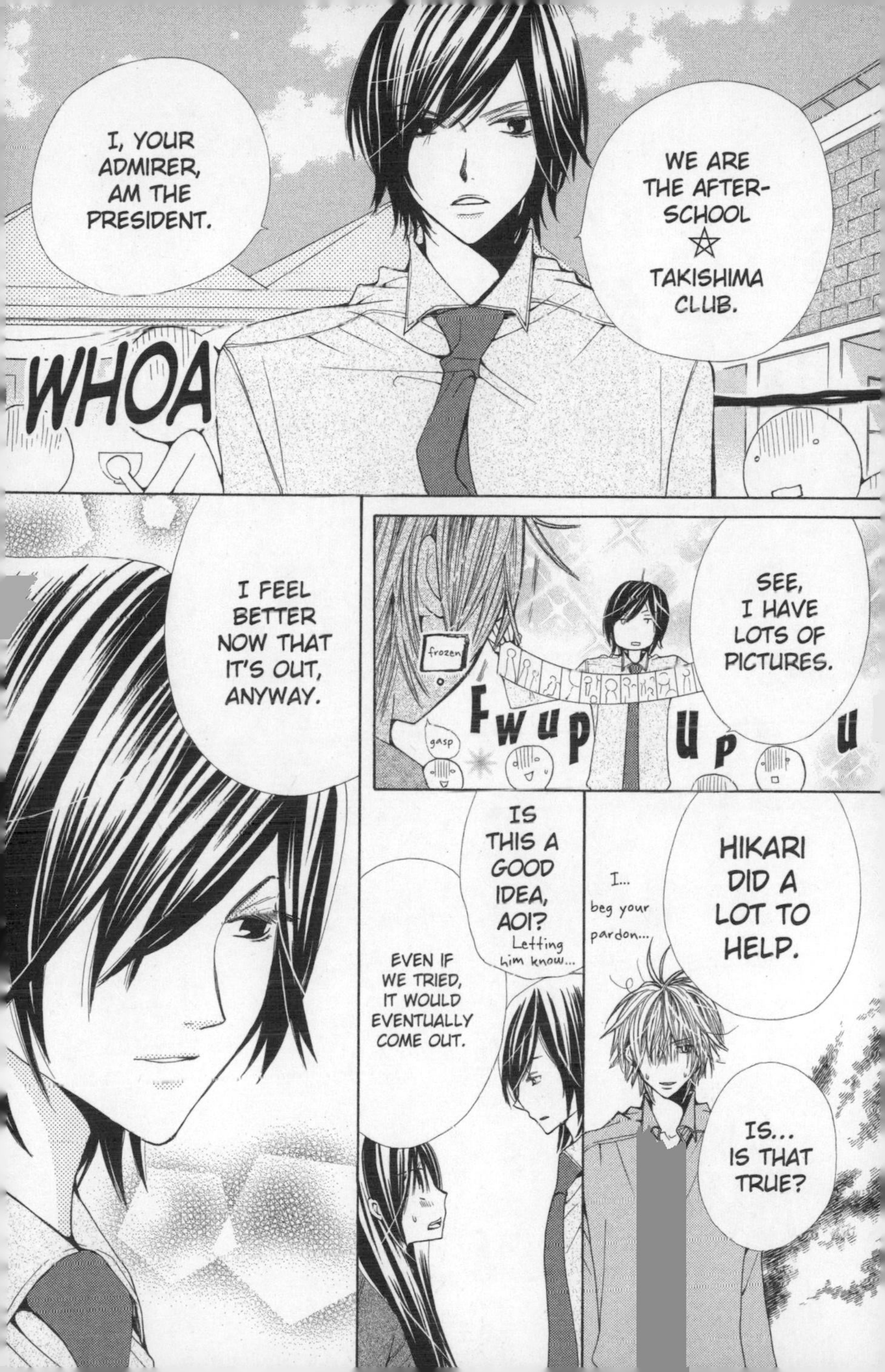
WE ARE THE AFTER-SCHOOL ☆ TAKISHIMA CLUB.
I, YOUR ADMIRER, AM THE PRESIDENT.
WHOA
SEE, I HAVE LOTS OF PICTURES.
frozen
Fwup Up u
gasp
HIKARI DID A LOT TO HELP.
I... beg your pardon...
IS... IS THAT TRUE?
IS THIS A GOOD IDEA, AOI?
Letting him know...
EVEN IF WE TRIED, IT WOULD EVENTUALLY COME OUT.
I FEEL BETTER NOW THAT IT'S OUT, ANYWAY.

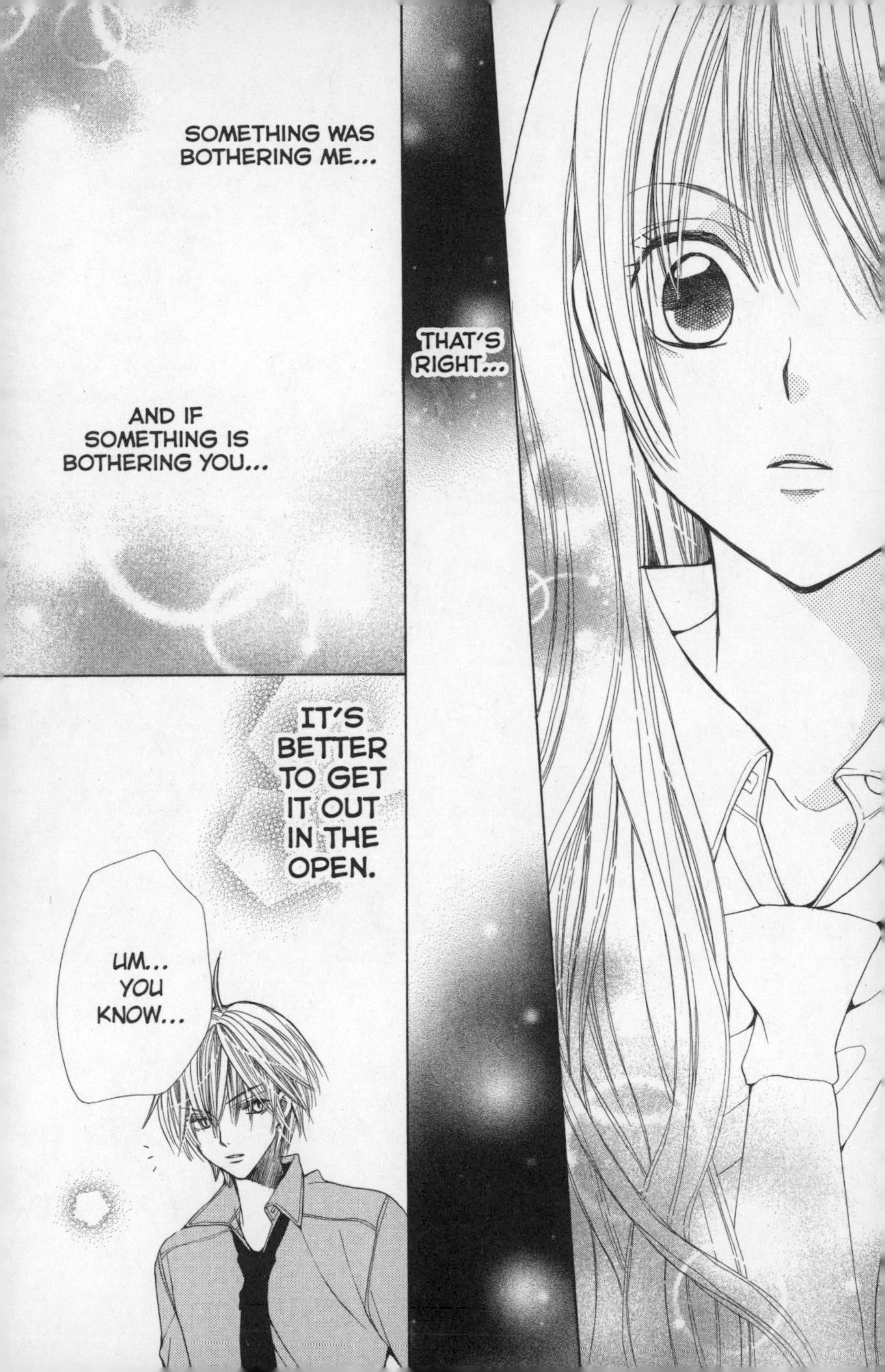
THAT'S RIGHT...
SOMETHING WAS BOTHERING ME...
AND IF SOMETHING IS BOTHERING YOU...
IT'S BETTER TO GET IT OUT IN THE OPEN.
UM... YOU KNOW...

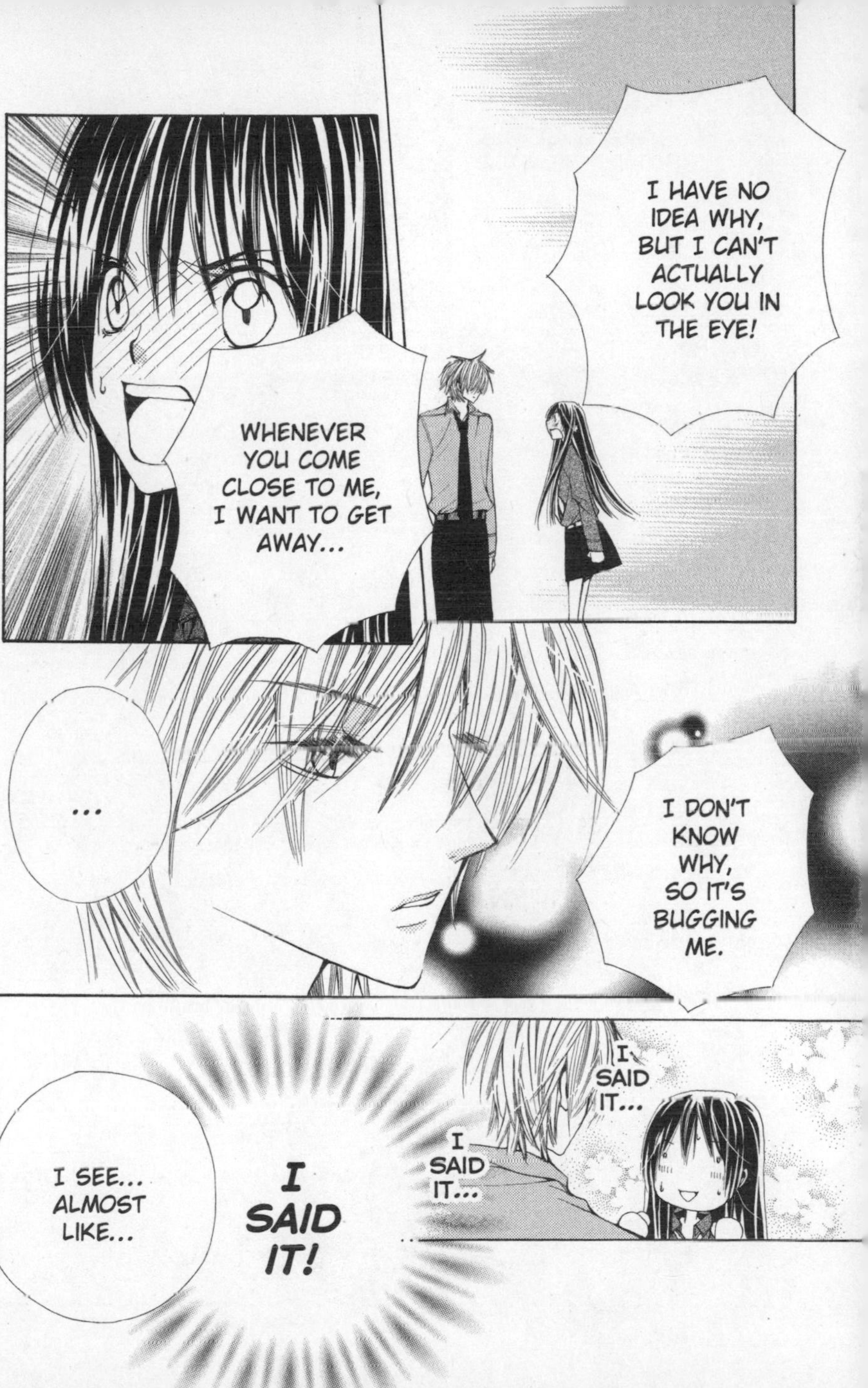
I HAVE NO IDEA WHY, BUT I CAN'T ACTUALLY LOOK YOU IN THE EYE!
WHENEVER YOU COME CLOSE TO ME, I WANT TO GET AWAY...
I DON'T KNOW WHY, SO IT'S BUGGING ME.
...
I SAID IT...
I SAID IT...
I SAID IT!
I SEE... ALMOST LIKE...

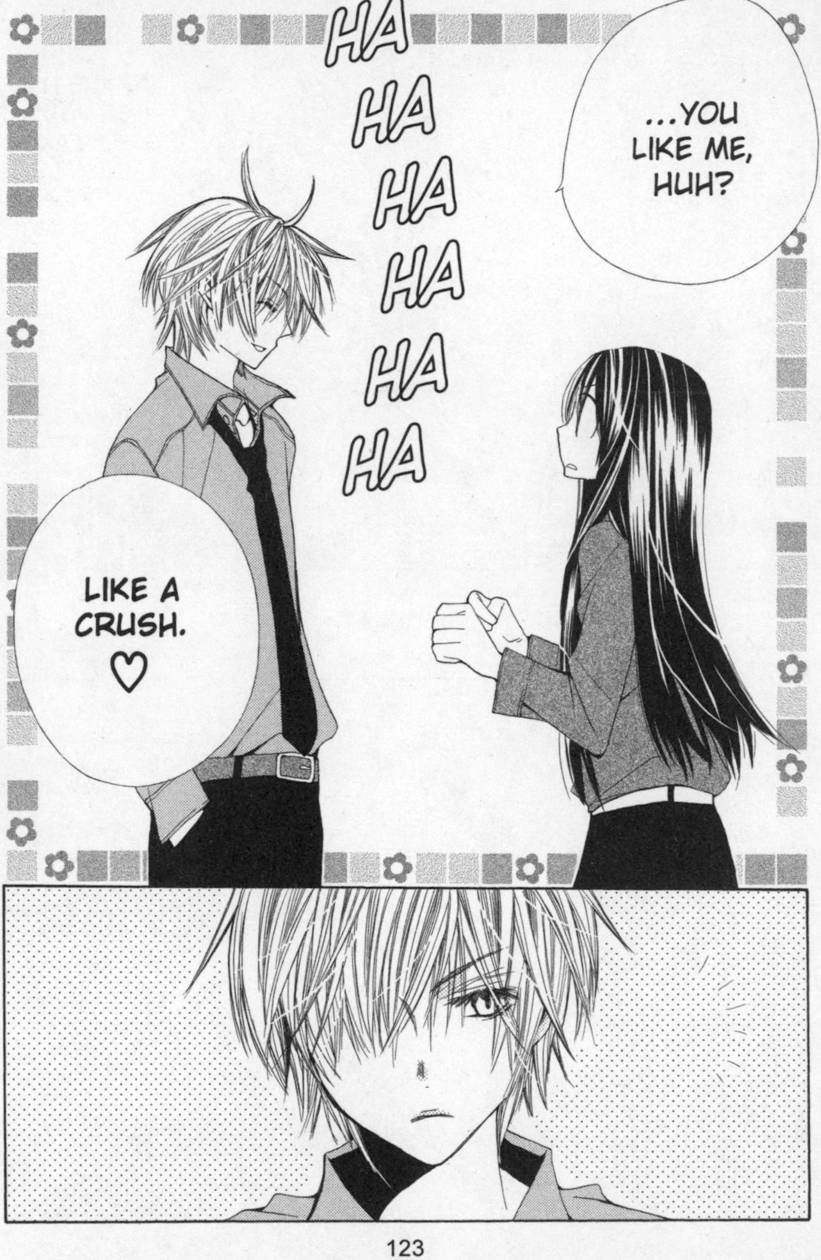
...YOU LIKE ME, HUH?
HA HA HA HA HA HA
LIKE A CRUSH. ♡

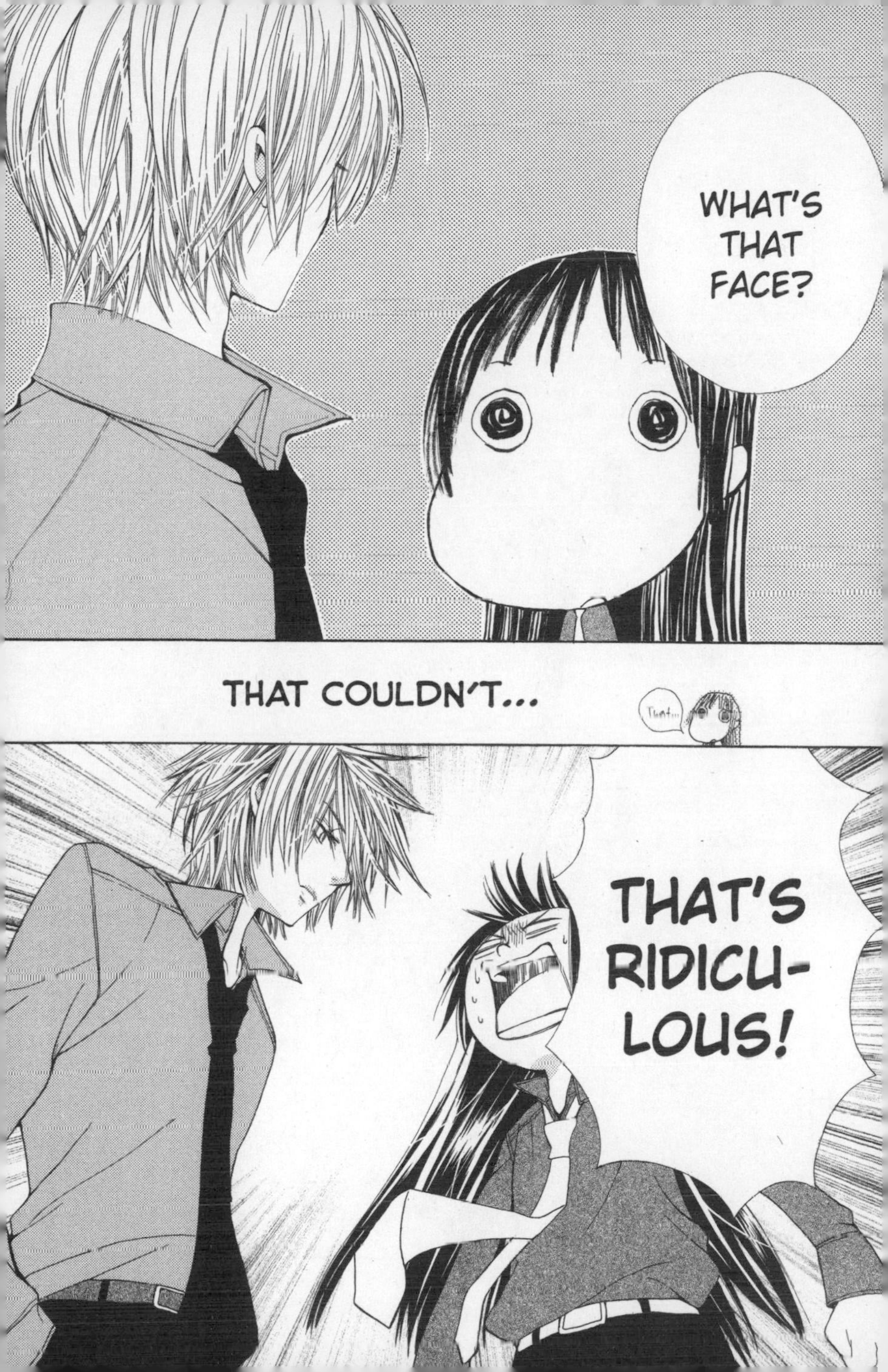
WHAT'S THAT FACE?
That...
THAT COULDN'T...
THAT'S RIDICULOUS!

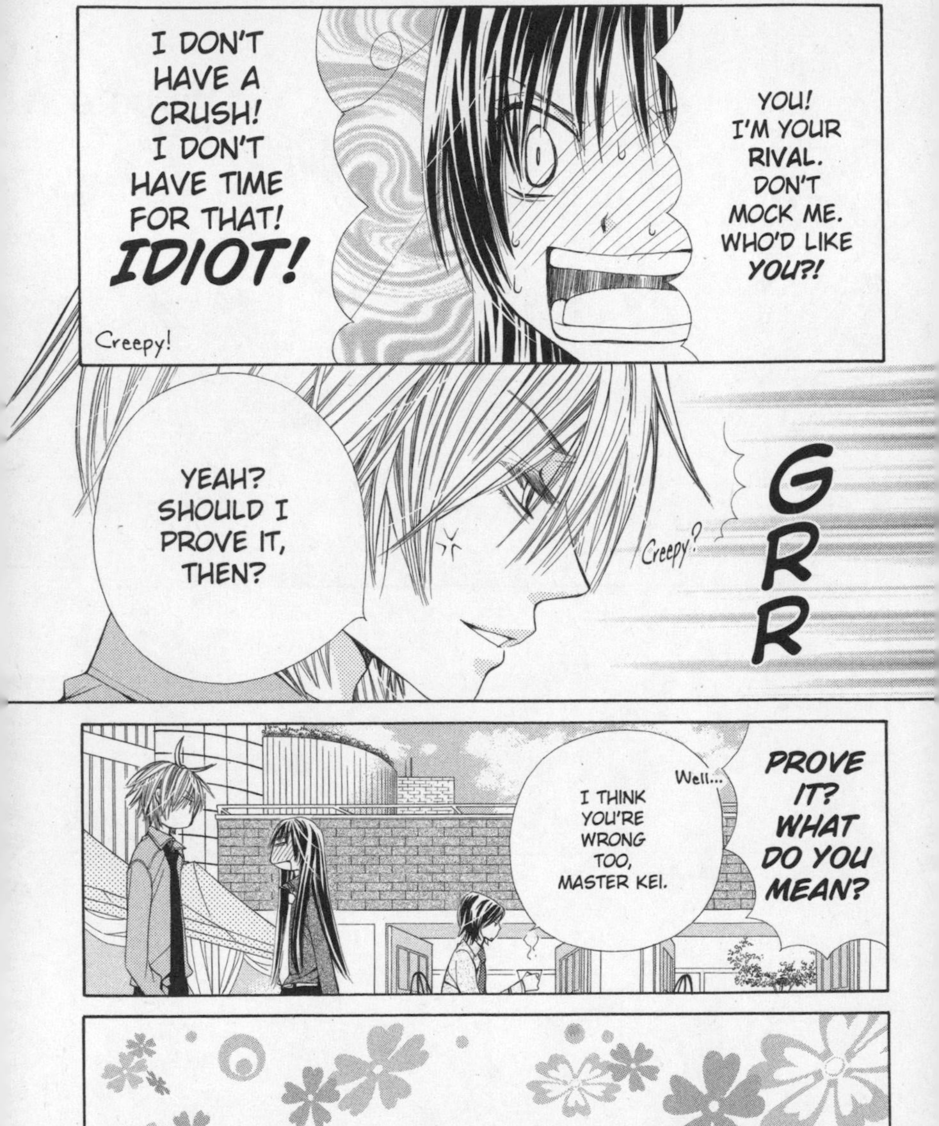
YOU! I'M YOUR RIVAL. DON'T MOCK ME. WHO'D LIKE *YOU?!*
I DON'T HAVE A CRUSH! I DON'T HAVE TIME FOR THAT! ***IDIOT!***
Creepy!
GRR
Creepy?
YEAH? SHOULD I PROVE IT, THEN?
PROVE IT? WHAT DO YOU MEAN?
Well...
I THINK YOU'RE WRONG TOO, MASTER KEI.

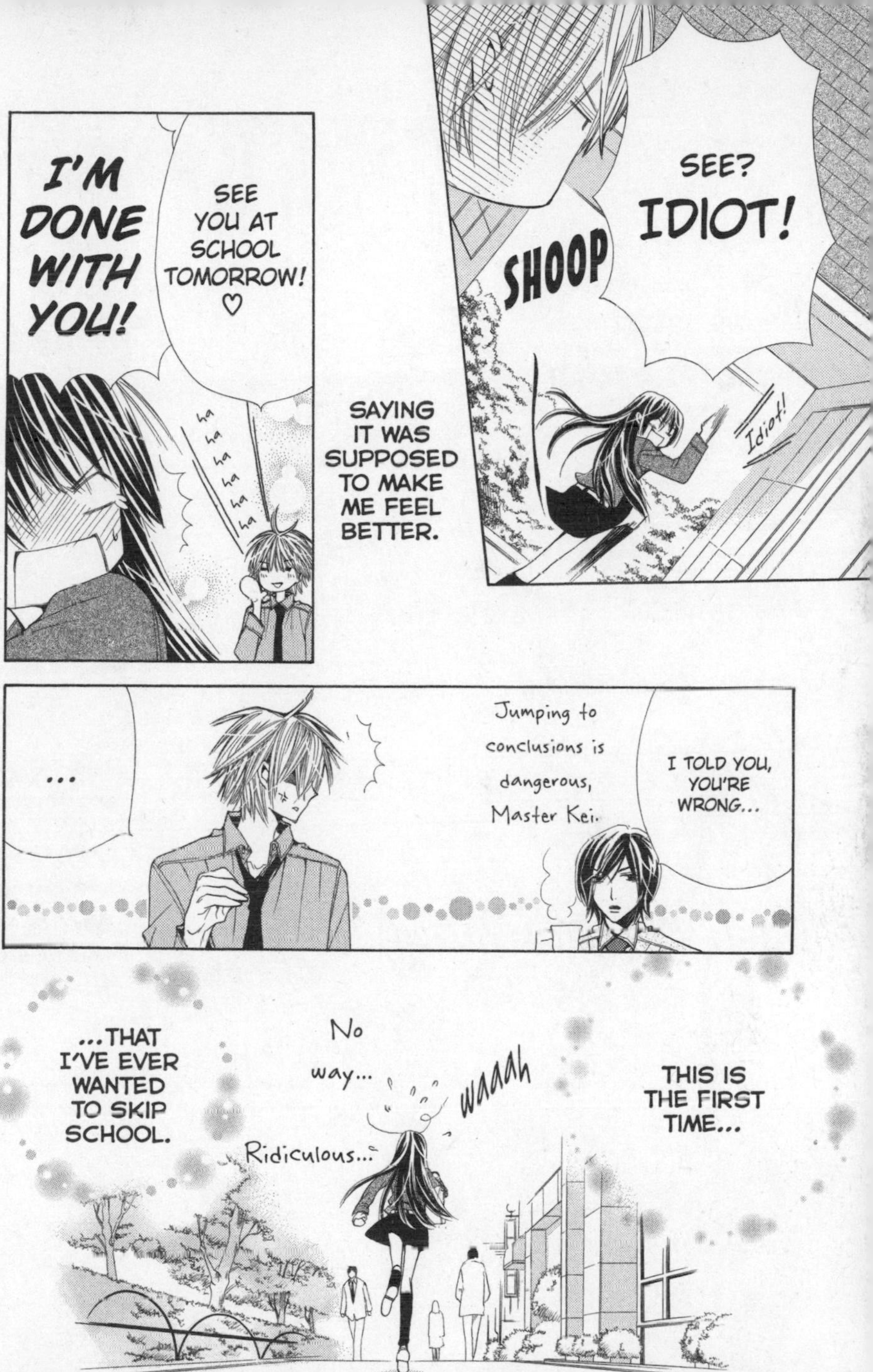
SEE? IDIOT!
SHOOP
Idiot!
SAYING IT WAS SUPPOSED TO MAKE ME FEEL BETTER.
SEE YOU AT SCHOOL TOMORROW! ♡
ha ha ha ha ha ha
I'M DONE WITH YOU!
I TOLD YOU, YOU'RE WRONG...
Jumping to conclusions is dangerous, Master Kei.
...
THIS IS THE FIRST TIME...
waaah
No way...
Ridiculous...
...THAT I'VE EVER WANTED TO SKIP SCHOOL.

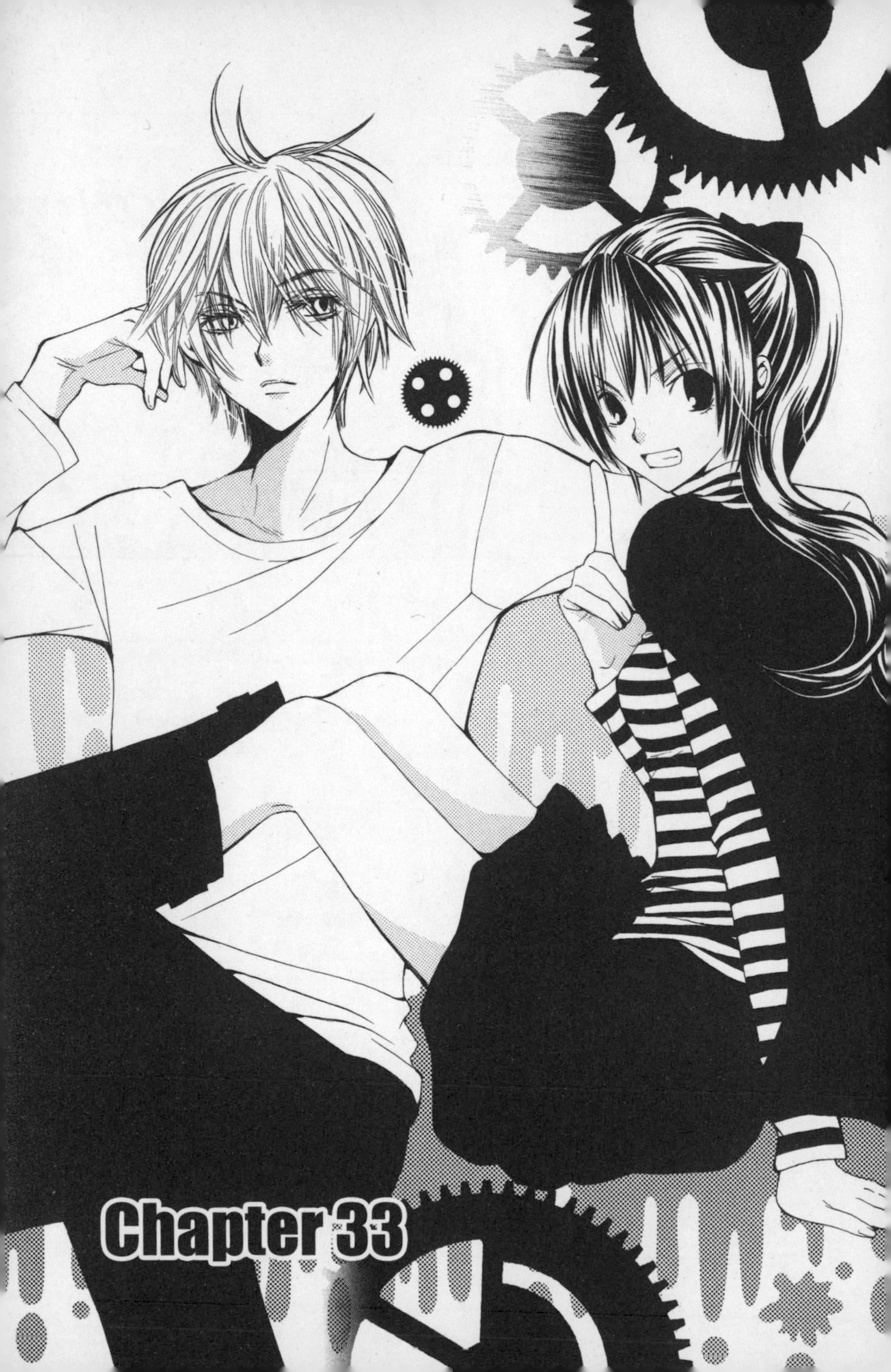
Chapter 33

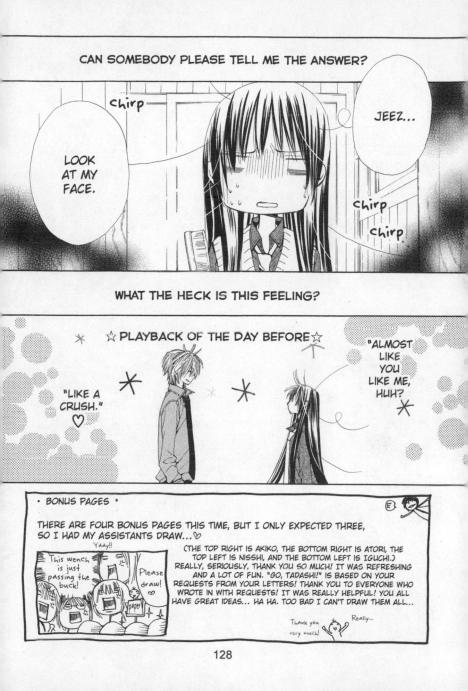

CAN SOMEBODY PLEASE TELL ME THE ANSWER?

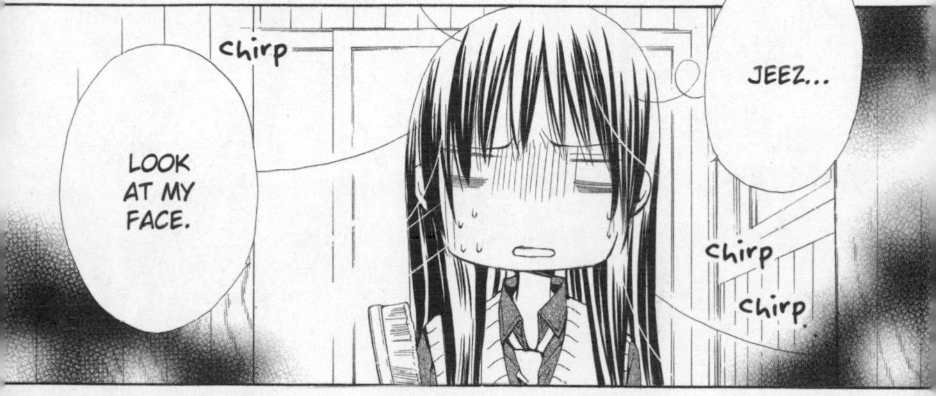
JEEZ...
chirp
chirp
LOOK AT MY FACE.
chirp

WHAT THE HECK IS THIS FEELING?

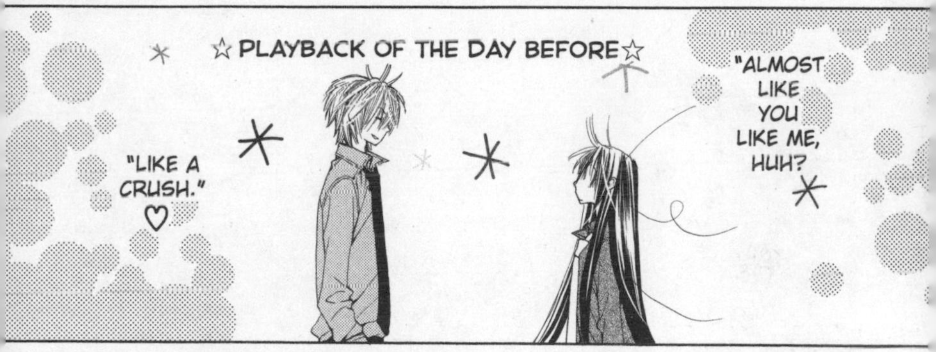
☆PLAYBACK OF THE DAY BEFORE☆
"ALMOST LIKE YOU LIKE ME, HUH?"
"LIKE A CRUSH." ♡

• BONUS PAGES •

THERE ARE FOUR BONUS PAGES THIS TIME, BUT I ONLY EXPECTED THREE, SO I HAD MY ASSISTANTS DRAW...♡

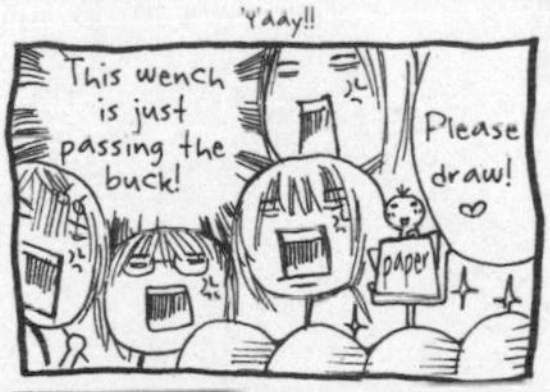
Y'ady!!
Please draw! ♡
This wench is just passing the buck!
paper

(THE TOP RIGHT IS AKIKO, THE BOTTOM RIGHT IS ATORI, THE TOP LEFT IS NISSHI, AND THE BOTTOM LEFT IS IGUCHI.) REALLY, SERIOUSLY, THANK YOU SO MUCH! IT WAS REFRESHING AND A LOT OF FUN. "GO, TADASHI!" IS BASED ON YOUR REQUESTS FROM YOUR LETTERS! THANK YOU TO EVERYONE WHO WROTE IN WITH REQUESTS! IT WAS REALLY HELPFUL! YOU ALL HAVE GREAT IDEAS... HA HA. TOO BAD I CAN'T DRAW THEM ALL...

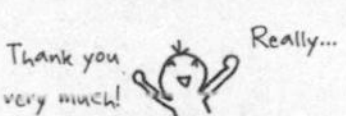
Really...
Thank you very much!

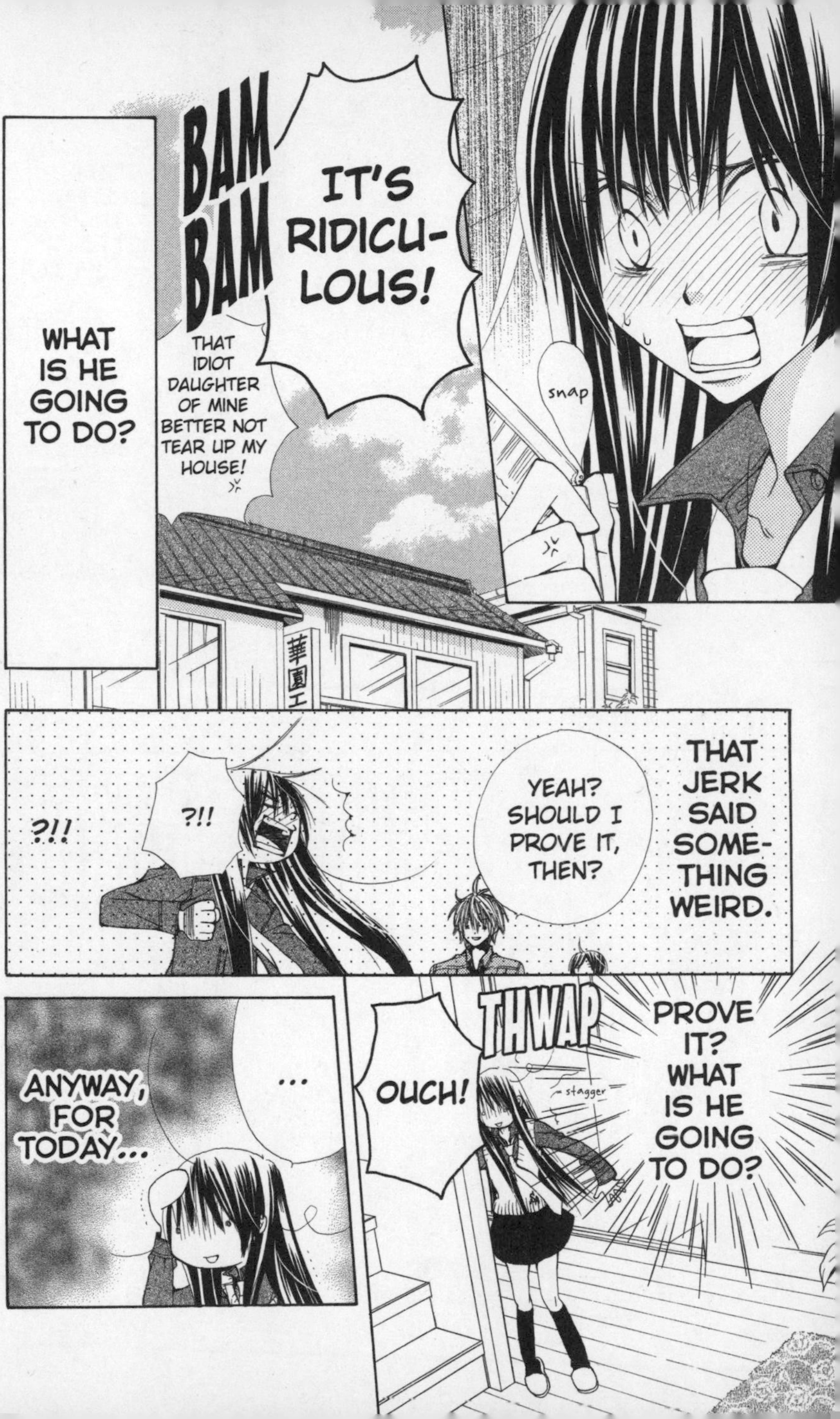
IT'S RIDICULOUS!
snap
BAM BAM
THAT IDIOT DAUGHTER OF MINE BETTER NOT TEAR UP MY HOUSE!
WHAT IS HE GOING TO DO?
THAT JERK SAID SOMETHING WEIRD.
YEAH? SHOULD I PROVE IT, THEN?
?!!
?!!
PROVE IT? WHAT IS HE GOING TO DO?
THWAP
stagger
OUCH!
...
ANYWAY, FOR TODAY...

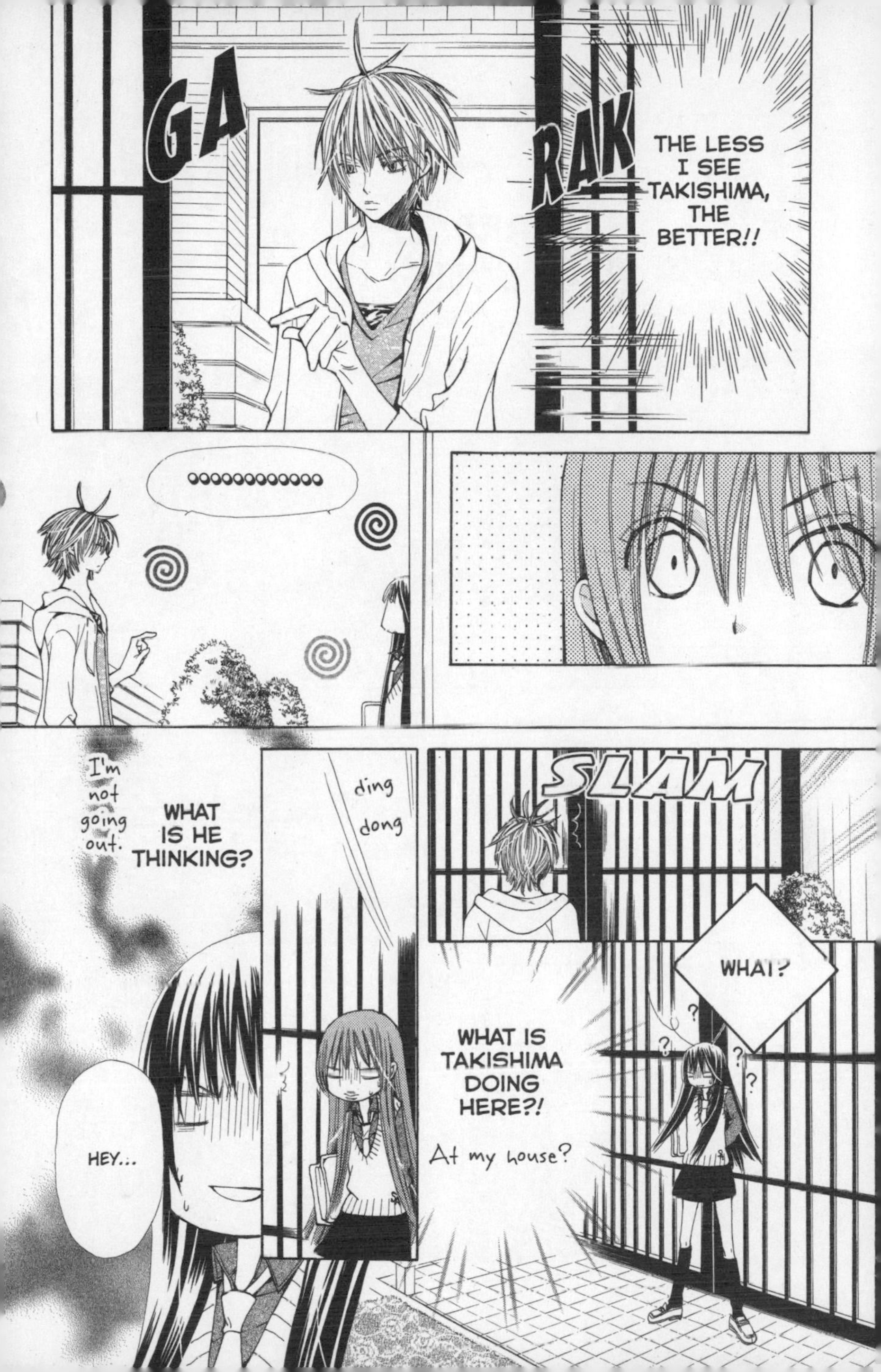
THE LESS I SEE TAKISHIMA, THE BETTER!!
GA
RAK
....
SLAM
WHAT?
WHAT IS TAKISHIMA DOING HERE?!
At my house?
ding dong
I'm not going out.
WHAT IS HE THINKING?
HEY...

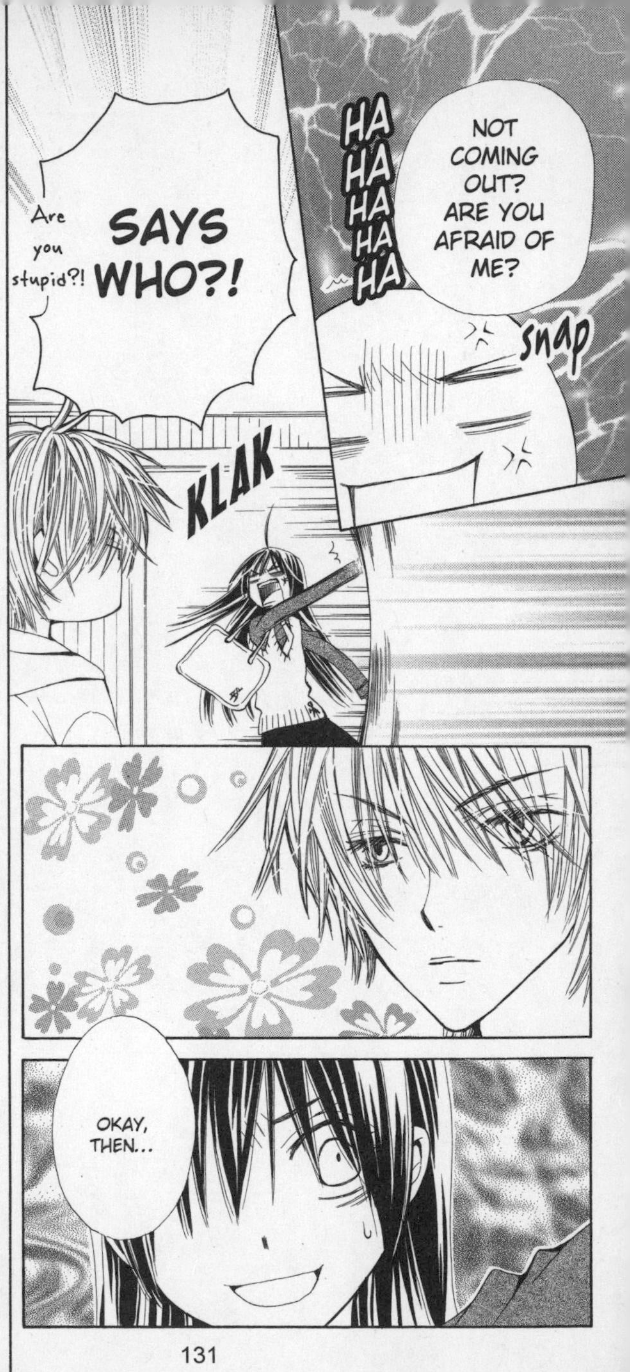
NOT COMING OUT? ARE YOU AFRAID OF ME?
HA HA HA HA HA
snap
SAYS WHO?!
Are you stupid?!
KLAK
OKAY, THEN...

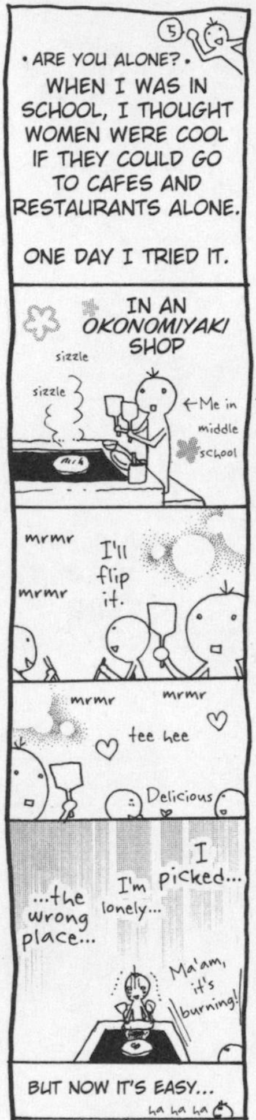
5
• ARE YOU ALONE? •
WHEN I WAS IN SCHOOL, I THOUGHT WOMEN WERE COOL IF THEY COULD GO TO CAFES AND RESTAURANTS ALONE.
ONE DAY I TRIED IT.
IN AN OKONOMIYAKI SHOP
sizzle
sizzle
←Me in middle school
mrmr
mrmr
I'll flip it.
mrmr
mrmr
tee hee
Delicious
I picked...
I'm lonely...
...the wrong place...
Ma'am, it's burning!
BUT NOW IT'S EASY...
ha ha ha

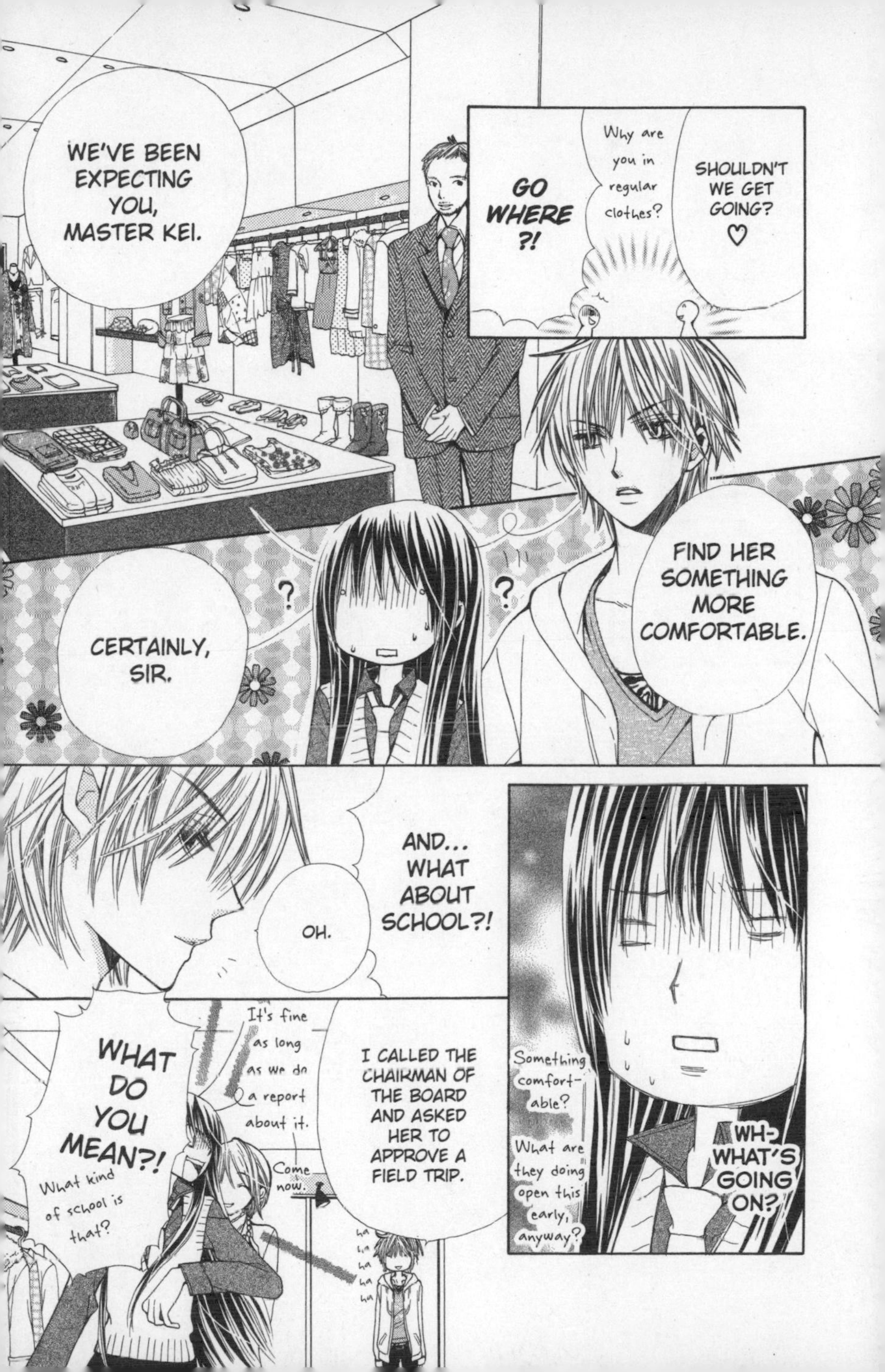
SHOULDN'T WE GET GOING? ♡
Why are you in regular clothes?
GO WHERE?!
WE'VE BEEN EXPECTING YOU, MASTER KEI.
FIND HER SOMETHING MORE COMFORTABLE.
CERTAINLY, SIR.
WH-WHAT'S GOING ON?
Something comfortable?
What are they doing open this early, anyway?
AND... WHAT ABOUT SCHOOL?!
OH.
I CALLED THE CHAIRMAN OF THE BOARD AND ASKED HER TO APPROVE A FIELD TRIP.
It's fine as long as we do a report about it.
Come now.
WHAT DO YOU MEAN?!
What kind of school is that?
ha ha ha ha ha

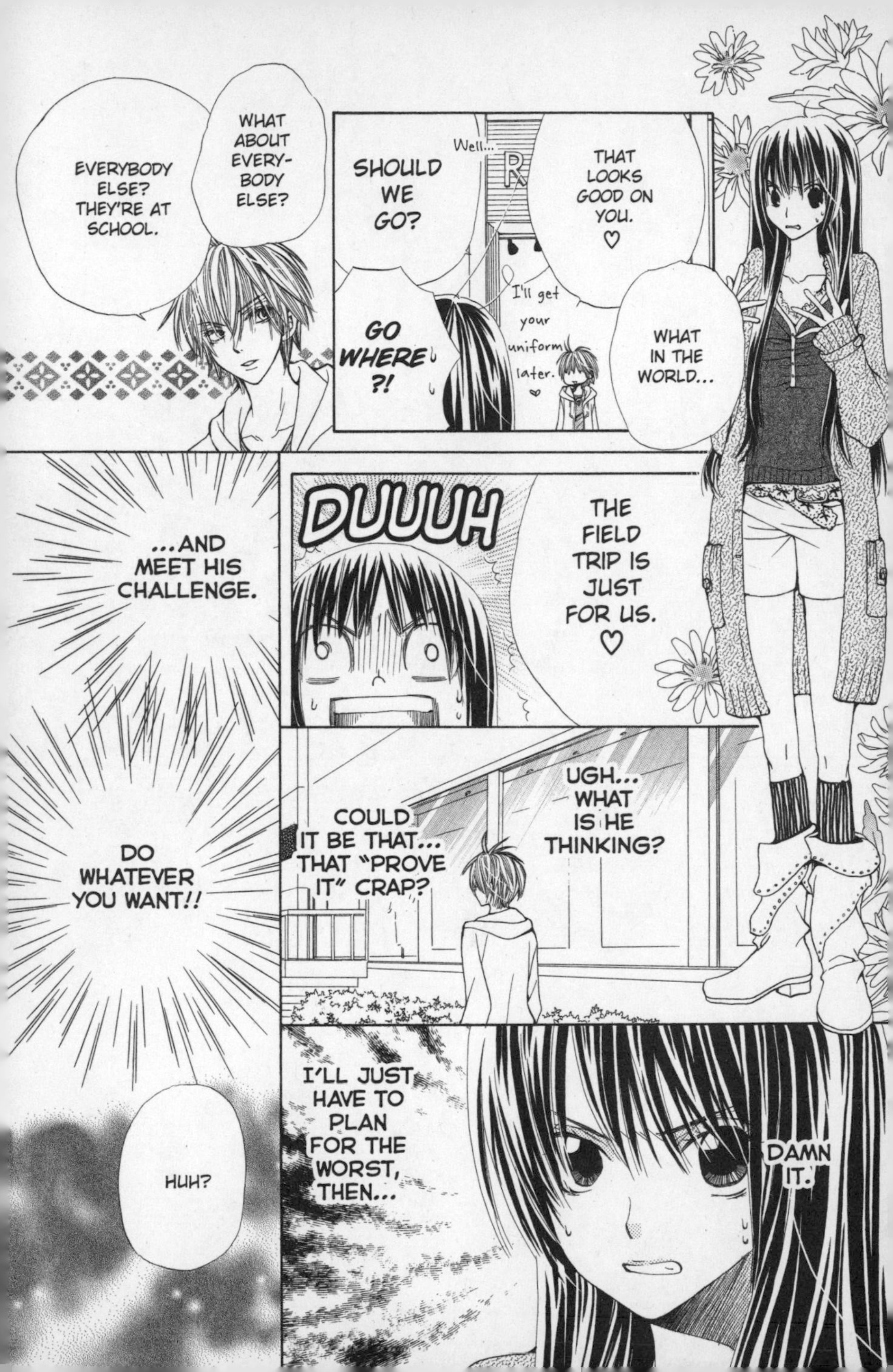
WHAT IN THE WORLD...
THAT LOOKS GOOD ON YOU. ♡
Well...
I'll get your uniform later. ♥
SHOULD WE GO?
GO WHERE?!
WHAT ABOUT EVERYBODY ELSE?
EVERYBODY ELSE? THEY'RE AT SCHOOL.
THE FIELD TRIP IS JUST FOR US. ♡
DUUUH
UGH... WHAT IS HE THINKING?
COULD IT BE THAT... THAT "PROVE IT" CRAP?
DAMN IT.
I'LL JUST HAVE TO PLAN FOR THE WORST, THEN...
...AND MEET HIS CHALLENGE.
DO WHATEVER YOU WANT!!
HUH?

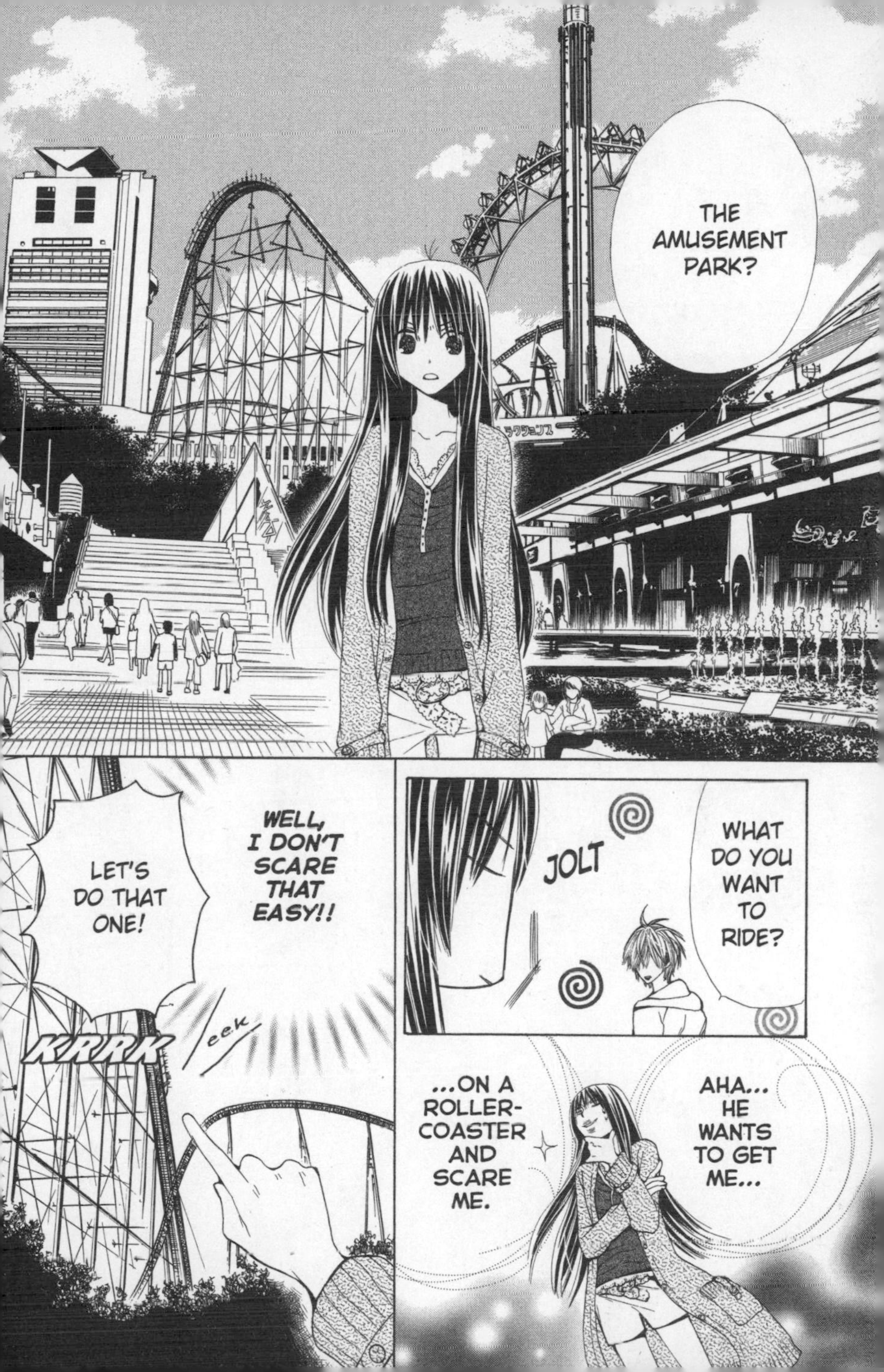
THE AMUSEMENT PARK?
WHAT DO YOU WANT TO RIDE?
JOLT
AHA... HE WANTS TO GET ME...
...ON A ROLLER-COASTER AND SCARE ME.
WELL, I DON'T SCARE THAT EASY!!
LET'S DO THAT ONE!
eek
KRRK

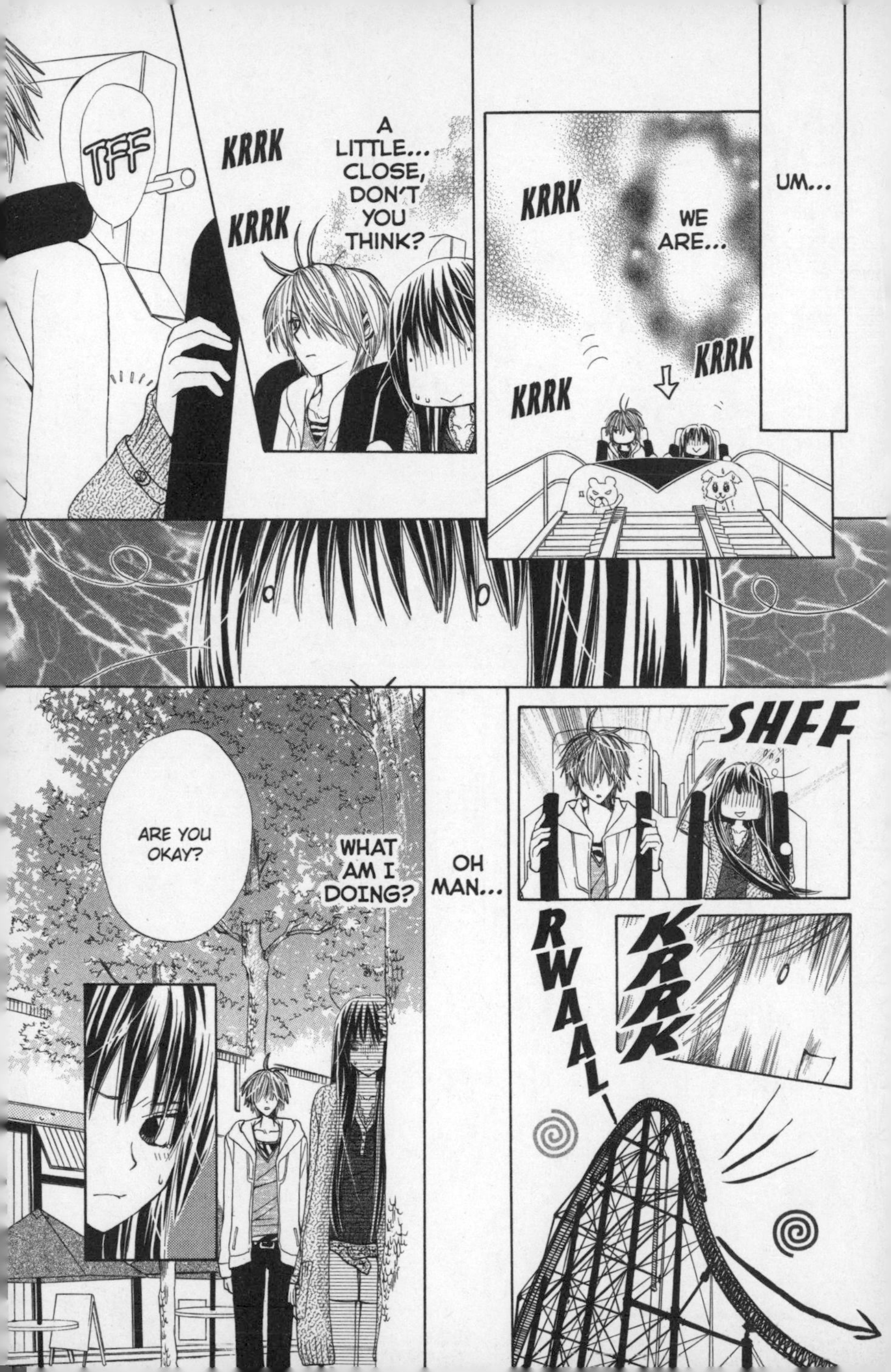
UM...
WE ARE...
KRRK
KRRK
KRRK
A LITTLE... CLOSE, DON'T YOU THINK?
KRRK
KRRK
TFF
SHFF
KRRK
RWAAL
OH MAN...
WHAT AM I DOING?
ARE YOU OKAY?

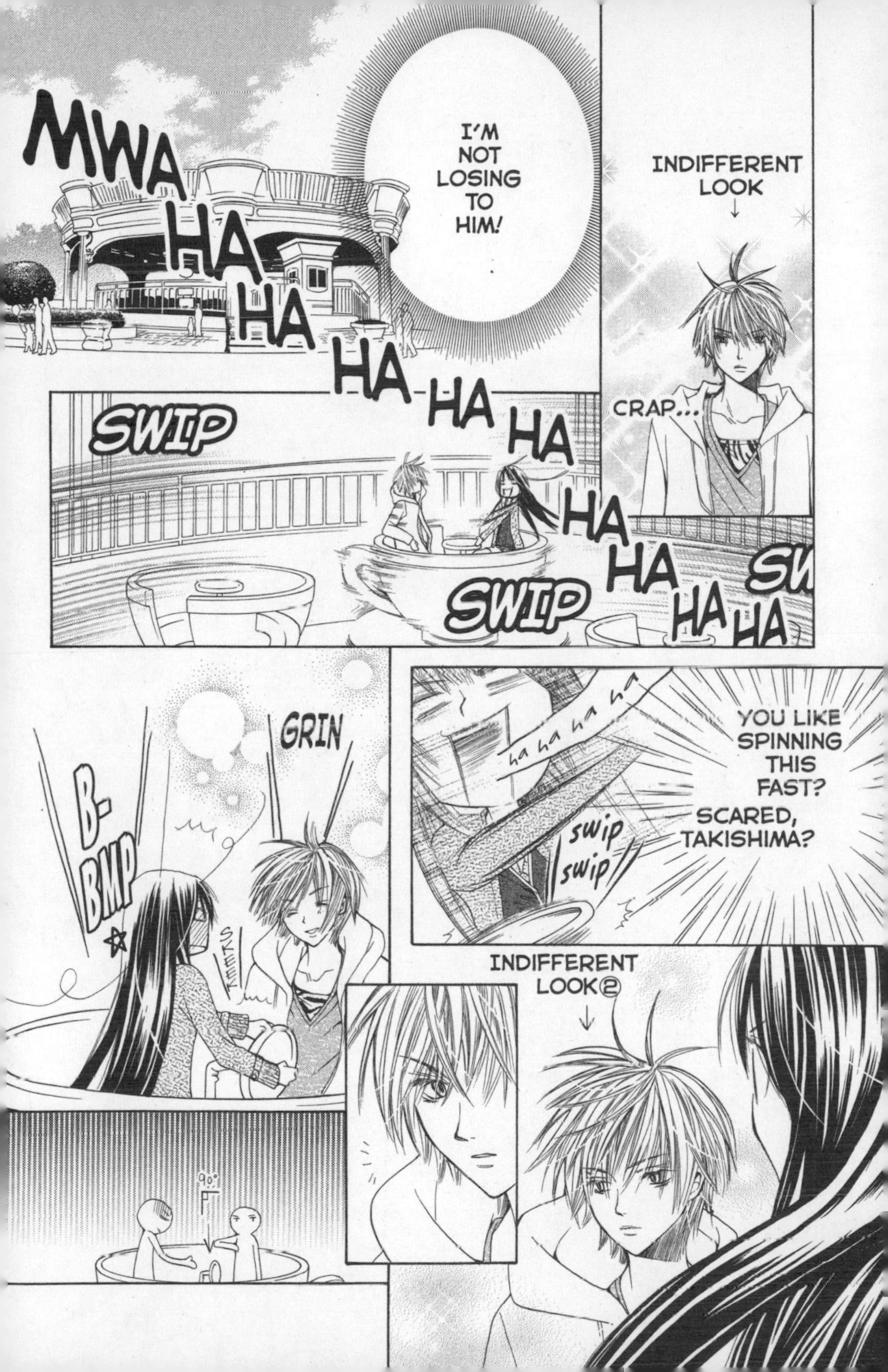

INDIFFERENT LOOK
↓
CRAP...
MWA HA HA HA HA HA HA HA HA HA
I'M NOT LOSING TO HIM!
SWIP
SWIP
SW
ha ha ha ha ha
YOU LIKE SPINNING THIS FAST?
SCARED, TAKISHIMA?
swip swip
GRIN
B-BMP
SKREE
INDIFFERENT LOOK②
↓
90°

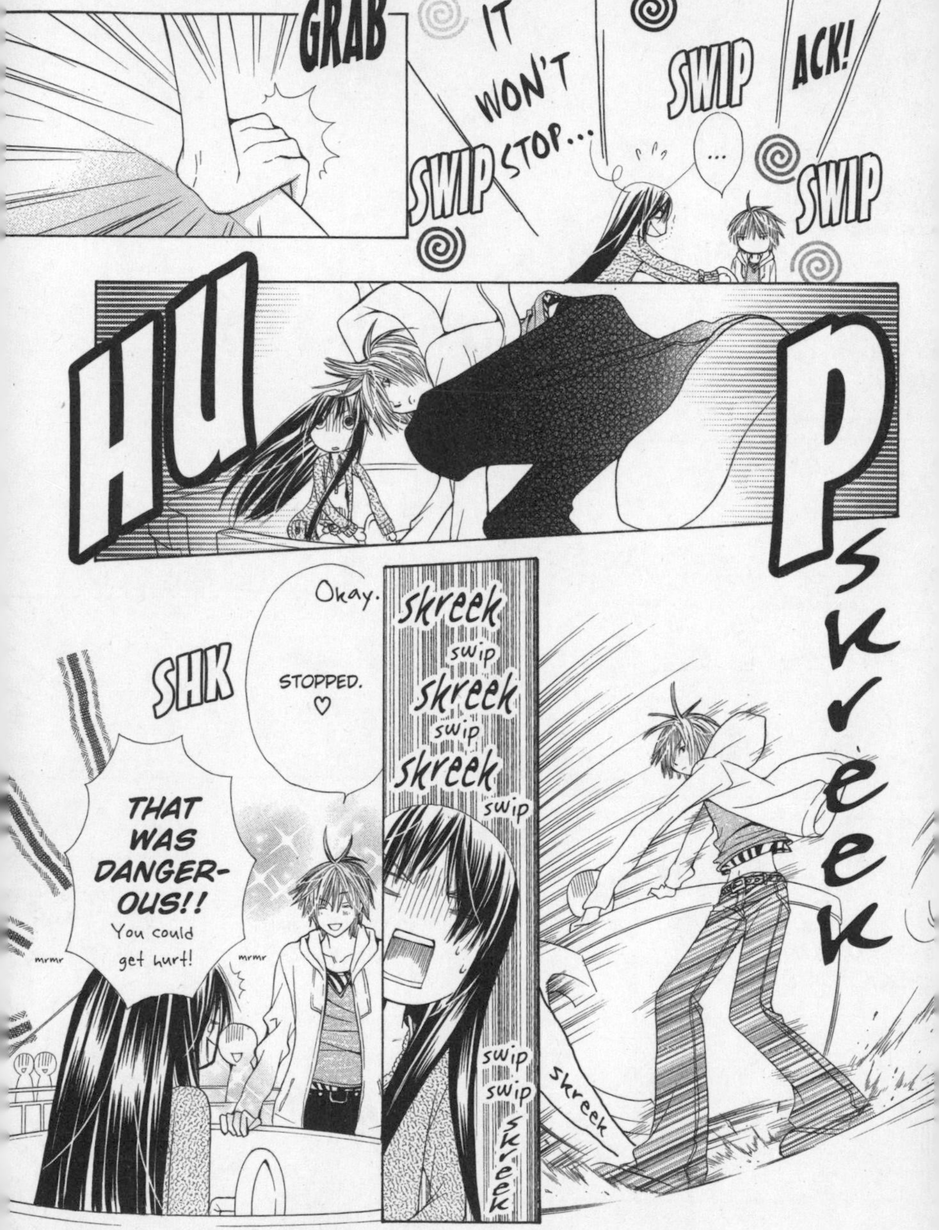
ACK!
SWIP
SWIP
...
IT WON'T STOP...
SWIP
GRAB
HUP
skreek
skreek swip skreek swip skreek swip
swip swip skreek
skreek
Okay.
STOPPED. ♡
SHK
THAT WAS DANGER-OUS!! You could get hurt!
mrmr
mrmr

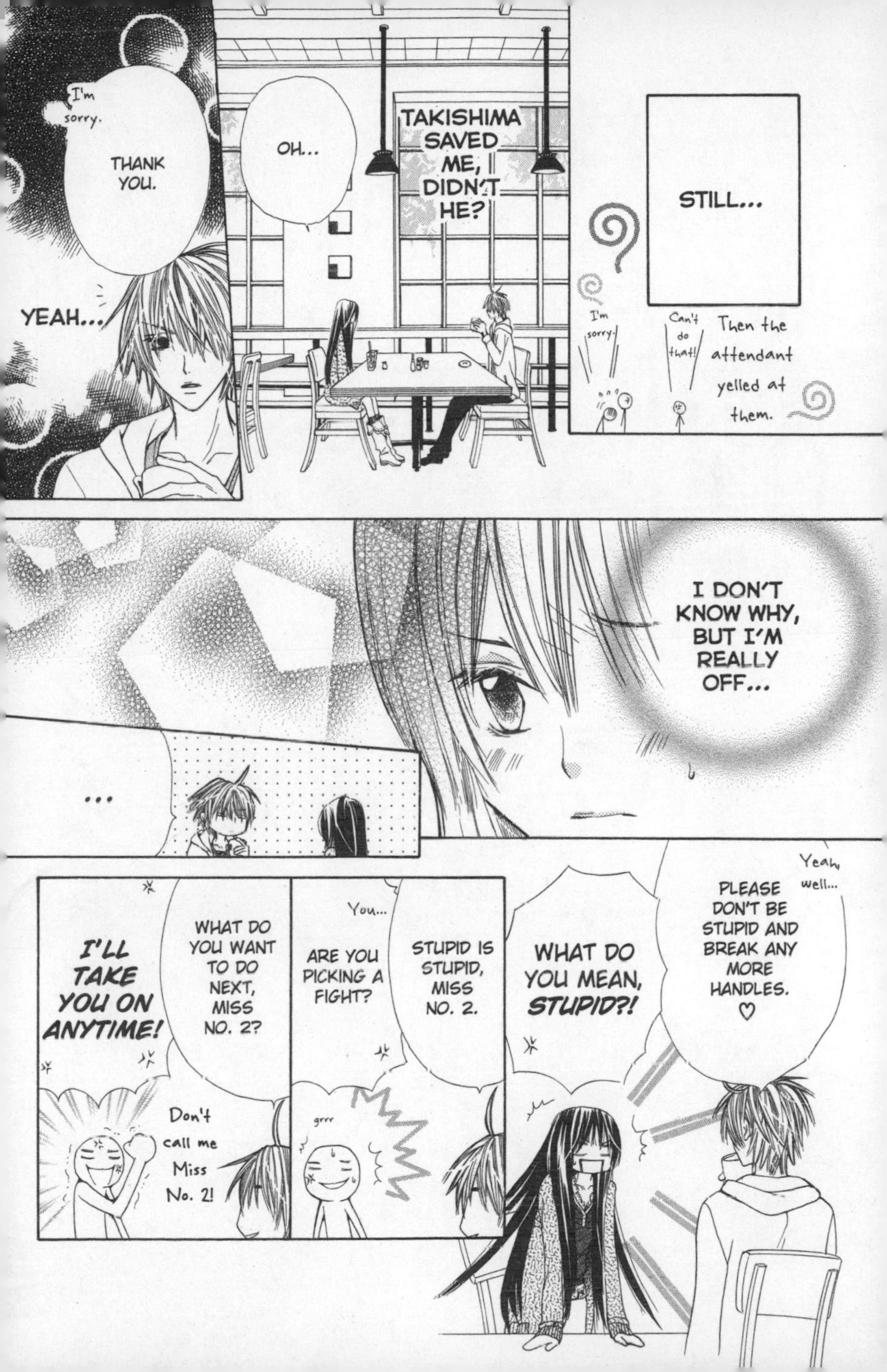
STILL...
Then the attendant yelled at them.
Can't do that!
I'm sorry.
TAKISHIMA SAVED ME, DIDN'T HE?
OH...
I'm sorry.
THANK YOU.
YEAH...
I DON'T KNOW WHY, BUT I'M REALLY OFF...
...
Yeah, well...
PLEASE DON'T BE STUPID AND BREAK ANY MORE HANDLES. ♡
WHAT DO YOU MEAN, STUPID?!
STUPID IS STUPID, MISS NO. 2.
You...
ARE YOU PICKING A FIGHT?
grrr
WHAT DO YOU WANT TO DO NEXT, MISS NO. 2?
I'LL TAKE YOU ON ANYTIME!
Don't call me Miss No. 2!

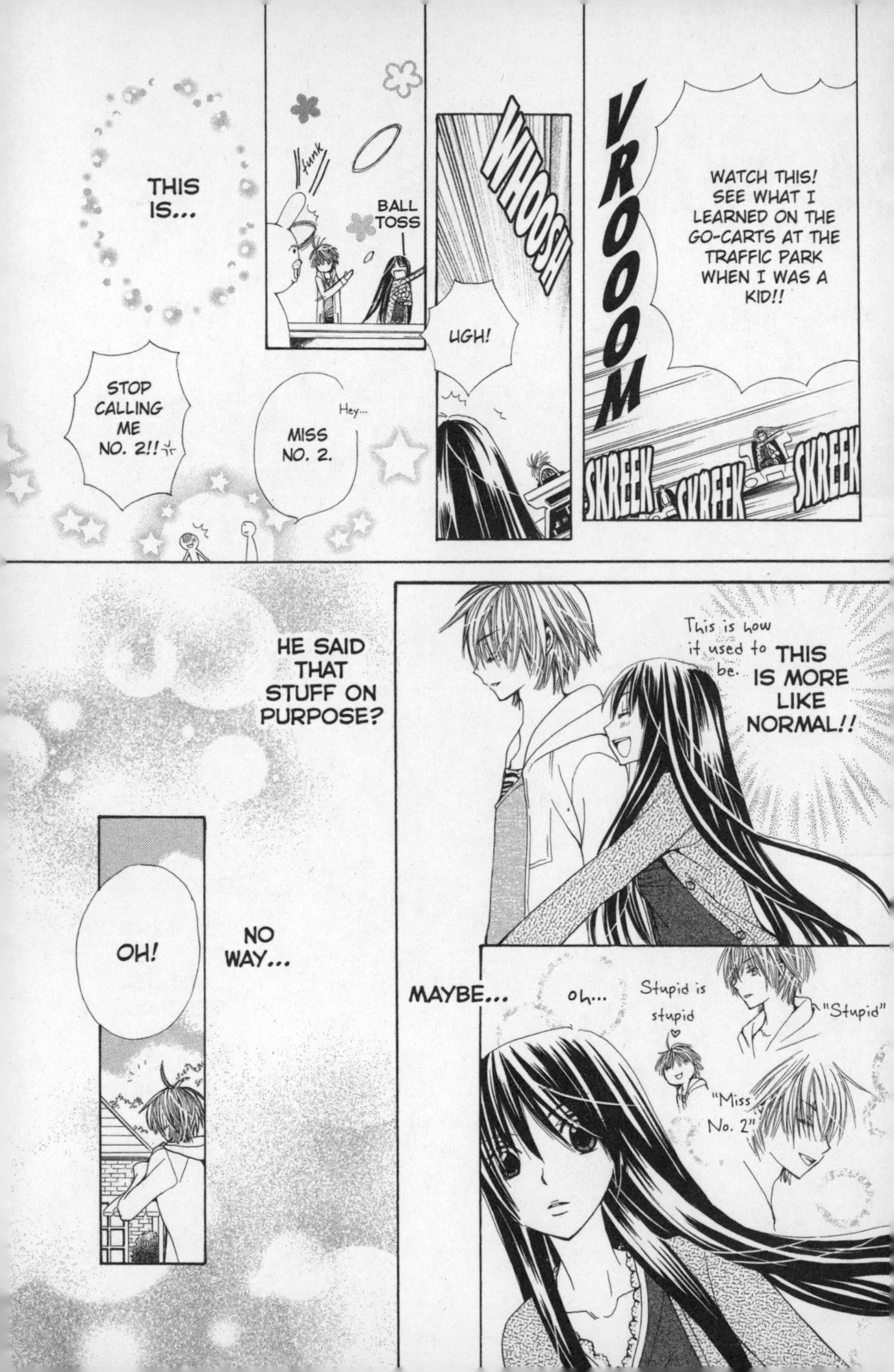
VROOOM
WATCH THIS! SEE WHAT I LEARNED ON THE GO-CARTS AT THE TRAFFIC PARK WHEN I WAS A KID!!
SKREEK
SKREEK
SKREEK
WHOOSH
UGH!
funk
BALL TOSS
THIS IS...
Hey...
MISS NO. 2.
STOP CALLING ME NO. 2!!
This is how it used to be...
THIS IS MORE LIKE NORMAL!!
MAYBE...
oh...
Stupid is stupid
"Stupid"
"Miss No. 2"
HE SAID THAT STUFF ON PURPOSE?
NO WAY...
OH!

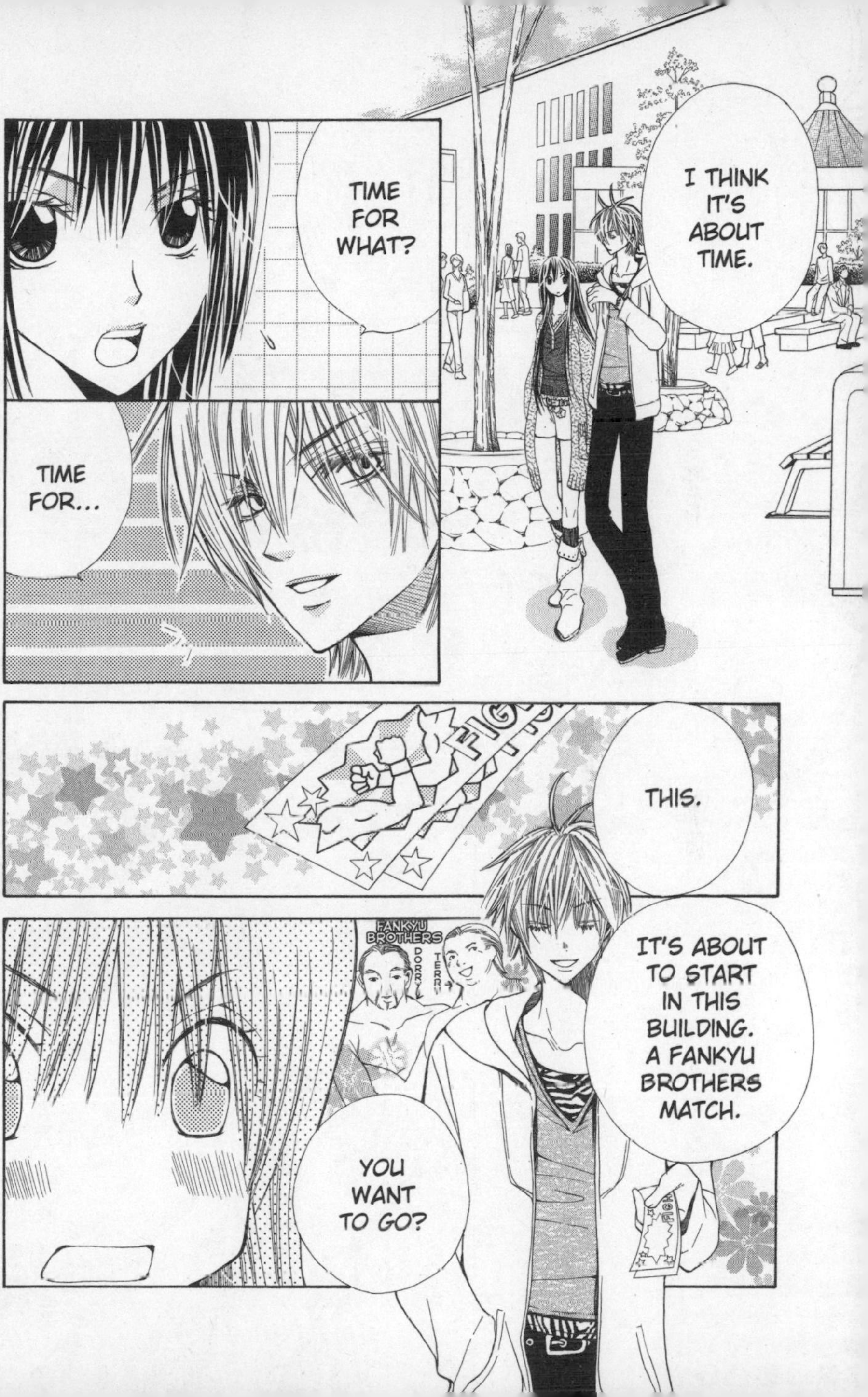
I THINK IT'S ABOUT TIME.
TIME FOR WHAT?
TIME FOR...
THIS.
IT'S ABOUT TO START IN THIS BUILDING. A FANKYU BROTHERS MATCH.
FANKYU BROTHERS
DORRY
TERRY
YOU WANT TO GO?

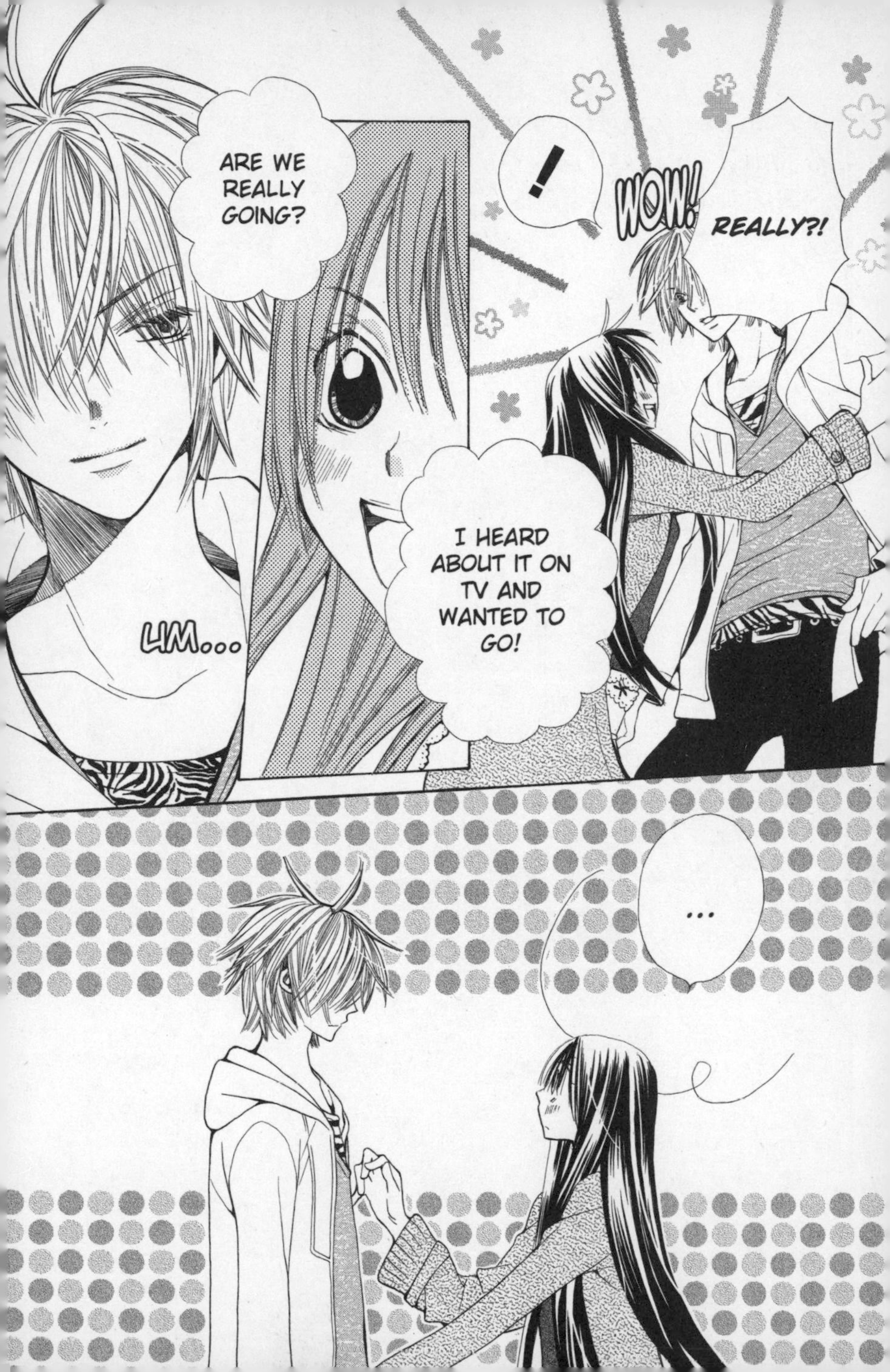
!
WOW!
REALLY?!
I HEARD ABOUT IT ON TV AND WANTED TO GO!
ARE WE REALLY GOING?
UM...
...

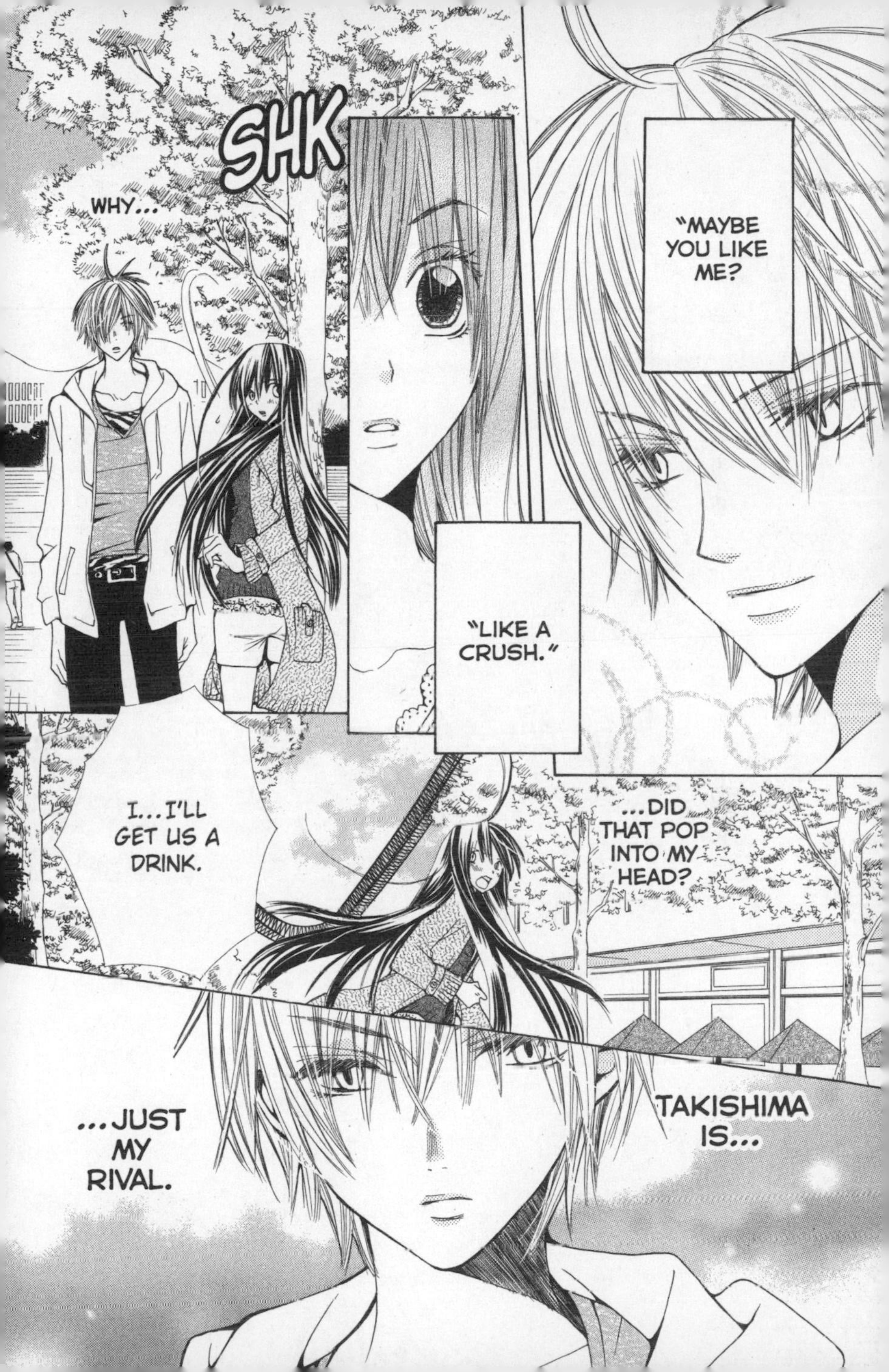
"MAYBE YOU LIKE ME?
"LIKE A CRUSH."
SHK
WHY...
...DID THAT POP INTO MY HEAD?
I...I'LL GET US A DRINK.
TAKISHIMA IS...
...JUST MY RIVAL.

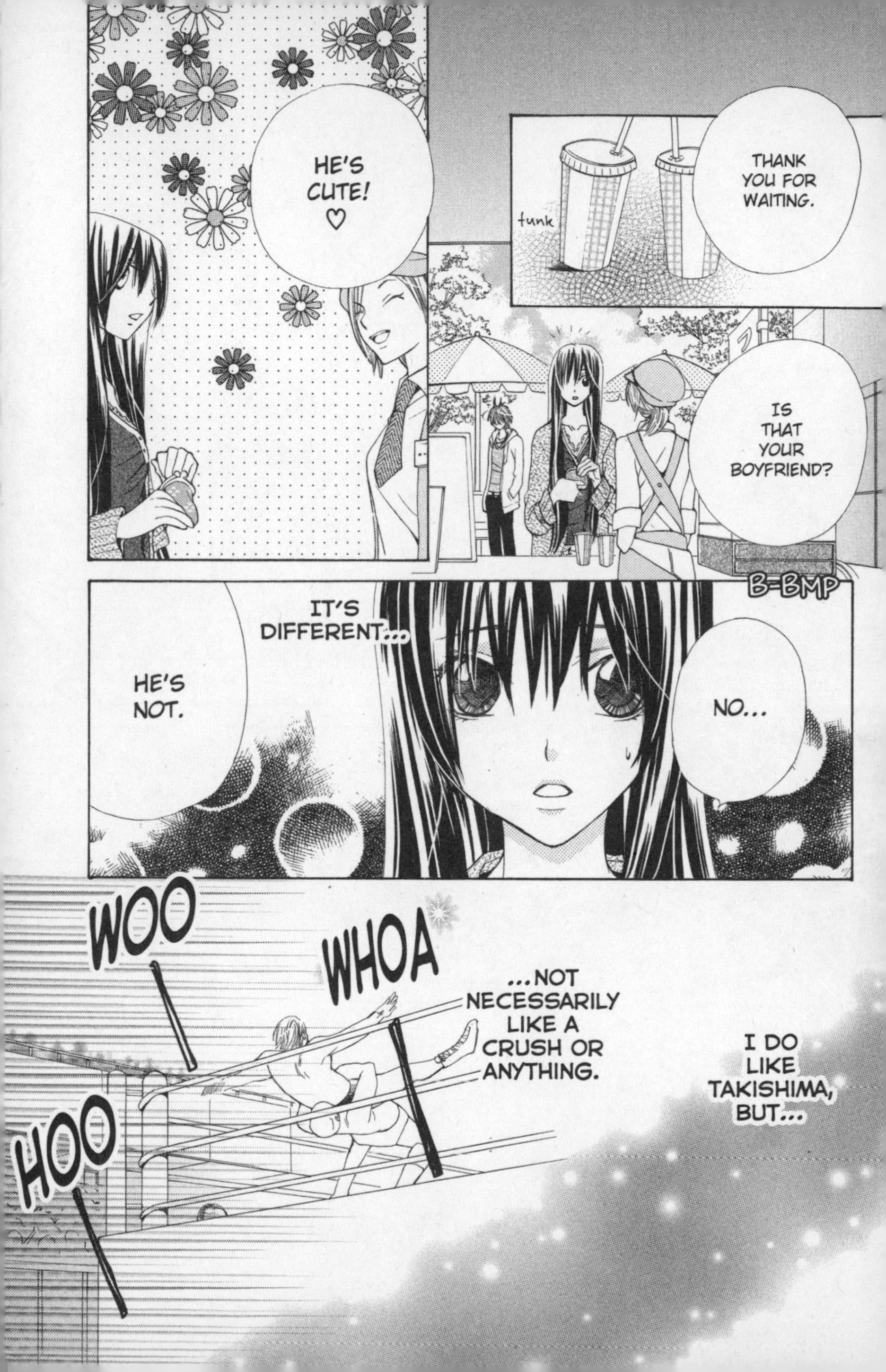
THANK YOU FOR WAITING.
funk
IS THAT YOUR BOYFRIEND?
HE'S CUTE! ♡
B-BMP
NO...
IT'S DIFFERENT...
HE'S NOT.
I DO LIKE TAKISHIMA, BUT...
...NOT NECESSARILY LIKE A CRUSH OR ANYTHING.
WOO
WHOA
HOO

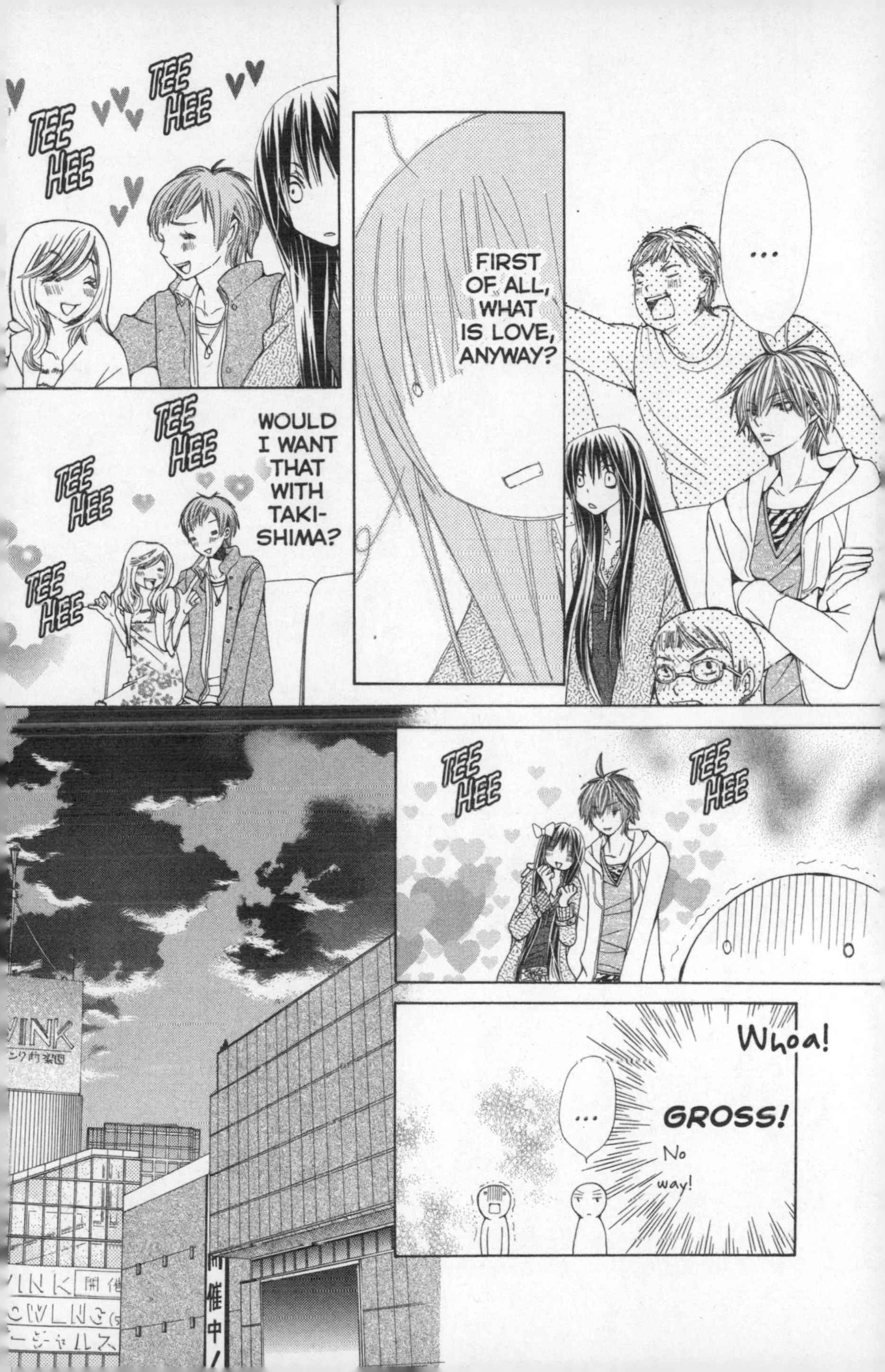
...
FIRST OF ALL, WHAT IS LOVE, ANYWAY?
TEE HEE
TEE HEE
WOULD I WANT THAT WITH TAKI-SHIMA?
TEE HEE
TEE HEE
TEE HEE
TEE HEE
TEE HEE
Whoa!
GROSS!
No way!
...

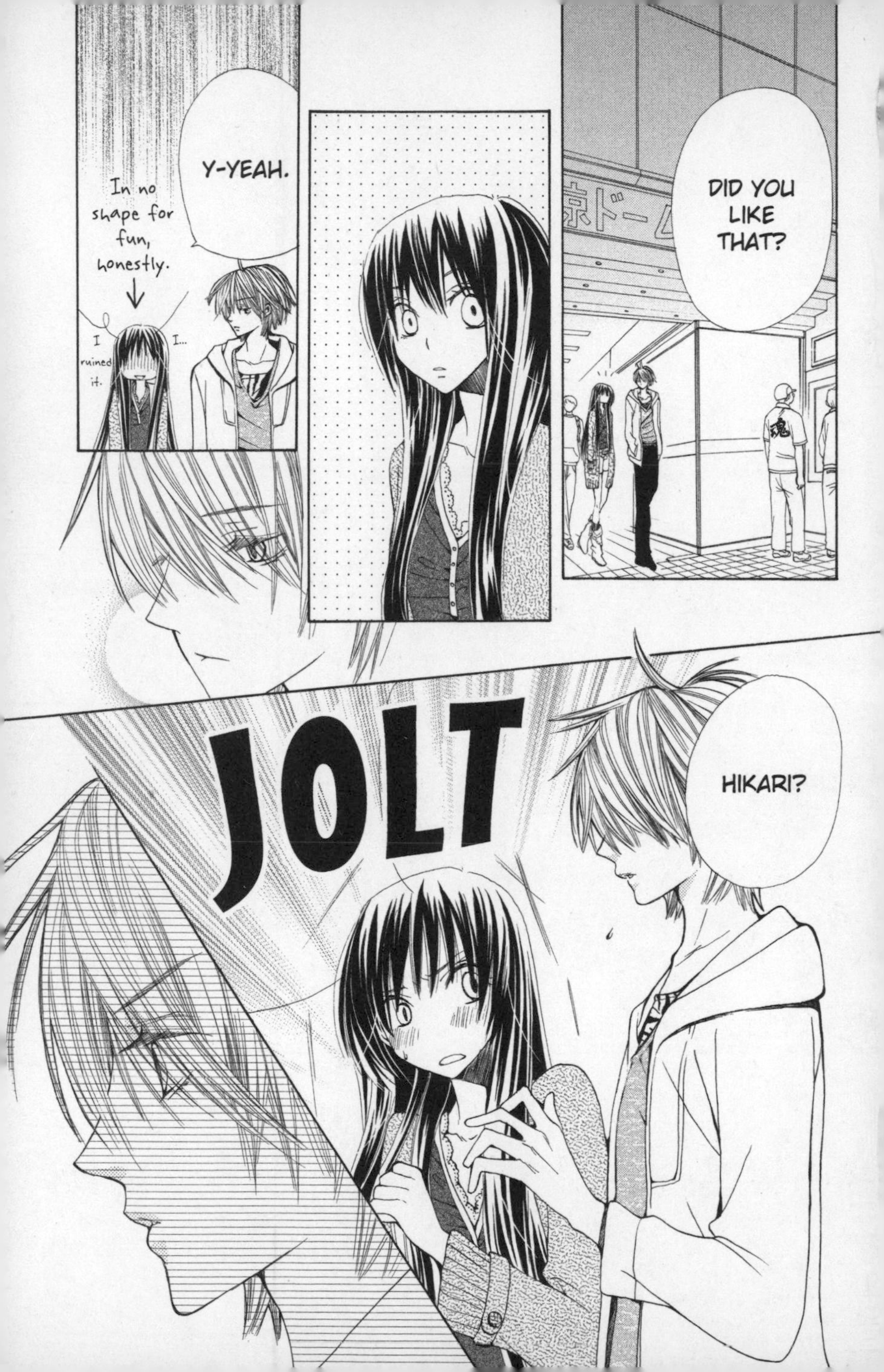
DID YOU LIKE THAT?
Y-YEAH.
In no shape for fun, honestly.
I...
I ruined it.
HIKARI?
JOLT

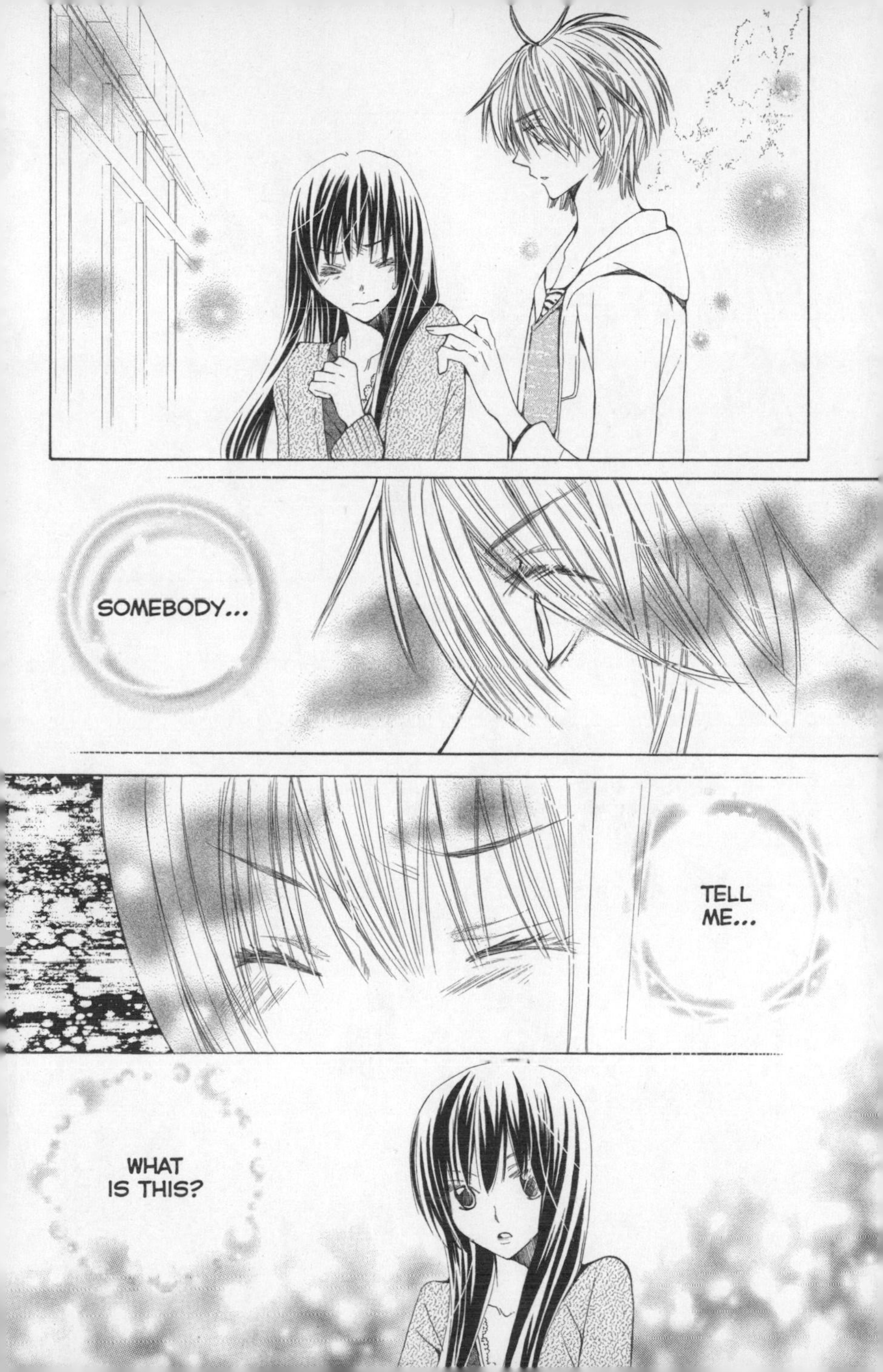
SOMEBODY...
TELL ME...
WHAT IS THIS?

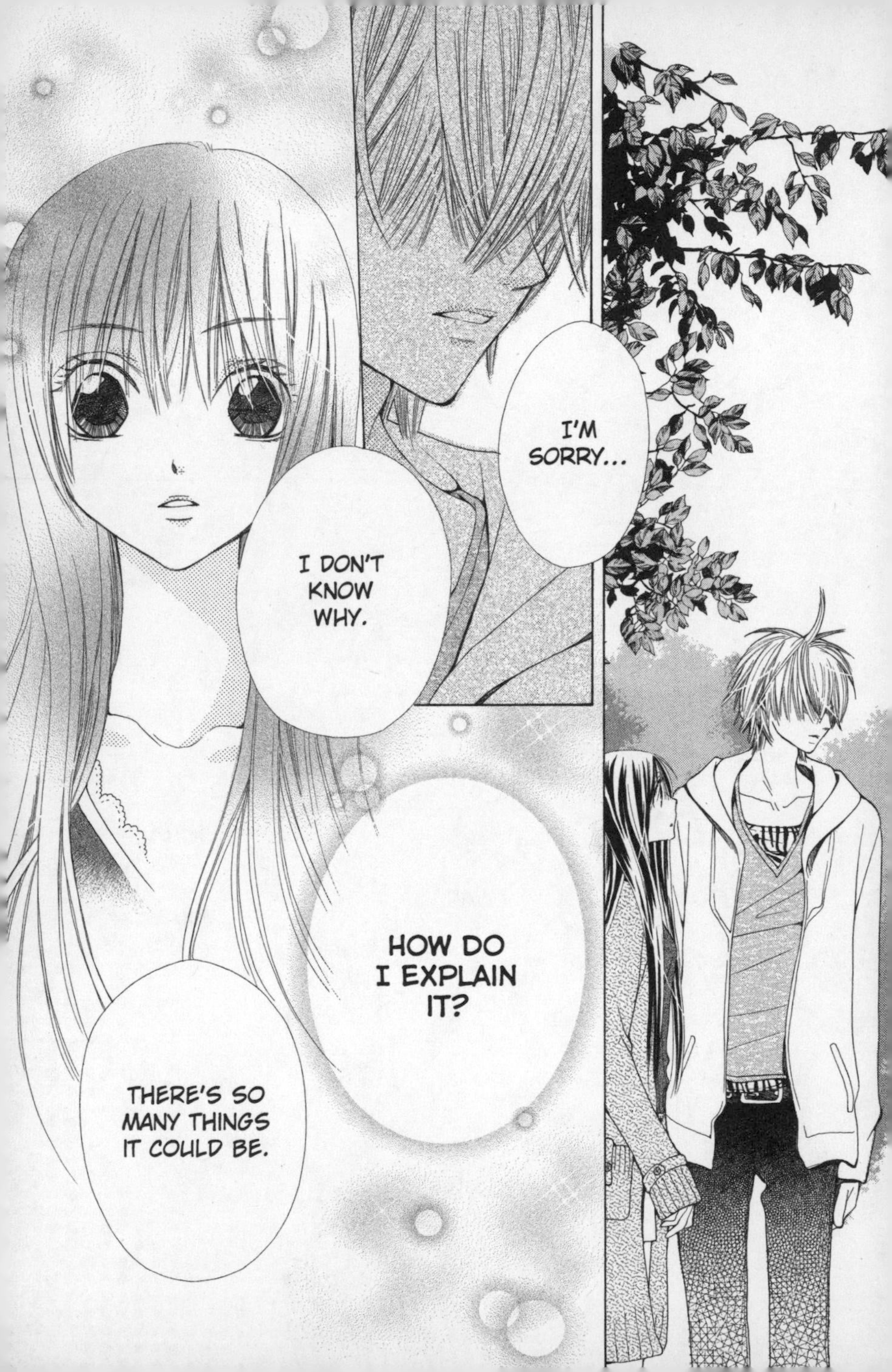
I'M SORRY...
I DON'T KNOW WHY.
HOW DO I EXPLAIN IT?
THERE'S SO MANY THINGS IT COULD BE.

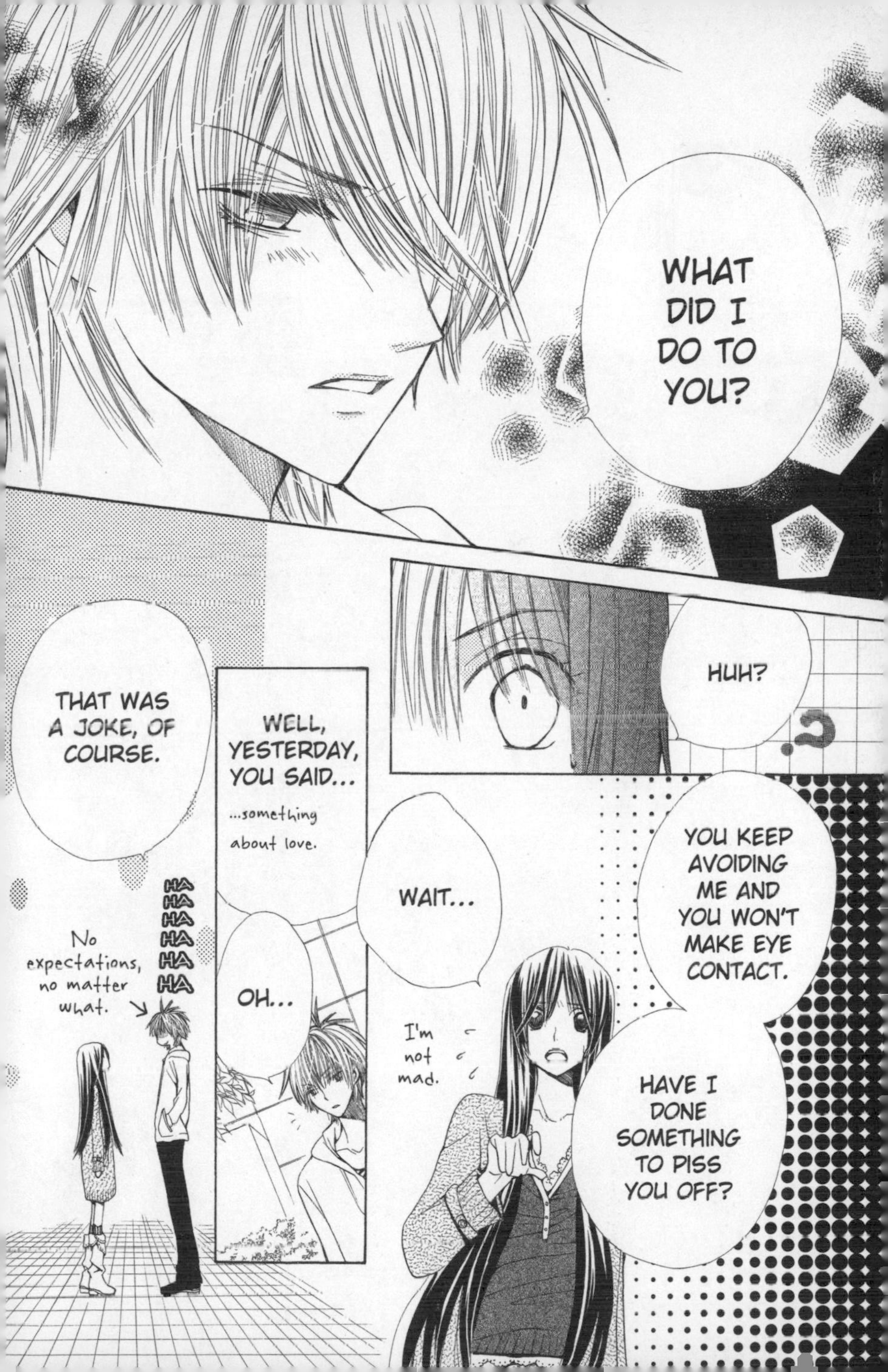
WHAT DID I DO TO YOU?
HUH?
YOU KEEP AVOIDING ME AND YOU WON'T MAKE EYE CONTACT.
HAVE I DONE SOMETHING TO PISS YOU OFF?
I'm not mad.
WAIT...
OH...
WELL, YESTERDAY, YOU SAID...
...something about love.
THAT WAS A JOKE, OF COURSE.
HA HA HA HA HA HA
No expectations, no matter what.

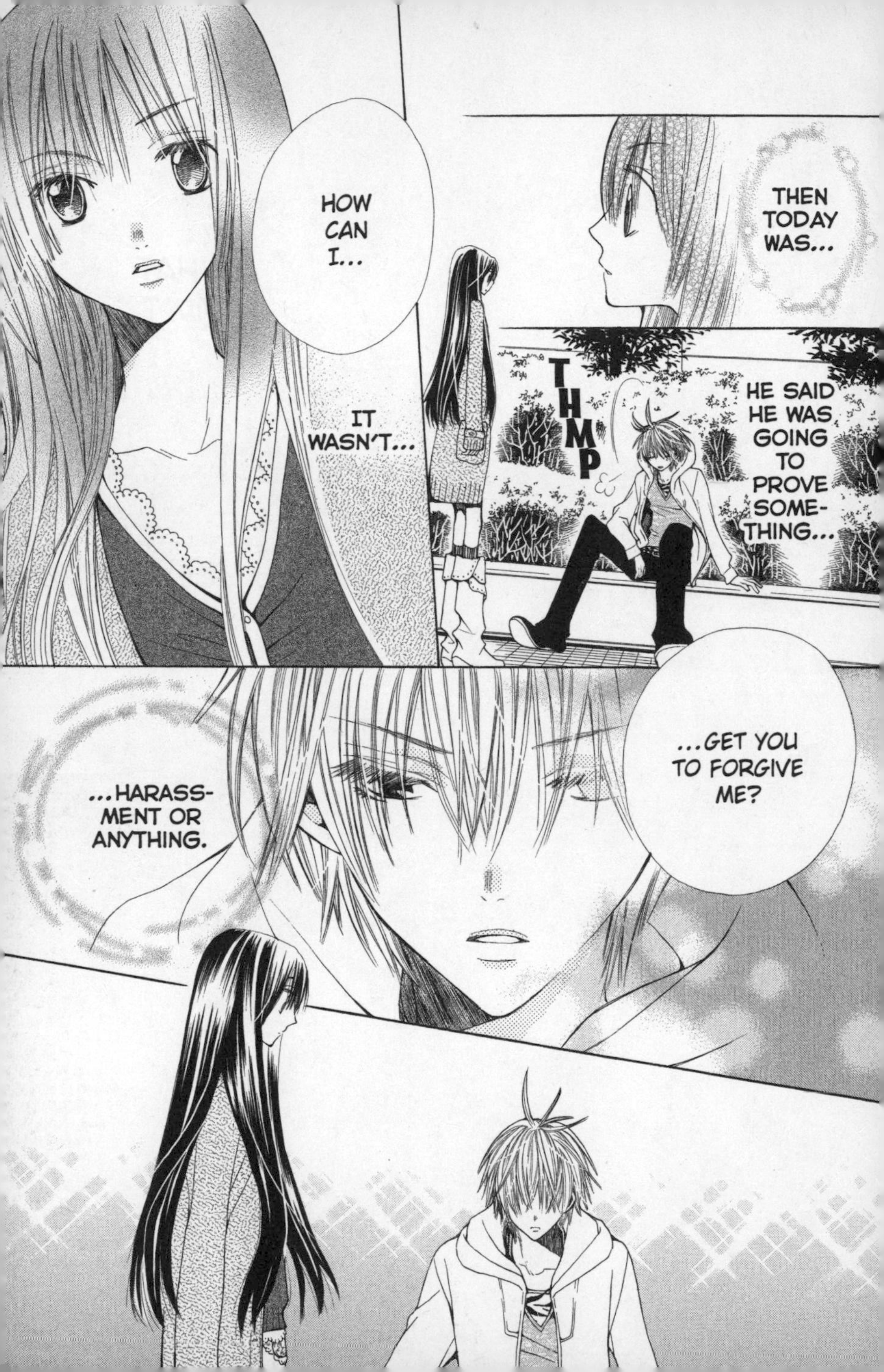
THEN TODAY WAS...
HE SAID HE WAS GOING TO PROVE SOME-THING...
THMP
HOW CAN I...
IT WASN'T...
...GET YOU TO FORGIVE ME?
...HARASS-MENT OR ANYTHING.

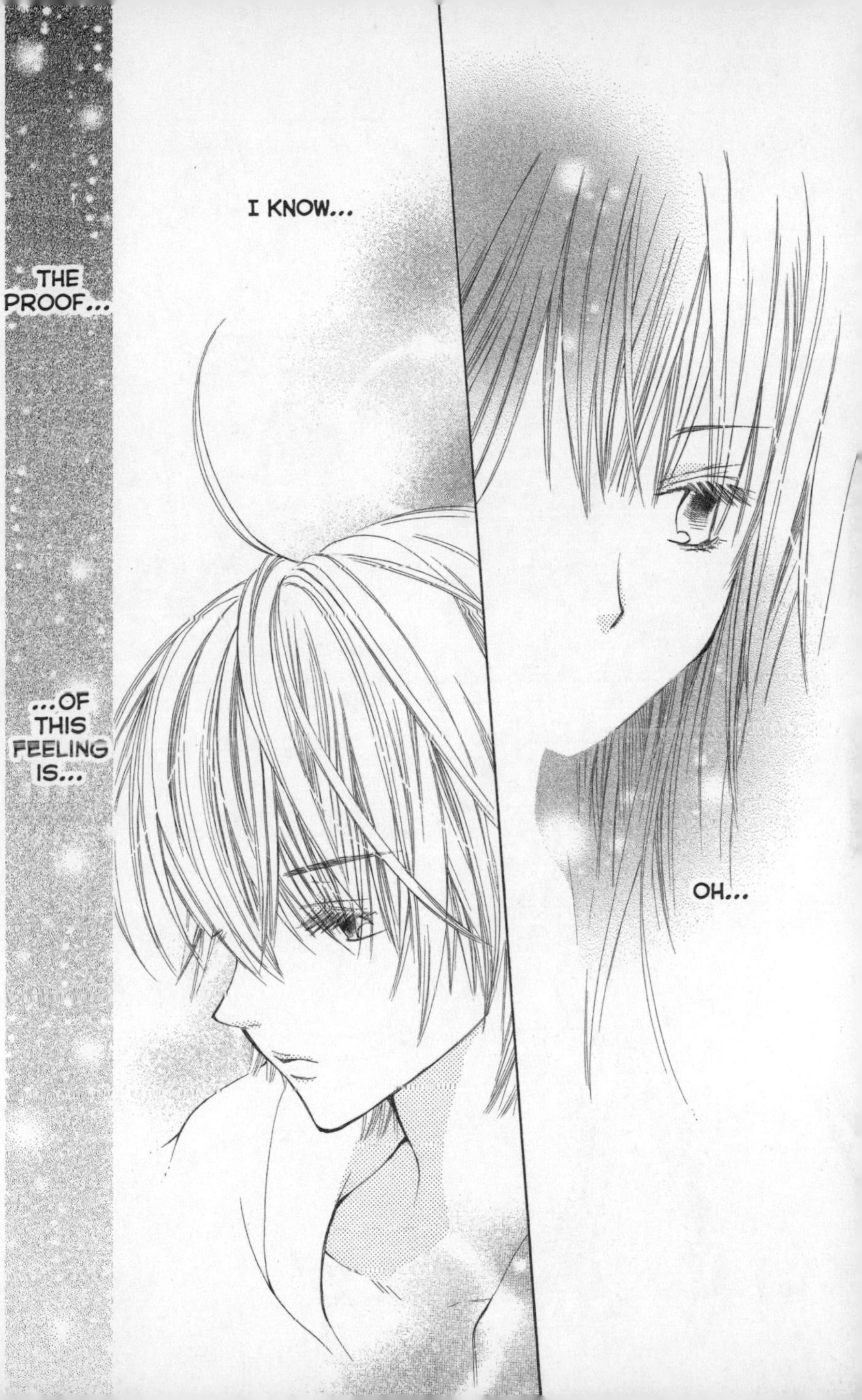
OH...
I KNOW...
THE PROOF...
...OF THIS FEELING IS...

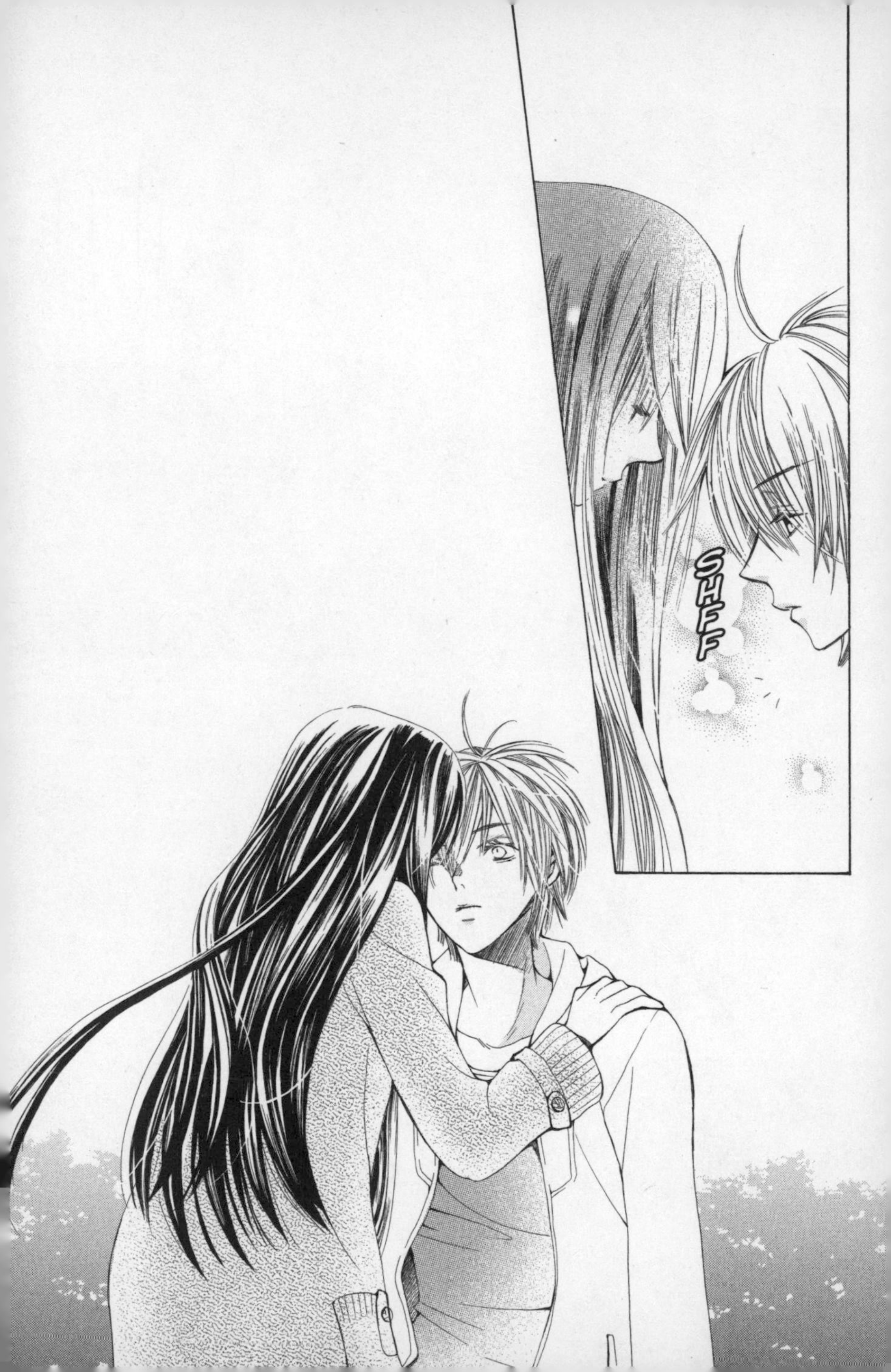
SHFF

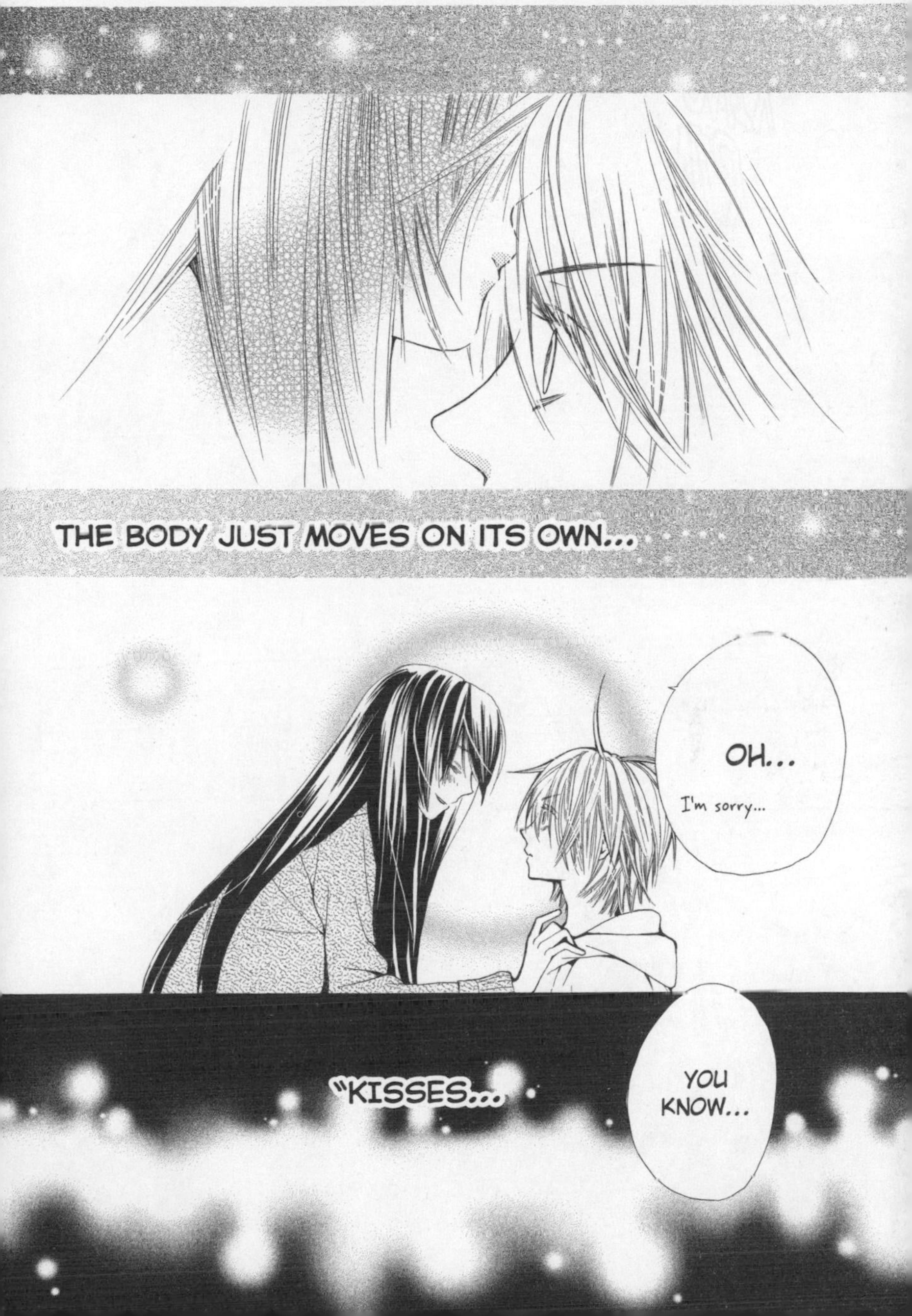
THE BODY JUST MOVES ON ITS OWN...
OH...
I'm sorry...
YOU KNOW...
"KISSES...

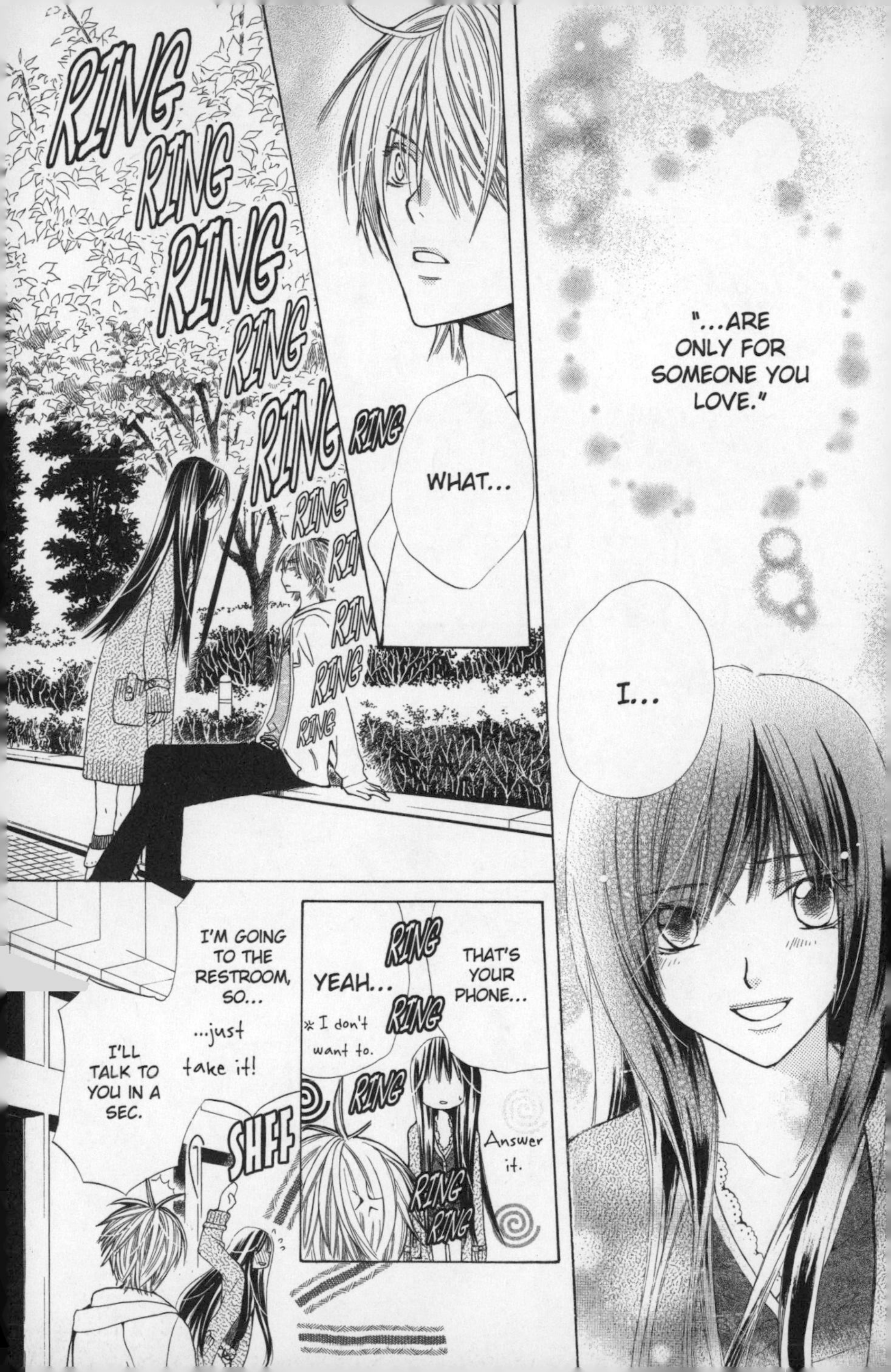
"...ARE ONLY FOR SOMEONE YOU LOVE."
I...
WHAT...
RING RING RING RING RING RING RING RING RING RING RING
Answer it.
THAT'S YOUR PHONE...
RING
YEAH...
RING
*I don't want to.
RING
RING RING
I'M GOING TO THE RESTROOM, SO...
...just take it!
I'LL TALK TO YOU IN A SEC.
SHFF

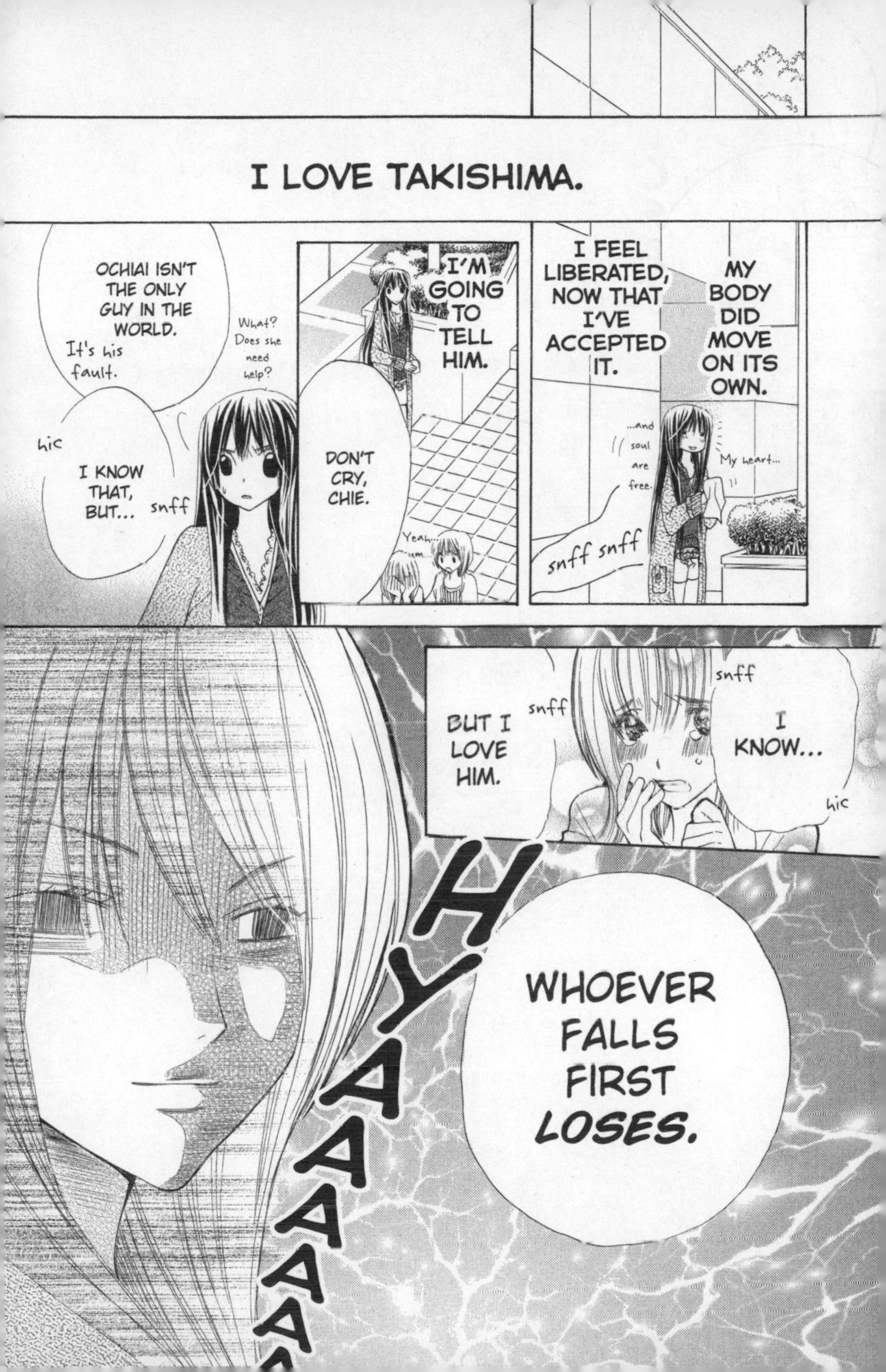
I LOVE TAKISHIMA.
MY BODY DID MOVE ON ITS OWN.
I FEEL LIBERATED, NOW THAT I'VE ACCEPTED IT.
My heart...
...and soul are free.
snff snff
I'M GOING TO TELL HIM.
DON'T CRY, CHIE.
Yeah... um...
What? Does she need help?
OCHIAI ISN'T THE ONLY GUY IN THE WORLD.
It's his fault.
hic
I KNOW THAT, BUT...
snff
snff
I KNOW...
hic
snff
BUT I LOVE HIM.
HYAAAAAA
WHOEVER FALLS FIRST LOSES.

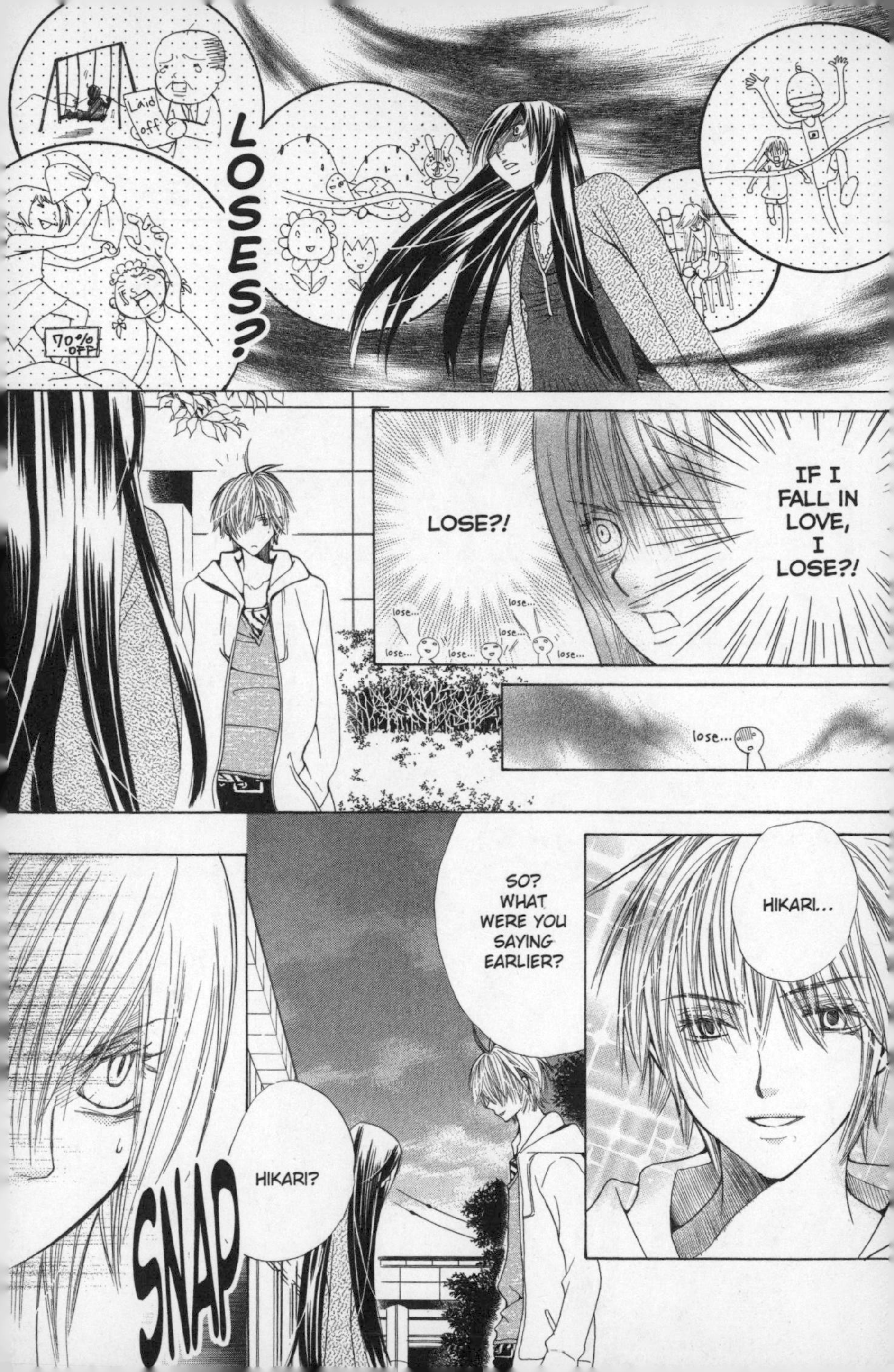
Laid off
70% OFF
LOSES?!
IF I FALL IN LOVE, I LOSE?!
LOSE?!
lose...
lose...
lose...
lose...
lose...
lose...
lose...
HIKARI...
SO? WHAT WERE YOU SAYING EARLIER?
HIKARI?
SNAP

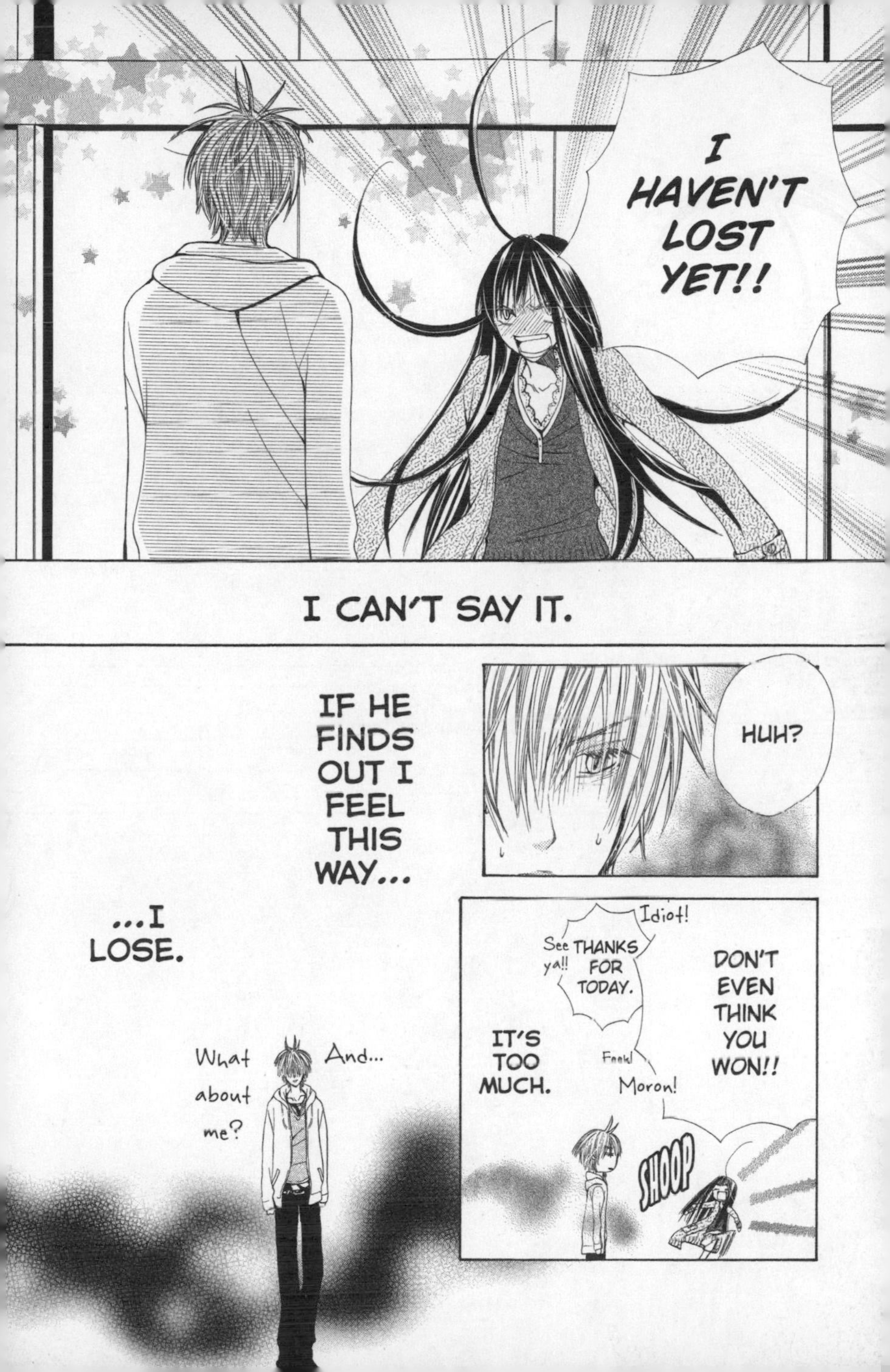
I HAVEN'T LOST YET!!
I CAN'T SAY IT.
HUH?
IF HE FINDS OUT I FEEL THIS WAY...
DON'T EVEN THINK YOU WON!!
Idiot!
THANKS FOR TODAY.
See ya!!
Fool!
Moron!
SHOOP
IT'S TOO MUCH.
...I LOSE.
And...
What about me?

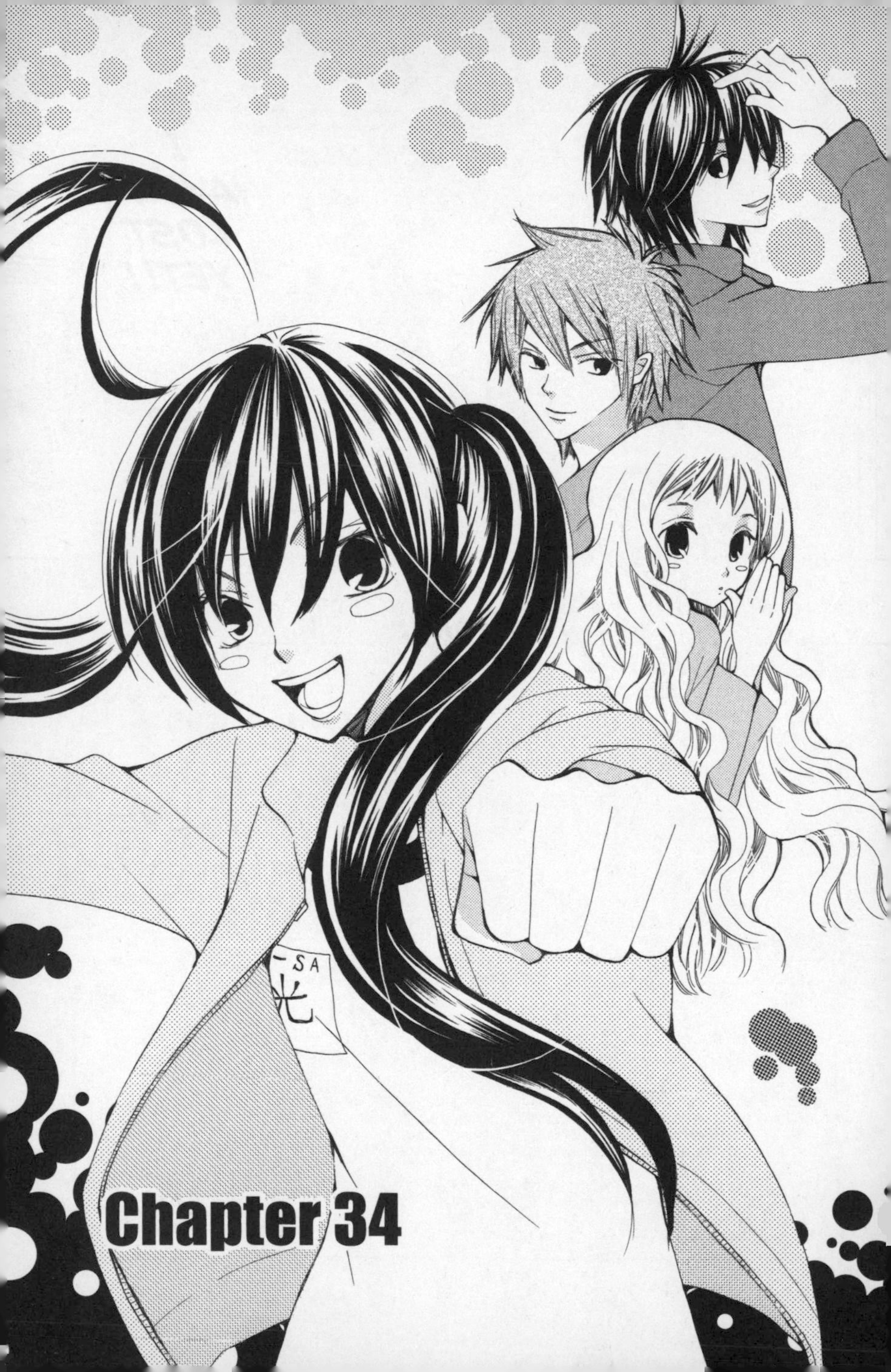
SA
光
Chapter 34

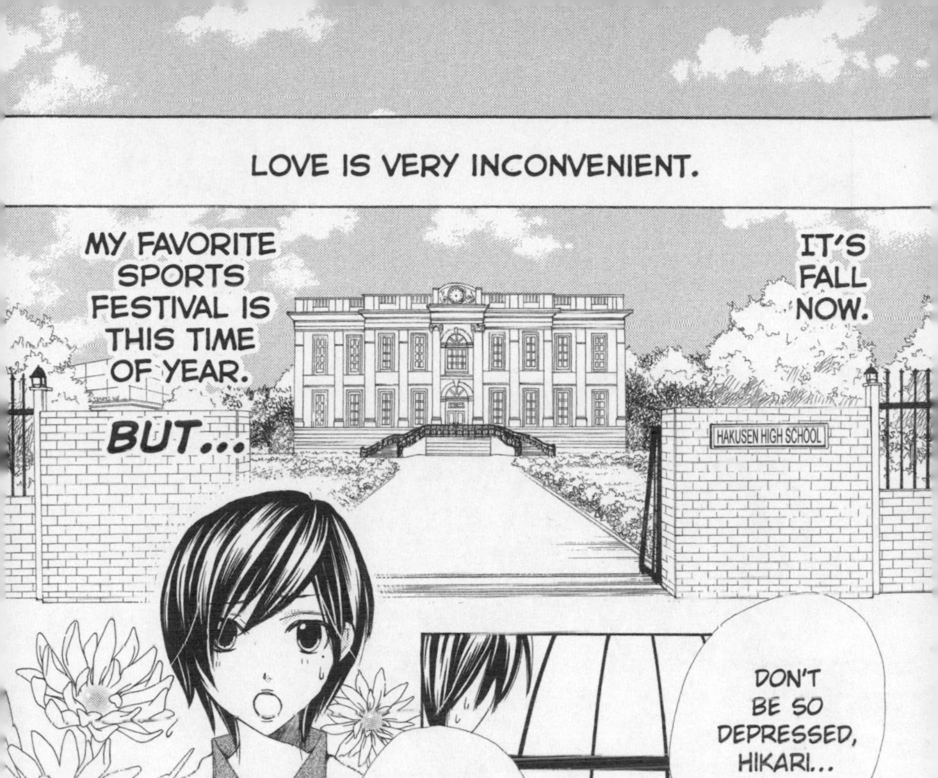
LOVE IS VERY INCONVENIENT.
IT'S FALL NOW.
MY FAVORITE SPORTS FESTIVAL IS THIS TIME OF YEAR.
BUT...
HAKUSEN HIGH SCHOOL
DON'T BE SO DEPRESSED, HIKARI...
IT WAS JUST A FLUKE THAT YOU DIDN'T DO WELL.

• THIS AND THAT •

• THANK YOU SO MUCH FOR READING *S•A!* I WANT TO GET BETTER SO THAT YOU CAN ENJOY IT MORE AND MORE.

• AND TO MY ASSISTANTS WHO DRAW THE BACKGROUNDS AND FINISH UP THE PICTURES, TO THE EDITORS WHO HELP WITH MY WORK, TO MY FAMILY, MY FRIENDS AND--AND ESPECIALLY TO ALL OF YOU WHO READ MY WORK, THANK YOU SO, SO MUCH! I SIMPLY CANNOT EXPRESS HOW THANKFUL I AM! THANK YOU VERY MUCH!

YOUR LETTERS AND SUPPORT REALLY MAKE ME HAPPY. I'M VERY SORRY FOR TAKING SO LONG TO RESPOND AND FOR USING PRE-PRINTED POSTCARDS...I REALLY WANT TO DO BETTER..

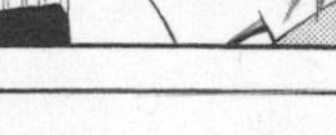
Thank you...
...very much!

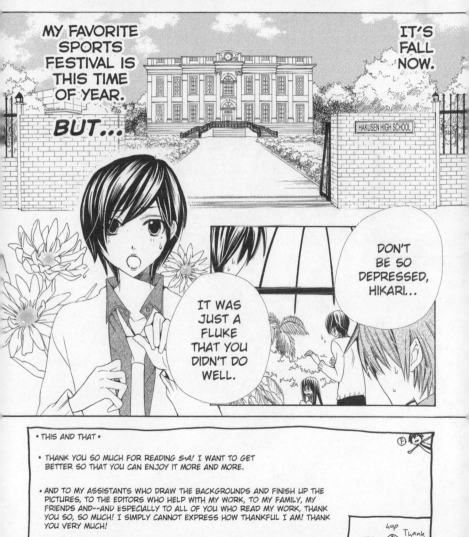

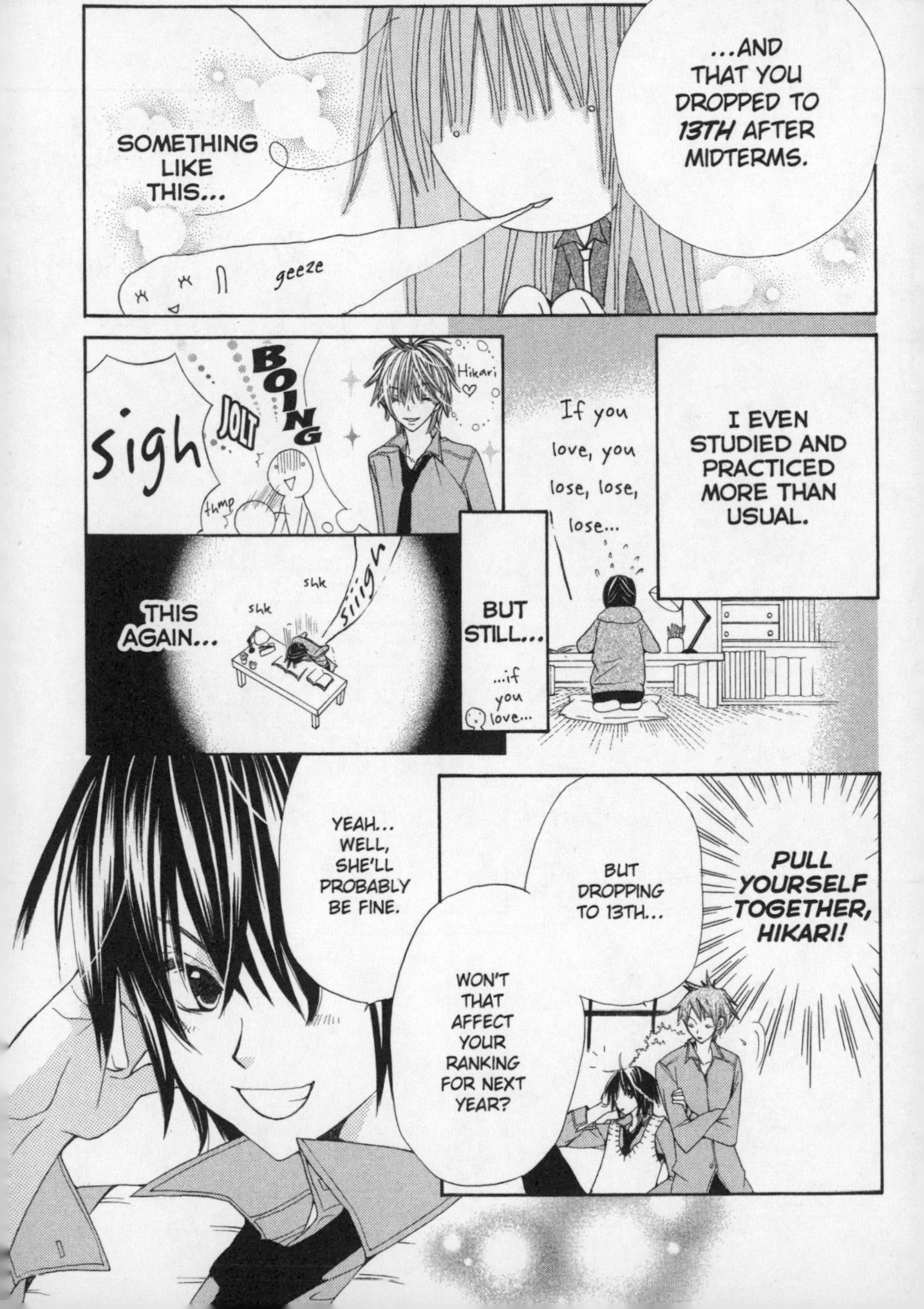
...AND THAT YOU DROPPED TO 13TH AFTER MIDTERMS.
SOMETHING LIKE THIS...
geeze
I EVEN STUDIED AND PRACTICED MORE THAN USUAL.
If you love, you lose, lose, lose...
Hikari ♡
BOING
JOLT
sigh
thmp
BUT STILL...
...if you love...
THIS AGAIN...
shk
shk
siiigh
PULL YOURSELF TOGETHER, HIKARI!
BUT DROPPING TO 13TH...
WON'T THAT AFFECT YOUR RANKING FOR NEXT YEAR?
YEAH... WELL, SHE'LL PROBABLY BE FINE.

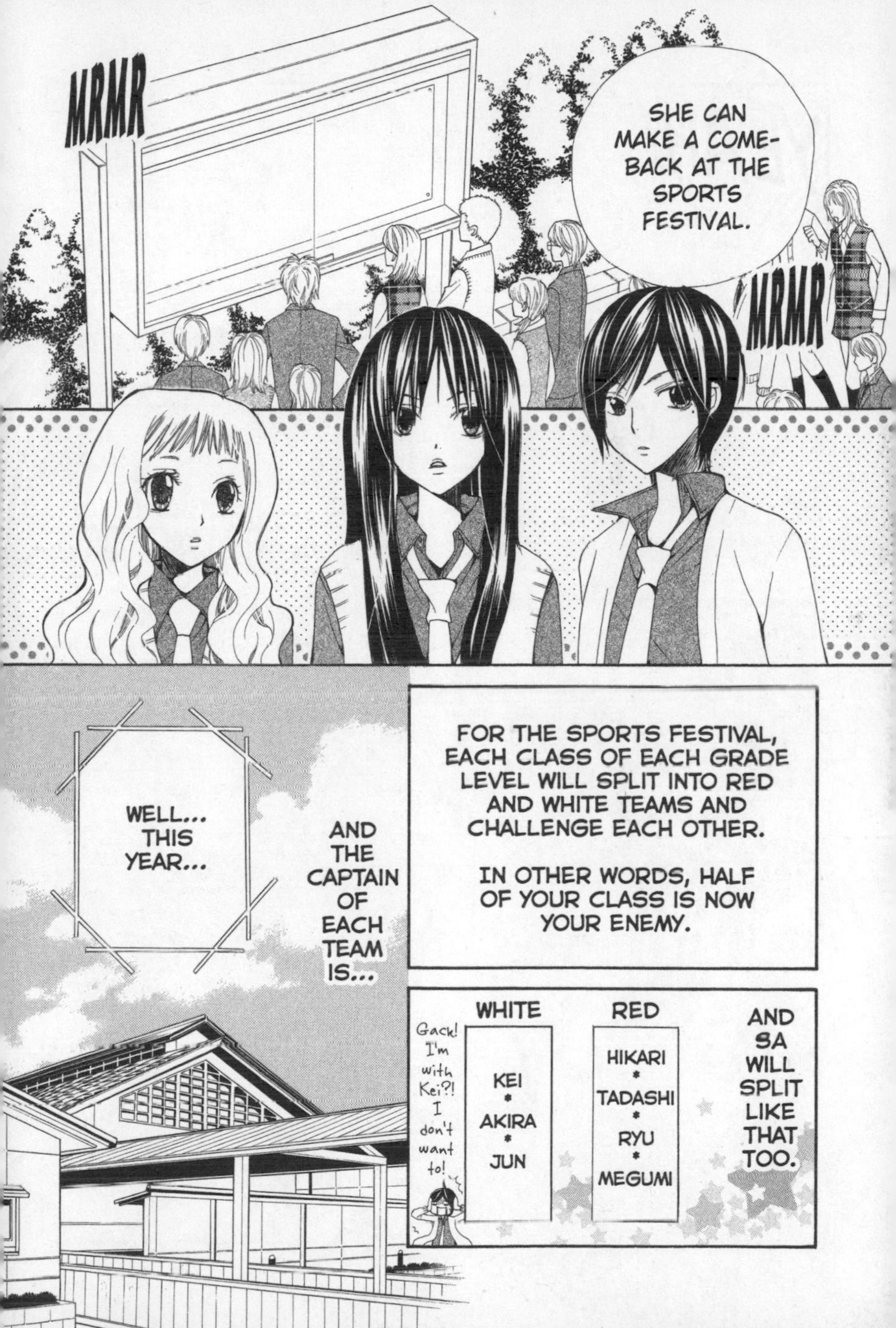
SHE CAN MAKE A COME-BACK AT THE SPORTS FESTIVAL.
MRMR
MRMR
FOR THE SPORTS FESTIVAL, EACH CLASS OF EACH GRADE LEVEL WILL SPLIT INTO RED AND WHITE TEAMS AND CHALLENGE EACH OTHER.
IN OTHER WORDS, HALF OF YOUR CLASS IS NOW YOUR ENEMY.
AND SA WILL SPLIT LIKE THAT TOO.
RED
HIKARI • TADASHI • RYU • MEGUMI
WHITE
KEI • AKIRA • JUN
Gack! I'm with Kei?! I don't want to!
AND THE CAPTAIN OF EACH TEAM IS...
WELL... THIS YEAR...

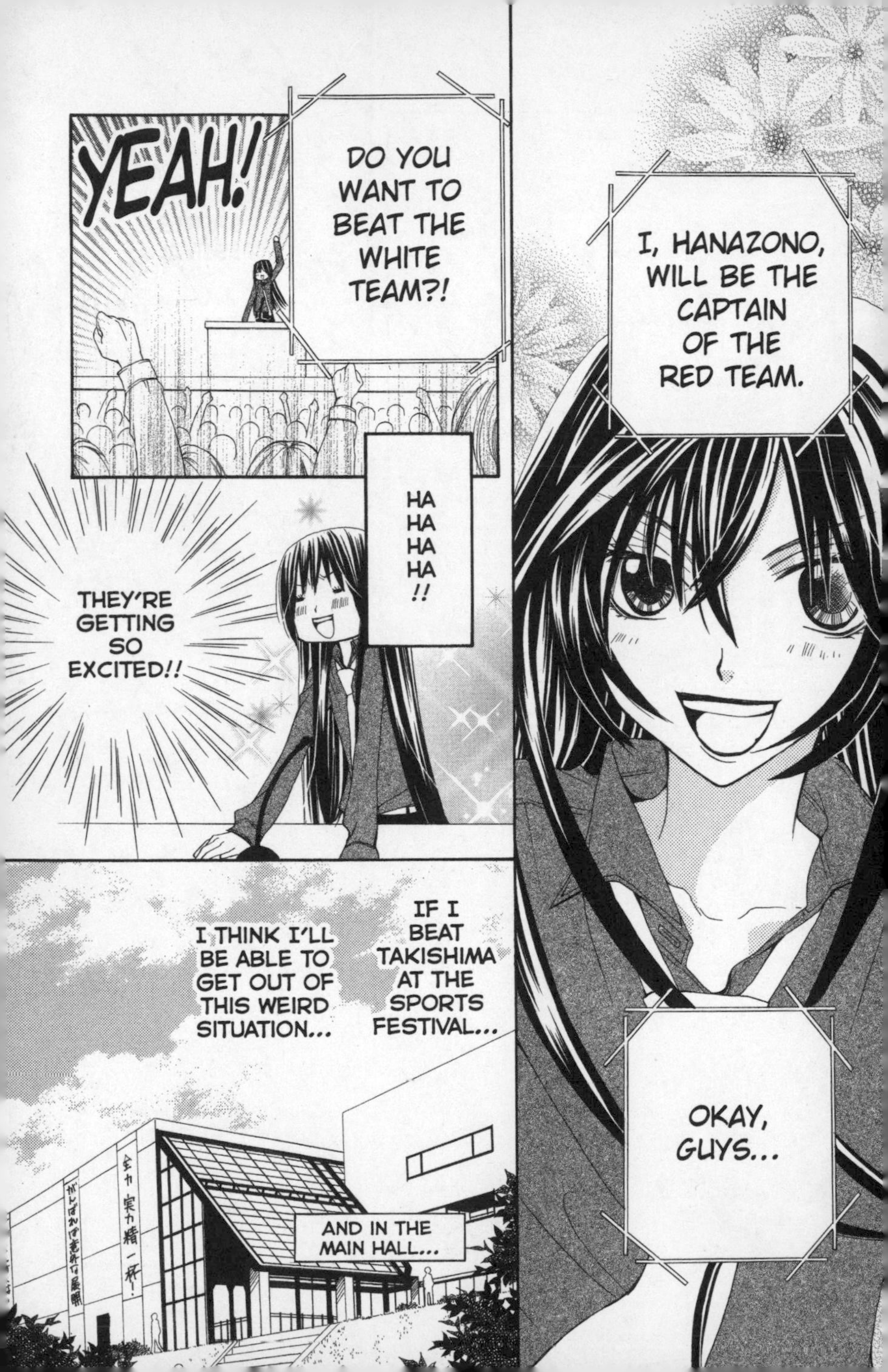
I, HANAZONO, WILL BE THE CAPTAIN OF THE RED TEAM.
OKAY, GUYS...
DO YOU WANT TO BEAT THE WHITE TEAM?!
YEAH!
HA HA HA HA!!
THEY'RE GETTING SO EXCITED!!
IF I BEAT TAKISHIMA AT THE SPORTS FESTIVAL...
I THINK I'LL BE ABLE TO GET OUT OF THIS WEIRD SITUATION...
AND IN THE MAIN HALL...

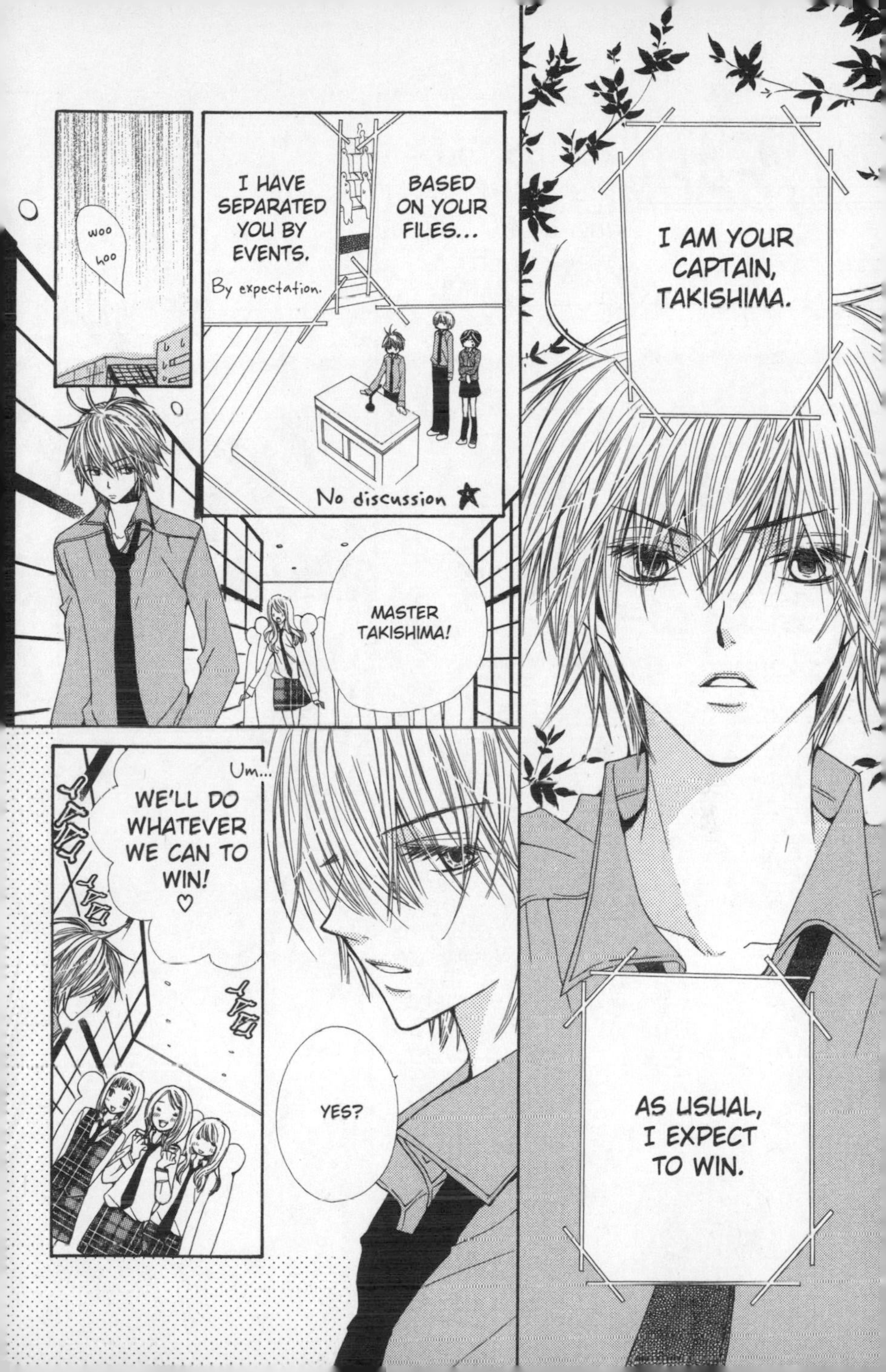
I AM YOUR CAPTAIN, TAKISHIMA.
AS USUAL, I EXPECT TO WIN.
BASED ON YOUR FILES...
I HAVE SEPARATED YOU BY EVENTS.
By expectation.
No discussion ★
woo hoo
MASTER TAKISHIMA!
YES?
Um...
WE'LL DO WHATEVER WE CAN TO WIN! ♡

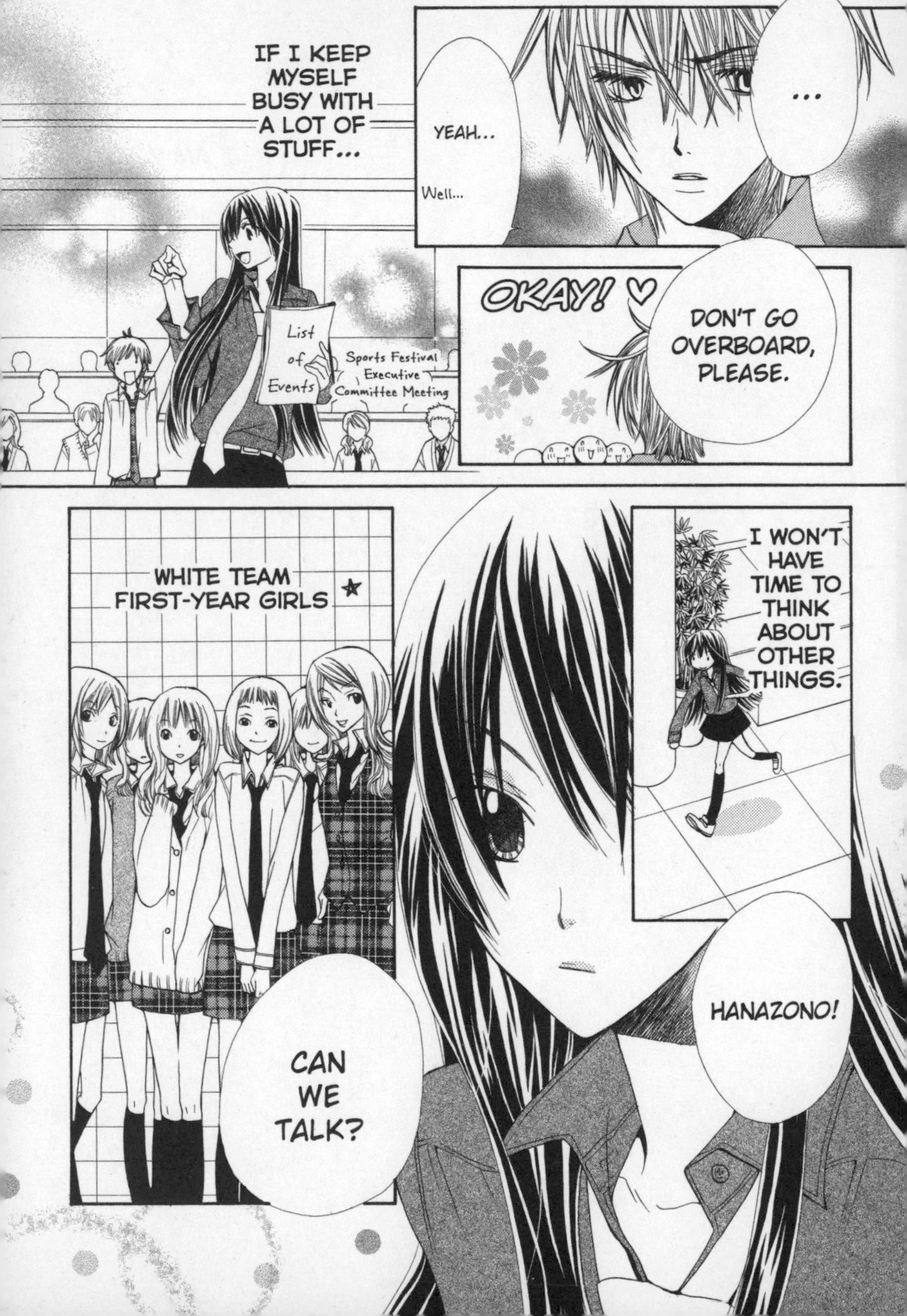
...
YEAH...
Well...
DON'T GO OVERBOARD, PLEASE.
OKAY! ♥
IF I KEEP MYSELF BUSY WITH A LOT OF STUFF...
List of Events
Sports Festival Executive Committee Meeting
I WON'T HAVE TIME TO THINK ABOUT OTHER THINGS.
HANAZONO!
WHITE TEAM FIRST-YEAR GIRLS
CAN WE TALK?

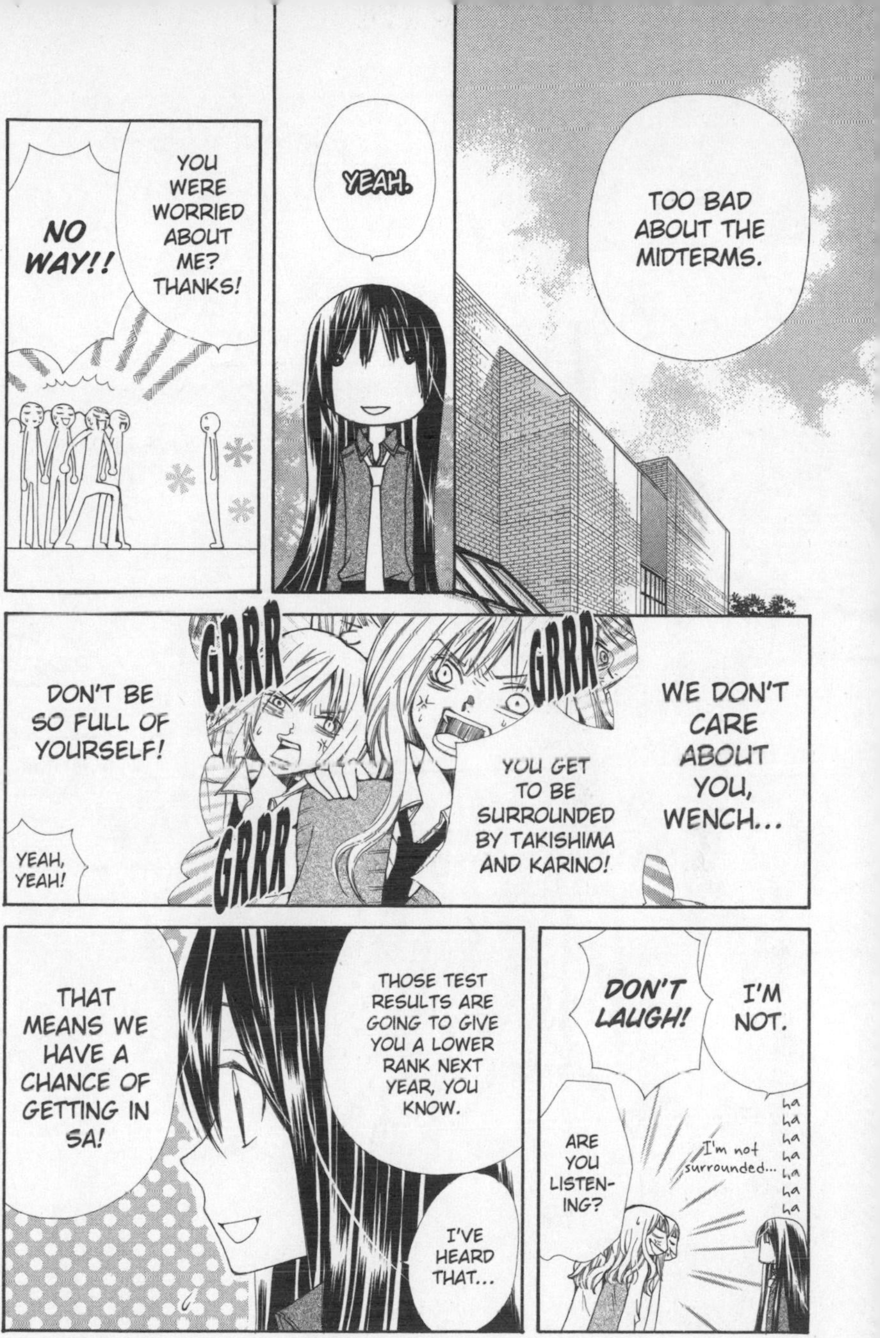
TOO BAD ABOUT THE MIDTERMS.
YEAH.
YOU WERE WORRIED ABOUT ME? THANKS!
NO WAY!!
WE DON'T CARE ABOUT YOU, WENCH...
GRRR
YOU GET TO BE SURROUNDED BY TAKISHIMA AND KARINO!
GRRR
DON'T BE SO FULL OF YOURSELF!
GRRR
YEAH, YEAH!
I'M NOT.
DON'T LAUGH!
ha ha ha ha ha ha ha
I'm not surrounded...
ARE YOU LISTENING?
THOSE TEST RESULTS ARE GOING TO GIVE YOU A LOWER RANK NEXT YEAR, YOU KNOW.
THAT MEANS WE HAVE A CHANCE OF GETTING IN SA!
I'VE HEARD THAT...

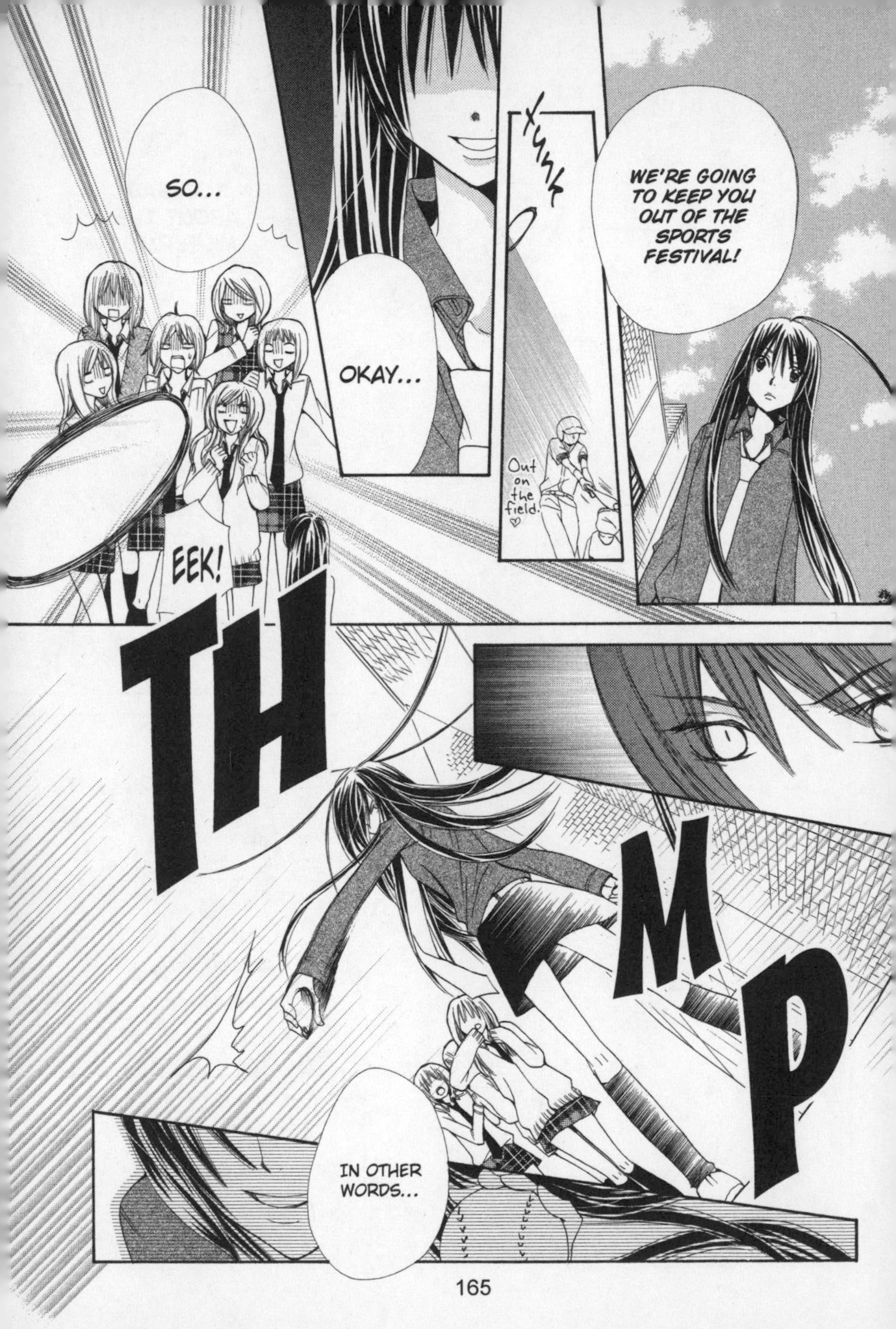
WE'RE GOING TO KEEP YOU OUT OF THE SPORTS FESTIVAL!
YANK
Out on the field. ♡
OKAY...
SO...
EEK!
THUMP
IN OTHER WORDS...

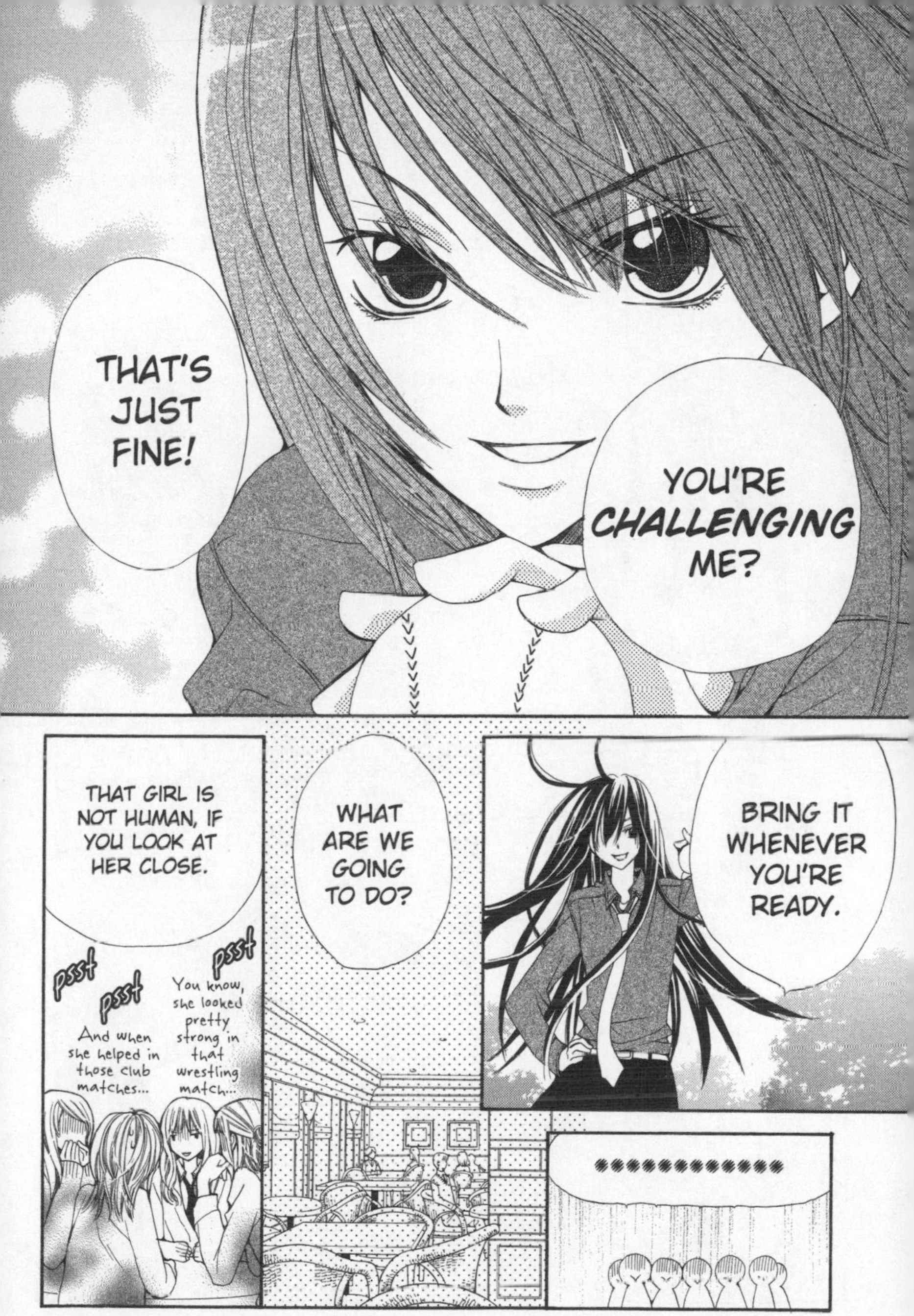
YOU'RE *CHALLENGING* ME?
THAT'S JUST FINE!
BRING IT WHENEVER YOU'RE READY.
••••••••••••
WHAT ARE WE GOING TO DO?
THAT GIRL IS NOT HUMAN, IF YOU LOOK AT HER CLOSE.
psst
You know, she looked pretty strong in that wrestling match...
psst
psst
And when she helped in those club matches...

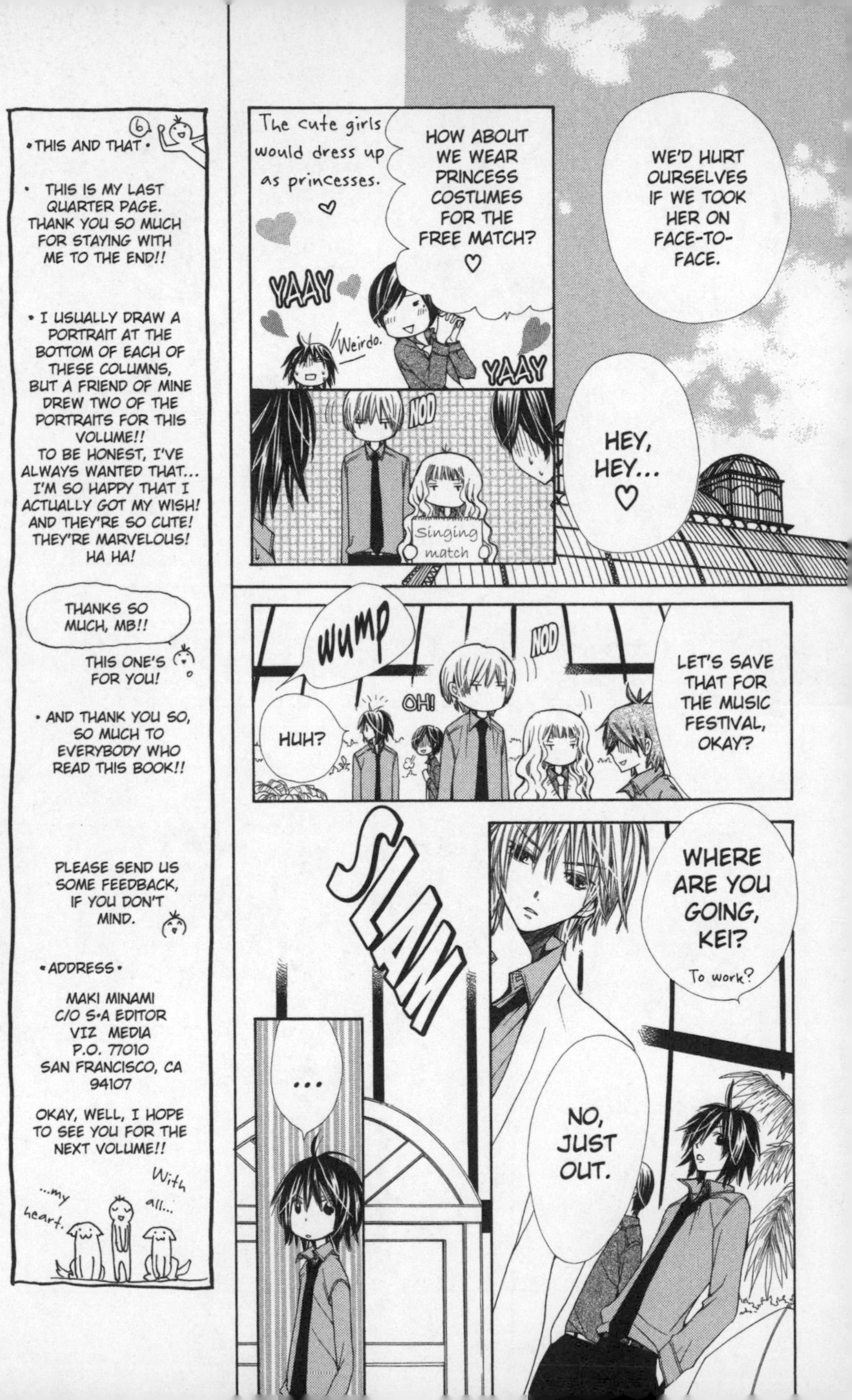
WE'D HURT OURSELVES IF WE TOOK HER ON FACE-TO-FACE.
HEY, HEY... ♡
HOW ABOUT WE WEAR PRINCESS COSTUMES FOR THE FREE MATCH? ♡
The cute girls would dress up as princesses. ♡
YAAY
YAAY
Weirdo.
NOD
Singing match
LET'S SAVE THAT FOR THE MUSIC FESTIVAL, OKAY?
NOD
wump
OH!
HUH?
WHERE ARE YOU GOING, KEI?
To work?
SLAM
NO, JUST OUT.
...

⑥ •THIS AND THAT•

- THIS IS MY LAST QUARTER PAGE. THANK YOU SO MUCH FOR STAYING WITH ME TO THE END!!

- I USUALLY DRAW A PORTRAIT AT THE BOTTOM OF EACH OF THESE COLUMNS, BUT A FRIEND OF MINE DREW TWO OF THE PORTRAITS FOR THIS VOLUME!! TO BE HONEST, I'VE ALWAYS WANTED THAT... I'M SO HAPPY THAT I ACTUALLY GOT MY WISH! AND THEY'RE SO CUTE! THEY'RE MARVELOUS! HA HA!

THANKS SO MUCH, MB!!

THIS ONE'S FOR YOU!

- AND THANK YOU SO, SO MUCH TO EVERYBODY WHO READ THIS BOOK!!

PLEASE SEND US SOME FEEDBACK, IF YOU DON'T MIND.

•ADDRESS•

MAKI MINAMI
C/O S•A EDITOR
VIZ MEDIA
P.O. 77010
SAN FRANCISCO, CA
94107

OKAY, WELL, I HOPE TO SEE YOU FOR THE NEXT VOLUME!!

With all... ...my heart.

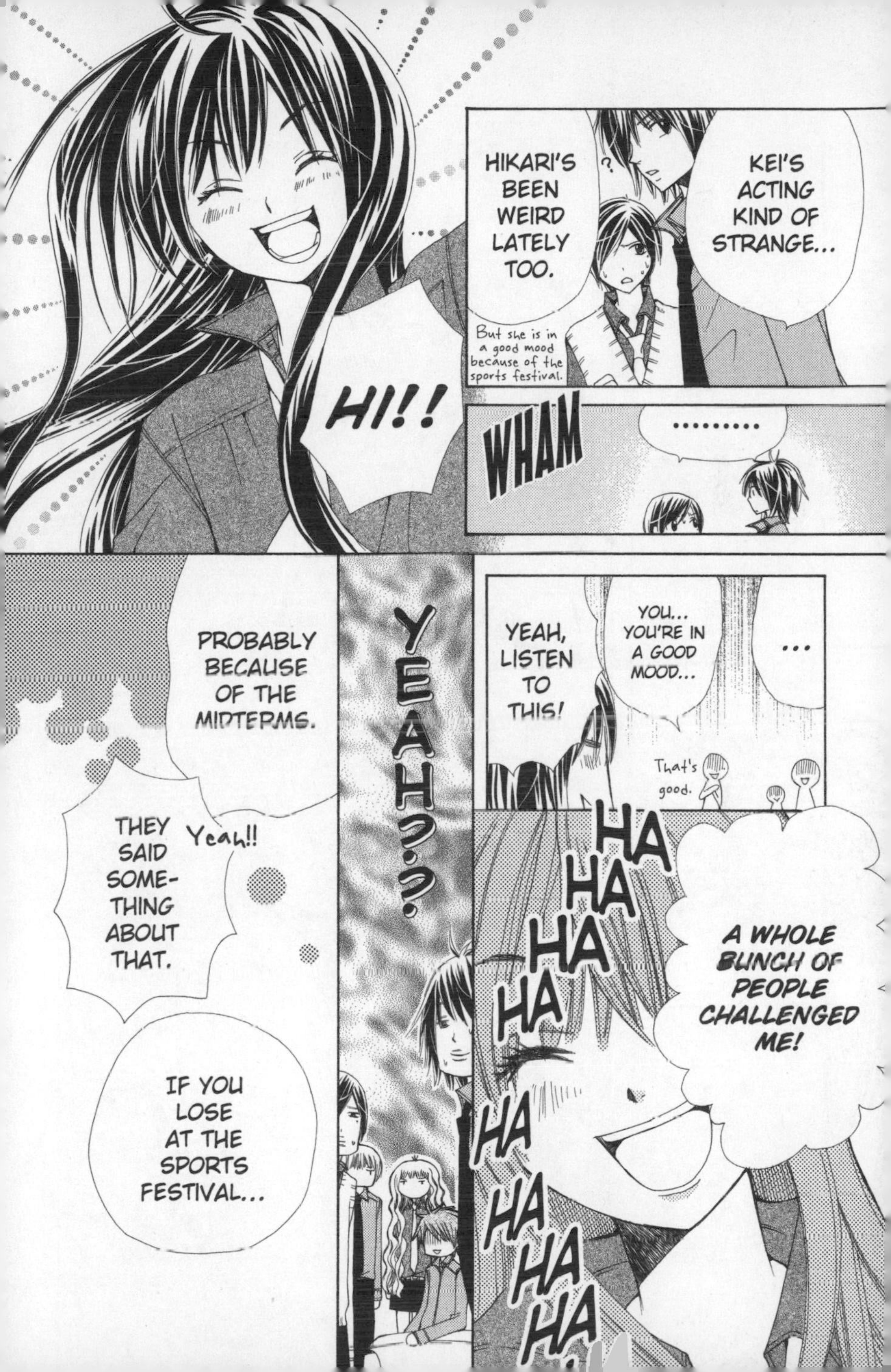
KEI'S ACTING KIND OF STRANGE...
HIKARI'S BEEN WEIRD LATELY TOO.
But she is in a good mood because of the sports festival.
WHAM
....
HI!!
...
YOU... YOU'RE IN A GOOD MOOD...
YEAH, LISTEN TO THIS!
That's good.
A WHOLE BUNCH OF PEOPLE CHALLENGED ME!
HA HA HA HA HA HA HA HA HA HA HA...
YEAH??
PROBABLY BECAUSE OF THE MIDTERMS.
THEY SAID SOMETHING ABOUT THAT.
Yeah!!
IF YOU LOSE AT THE SPORTS FESTIVAL...

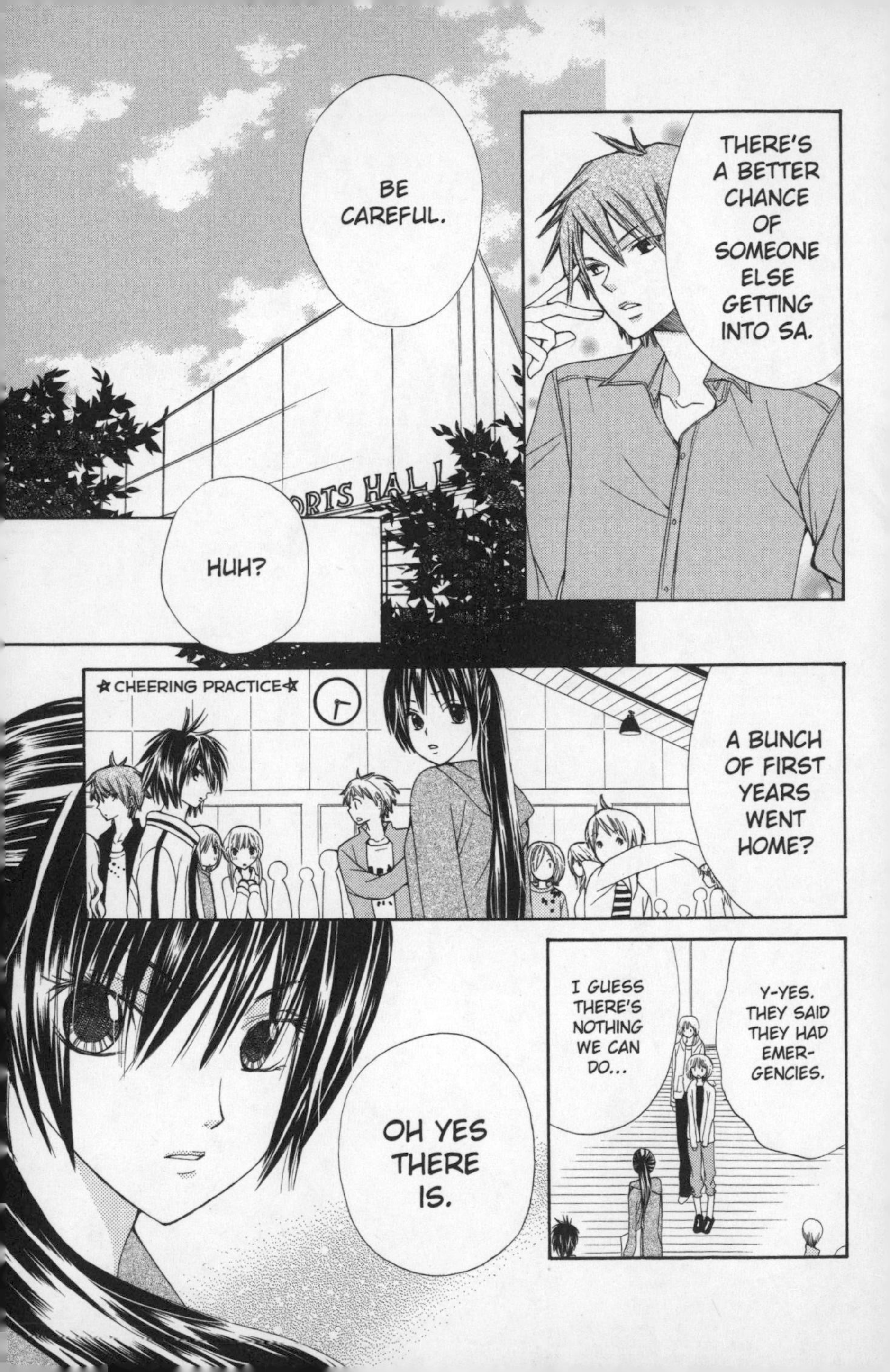
THERE'S A BETTER CHANCE OF SOMEONE ELSE GETTING INTO SA.
BE CAREFUL.
ORTS HALL
HUH?
A BUNCH OF FIRST YEARS WENT HOME?
☆CHEERING PRACTICE☆
Y-YES. THEY SAID THEY HAD EMER-GENCIES.
I GUESS THERE'S NOTHING WE CAN DO...
OH YES THERE IS.

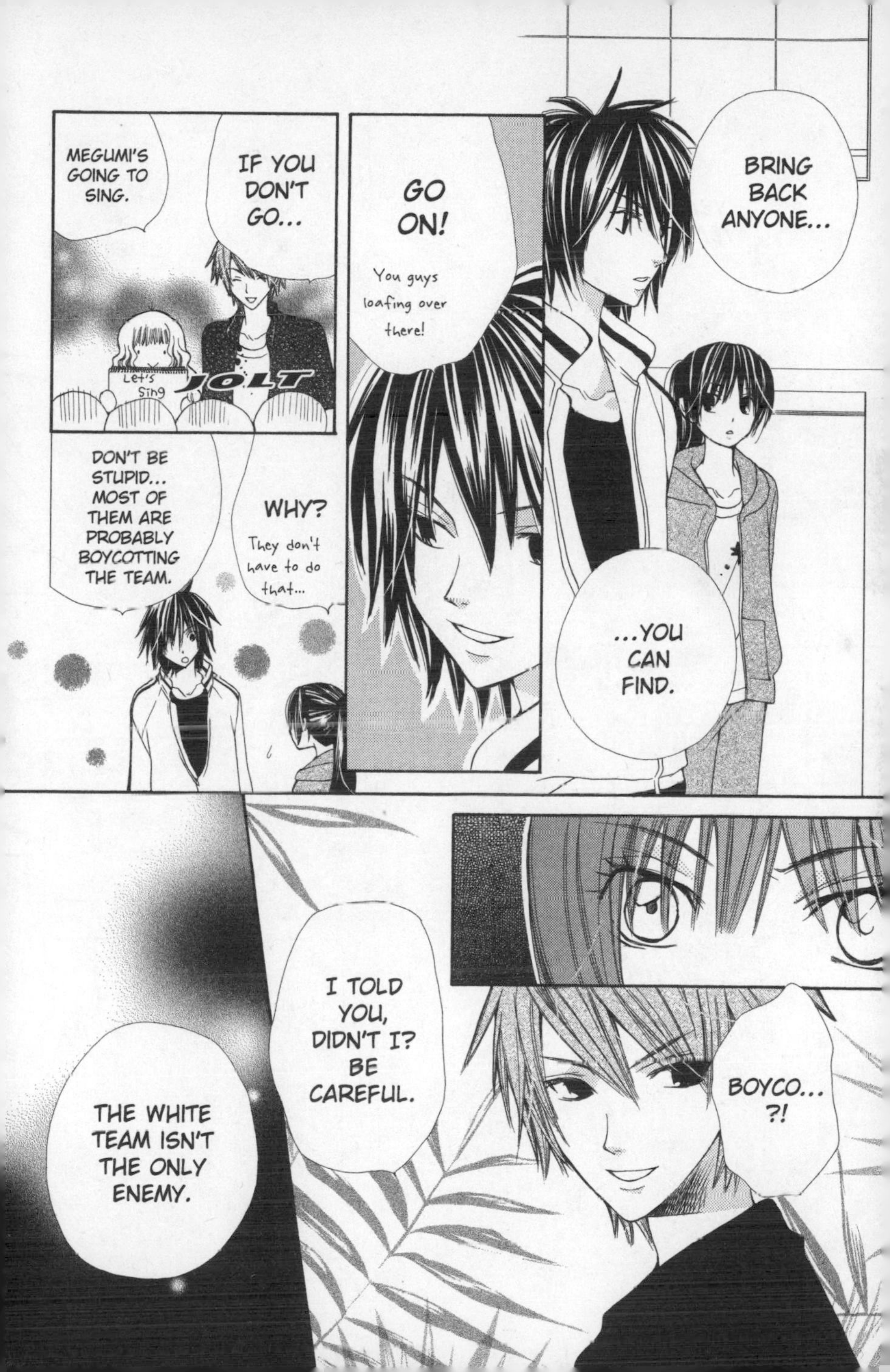
BRING BACK ANYONE...
...YOU CAN FIND.
GO ON!
You guys loafing over there!
IF YOU DON'T GO...
MEGUMI'S GOING TO SING.
Let's Sing
JOLT
WHY?
They don't have to do that...
DON'T BE STUPID... MOST OF THEM ARE PROBABLY BOYCOTTING THE TEAM.
BOYCO...?!
I TOLD YOU, DIDN'T I? BE CAREFUL.
THE WHITE TEAM ISN'T THE ONLY ENEMY.

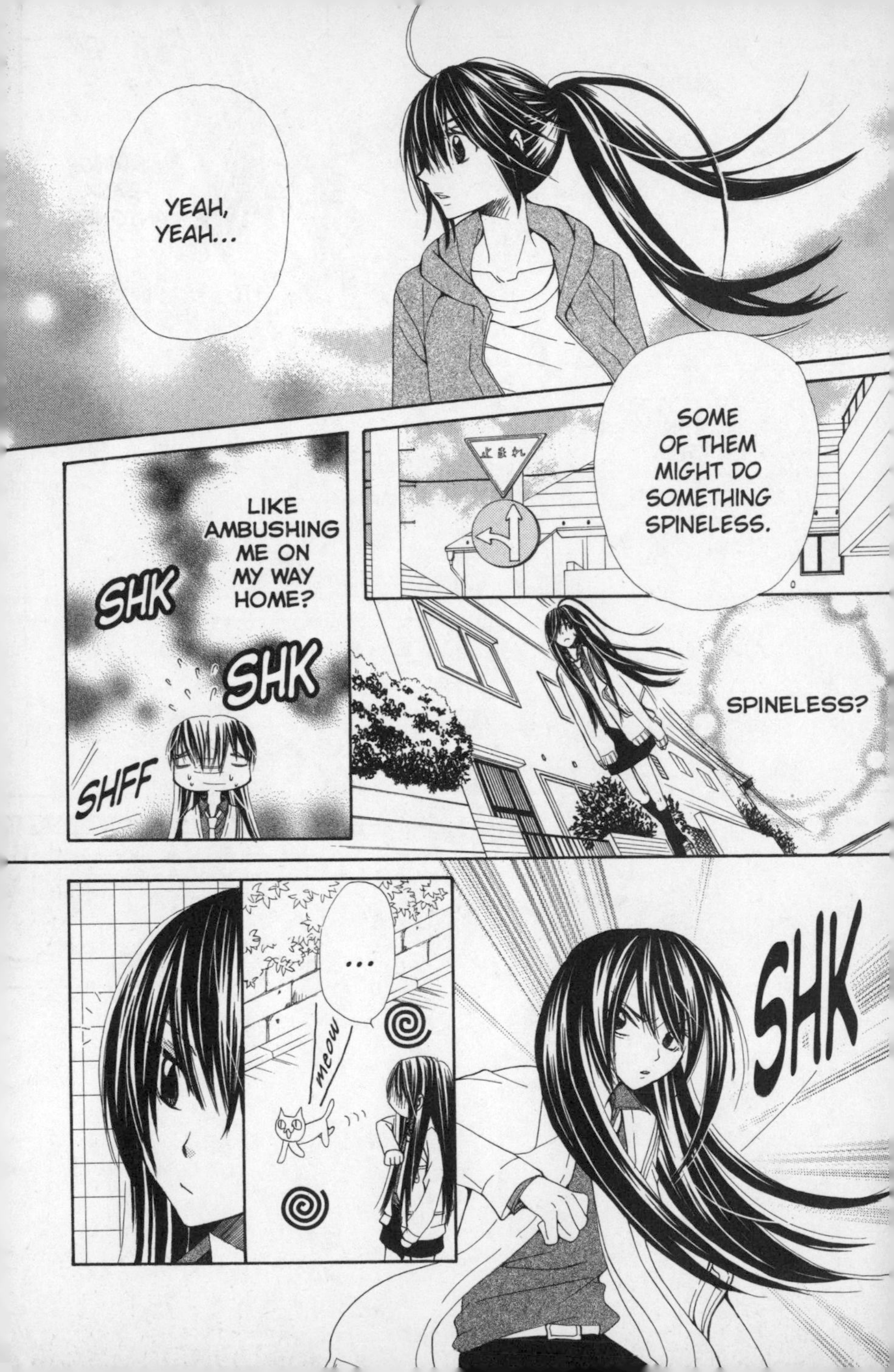
YEAH, YEAH...
SOME OF THEM MIGHT DO SOMETHING SPINELESS.
SPINELESS?
LIKE AMBUSHING ME ON MY WAY HOME?
SHK
SHK
SHFF
SHK
...
meow

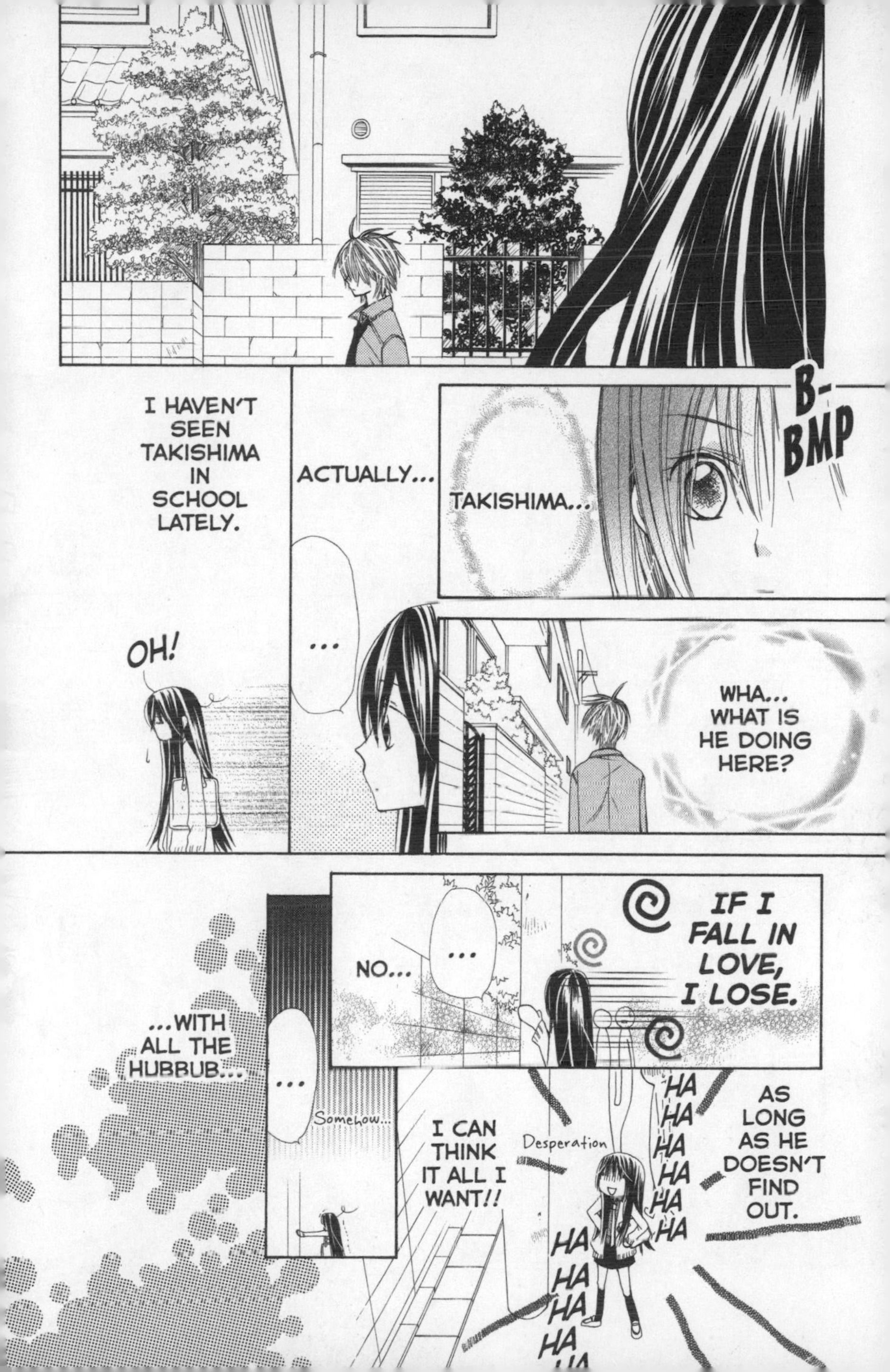
B-BMP
TAKISHIMA...
WHA... WHAT IS HE DOING HERE?
...
ACTUALLY...
I HAVEN'T SEEN TAKISHIMA IN SCHOOL LATELY.
OH!
IF I FALL IN LOVE, I LOSE.
...
NO...
AS LONG AS HE DOESN'T FIND OUT.
HA HA HA HA HA HA HA
HA HA HA HA HA
Desperation
I CAN THINK IT ALL I WANT!!
Somehow...
...
...WITH ALL THE HUBBUB...

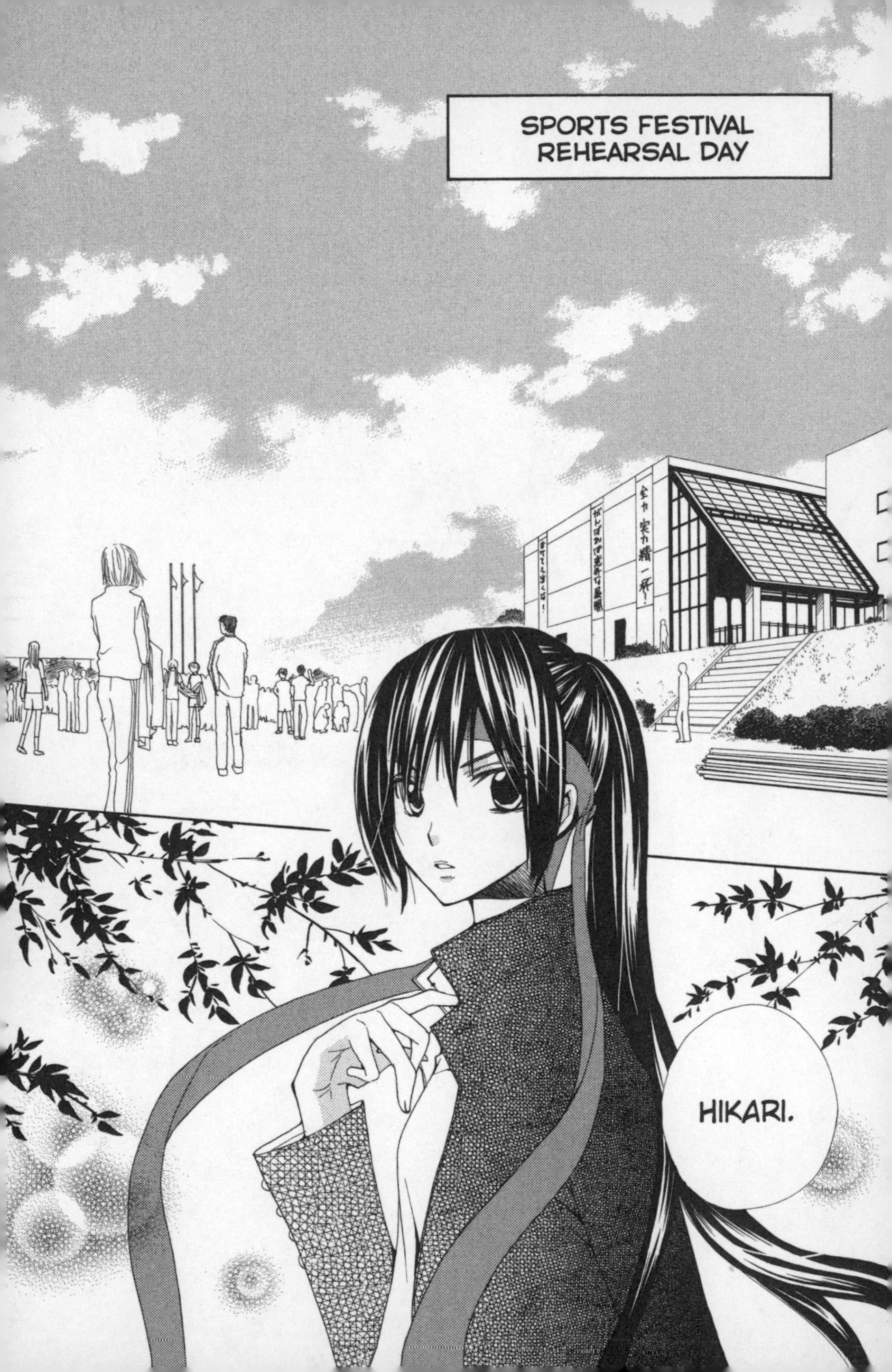
SPORTS FESTIVAL REHEARSAL DAY
HIKARI.

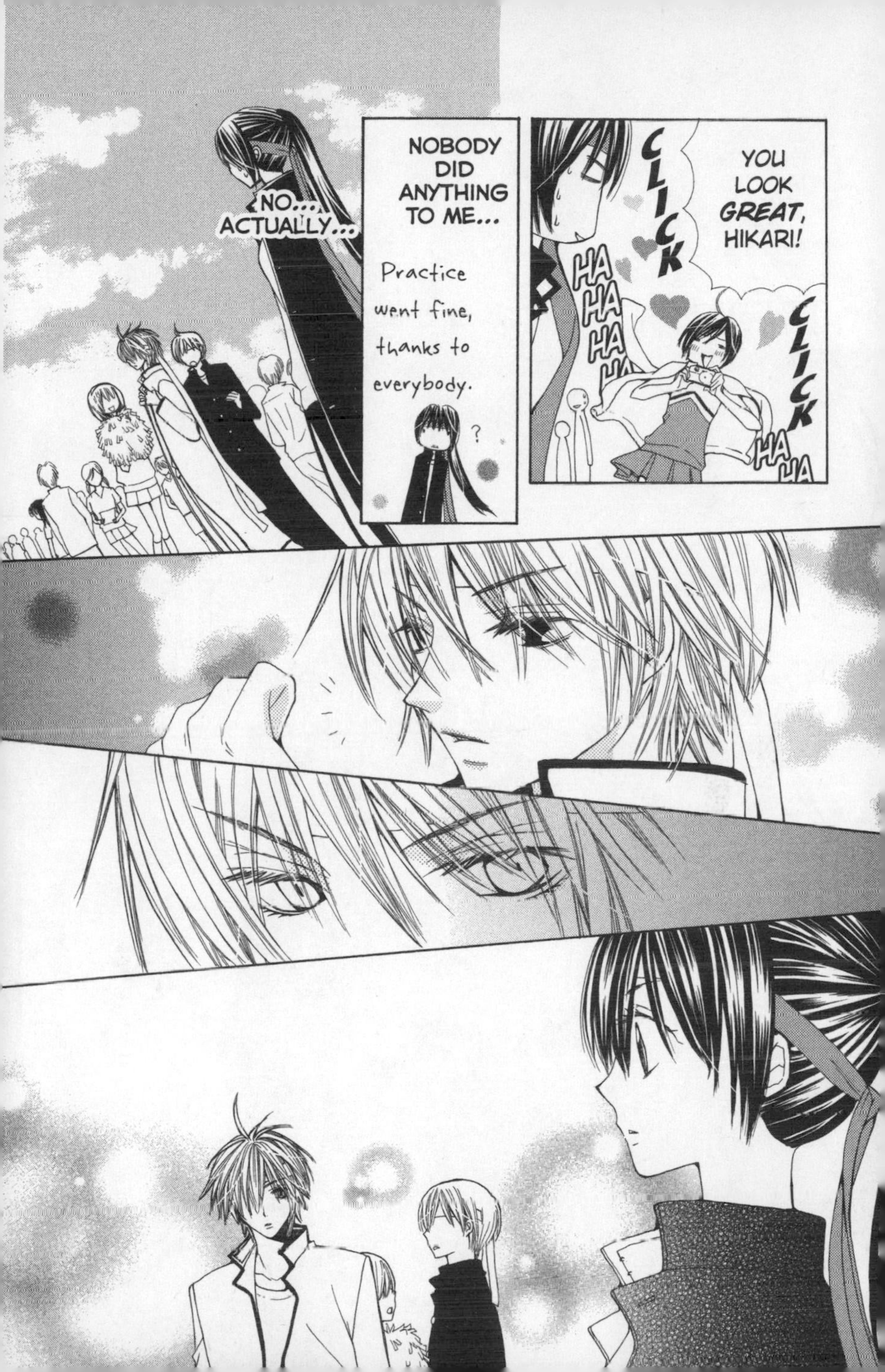
CLICK
YOU LOOK GREAT, HIKARI!
HA HA HA HA
CLICK
HA HA
NOBODY DID ANYTHING TO ME...
Practice went fine, thanks to everybody.
?
NO... ACTUALLY...

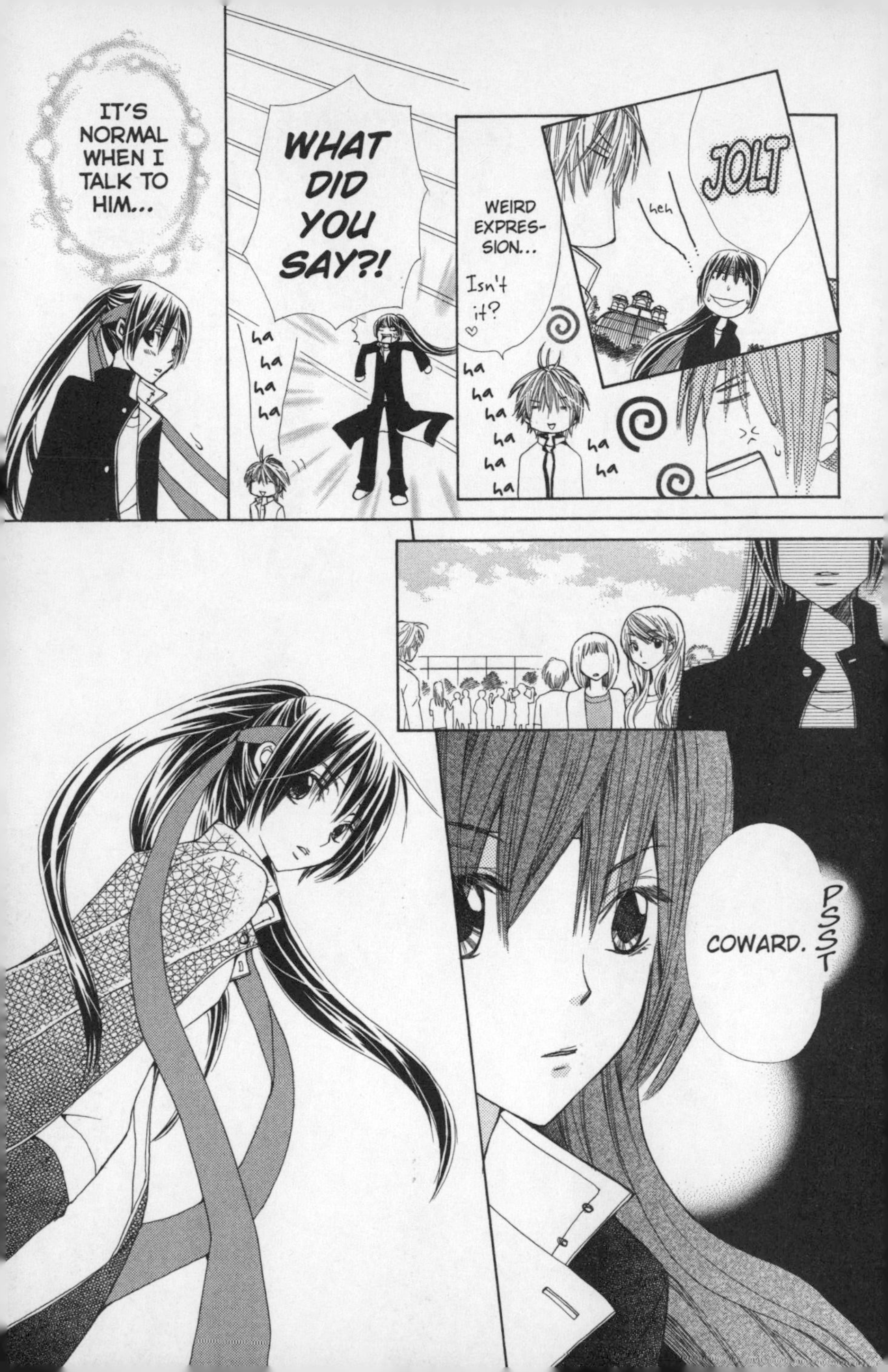
JOLT
heh
WEIRD EXPRES-SION...
Isn't it?
ha ha ha ha ha ha
ha ha
WHAT DID YOU SAY?!
ha ha ha ha
IT'S NORMAL WHEN I TALK TO HIM...
PSST
COWARD.

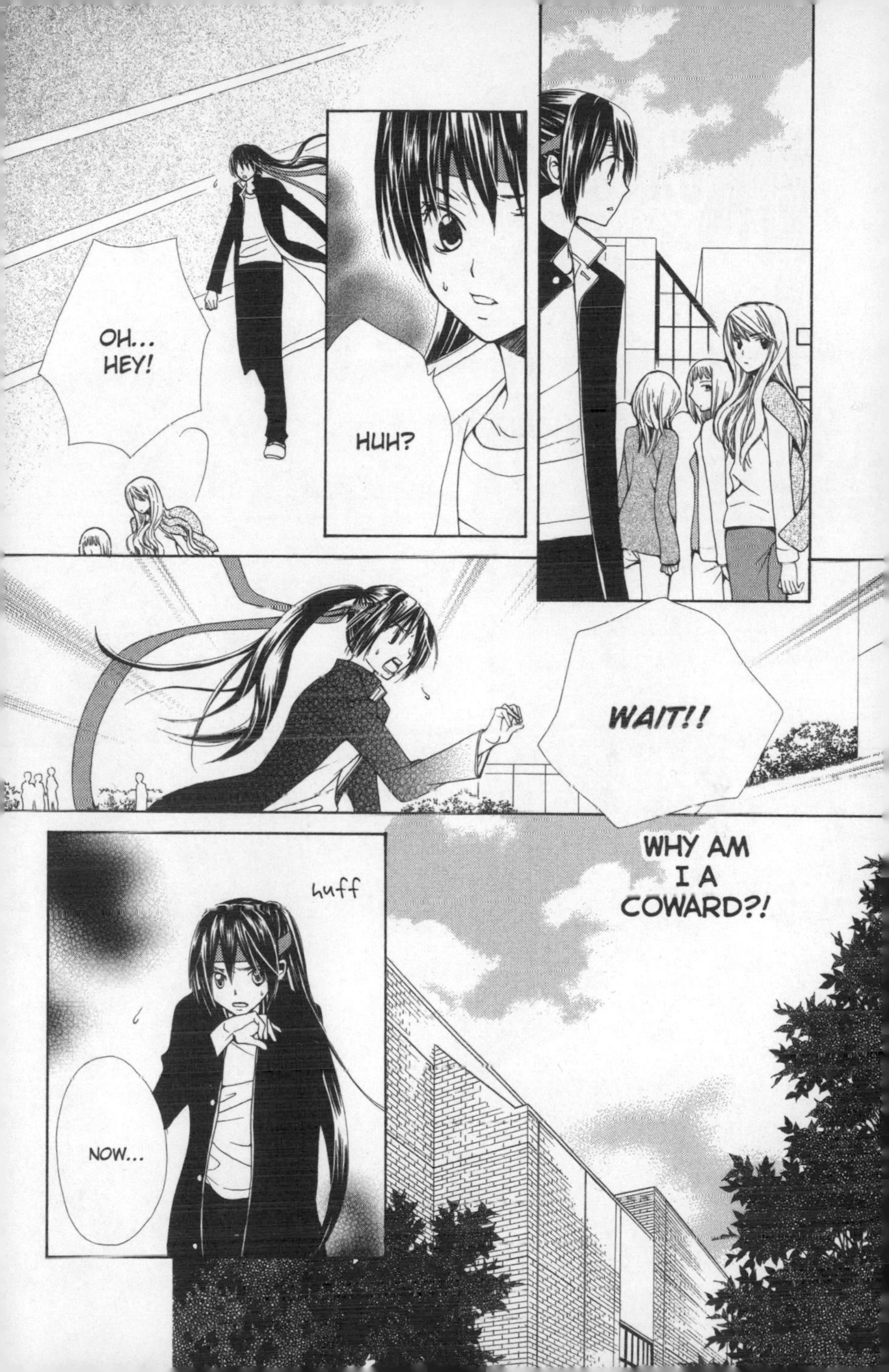
HUH?
OH... HEY!
WAIT!!
WHY AM I A COWARD?!
huff
NOW...

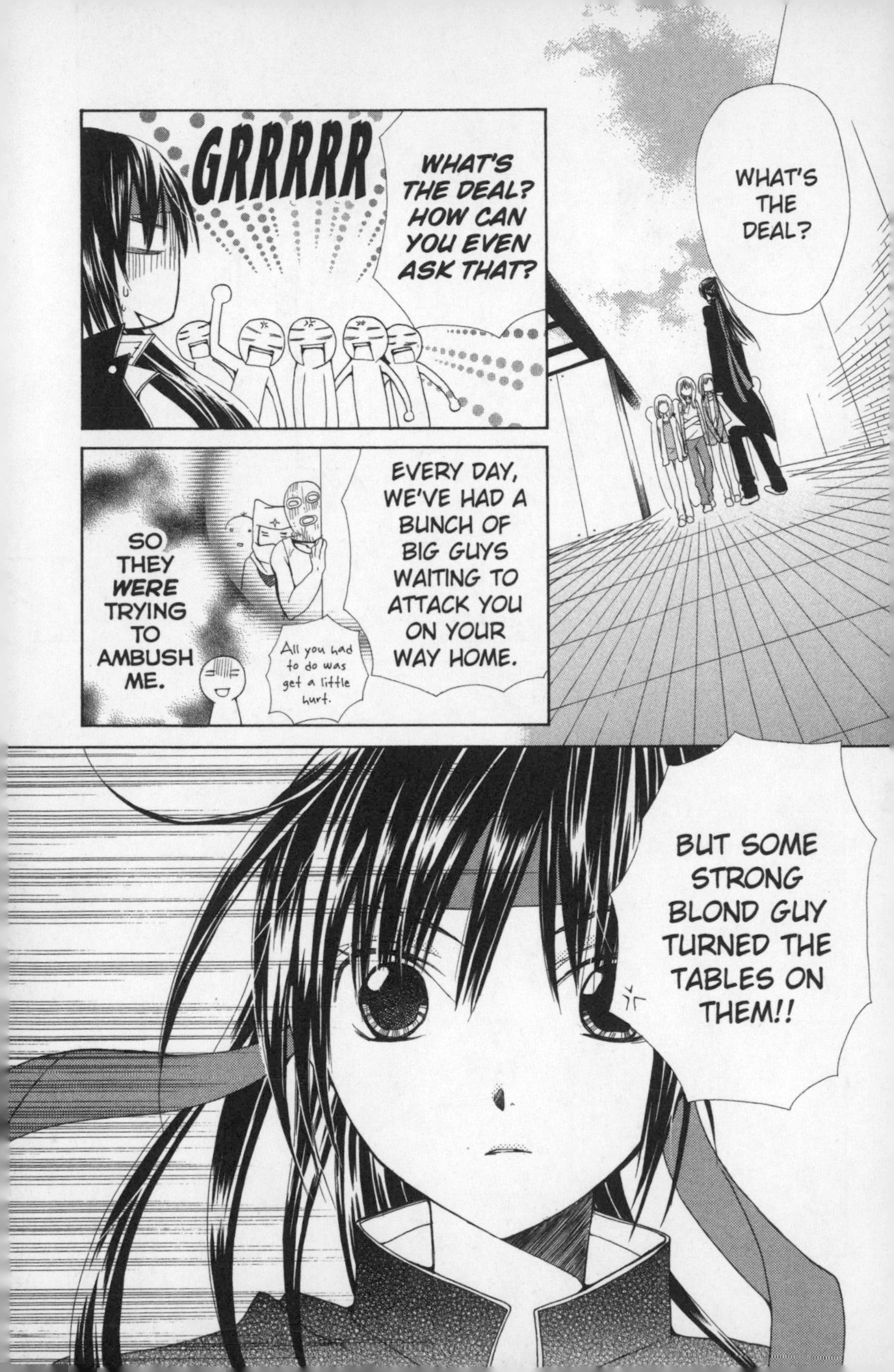
WHAT'S THE DEAL?
WHAT'S THE DEAL? HOW CAN YOU EVEN ASK THAT?
GRRRRR
EVERY DAY, WE'VE HAD A BUNCH OF BIG GUYS WAITING TO ATTACK YOU ON YOUR WAY HOME.
All you had to do was get a little hurt.
SO THEY WERE TRYING TO AMBUSH ME.
BUT SOME STRONG BLOND GUY TURNED THE TABLES ON THEM!!

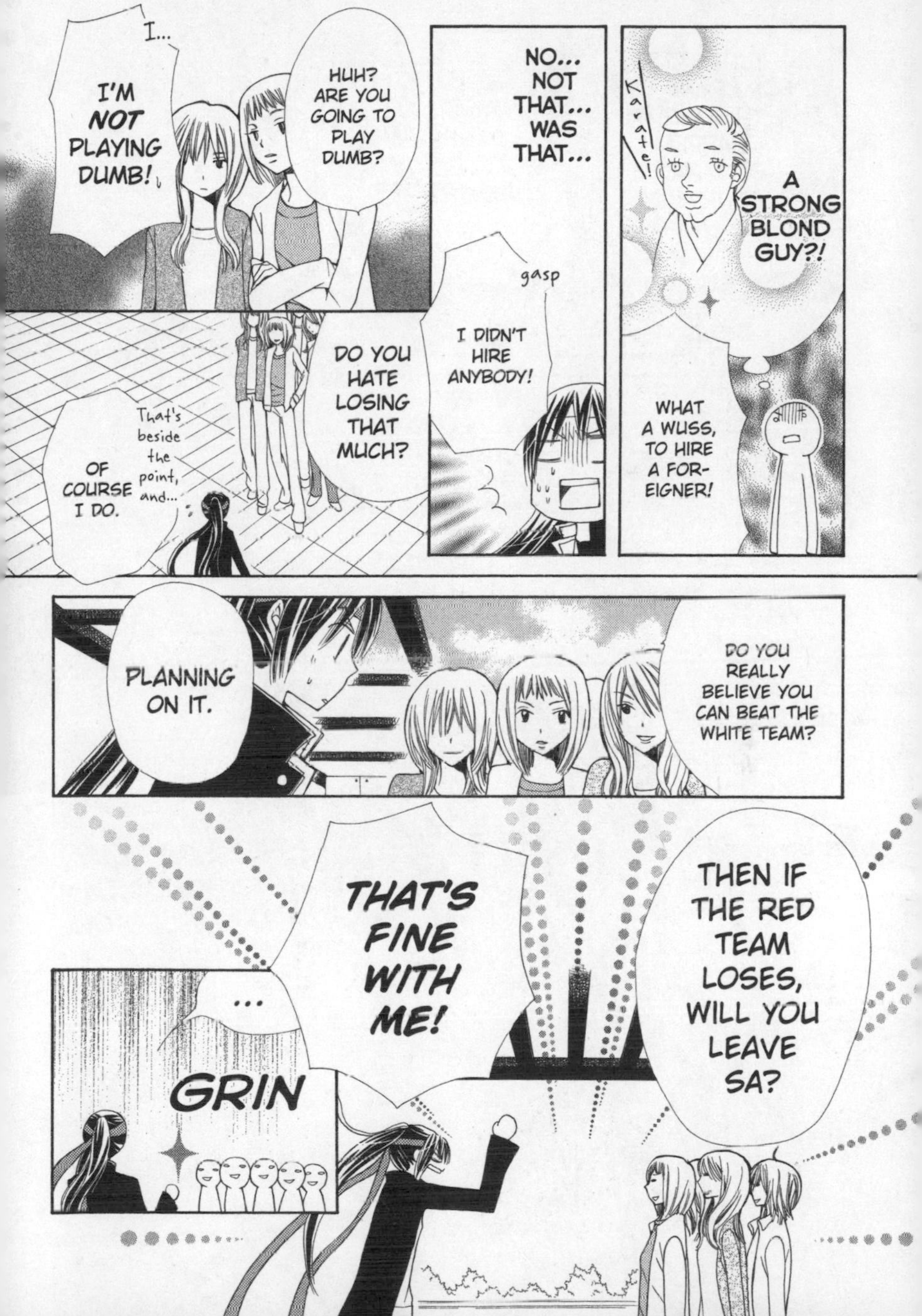
Karate!
A STRONG BLOND GUY?!
WHAT A WUSS, TO HIRE A FOR-EIGNER!
NO... NOT THAT... WAS THAT...
gasp
I DIDN'T HIRE ANYBODY!
HUH? ARE YOU GOING TO PLAY DUMB?
I...
I'M *NOT* PLAYING DUMB!
DO YOU HATE LOSING THAT MUCH?
OF COURSE I DO.
That's beside the point, and...
DO YOU REALLY BELIEVE YOU CAN BEAT THE WHITE TEAM?
PLANNING ON IT.
THEN IF THE RED TEAM LOSES, WILL YOU LEAVE SA?
THAT'S FINE WITH ME!
...
GRIN

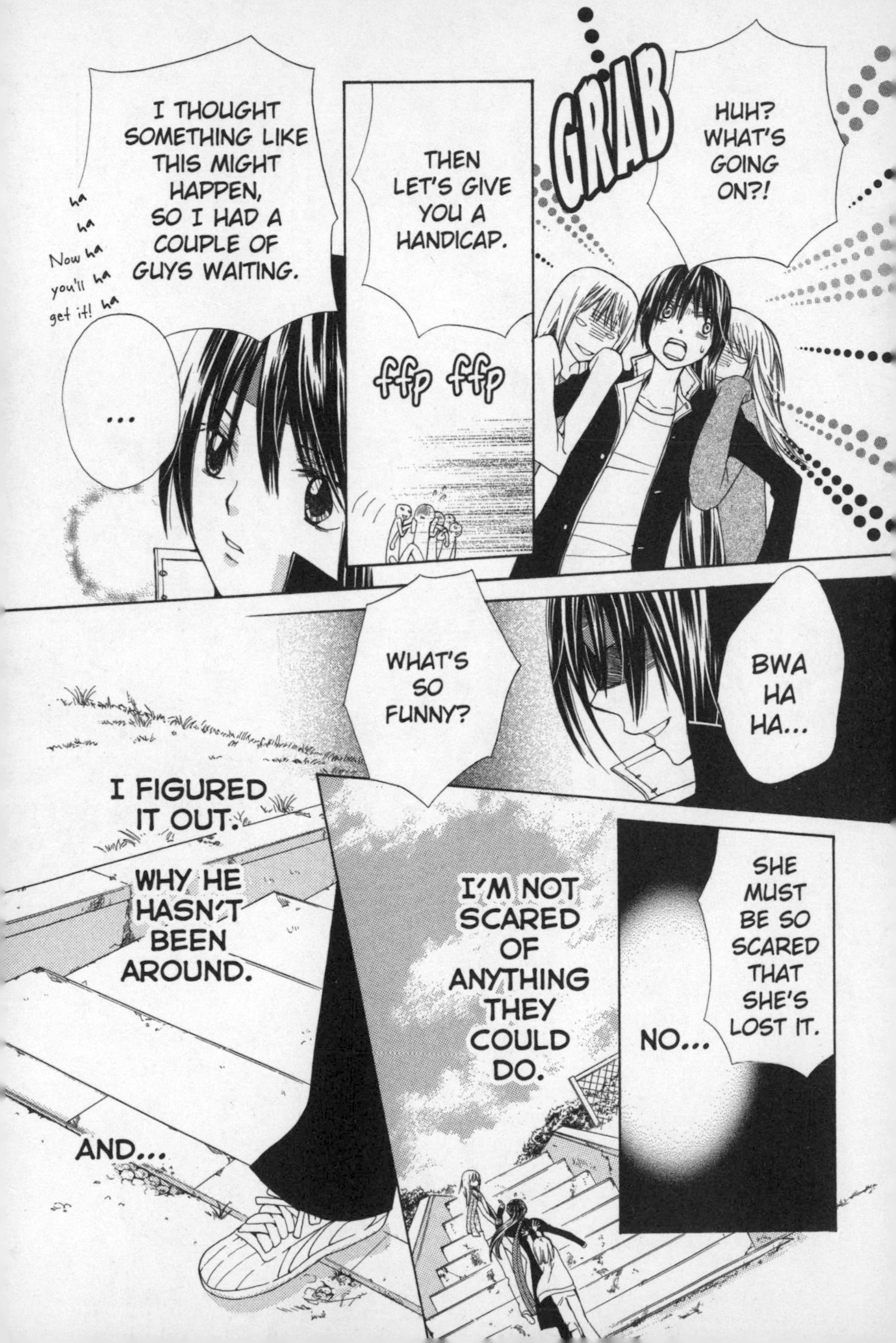
GRAB
HUH? WHAT'S GOING ON?!
THEN LET'S GIVE YOU A HANDICAP.
ffp ffp
I THOUGHT SOMETHING LIKE THIS MIGHT HAPPEN, SO I HAD A COUPLE OF GUYS WAITING.
ha ha Now ha you'll ha get it! ha
...
BWA HA HA...
WHAT'S SO FUNNY?
SHE MUST BE SO SCARED THAT SHE'S LOST IT.
NO...
I'M NOT SCARED OF ANYTHING THEY COULD DO.
I FIGURED IT OUT.
WHY HE HASN'T BEEN AROUND.
AND...

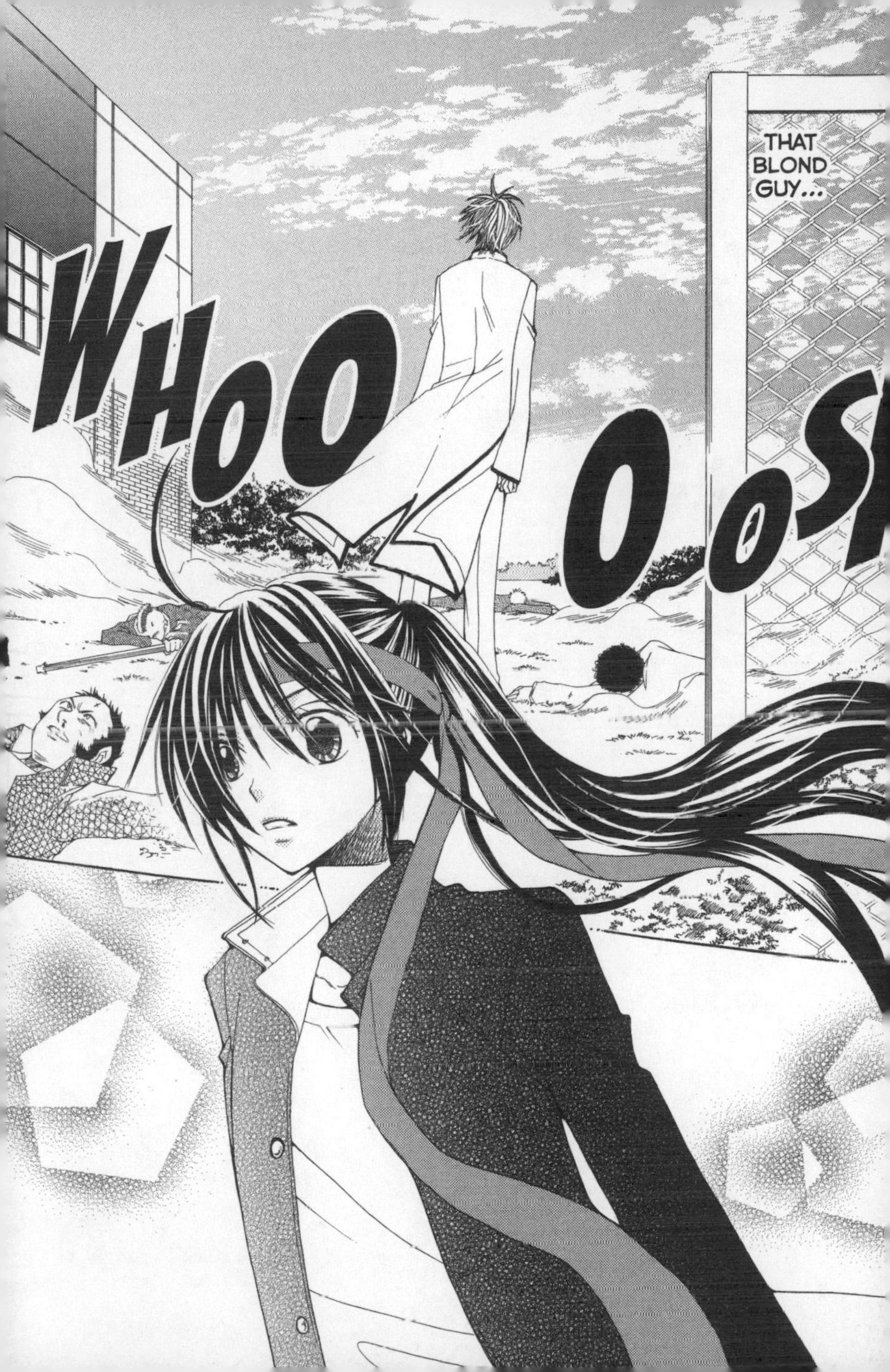
THAT BLOND GUY...
WHOOOOOSH

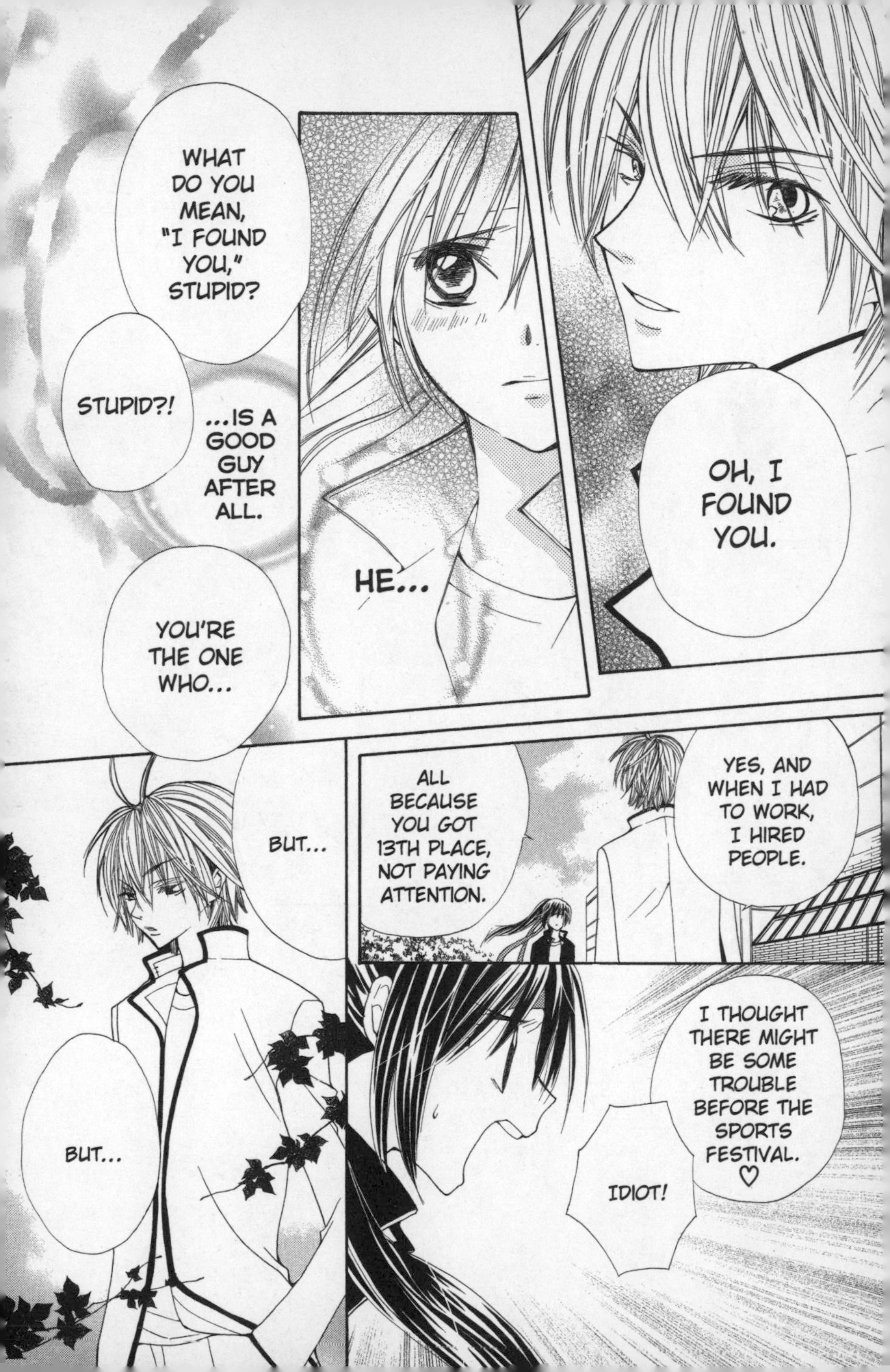
OH, I FOUND YOU.
HE...
...IS A GOOD GUY AFTER ALL.
WHAT DO YOU MEAN, "I FOUND YOU," STUPID?
STUPID?!
YOU'RE THE ONE WHO...
YES, AND WHEN I HAD TO WORK, I HIRED PEOPLE.
ALL BECAUSE YOU GOT 13TH PLACE, NOT PAYING ATTENTION.
I THOUGHT THERE MIGHT BE SOME TROUBLE BEFORE THE SPORTS FESTIVAL. ♡
IDIOT!
BUT...
BUT...

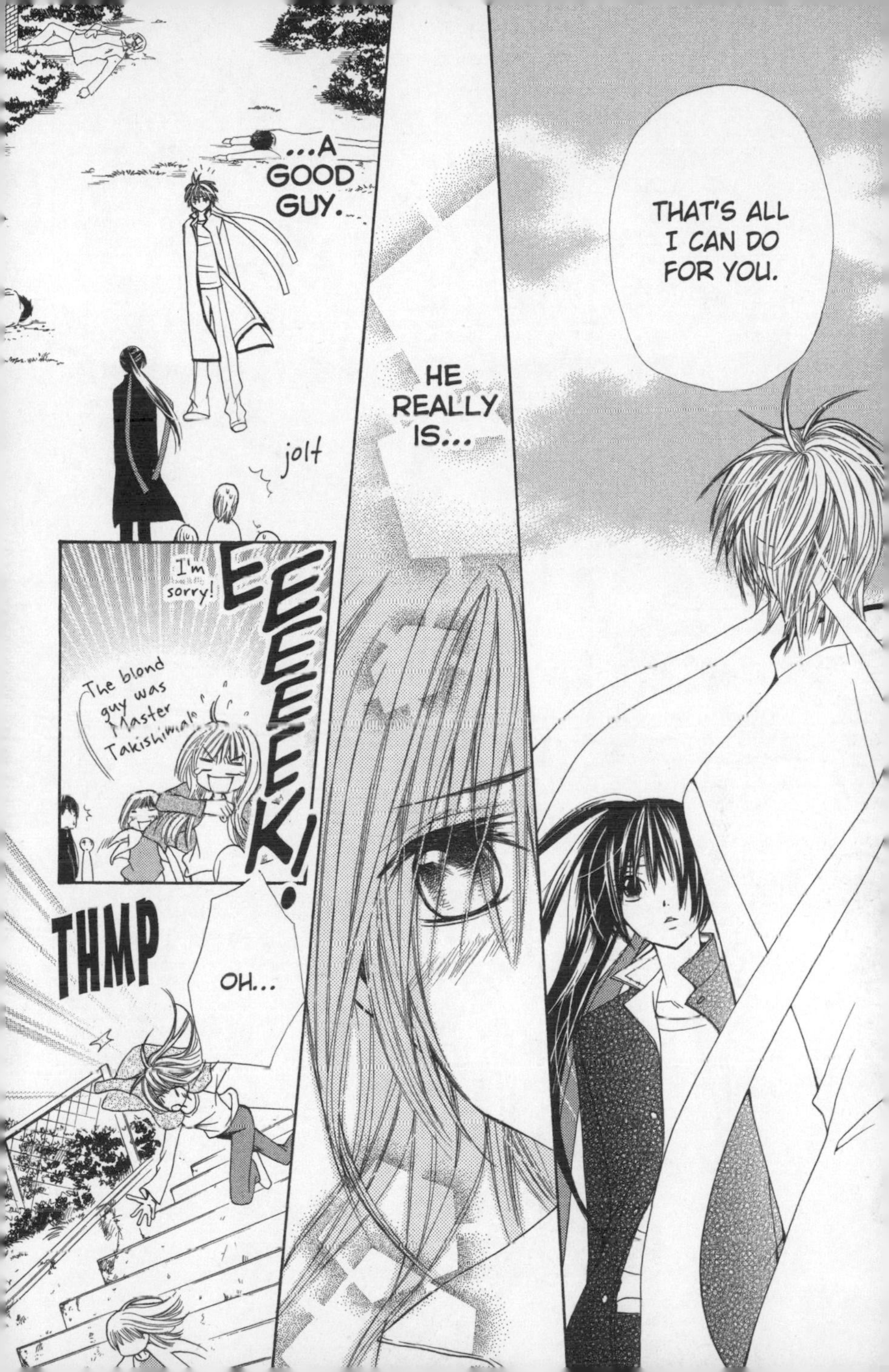
THAT'S ALL I CAN DO FOR YOU.
HE REALLY IS...
...A GOOD GUY.
jolt
EEEEEK!
I'm sorry!
The blond guy was Master Takishima!
THMP
OH...

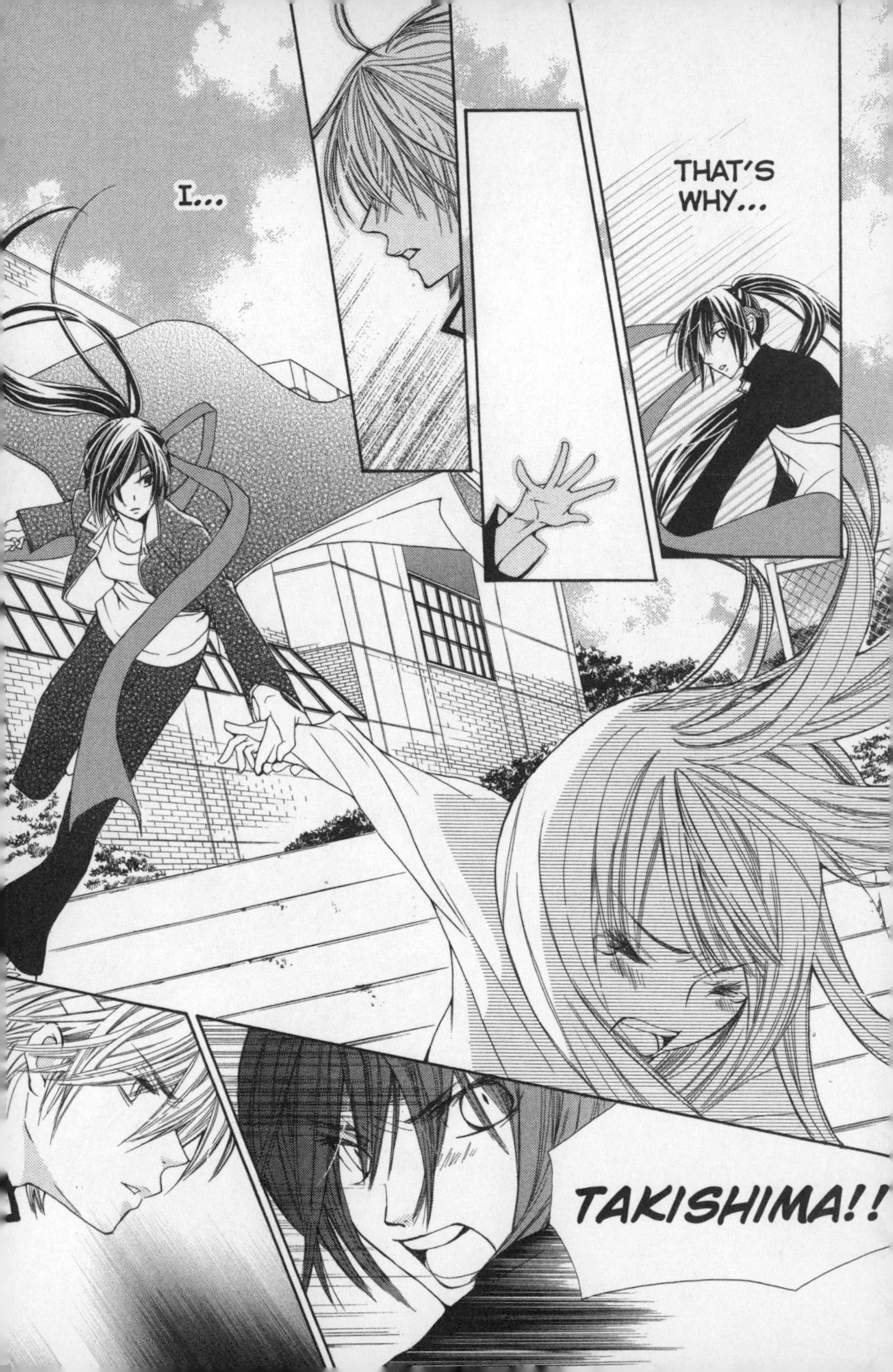
THAT'S WHY...
I...
TAKISHIMA!!

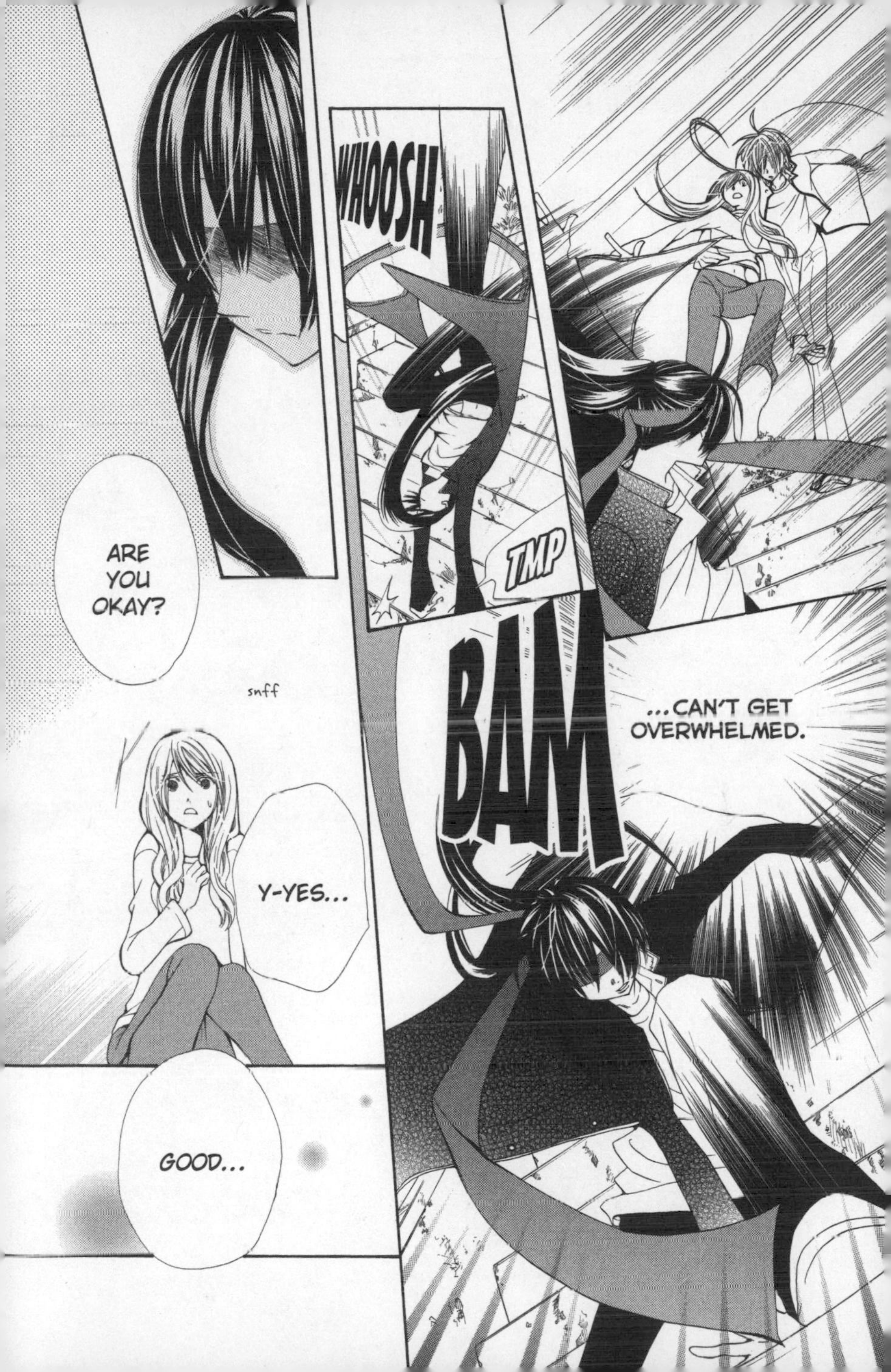
WHOOSH
TMP
BAM
...CAN'T GET OVERWHELMED.
ARE YOU OKAY?
snff
Y-YES...
GOOD...

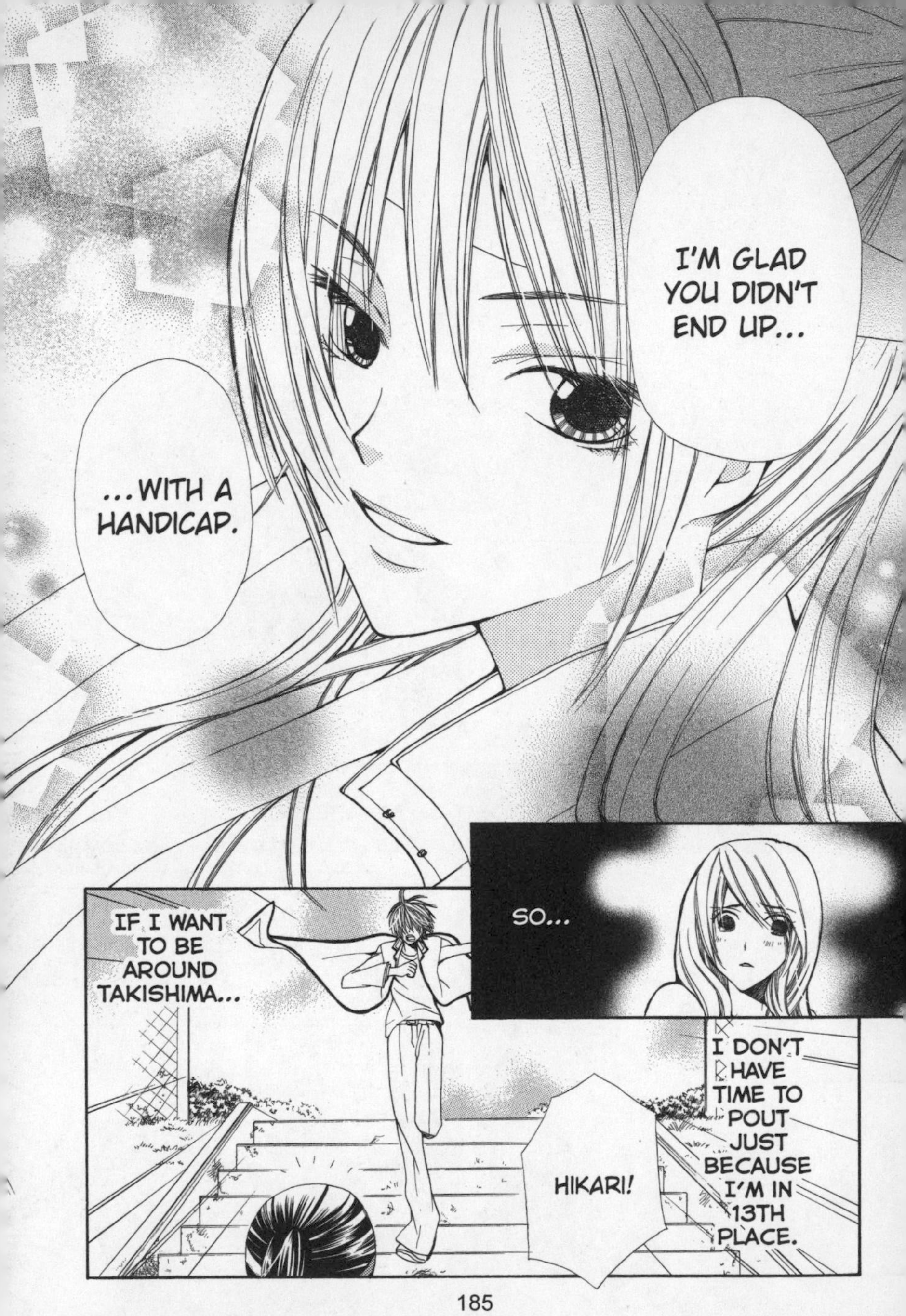

I'M GLAD YOU DIDN'T END UP...
...WITH A HANDICAP.
SO...
IF I WANT TO BE AROUND TAKISHIMA...
I DON'T HAVE TIME TO POUT JUST BECAUSE I'M IN 13TH PLACE.
HIKARI!

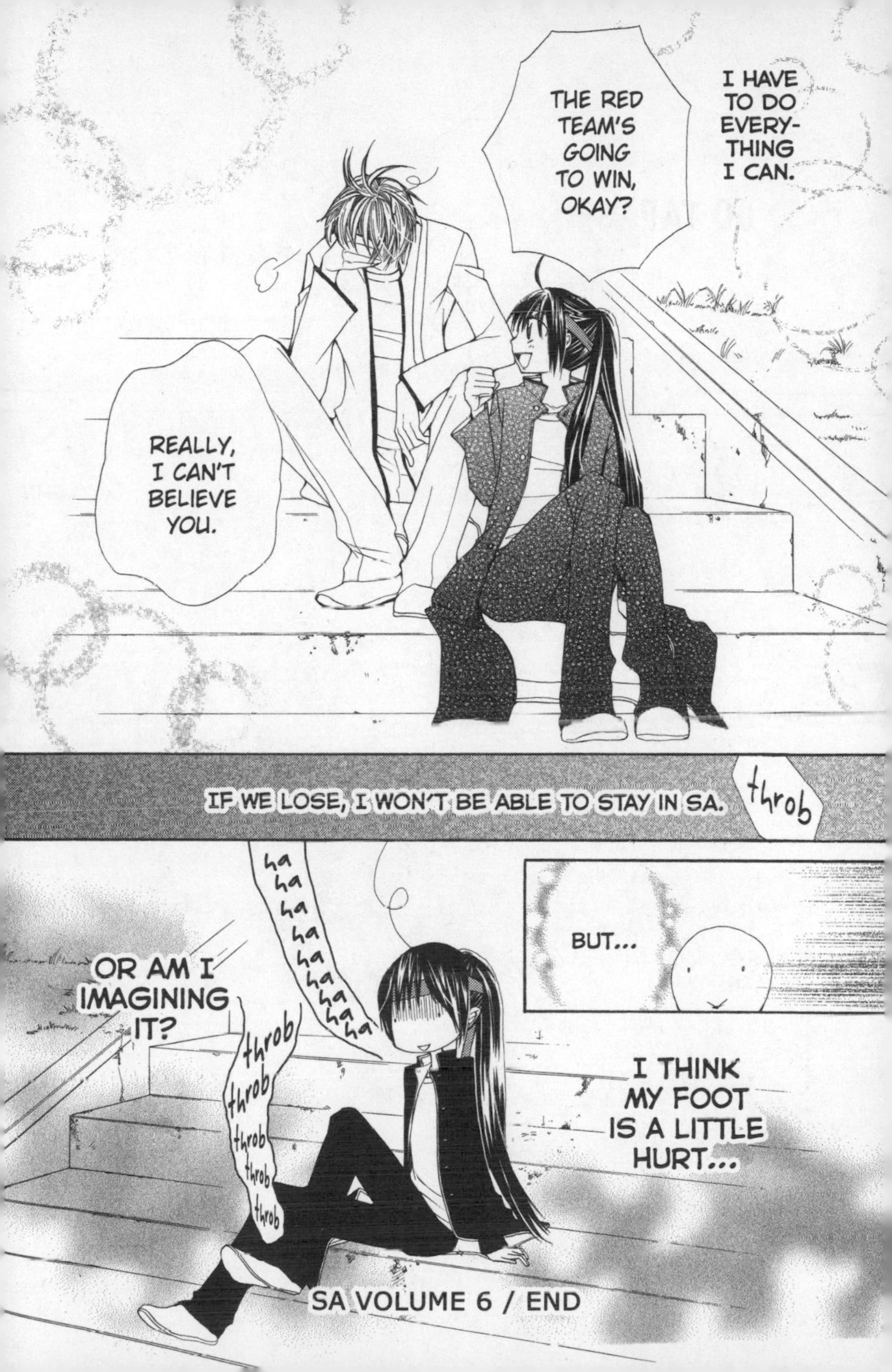
I HAVE TO DO EVERY-THING I CAN.
THE RED TEAM'S GOING TO WIN, OKAY?
REALLY, I CAN'T BELIEVE YOU.
throb
IF WE LOSE, I WON'T BE ABLE TO STAY IN SA.
BUT...
I THINK MY FOOT IS A LITTLE HURT...
ha ha ha ha ha ha ha ha ha
OR AM I IMAGINING IT?
throb throb throb throb throb
SA VOLUME 6 / END

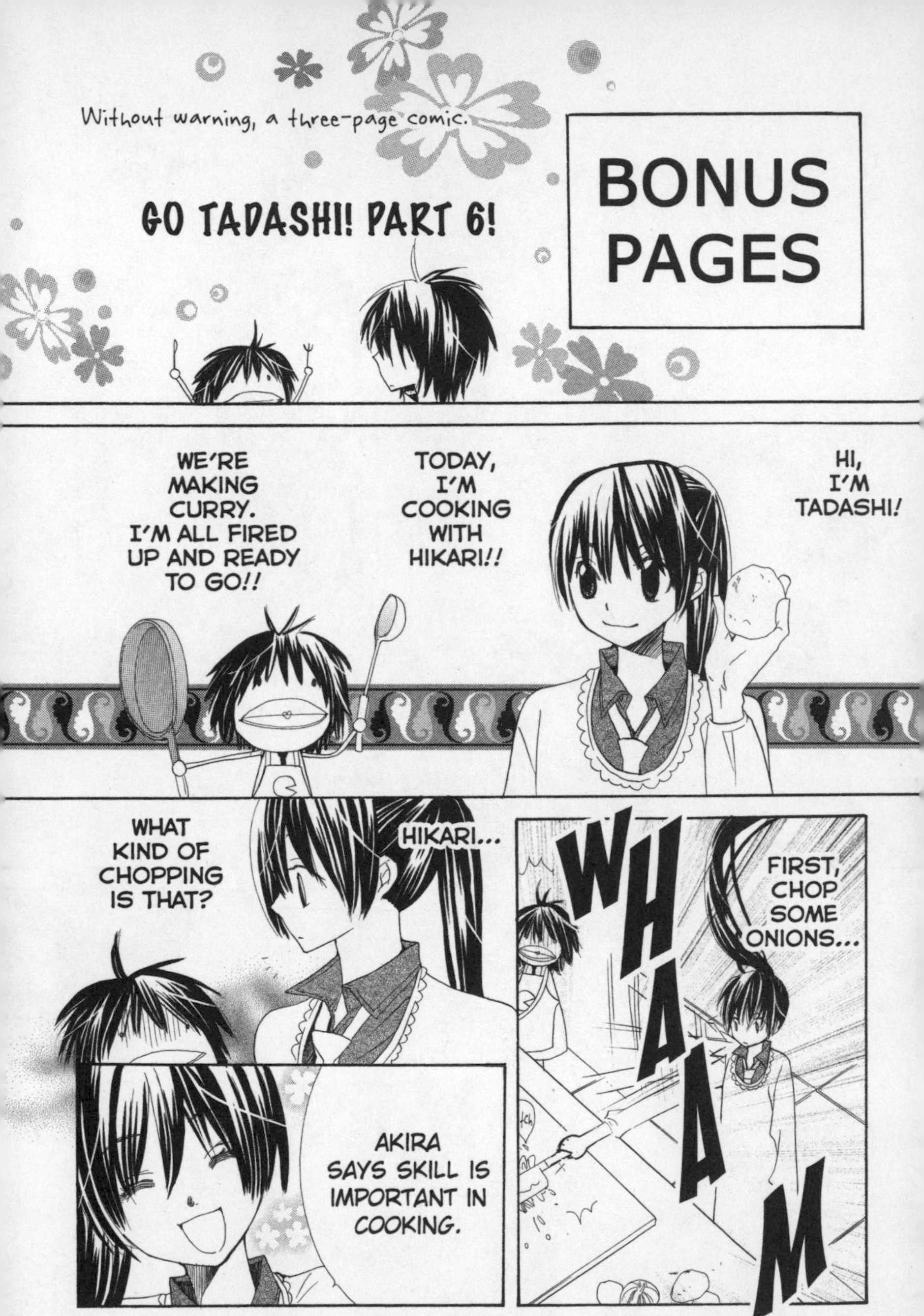
BONUS PAGES
Without warning, a three-page comic.
GO TADASHI! PART 6!
HI, I'M TADASHI!
TODAY, I'M COOKING WITH HIKARI!!
WE'RE MAKING CURRY. I'M ALL FIRED UP AND READY TO GO!!
FIRST, CHOP SOME ONIONS...
WHAAAM
HIKARI...
WHAT KIND OF CHOPPING IS THAT?
AKIRA SAYS SKILL IS IMPORTANT IN COOKING.

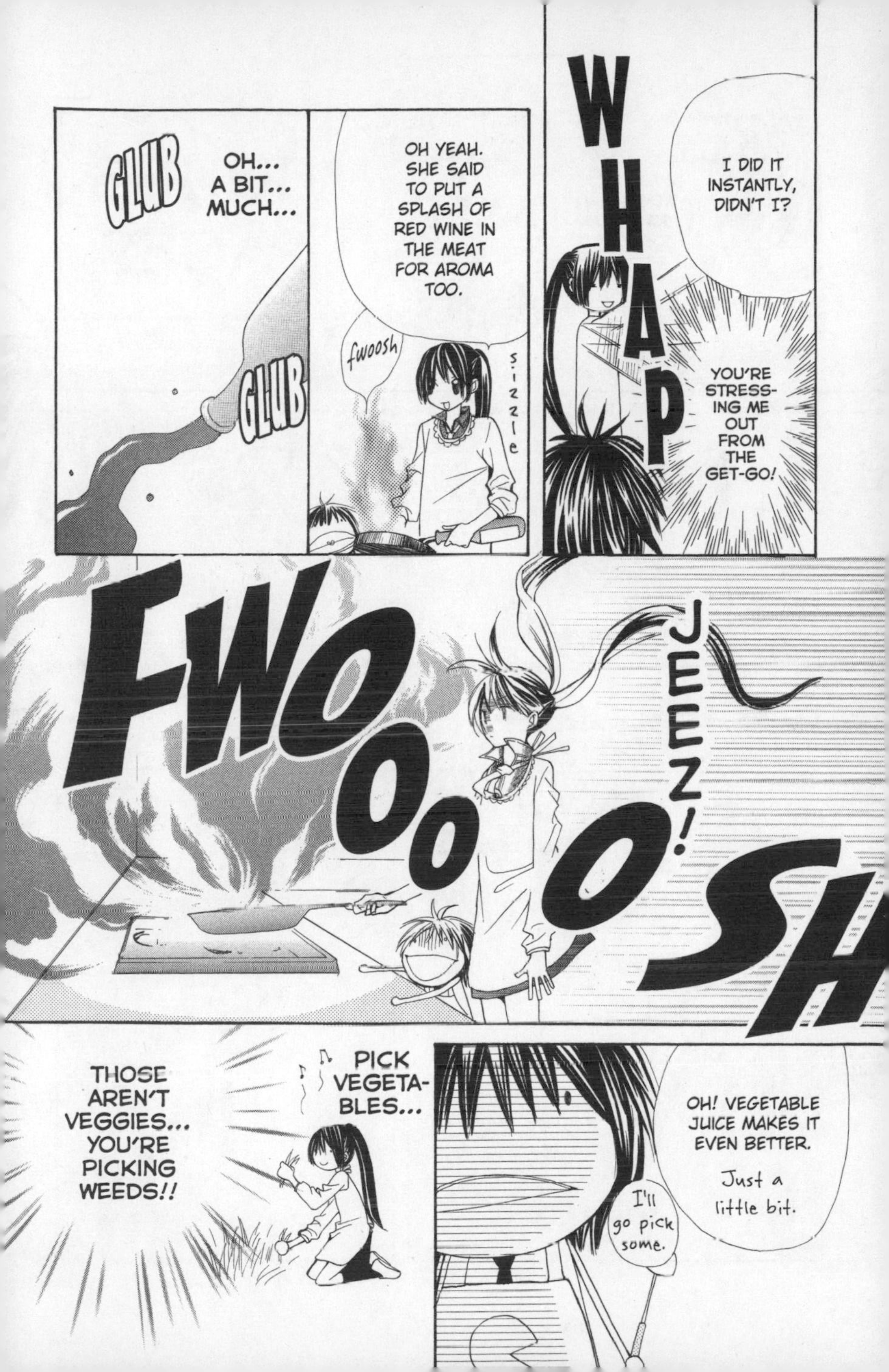
I DID IT INSTANTLY, DIDN'T I?
WHAP
YOU'RE STRESSING ME OUT FROM THE GET-GO!
OH YEAH. SHE SAID TO PUT A SPLASH OF RED WINE IN THE MEAT FOR AROMA TOO.
sizzle
fwoosh
OH... A BIT... MUCH...
GLUB
GLUB
JEEZ!
FWOOOOSH
OH! VEGETABLE JUICE MAKES IT EVEN BETTER.
Just a little bit.
I'll go pick some.
PICK VEGETABLES...
THOSE AREN'T VEGGIES... YOU'RE PICKING WEEDS!!

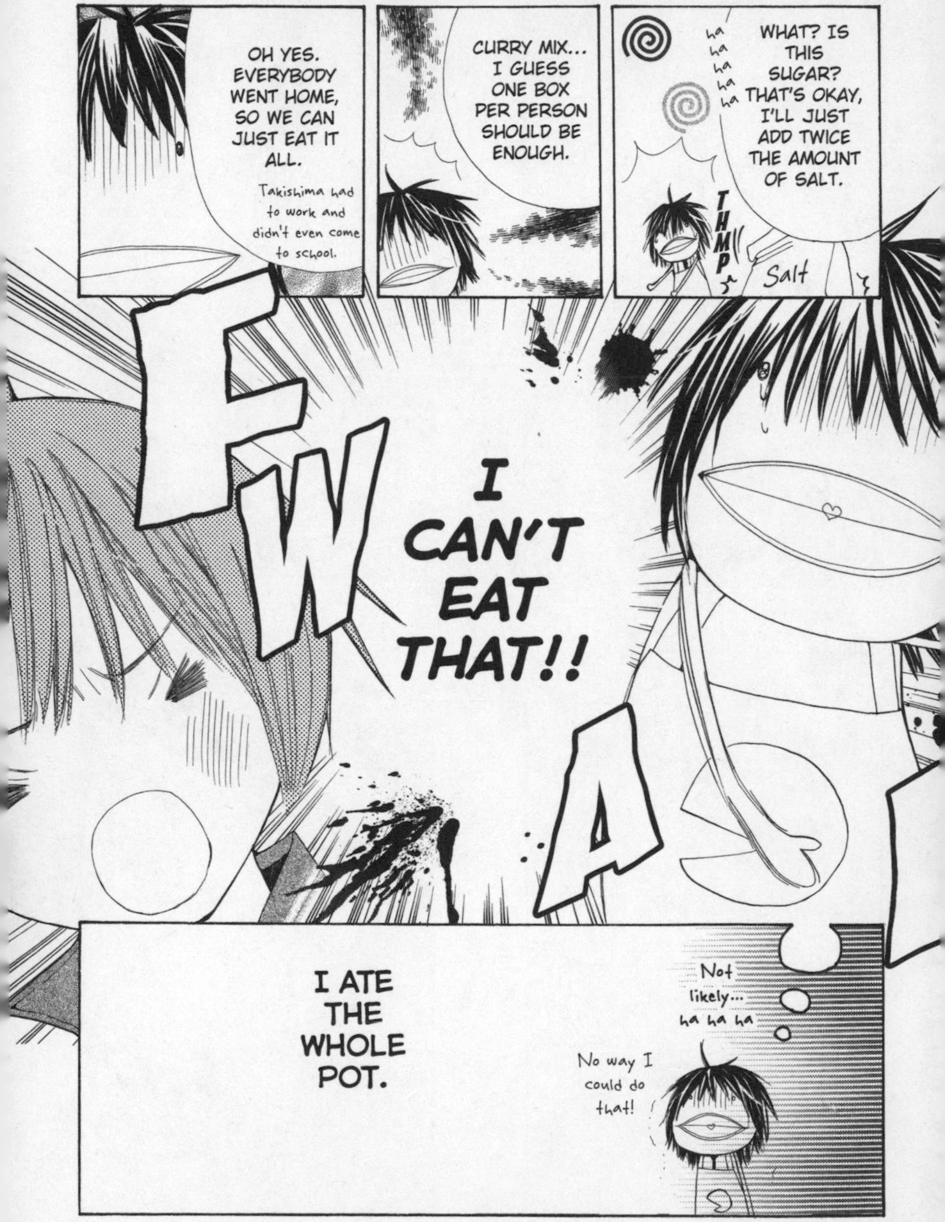
WHAT? IS THIS SUGAR? THAT'S OKAY, I'LL JUST ADD TWICE THE AMOUNT OF SALT.
ha ha ha ha ha
THMP
Salt
CURRY MIX... I GUESS ONE BOX PER PERSON SHOULD BE ENOUGH.
OH YES. EVERYBODY WENT HOME, SO WE CAN JUST EAT IT ALL.
Takishima had to work and didn't even come to school.
I CAN'T EAT THAT!!
FWA
Not likely... ha ha ha
No way I could do that!
I ATE THE WHOLE POT.

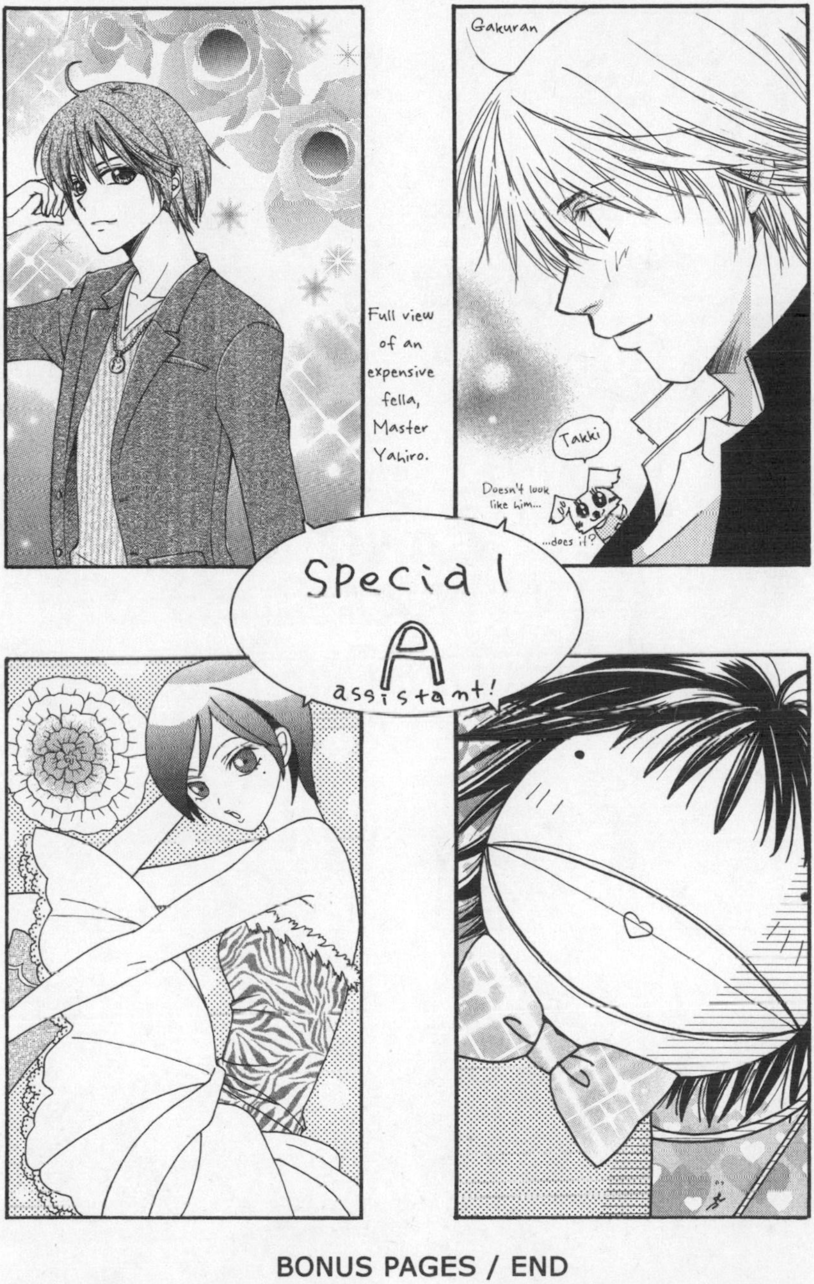
Gakuran
Takki
Doesn't look like him...
...does it?
Full view of an expensive fella, Master Yahiro.
Special A assistant!

BONUS PAGES / END

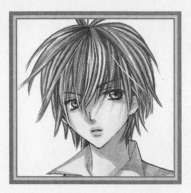

Maki Minami is from Saitama prefecture in Japan. She debuted in 2001 with *Kanata no Ao* (Faraway Blue). Her other works include *Kimi wa Girlfriend* (You're My Girlfriend), *Mainichi ga Takaramono* (Every Day Is a Treasure) and *Yuki Atataka* (Warm Winter). *S•A* is her current series in Japan's *Hana to Yume* magazine.

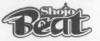

S•A
Vol. 6
The Shojo Beat Manga Edition

STORY & ART BY
MAKI MINAMI

English Adaptation/Amanda Hubbard
Translation/JN Productions
Touch-up Art & Lettering/Elizabeth Watasin
Cover Design/Izumi Hirayama
Interior Design/Deirdre Shiozawa
Editors/Carol Fox & Jonathan Tarbox

Editor in Chief, Books/Alvin Lu
Editor in Chief, Magazines/Marc Weidenbaum
VP of Publishing Licensing/Rika Inouye
VP of Sales/Gonzalo Ferreyra
Sr. VP of Marketing/Liza Coppola
Publisher/Hyoe Narita

Printed in Canada

Published by VIZ Media, LLC
P.O. Box 77010
San Francisco, CA 94107

Shojo Beat Manga Edition
10 9 8 7 6 5 4 3 2 1
First printing, September 2008

www.viz.com
store.viz.com

RATED T FOR TEEN

PARENTAL ADVISORY
S•A is rated T for Teen and is recommended for ages 13 and up.

ratings.viz.com

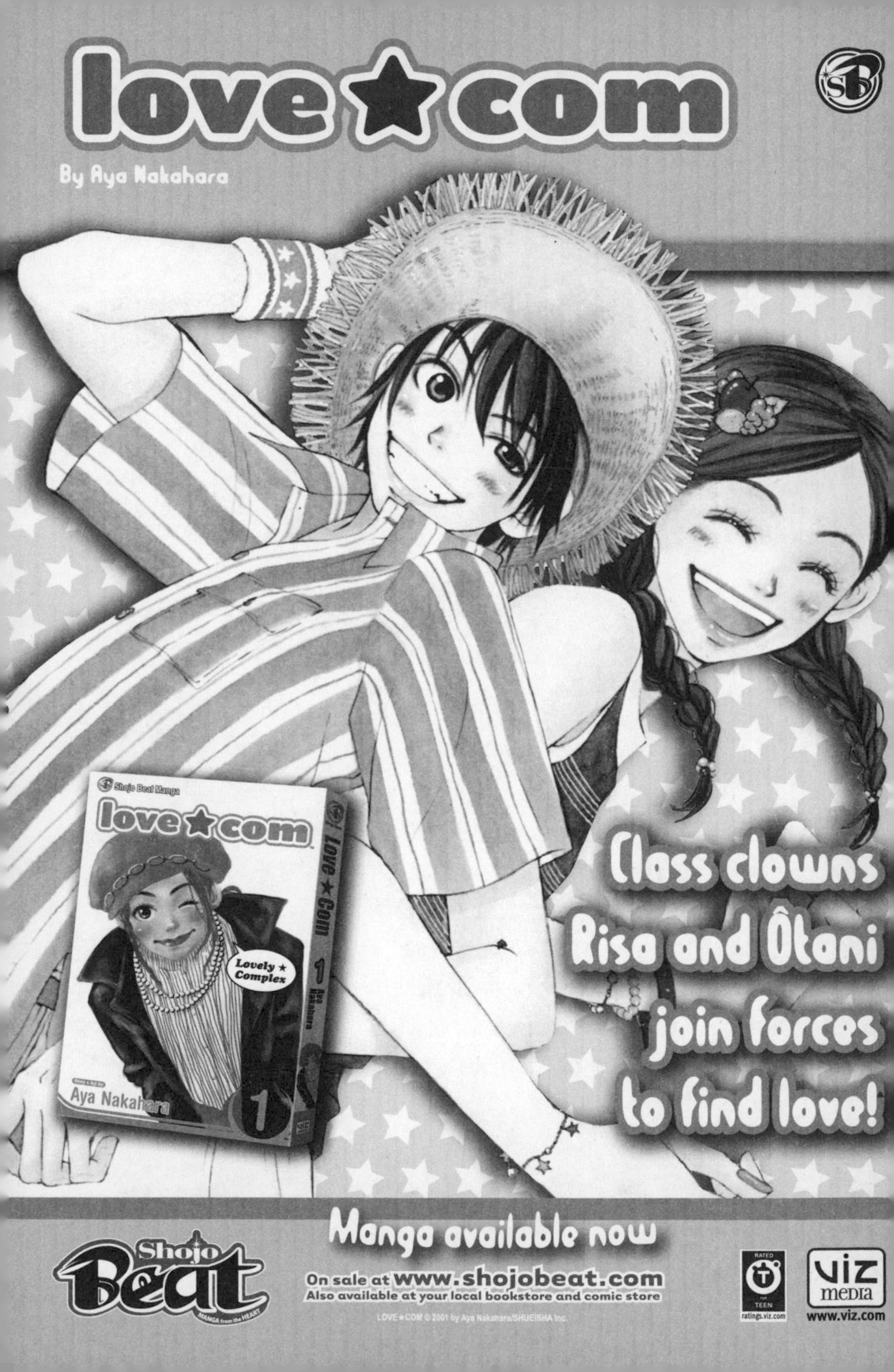
love★com
By Aya Nakahara
Shojo Beat Manga
love★com
Love★Com
1
Aya Nakahara
Lovely ★ Complex
Aya Nakahara
1
Class clowns Risa and Ôtani join forces to find love!
Manga available now
Shojo Beat
MANGA from the HEART
On sale at www.shojobeat.com
Also available at your local bookstore and comic store
LOVE★COM © 2001 by Aya Nakahara/SHUEISHA Inc.
RATED
T
TEEN
ratings.viz.com
VIZ MEDIA
www.viz.com

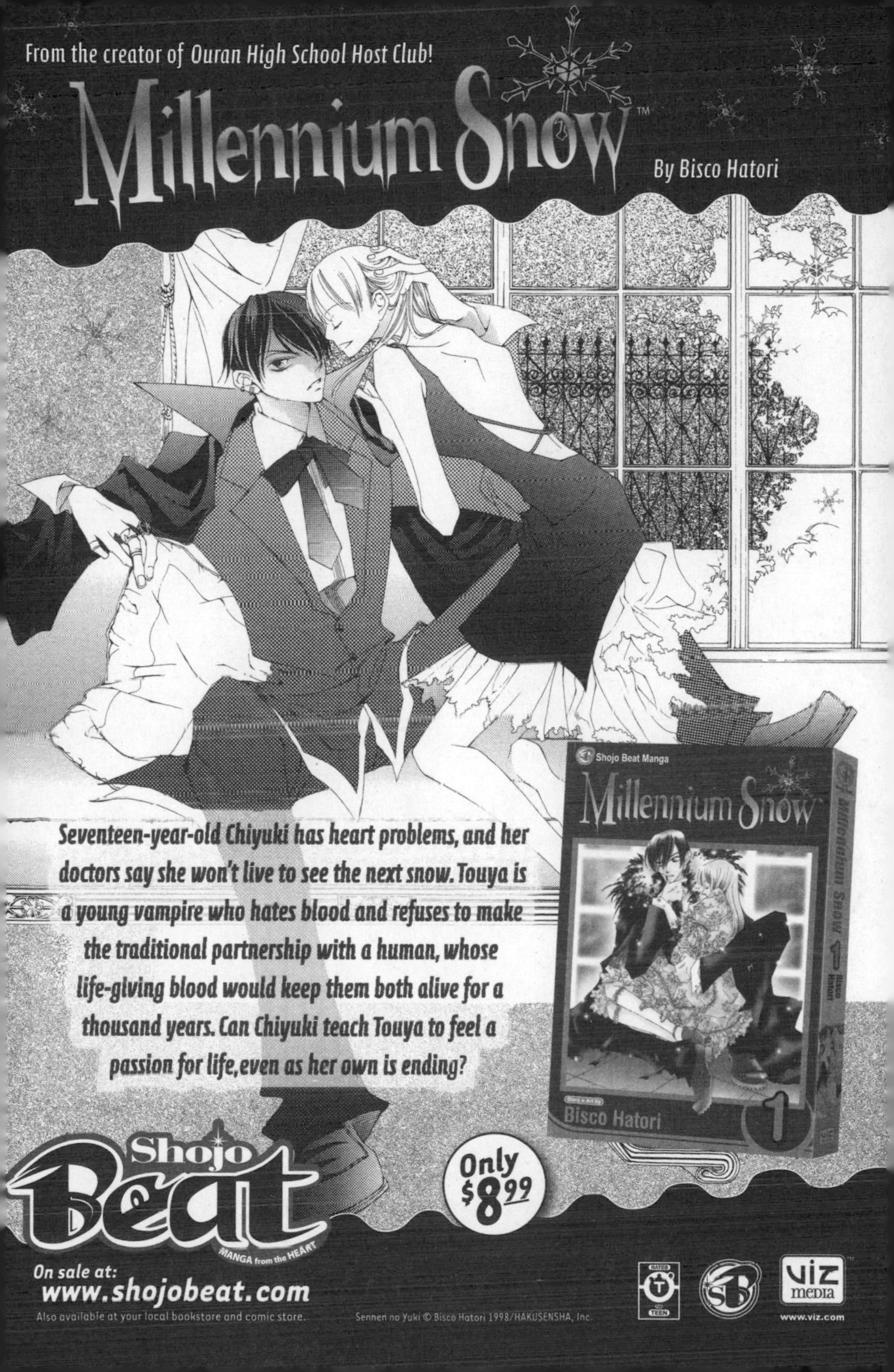
From the creator of Ouran High School Host Club!
Millennium Snow™
By Bisco Hatori
Seventeen-year-old Chiyuki has heart problems, and her doctors say she won't live to see the next snow. Touya is a young vampire who hates blood and refuses to make the traditional partnership with a human, whose life-giving blood would keep them both alive for a thousand years. Can Chiyuki teach Touya to feel a passion for life, even as her own is ending?
Shojo Beat Manga
Millennium Snow
1
Bisco Hatori
Shojo Beat
MANGA from the HEART
Only $8.99
On sale at:
www.shojobeat.com
Also available at your local bookstore and comic store.
Sennen no Yuki © Bisco Hatori 1998/HAKUSENSHA, Inc.
RATED T TEEN
VIZ media
www.viz.com

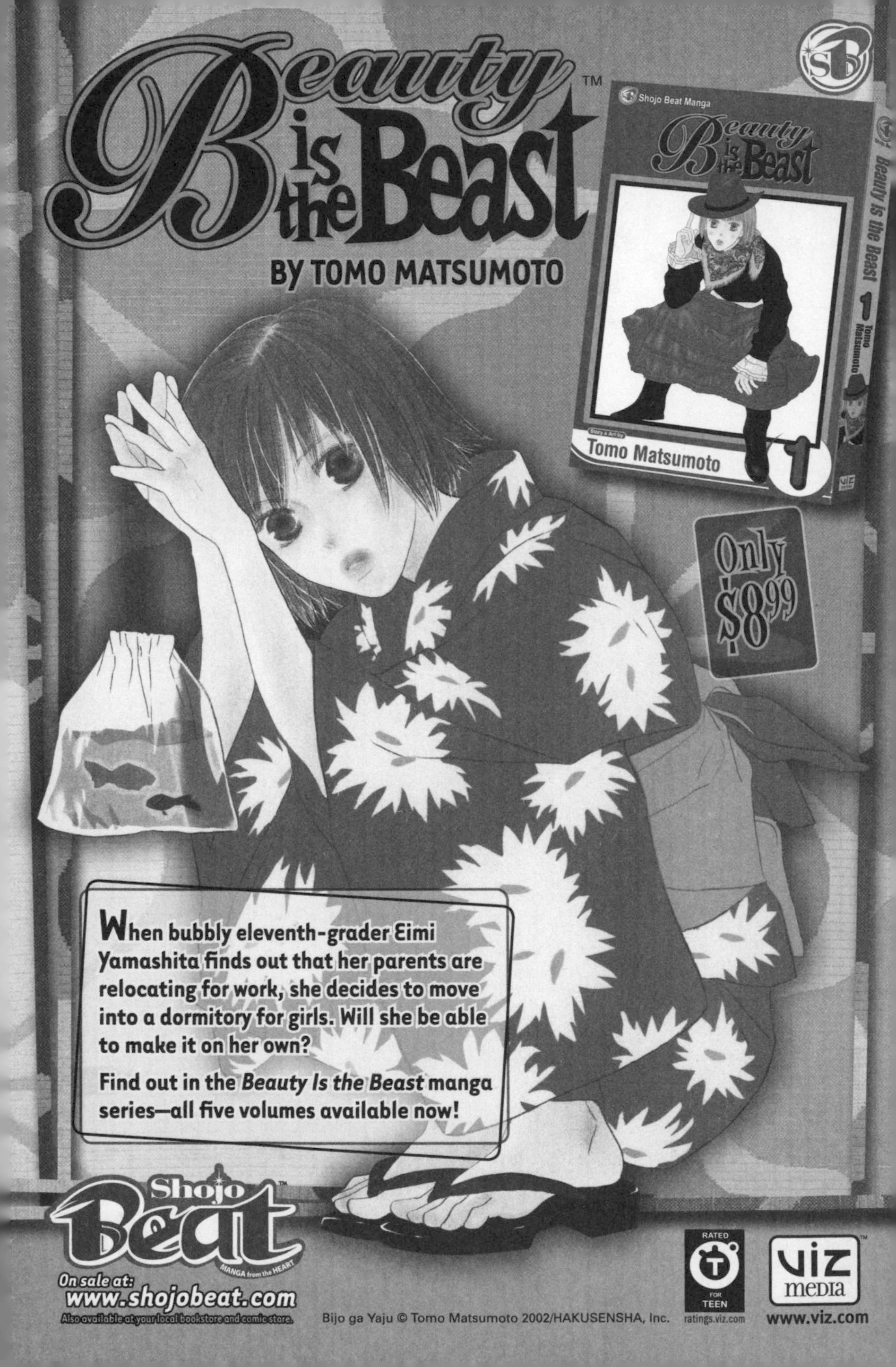
Beauty is the Beast™
BY TOMO MATSUMOTO
Shojo Beat Manga
Beauty is the Beast
Tomo Matsumoto
1
Only $8.99
When bubbly eleventh-grader Eimi Yamashita finds out that her parents are relocating for work, she decides to move into a dormitory for girls. Will she be able to make it on her own?
Find out in the *Beauty Is the Beast* manga series—all five volumes available now!
Shojo Beat™
MANGA from the HEART
On sale at:
www.shojobeat.com
Also available at your local bookstore and comic store.
Bijo ga Yaju © Tomo Matsumoto 2002/HAKUSENSHA, Inc.
RATED T FOR TEEN
ratings.viz.com
VIZ media
www.viz.com

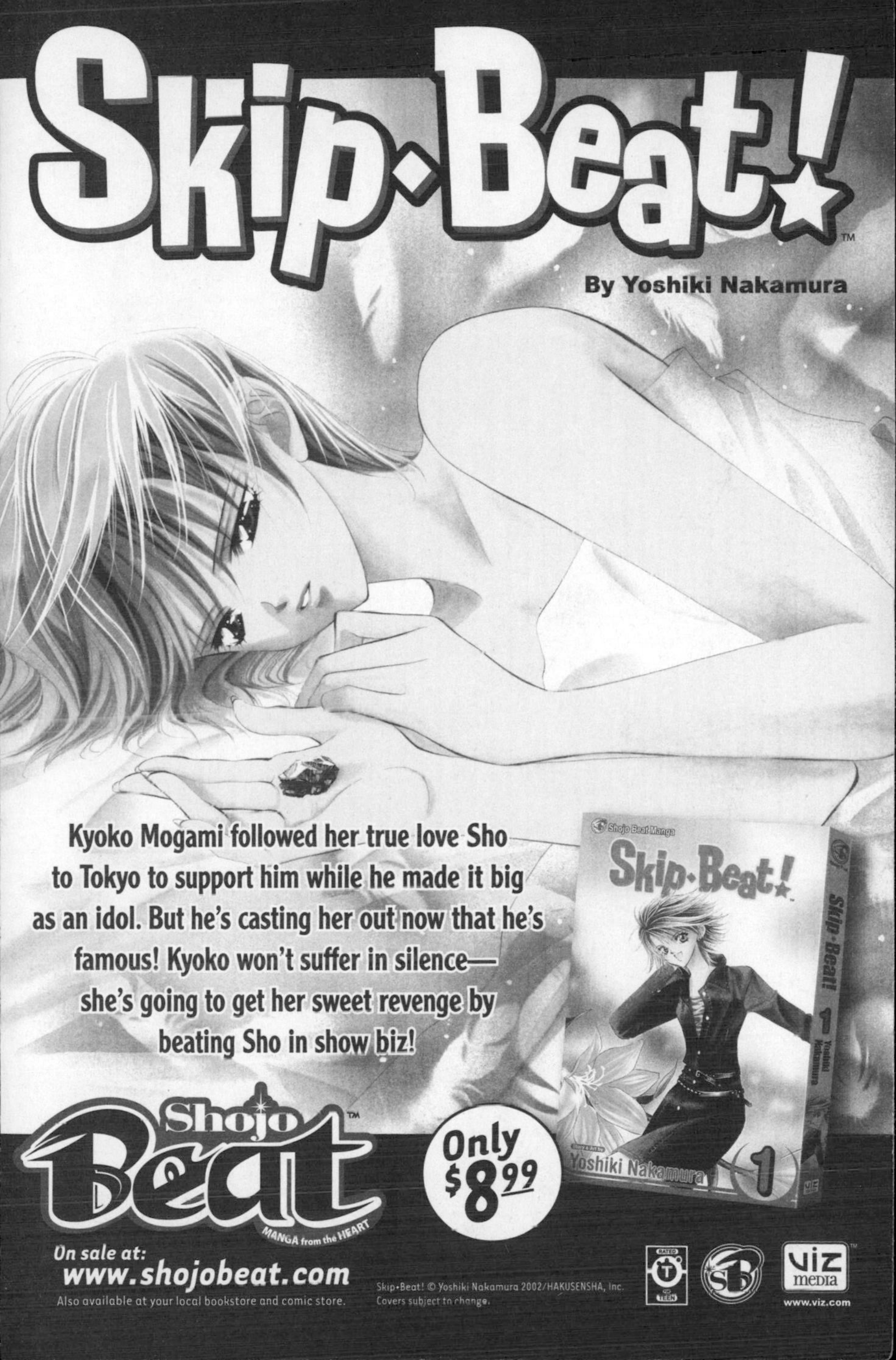
Skip·Beat!
TM
By Yoshiki Nakamura
Kyoko Mogami followed her true love Sho to Tokyo to support him while he made it big as an idol. But he's casting her out now that he's famous! Kyoko won't suffer in silence—she's going to get her sweet revenge by beating Sho in show biz!
Shojo Beat Manga
Skip·Beat!
Yoshiki Nakamura
1
Shojo Beat
TM
MANGA from the HEART
Only $8.99
On sale at:
www.shojobeat.com
Also available at your local bookstore and comic store.
Skip·Beat! © Yoshiki Nakamura 2002/HAKUSENSHA, Inc.
Covers subject to change.
RATED T TEEN
SB
VIZ media
www.viz.com

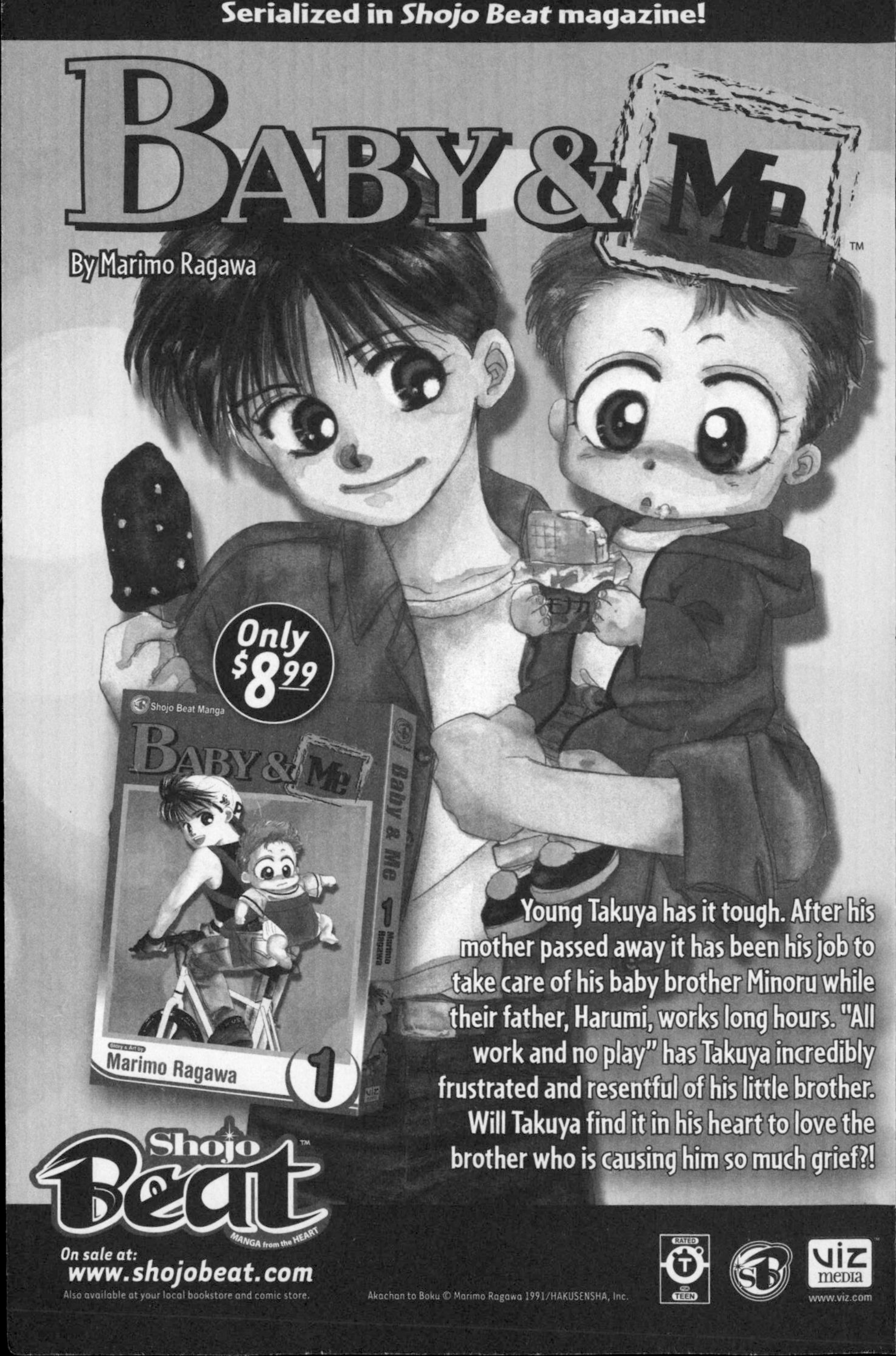
Serialized in Shojo Beat magazine!
BABY & Me™
By Marimo Ragawa
Only $8.99
Shojo Beat Manga
BABY & Me
Baby & Me 1 Marimo Ragawa
Marimo Ragawa
1
Young Takuya has it tough. After his mother passed away it has been his job to take care of his baby brother Minoru while their father, Harumi, works long hours. "All work and no play" has Takuya incredibly frustrated and resentful of his little brother. Will Takuya find it in his heart to love the brother who is causing him so much grief?!
Shojo Beat™
MANGA from the HEART
On sale at:
www.shojobeat.com
Also available at your local bookstore and comic store.
Akachan to Boku © Marimo Ragawa 1991/HAKUSENSHA, Inc.
RATED T FOR TEEN
viz media
www.viz.com

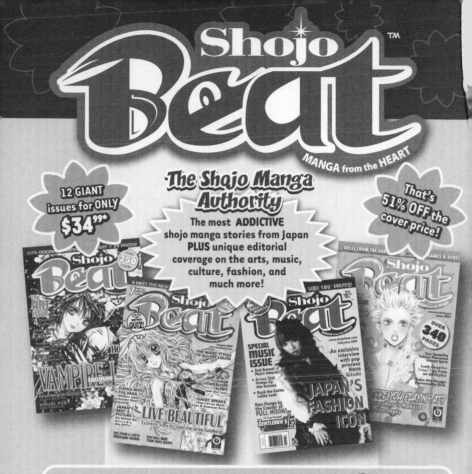

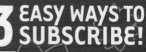